DEDUCTION AND DECLARATIVE PROGRAMMING

Cambridge Tracts in Theoretical Computer Science

Titles in the series

1. G. Chaitin *Algorithmic Information Theory*
2. L.C. Paulson *Logic and Computation*
3. M. Spivey *Understanding Z*
4. G. Revesz *Lambda Calculus, Combinators and Functional Programming*
5. A. Ramsay *Formal Methods in Artificial Intelligence*
6. S. Vickers *Topology via Logic*
7. J-Y. Girard, Y. Lafont & P. Taylor *Proofs and Types*
8. J. Clifford *Formal Semantics & Pragmatics for Natural Language Processing*
9. M. Winslett *Updating Logical Databases*
10. K. McEvoy & J.V. Tucker (eds) *Theoretical Foundations of VLSI Design*
11. T.H. Tse *A Unifying Framework for Stuctured Analysis and Design Models*
12. G. Brewka *Nonmonotonic Reasoning*
14. S.G. Hoggar *Mathematics for Computer Graphics*
15. S. Dasgupta *Design Theory and Computer Science*
17. J.C.M. Baeten (ed) *Applications of Process Algebra*
18. J.C.M. Baeten & W. P. Weijland *Process Algebra*
23. E.-R. Olderog *Nets, Terms and Formulas*
26. P.D. Mosses *Action Semantics*
27. W.H. Hesselink *Programs, Recursion and Unbounded Choice*
28. P. Padawitz *Deduction and Declarative Programming*
29. P. Gärdenfors (ed) *Belief Revision*
30. M. Anthony & N. Biggs *Computational Learning Theory*
33. E.G. Manes *Predicate Transformer Semantics*
34. F. Nielson & H.R. Nielson *Two Level Functional Languages*
35. L. Feijs & H. Jonkers *Formal Specification and Design*

DEDUCTION AND DECLARATIVE PROGRAMMING

PETER PADAWITZ
Department of Computer Science
University of Dortmund

CAMBRIDGE
UNIVERSITY PRESS

CAMBRIDGE UNIVERSITY PRESS
Cambridge, New York, Melbourne, Madrid, Cape Town, Singapore, São Paulo

Cambridge University Press
The Edinburgh Building, Cambridge CB2 2RU, UK

Published in the United States of America by Cambridge University Press, New York

www.cambridge.org
Information on this title: www.cambridge.org/9780521417235

First published 1992
This digitally printed first paperback version 2006

A catalogue record for this publication is available from the British Library

ISBN-13 978-0-521-41723-5 hardback
ISBN-10 0-521-41723-6 hardback

ISBN-13 978-0-521-03251-3 paperback
ISBN-10 0-521-03251-2 paperback

Contents

0: Introduction

This monograph promotes specification and programming on the basis of Horn logic with equality. As was pointed out in [Pad88a], this theoretical background equips us with a number of deductive methods for reasoning about specifications and designing correct programs. The term *declarative programming* stands for the combination of functional (or applicative) and relational (or logic) programming. This does not rule out the design of imperative programs with conditionals, loops and sequences of variable assignments, since all these features have functional or relational equivalents. In particular, variables become "output parameters" of functions. Hence the *static* view of declarative programming is not really a restriction. Only if correctness conditions concerned with liveness or synchronization are demanded, transition relations must be specified for fixing the *dynamics* of program execution (cf. Sect. 6.6).

0.1 Design specifications

With regard to the overall software design process, the methods considered here are tailored to *design specifications,* each consisting of a many-sorted signature *SIG* denoting data, functions and predicates to be specified and a set of Horn clauses over SIG, allowing more or less abstract presentations of declarative programs and the data structures they use and manipulate (cf. Sects. 1.1 and 1.2). Associated with a design specification *DS* is a *requirement specification,* the *conjecture section* of DS, which consists of correctness conditions on DS. In contrast to design axioms, Horn clauses are not always sufficient for specifying requirements. Hence we admit positive *Gentzen clauses,* which may involve disjunctions and existential quantifiers, in a requirement specification (cf. Sect. 1.4).

Syntactically, each object specified by DS is denoted by a ground, i.e. variable-free, term over SIG. A Gentzen clause c from the conjecture section of DS is satisfied if c is *inductively valid w.r.t. DS,* i.e., if c is valid in the *initial DS-structure* (cf. Sect. 3.1). The initial DS-structure is a model of DS that realizes the *closed world assumption*: a *fact,* i.e., a ground atomic formula p over SIG is valid in this structure if and only if p is derivable from DS. Certain clauses of DS *define* a predicate P if they determine the interpretation of P in the initial DS-structure (cf. Sect. 1.5).

Let A be the model of DS one has in mind when building DS. DS is called *initially correct w.r.t. A* if A is isomorphic to the initial DS-structure (cf. Sect. 3.2). For proving initial correctness with the help of a theorem prover, A should be given as a *canonical term structure* (cf. Sect. 3.3). The actual construction of A and the correctness proof of DS can be restricted to the *sort building part* of DS. The remaining (sometimes partial) functions and predicates of A usually constitute *algorithms* on the sort building part. This motivates the distinction of a *base specification BS* and the proof obligation that DS is a *conservative extension of BS* (cf. Sect. 3.4). The distinction allows us to compare several extensions of BS with each other and thus provides a formal setting for proving program equivalence (cf. Sect. 3.5). In some cases, a program can be derived from the proof of its correctness conditions, expressed in terms of given programs (cf. Sect. 2.1).

0.2 Functional versus logic programs

What separates a functional program from a logic program? Not much. A functional program is a set of (conditional) equations defining a function F, such as

```
insert(x,ε) ≡ x&ε
insert(x,y&s) ≡ x&y&s   ⇐   x ≤ y
insert(x,y&s) ≡ y&insert(x,s)   ⇐   x > y.
```

Usually, the definition is recursive and the recursive calls of F are part of the equations' right-hand sides. A logic program is a set of Horn clauses defining a predicate P, e.g.,

```
sorted(ε)
sorted(x&ε)
sorted(x&y&s)   ⇐   x ≤ y, sorted(y&s).
```

Recursive calls of P are part of the clauses' premises. Since the equations of a functional program may also be equipped with conditions, we should make a difference between conditions of a functional program and premises of a logic program. In fact, the latter involve recursive calls, the former do not. Syntactic manipulations allow us to shift recursive function calls from the right-hand side of an equation to a condition, while predicates can be turned into Boolean functions such that the premise of a logic program becomes the body of a functional program. If one does not use (non-strict) conditional operators (cf. Sect. 2.6), a part of the premise may be left, called a *guard* because it guards recursive function or predicate calls, while the part that can be shifted to the conclusion is called the body or *generator*, since it usually includes recursive calls that are expected to generate solutions in certain *output variables*. The *commit operator* ":" separates the guard from the generator:

```
div(x,y) ≡ (0,x)    ⇐  x < y
div(x,y) ≡ (q+1,r)  ⇐  x ≥ y, y > 0 : div(x-y,y) ≡ (q,r)
```

In parallel logic programming languages, such *guarded (Horn) clauses* are associated with a particular evaluation strategy (cf. [Ued86], [Sha89]). Under certain conditions, a set CS of guarded clauses is inductively equivalent to the Gentzen clause c that results from shifting the generators to the conclusions of CS. Proving c is often more *goal-directed* than proving CS, in particular, if the proof is to reveal axioms for a program to be synthesized (cf. Sect. 2.1). Conditions admitting the theory-preserving translation of CS mainly concern the generators of CS (cf. Sect. 2.2). Actually, the generators should be equations whose right-hand sides constitute a *set of constructor terms* (cf. Sects. 2.3 and 2.4). In contrast to the translation of Horn clauses into a Gentzen clause, the converse transformation of an arbitrary Gentzen clause into Horn clauses goes through without assumptions. We only need an additional *conjecture predicate* (cf. Sect. 2.5).

Hence guarded clauses cover functional as well as logic programs. However, aside from the viewpoint of what these programs *declare*, one may classify the programs with regard to what they *compute*. Here is an actual difference between functional and logic programs: the former return function values, the latter compute solutions or bindings, formally presented as substitutions, i.e., term assignments to variables. The distinction between the two is reflected in the way current run-time systems for respectively functional and logic programming languages handle their input. Just as Horn logic with equality allows us to *verify* functional and logic programs using the same methods, future programming environments will combine program execution with other deductive tasks and thus may dissolve the *computational* difference as well. EQLOG (cf. [GM85]) was the first language that rigorously combined both styles. [Pad88a], the forerunner of this book, argues along the same line.

Beyond the rough distinction considered here, [GL90] classifies current declarative languages in more detail.

0.3 Goal-directed reasoning

Whether we want to evaluate a functional expression, compute a solution or prove a theorem, a procedure for performing such tasks should work top-down or *goal-directed*, i.e., transform the expression to be evaluated, the formula to be solved or the theorem to be proved via a sequence of deduction steps into a value, a solution or another satisfactory answer to the question associated with the given goal. For instance, proving a Horn clause $c = \gamma \Leftarrow \delta$ in a goal-directed way means transforming the conclusion γ into the premise δ. We call the sequence of intermediate goals as well as the process of deriving them an *expansion* for appealing to the coincidence of applying Horn clauses and expanding logic programs.

The basic inference rules for carrying out an expansion are *resolution* and *paramodulation*. Resolution captures the logic way of reasoning: a goal, i.e., a set of atomic formulas, is decomposed into subgoals. Paramodulation captures the algebraic way: a goal is transformed into equivalent ones by successive term replacements. The computation sequence from a functional expression to a "normal form" is an example of an exclusively paramodulating expansion. In general, the way from a goal γ to one of its solutions is recorded by a *solving expansion*, i.e., a sequence of pairs of a goal and a substitution, beginning with γ and the identity substitution and, if successful, ending with the empty goal and a solution of γ (cf. Chapter 4).

A *proving expansion* of $\gamma \Leftarrow \delta$, on the other hand, is a sequence of goal *sets* regarded as disjunctions: each ground substitution satisfying δ solves *some* element of each goal set in the sequence. Disjunctions arise when a subgoal φ is split into several goals, due to a case analysis. This happens if φ is resolved or paramodulated upon several lemmas in parallel all of which are inductively valid w.r.t. DS. Lemmas are collected in the *theorem section* of DS. Like conjectures, lemmas may be arbitrary Gentzen clauses. In particular, the conclusion of a lemma may be a disjunction of several goals. Resolving such a lemma upon a goal set G means resolving each summand of the lemma upon an element of G such that several elements of G are joined into a single goal and the expansion turns locally into a contraction (cf. Sect. 5.1).

Induction steps in such a proof are resolution or paramodulation steps upon the conjecture $\gamma \Leftarrow \delta$ (cf. Sect. 5.2). They are often necessary for obtaining a finite proof. For performing an induction step, the expansion must be directed towards an induction hypothesis, i.e., towards an instance of γ. Moreover, the expansion must end up with (a subset of) δ. Hence δ should be kept small. Here one takes advantage of embedding $\gamma \Leftarrow \delta$ into a set CS of guarded clauses, since, by translating CS into a Gentzen clause (cf. Sect. 0.2), the generator of $\gamma \Leftarrow \delta$ is shifted from δ to γ (cf. Sect. 5.3). Resolution or paramodulation upon lemmas and conjectures form the calculus of *inductive expansion*. Examples are carried out in Sects. 5.3, 5.5, 8.5-8.7 and 9.2.

0.4 Confluent specifications

The theory of term rewriting (cf. [HO80], [DJ90]) has led to *(inductive) completion* as another way of proving a set CS of requirements to a design specification DS. The main idea is to transform the union of DS and CS into a confluent system R of rewrite rules and to deduce that R and thus DS∪CS is a conservative extension of DS. In Chapters 6 and 7, this approach is generalized to Horn logic with equality. Since we want to compare it with the expansion approach (cf. Sect. 7.5), rewriting must be regarded as a process of transforming goals rather than terms. Hence we introduce the calculus of *goal reduction* (cf. Chapter 6) and prove a Church-Rosser theorem for Horn logic: the calculus is complete for valid ground goals iff DS is *ground confluent* and iff inductive validity w.r.t. DS is equivalent to *reductive validity* (cf. Section 6.1). The latter notion generalizes *convergence*, i.e., reducibility to the empty goal, from ground goals to Horn clauses. For proofs of ground confluence, we provide an appropriate superposition theorem: a *strongly terminating* specification DS is ground confluent iff DS is *critical clause convergent* (cf. Sect. 6.3). Strong termination requires a *reduction ordering*, i.e., a Noetherian ordering on the set of convergent ground goals. The *path calculus* based on an ordering of function and predicate symbols yields a standard schema for deriving a reduction ordering from Noetherian predicates of DS (cf. Sect. 6.2).

If there is a finite set CS of Horn clauses subsuming all critical clauses, critical clause convergence can be inferred from the reductive validity of CS. For proving that a Horn clause $p \Leftarrow \gamma$ is reductively valid, we introduce the *sub-p-reductive expansion calculus*, which, like inductive expansion, employs resolution and paramodulation as the basic inference rules (cf. Sect. 6.4). Each goal γ of a sub-p-reductive expansion is *p-bounded* w.r.t. its direct successors in the expansion, i.e., for each ground substitution f such that the f-instance of a successor is convergent the f-instance of γ is smaller than the f-instance of p w.r.t. a given reduction ordering. P-boundedness ensures that the expansion proof does not run into a circular argument.

To sum up: the sub-p-reductive expansion calculus serves for proving critical clause convergence and thus ground confluence (cf. Sect. 6.5).

The advantages of a ground confluent design specification are manifold. First, the solving expansion calculi *directed expansion* and *strategic expansion* are complete w.r.t. all goal solutions (cf. Sects. 6.1 and 7.1). Second, *narrowing* is complete w.r.t. *reduced* goal solutions (cf. Sect. 7.2). Third, one obtains simple syntactic criteria for a set of terms to be a set of constructors (cf. Sect. 7.3). The last two results are used for augmenting the *inductive* expansion calculus with two rules that check a goal for unsolvability: the *failure rule* and the *clash rule*.

Ground confluence is not the only proof obligation to be handled by sub-p-reductive expansion. This calculus can be extended to a method for proving inductive validity, which competes with inductive expansion and reflects the idea of inductive completion (see above). For justifying the method, one starts out from the fact that a clause set CS is inductively valid w.r.t. DS iff DS∪CS is a conservative extension of DS. The latter property amounts to *reductive consistency* as long as DS∪CS is ground confluent (cf. Sect. 6.4). Provided that DS is already ground confluent and DS∪CS is strongly terminating, DS∪CS is reductively consistent and ground confluent iff CS is *inductively convergent*. The inductive convergence of $p \Leftarrow \gamma \in CS$ is proved by establishing a *reductive expansion*, i.e., a set of goal reductions of p into goals $\gamma_1,\dots,\gamma_n$, respectively, followed by a sub-p-reductive expansion of $\{\gamma_1,\dots,\gamma_n\}$ into $\{\gamma\}$ upon DS *and* CS (cf. Sect. 7.4).

Hence the reductive expansion of $p \Leftarrow \gamma$ allows us to apply instances of CS without identifying them as induction hypotheses. (This led to the notion "inductionless induction".) However, since the goals of the expansion of $\{\gamma_1,\dots,\gamma_n\}$ into $\{\gamma\}$ must be p-bounded w.r.t. a reduction ordering, inductionless induction is not very different from explicit induction: descent conditions of inductive expansions (cf. Section 5.2) recur as boundary conditions in reductive expansions. At the least, inductive expansions can be transformed into reductive ones and, conversely, a sort of specification renaming reduces the crucial boundary conditions of reductive expansions to descent conditions (cf. Sect. 7.5).

0.5 Miscellaneous

Section 6.6 distinguishes the rewriting-oriented calculi of Chapters 6 and 7 from a *rewriting logic*, which yields the rule-based semantics of a language in terms of an abstract machine rather than serving particular proof-theoretical purposes. Section 7.6 provides a simple notion of *implementation correctness* along with deductive criteria based on the results of Chapter 6. Chapter 8 presents a number of design specifications, ranging from attributed grammars via deterministic algorithms on numbers, sequences, trees and graphs to stream-processing networks with non-deterministic functions. Expansion proofs of non-trivial requirements to some of these specifications are carried out in detail. EXPANDER, a running Standard ML implementation of inductive expansion is documented in Chapter 9.

The book developed from our research and teaching on specification and programming carried out over the period 1988-1991. It also covers some of the material presented in an earlier book on Horn logic with equality ([Pad88a]). However, there are essential differences with regard to both content and goal. In [Pad88a], the aim was to unify as much as possible from the current research on term rewriting with goal-directed calculi used in automated deduction and logic programming. In the present book, the key notions have been emphasized and only these were worked out in detail. Special issues, such as resolution and rewriting modulo an equational theory, inference strategies and optimized calculi, are not treated here. The emphasis is put on deductive methods that are sufficiently general, simple and flexible and thus *ready to hand* when design specifications are developed and proved correct (cf. [WF86]).

A second forerunner of this monograph is the paper [Pad91]. It includes a more detailed discussion of *partial* program correctness and *computational* induction in the framework of inductive expansion (cf. Sect. 1.2).

Essential are the calculi of inductive and sub-p-reductive expansions for proving respectively inductive validity and sub-p-reductive validity. Most of the meta-level proof obligations, such as confluence, consistency, unsolvability, initial correctness, program equivalence, implementation correctness, or the constructor property, involve the inductive or sub-p-reductive validity of certain Gentzen clauses. Inductive theorems may be proved either explicity by inductive expansion or implicitly by reductive expansion, which combines goal reduction with sub-p-reductive expansion (cf. Section 0.4). These methods should be compared with each other in more detail. In fact, correctness conditions, of which a proof by reductive expansion is an improvement over a proof by inductive expansion, are still missing.

I am very grateful to Alfons Geser, Dieter Hofbauer and Thomas Streicher who provided a number of valuable comments on previous versions of this book. When I was implementing EXPANDER, Stefan Gastinger and Robert Stabl were patient enough to answer all my silly questions concerning the SML system.

1: Preliminaries

Given a set S, an *S-sorted set* A is a family of sets, i.e. $A = \{A_s \mid s \in S\}$. A *signature* SIG = (S,OP,PR) consists of a set S of *sorts* and two S^+-sorted sets OP and PR of *function* and *predicate symbols,* respectively. S-sorted function symbols are called *constants.*

Cartesian products of sorts yield further sorts. Corresponding tupling operators denoted by (_,...,_) provide further function symbols. We assume that for all $s \in S$, PR_{ss} implicitly contains a predicate symbol $\equiv_s$, called the *equality predicate for* s. We also fix an S-sorted set X of *(individual) variables* such that for all $s \in S$, X_s is countably infinite. Typical variables or finite sequences of variables are *x,y,z*.

Example 1.1 The signature for most of our sample proofs provides sorts, functions and predicates for natural numbers, pairs (of arbitrary elements), sequences and bags (multisets) of natural numbers. Appropriate axioms are given later.

NSB

sorts	nat, seq, bag		
	symbol	*type*	
functs	0	nat	
	1	nat	
	_+1	nat ⟶ nat	
	_+2	nat ⟶ nat	
	_+_	nat,nat ⟶ nat	
	_-_	nat,nat ⟶ nat	
	_*2	nat ⟶ nat	
	div	nat,nat ⟶ nat×nat	(quotient and remainder)
	ε	seq	
	_&_	nat,seq ⟶ seq	
	∅	bag	
	add	nat,bag⟶ bag	
	makeBag	seq ⟶ bag	
	insert	nat,seq ⟶ seq	
preds	_ ≤ _	nat,nat	
	_ ≥ _	nat,nat	
	_ < _	nat,nat	
	_ > _	nat,nat	

_ ≠ _	nat,nat
sorted	seq
Def	nat
Def	nat×nat
Def	seq

We hope that the notation is self-explanatory. ∎

Apart from concrete examples like 1.1, function and predicate symbols are always denoted by capital roman letters.

Let us fix a signature SIG = (S,OP,PR).

1.1 Terms and substitutions

T(SIG) denotes the S^*-sorted set of terms (and term tuples) over SIG and X. Given a term t, *var(t)* is the set of variables of t. t is *ground* if var(t) is empty. The function symbols of t form the set *op(t)*. *GT(SIG)* denotes the set of ground terms over SIG. SIG is assumed to be *inhabited,* i.e., for all s ∈ S, $GT(SIG)_s \neq \emptyset$.

When talking about terms in general, we employ the prefix notation. In some examples, however, the layout of terms is adapted to the underlying signature where infix, postfix or mixfix notations may occur as well. For instance, `0+1`, `(0,0*2)` and `0&ε` are ground terms over NSB.

Given S-sorted sets A and B, a set of functions $f_s : A_s \longrightarrow B_s$, s ∈ S, is an *S-sorted function,* denoted by f : A⟶B. Given $w = (s_1,...,s_n) \in S^+$ and $(a_1,...,a_n) \in A_w = A_{s1} \times ... \times A_{sn}$, f is extended to an S^+-sorted function by defining $f_w(a_1,...,a_n) = (f_{s1}a_1,...,f_{sn}a_n)$.

We denote by id^A the identity function on A, and by ∘ the operator for the sequential composition of functions (from right to left) and relations (from left to right). Function application brackets, the composition operator and sort indices are omitted when they are clear from the context. The set of all S-sorted functions from X to A is denoted by A^X.

An S-sorted function f : X⟶T(SIG) is called a *substitution.* The *domain of f, dom(f),* is the set of all x ∈ X such that fx ≠ x. If dom(f) is empty, then f is called the *identity substitution* and denoted by *id.* If dom(f) = $\{x_1,...,x_n\}$ and for all 1≤i≤n, $fx_i = t_i$, then f is also written as the set $\{t_1/x_1,...,t_n/x_n\}$. Given V ⊆ X, f|V, the *restriction of f to V,* is defined by (f|V)(x) = fx for all x ∈ V and by (f|V)(x) = x for all x ∈ X-V.

A substitution f is *ground* if f(X), the image of X under f, consists of ground terms. The set of ground substitutions over a given signature SIG is denoted by *GS*.

The *instance of a term t by f*, denoted by *t[f]*, is the term obtained from t by replacing each variable of t by its value under f. Conversely, one says that *t subsumes t[f]* or that *t is a prefix of t[f]*. *A term set T subsumes a term t'* if some $t \in T$ subsumes t'. *f unifies terms t and t'*, or *f is a unifier of t and t'*, if t[f] = t'[f]. A unifier f of terms t and t' is *most general* if f is a prefix of every unifier of t and t'. The substitution operator _[_] is inductively defined on the term structure:

- for all $x \in X$, x[f] = f(x),
- for all $w \in S^*$, $s \in S$, $F \in OP_{ws}$ and $t \in T(SIG)_w$, (Ft)[f] = F(t[f]).

Given two substitutions f and g, the sequential composition *f[g]* is defined as f[g](x) = f(x)[g] for all $x \in X$. The parallel composition *f+g*, is defined only if f and g have disjoint domains. Then (f+g)(x) = fx if $x \in$ dom(f), and (f+g)(x) = gx otherwise.

1.2 Atoms, goals and Horn clauses

Given $w \in S^+$, $P \in PR_w$ and $u \in T(SIG)_w$, the expression Pu is called an *atom (over SIG)*. If P is the equality predicate for $s \in S$ and thus u = (t,t') for some t,t' $\in T(SIG)_s$, then Pu is an *equation*, written as *t≡t'*. An equation of the form t≡t is called *reflexive*. Given a substitution f, *EQ(f)* denotes the set of all equations x≡fx such that $x \in$ dom(f).

Note the difference between the formula t≡t' and the structural identity of two terms t,t' denoted by *t = t'*. ≡ is a predicate *symbol*, while = *means* equality. Examples of structural identities between equations are, for instance,

$$Ft \equiv t' \;=\; Fx[t/x] \equiv t' \;=\; (Fx \equiv y)[t/x, t'/y] \;=\; (Fx \equiv y)[f]$$

where fx = t and fy = t'.

The notions *var, instance, prefix, unifier* and *ground* extend from terms to atoms as if predicate symbols were function symbols.

At(SIG) and *GAt(SIG)* denote respectively the sets of atoms and ground atoms over SIG. Sets of atoms are called *goals*.

Small Latin letters may stand for terms, atoms or substitutions. Small Greek letters are reserved for goals.

A *Horn clause* $c = p \Leftarrow \delta$ consists of an atom p, the *conclusion* of c, and a goal δ, the *premise* of c. If p is an equation, then c is a *conditional equation*. If δ is empty, then c is identified with p. The set brackets of a premise are mostly omitted.

Given goals γ,δ, the formula $\gamma \Leftarrow \delta$ stands for the set $\{p \Leftarrow \delta \mid p \in \gamma\}$ of Horn clauses. Given goals $\delta_1,\ldots,\delta_n$, the goal set $\{\delta_1,\ldots,\delta_n\}$ stands for the disjunction of $\delta_1,\ldots,\delta_n$. Given $Z \subseteq X$, the formula $\forall Z\delta$ stands for the goal $\cup\{\delta[f|Z] \mid f \in GS\}$. $\forall Z\delta$ is proved either by induction on GS or by deriving the goal $\delta[f|(X\text{-}Z)]$ via the cut calculus (see below). $\gamma \Leftarrow \delta$ and $\gamma \Leftarrow \forall Z\delta$ are also called Horn clauses.

For a typical example of a Horn clause with an infinite premise, consider the predicate *fair : stream* that checks whether a number stream contains infinitely many zeros (cf. Sect. 8.7):

```
fair(st)  ⇐  ∀ i : fairStep(i,st)
fairStep(0,st)
fairStep(i+1,st)  ⇐  st ≡ s•(0&st'), fairStep(i,st').
```

fairStep(i,st) holds true if st contains at least i zeros. Step functions are also convenient for making "non-terminating" functions amenable to inductive proofs without changing the simple semantics of Horn clause specifications (cf. Sect. 3.1). For instance, a function *eval : prog,state⟶ state* that evaluates iterative programs can be axiomatized without any reference to lattice theory:

```
eval(p, s) ≡ s'  ⇐  evalStep(i, p, s) ≡ s', Def(s')
evalStep(i, p;p', s) ≡ evalStep(i, p', s')  ⇐  evalStep(i, p, s) ≡ s'

evalStep(i, while b do p od, s) ≡ s  ⇐  evalStep(i, b, s) ≡ false
evalStep(i+1, while b do p od, s) ≡ evalStep(i, while b do p od, s')

              ⇐  evalStep(i+1, b, s) ≡ true, evalStep(i+1, p, s) ≡ s'.
```

The use of step functions in partial correctness proofs is illustrated in [Pad91], Section 8.

Definition A *(design) specification* is a pair (SIG,AX), consisting of a signature SIG and a set AX of Horn clauses, constituting the axioms of the specification. ▮

In concrete specifications, (SIG,AX) is often identified with AX.

Example 1.1 (continued) The axioms of NSB read as follows.

```
vars    x,y,q,r : nat;  s : seq;  b : bag
axms    1 ≡ 0+1
        x+2 ≡ x+1+1
        x+0 ≡ x                                                      (N1)
        x+(y+1) ≡ (x+y)+1                                            (N2)
        0-y ≡ 0                                                      (N3)
        (x+1)-0 ≡ x+1                                                (N4)
        (x+1)-(y+1) ≡ x-y                                            (N5)
        div(x,y) ≡ (0,x)   ⇐   x < y                                 (N6)
        div(x,y) ≡ (q+1,r)   ⇐   x ≥ y,  y > 0,  div(x-y,y) ≡ (q,r)  (N7)
        0*2 ≡ 0                                                      (DB1)
        (x+1)*2 ≡ (x*2)+2                                            (DB2)
        makeBag(ε) ≡ Ø                                               (BA1)
        makeBag(x&s) ≡ add(x,makeBag(s))                             (BA2)
        add(x,add(y,b)) ≡ add(y,add(x,b))   ⇐   x > y                (BA3)
        insert(x,ε) ≡ x&ε                                            (IN1)
        insert(x,y&s) ≡ x&y&s   ⇐   x ≤ y                            (IN2)
        insert(x,y&s) ≡ y&insert(x,s)   ⇐   x > y                    (IN3)
        0 ≤ y                                                        (LE1)
        x+1 ≤ y+1   ⇐   x ≤ y                                        (LE2)
        x ≥ y   ⇐   y ≤ x                                            (GE)
        x < y   ⇐   x+1 ≤ y                                          (LT)
        x > y   ⇐   y < x                                            (GT)
        x ≢ y   ⇐   x < y                                            (NE1)
        x ≢ y   ⇐   x > y                                            (NE2)
        sorted(ε)                                                    (SO1)
        sorted(x&ε)                                                  (SO2)
        sorted(x&y&s)   ⇐   x ≤ y,  sorted(y&s)                      (SO3)
        Def(0)                                                       (DN1)
        Def(x+1)   ⇐   Def(x)                                        (DN2)
        Def((x,y))   ⇐   Def(x),  Def(y)                             (DNN)
        Def(ε)                                                       (DS1)
        Def(x&s)   ⇐   Def(s)                                        (DS2)
```

∎

Let us fix a specification (SIG,AX).

Definition The *cut calculus for Horn clauses* consists of the congruence axioms for all equality predicates of SIG and two inference rules: Let p,q be atoms and δ,δ' be goals.

(CUT)	$\{p \Leftarrow \delta \cup \{q\},\ q \Leftarrow \delta'\} \ \vdash\ p \Leftarrow \delta \cup \delta'$.
(SUB)	For all substitutions f, $p \Leftarrow \delta \ \vdash\ p[f] \Leftarrow \delta[f]$.

$\vdash_{cut}$ denotes the corresponding inference relation. A goal γ is *AX-valid* if AX $\vdash_{cut}$ γ. Two terms t and t' are called *AX-equivalent* if the equation t≡t' is AX-valid. $\equiv_{AX}$ denotes the corresponding congruence relation. Two substitutions f and g are *AX-equivalent* if for all x ∈ X, fx $\equiv_{AX}$ gx.

f solves a goal γ w.r.t. AX or is an *AX-solution of γ* if γ[f] is AX-valid. γ is *solvable w.r.t. AX* if some substitution solves γ w.r.t. AX. ∎

If there is a solution of γ, then there is also a ground solution of γ because we assume that (SIG,AX) is inhabited (cf. Sect. 1.1).

1.3 Models of a specification

For all s ∈ S, let $\sim_s$ be a binary relation on A_s. The family $\sim = \{\sim_s \mid s \in S\}$ is called an *S-sorted relation on A*. If all $\sim_s$, s ∈ S, are equivalence relations, then the *quotient of A by* $\sim$ is given by the family $A/\!\sim\; = \{A_s/\!\sim_s \mid s \in S\}$ of quotient sets. *nat* stands for the natural mapping from A to A/~ that assigns to a ∈ A the set of all a' ∈ A with a' ~ a.

Each substitution f induces an S-sorted function f^* : T(SIG)⟶T(SIG): For all t ∈ T(SIG), $f^*(t)$ is defined as the instance t[f] of t by f (cf. Sect. 1.1).

Definition A *SIG-structure* A consists of an S-sorted set, the *carrier set* of A, also denoted by A, a function $F^A : A_w \longrightarrow A_s$ for each function symbol F ∈ OP_{ws}, w ∈ S^*, s ∈ S, and a relation $P^A \subseteq A_w$ for each predicate symbol P ∈ PR_w, w ∈ S^+.

A is a SIG-structure *with identity* if for all s ∈ S, $\equiv_s^A$ is the identity on A_s. ∎

Structures with term carriers establish the link between the syntax and the semantics of a specification:

Definition Let C be an S-sorted subset of T(SIG). C is *contextually closed* if for all w ∈ S^*, s ∈ S and F ∈ OP_{ws}, t ∈ C_w implies Ft ∈ C_s. Hence contextually closed term sets differ only in the set of variables the terms include.

Let C be contextually closed. Then {Pt ∈ At(SIG) | t ∈ C^*} is called the *Herbrand universe* w.r.t. C. A subset HI of the Herbrand universe is called a *Herbrand interpretation*. The *Herbrand structure A = HS(C,HI)* is defined as follows:

- For all s ∈ S, $A_s = C_s$,
- for all w ∈ S^*, s ∈ S, F ∈ OP_{ws} and t ∈ C_w, $F^A(t)$ = Ft,
- for all w ∈ S^+ and P ∈ PR_w, P^A = {t ∈ C_w | Pt ∈ HI}. ∎

Definition Let A be a SIG-structure. Each $b \in A^X$ is extended to an S-sorted function $b^* : T(SIG) \longrightarrow A$ along the inductive definition of terms:

- For all $s \in S$ and $x \in X_s$, $b^*(x) = b(x)$,
- for all $s \in S$ and $F \in OP_s$, $b^*(F) = F^A$,
- for all $w \in S^+$, $s \in S$, $F \in OP_{ws}$ and $t \in T(SIG)_w$, $b^*(Ft) = F^A \circ b^*(t)$. ∎

Given $b \in A^X$, b^* *evaluates* a term t by, first, assigning values to the variables of t according to b, second, turning the function symbols of t into functions and, third, applying these functions stepwise inside out. Hence the instance t[f] of t by a substitution f can be evaluated in two equivalent ways:

- after substituting fx for $x \in var(t)$, evaluate t, or
- first evaluate fx, substitute the value for x and evaluate the resulting term afterwards.

Formally, this equivalence reads as follows:

Proposition 1.2 *Let A be a SIG-structure, $b \in A^X$, $t \in T(SIG)$ and f be a substitution. Then*

$$b^*(t[f]) = (b^* \circ f)^*(t).$$

Proof. By induction on size(t).

Case 1. t is a variable, say x. Then

$$b^*(t[f]) = b^*(x[f]) = b^*(fx) = (b^* \circ f)(x) = (b^* \circ f)^*(x) = (b^* \circ f)^*(t).$$

Case 2. t is a constant, say F. Then

$$b^*(t[f]) = b^*(F[f]) = b^*(F) = F^A = (b^* \circ f)^*(F) = (b^* \circ f)^*(t).$$

Case 3. t = Fu for some F and u. By the induction hypothesis, $b^*(u[f]) = (b^* \circ f)^*(u)$. Hence

$$b^*(t[f]) = b^*(Fu[f]) = (F^A \circ b^*)(u[f]) = (F^A \circ (b^* \circ f)^*)(u)$$
$$= (b^* \circ f)^*(Fu) = (b^* \circ f)^*(t). \ ∎$$

If t is ground, b^*t always returns the same value, regardless of the definition of b. This leads to the *evaluation mapping* $eval^A$ *of A*, which is defined as the restriction of any b^* to ground terms. A is *term-generated* if each $a \in A$ is the interpretation of a ground term, i.e., if $eval^A$ is surjective.

Definition Let A be a SIG-structure, $b \in A^X$ and $Pt \in At(SIG)$. *b solves Pt in A* if $b^*t \in P^A$. b solves a goal γ in A if b solves all $p \in \gamma$ in A.

An atom *p is valid in A* or *A satisfies p*, written $A \models p$, if all $b \in A^X$ solve p in A. A Horn clause $c = \gamma \Leftarrow \delta$ *is valid in A* or *A satisfies c*, written $A \models c$, if all solutions of δ in A solve γ in A. A class **C** of SIG-structures satisfies c if each A $\in$ **C** satisfies c.

A is a *SIG-model of AX* if A is a SIG-structure with identity and satisfies all clauses of AX. *Mod(SIG,AX)* denotes the class of all SIG-models of AX. *Gen(SIG,AX)* stands for the subclass of all term-generated SIG-models of AX. ∎

Mod(SIG,AX) satifies a Horn clause $p \Leftarrow \gamma$ if and only if p can be derived from $AX \cup \gamma$ via the cut calculus such that the variables of γ are not instantiated (cf. Cor. 3.2).

Definition Let A be a SIG-structure and R be an S-sorted binary relation on A. R is *OP-compatible* or *monotonic* if for all $w \in S^+$, $s \in S$ and $F \in OP_{ws}$, (a,b) $\in R_w$ implies $(F^A a, F^A b) \in R$. R is *PR-compatible* if for all $w \in S^+$, $s \in S$, $P \in PR_w$ and $a \in P^A$, $(a,b) \in R_w$ implies $b \in P^A$.

An OP- and PR-compatible equivalence relation ~ is a *SIG-congruence relation.* In that case, the quotient B = A/~ becomes a SIG-structure by defining

$$F^B \circ nat = nat \circ F^A \quad \text{and} \quad P^B = \{nat(a) \mid a \in P^A\}$$

where nat is the natural mapping from A to A/~. ∎

Note that, if A is a Herbrand structure with carrier set GT(SIG), then the evaluation mapping of A/~ agrees with nat.

1.4 Gentzen clauses and inductive theorems

For presenting and proving requirements to the design specification (SIG,AX), we provide the following additional notions.

Definition Given $X_1,\ldots,X_n \subseteq X$, atoms or goals $p_1,\ldots,p_n$ and a goal δ, the formula

$$c \;=\; \exists X_1 p_1 \vee \ldots \vee \exists X_n p_n \Leftarrow \delta \tag{1}$$

is called a *(positive) Gentzen clause.* W.l.o.g., the variables of δ are distinct from $X_1 \cup \ldots \cup X_n$. A summand of the form $\exists \emptyset p$ is identified with p.

c is *inductively valid w.r.t. AX,* an *inductive AX-theorem* or an *inductive consequence of AX* if for all $f \in GS$,

$$AX \vdash_{cut} \delta[f] \quad \text{implies} \quad AX \vdash_{cut} p_i[g]$$

for some $1 \le i \le n$ and $g \in GS$ with $g \mid (X-X_i) = f \mid (X-X_i)$.

The set of inductive AX-theorems is denoted by *ITh(AX)*. Two Gentzen clauses c and c' are *inductively AX-equivalent* if $c \in ITh(AX \cup \{c'\})$ and $c' \in ITh(AX \cup \{c\})$. ∎

The following Gentzen clauses are inductive consequences of NSB (cf. Ex. 1.1):

$$x \equiv 0 \lor \exists\{y\}\ x \equiv y+1 \ \Leftarrow\ Def(x) \qquad (DN^{-1})$$

$$s \equiv \varepsilon \lor \exists\{x,s'\}\ s \equiv x\&s' \ \Leftarrow\ Def(s) \qquad (DS^{-1})$$

$$x < y \lor x \equiv y \lor x > y \ \Leftarrow\ Def(x),\ Def(y) \qquad (C3)$$

$$\exists\{q,r\}\ \{x \equiv (q*y)+r,\ r < y\} \ \Leftarrow\ Def(x),\ Def(y),\ y > 0 \qquad (QUO)$$

Note that QUO is stronger than the conjunction of QUO1 and QUO2:

$$\exists\{q,r\}\ \{x \equiv (q*y)+r\} \ \Leftarrow\ Def(x),\ Def(y),\ y > 0 \qquad (QUO1)$$

$$\exists\{r\}\ \{r < y\} \ \Leftarrow\ Def(y),\ y > 0 \qquad (QUO2)$$

Inductive consequences of (SIG,AX) are often listed in a particular *theorems* section of (SIG,AX) (cf. Chapters 8 and 9).

1.5 Clause inversion

Inductive AX-validity agrees with validity in the initial (SIG,AX)-structure (cf. Sect. 3.1). Moreover, inductive validity complies with the *closed world assumption* of logic programming (cf. [Rei78]). Suppose we have axiomatized a predicate P by Horn clauses

$$P(t_{11},\ldots,t_{1n}) \ \Leftarrow\ \gamma_1 \qquad (c_1)$$

$$\ldots$$

$$P(t_{k1},\ldots,t_{kn}) \ \Leftarrow\ \gamma_k \qquad (c_k)$$

such that AX contains no further axioms with an occurrence of P in the conclusion. For all $1 \le i \le k$, let $z_1,\ldots,z_n$ be variables not occurring in $c_1,\ldots,c_k$,

$$\delta_i = \gamma_i \cup \{z_1 \equiv t_{i1},\ldots,z_n \equiv t_{in}\}$$

and $X_i = var(c_i)$. An *inverse of* $\{c_1,\ldots,c_k\}$ is given by a Gentzen clause

$$\exists X_1\delta_1' \lor \ldots \lor \exists X_k\delta_k' \ \Leftarrow\ P(z_1,\ldots,z_n) \qquad (c^{-1})$$

where $\delta_i' \subseteq \delta_i$ for all $1 \le i \le k$. c^{-1} is inductively valid w.r.t. AX because each ground instance p of $P(z_1,\ldots,z_n)$ can be derived from AX only if for some $1 \le i \le k$ and $g \in GS$, $\delta_i[g]$ is derivable as well: every derivation of p "passes" $\delta_i[g]$.

For instance, DN^{-1} and DS^{-1} (cf. Sect. 1.4) result from inverting {DN1,DN2} and {DS1,DS2} respectively (cf. Ex. 1.1). The specification of a *function* F by conditional equations

$$F(t_{11},\ldots,t_{1n}) \equiv t_1 \;\Leftarrow\; \gamma_1$$

$$\ldots$$

$$F(t_{k1},\ldots,t_{kn}) \equiv t_k \;\Leftarrow\; \gamma_k$$

can be inverted in a similar way, provided that for all $1 \le i \le k$, $F(t_{i1},\ldots,t_{in})$ is not unifiable with t_i.

2: Guards, Generators and Constructors

In Chapter 4, we will show how to prove an inductive theorem $\gamma \Leftarrow \delta$ by expanding γ into δ. The expansion fails if it is not directed towards a subset of δ. Hence δ should be kept small. This can often be achieved by splitting the atoms of δ into *guards* and *generators*. The distinction stems from parallel logic programming languages (cf. [Ued86]; [Llo87], p. 62; [Sha89]) where it determines the order of executing the atoms of a clause premise. Roughly said, guards come first, generators second. The *commit operator* ":" separates both parts of a premise.

A *guarded clause* $\gamma \Leftarrow \delta : \gamma'$ with guard δ and generator γ' has the same meaning as the Horn clause $c = \gamma \Leftarrow \delta \cup \gamma'$. If c is an *axiom* representing a program for a function or predicate F, then δ usually embodies a precondition, while γ' contains recursive calls of F and is thus related to γ in the same way as right-hand sides of equations defining a function are related to the corresponding left-hand sides.

Axioms N7 and SO3 of NSB (cf. Ex. 1.1) are typical examples of Horn clauses whose premises split into guards and generators. They may thus be equipped with the commit operator:

$$\mathrm{div}(x,y) \equiv (q+1,r) \Leftarrow x \geq y,\ y > 0 : \mathrm{div}(x-y,y) \equiv (q,r) \qquad \text{(N7)}$$

$$\mathrm{sorted}(x\&y\&s) \Leftarrow x \leq y : \mathrm{sorted}(y\&s). \qquad \text{(SO3)}$$

The correspondence between the body of a functional program and the generator (often also called the body) of a logic program provides the clue for distinguishing between the guard δ and the generator γ'. Semantically, γ' is part of the conclusion rather than of the premise. When applying this observation to *conjectures*, one expects to be able to prove c by expanding γ and γ' simultaneously into δ. Precise criteria for the correctness of this procedure are given in Sects. 2.2 and 2.3. Let us first illustrate how expansions of $\gamma \cup \gamma'$ into δ capture the idea of program synthesis.

2.1 From verification to synthesis

The sample expansion proofs given in Sect. 5.5 follow a program construction schema outlined below. Suppose that some function F is specified by an input/output relation InOut with precondition Pre:

$$F(x) \equiv y \;\Leftarrow\; InOut(x,y),\ Pre(x).$$

For instance, take DIVS (cf. Ex. 5.11):

$$divS(x,y) \equiv (q,r) \;\Leftarrow\; x \equiv (q*y)+r,\ r < y,\ y > 0.$$

Suppose further we want to construct an iterative program FLoop for F. Schematically, the verification condition may read as follows:

$$FLoop(x) \equiv F(x) \;\Leftarrow\; Pre(x), \tag{1}$$

e.g.,

$$divL(x,y) \equiv divS(x,y) \;\Leftarrow\; y > 0.$$

If we are satisfied with *partial* correctness, (1) can be weakened into

$$FLoop(x) \equiv F(x) \;\Leftarrow\; Pre(x),\ Def(F(x))$$

where Def recognizes all ground terms that are equivalent to *constructors* (cf. Sect. 2.3).

FLoop calls Loop, the function that accumulates the value of F(x) in its second argument, starting out from an initial value, say start:

$$FLoop(x) \equiv Loop(x,start), \tag{2}$$

e.g.,

$$divL(x,y) \equiv Loop(x,y,0,x).$$

To prove (1), it must be generalized into a property of *Loop*:

$$Loop(x,z) \equiv F(x) \;\Leftarrow\; Inv(x,z),\ Pre(x), \tag{3}$$

e.g.,

$$Loop(x,y,q,r) \equiv divS(x,y) \;\Leftarrow\; x \equiv (q*y)+r,\ y > 0.$$

In fact, if Inv(x,start) holds true, then (1) follows immediately from (2) and (3). Inv denotes the *loop invariant* that relates the input parameters x,y of Loop to the output parameters or *accumulators* q,r. The notion of a loop invariant is better known in *imperative* program verification by means of Hoare's assertion calculus (cf. [Hoa69]).

The equation Loop(x,z)≡F(x) can be expanded if axioms for Loop are not needed. In fact, they can often be derived from subgoals generated in the course of the proof, and we say that the program, consisting of (2) and the axioms for Loop, has been developed from the correctness proof.

Note that (3) has no generator. The entire premise of (3) yields a guard. One may add a generator and come up with:

$$\text{Loop}(x,z) \equiv z' \Leftarrow \text{Inv}(x,z), \text{Pre}(x) : F(x) \equiv z'.$$

$F(x)\equiv z'$ generates a substitution for the *output* variable z' that solves the equation $\text{Loop}(x,z)\equiv z'$.

A more general loop specification schema is given by:

$$\text{Loop}(x,z) \equiv G(z,z') \Leftarrow \text{Pre}(x) : F(x,z) \equiv C(z'), \qquad (4)$$

e.g.,

$$\text{Loop}(x,y,q,r) \equiv (q+q',r') \Leftarrow y > 0, \text{Def}(r), \text{Def}(y) : \text{div}(r,y) \equiv (q',r')$$

(cf. Ex. 5.9). If (4) satisfies the criteria developed in Sects. 2.2 and 2.3, then (4) can be proved by expanding the conclusion $\text{Loop}(x,z)\equiv G(z,z')$ and the generator $F(x,z)\equiv C(z')$ simultaneously into the guard $\{\text{Inv}(x), \text{Pre}(x)\}$.

In general, we search for conditions that allow us to reduce a proof of $\gamma\Leftarrow\delta:\gamma'$ to an expansion of $\gamma\cup\gamma'$ into δ, which admits program construction. For instance, the transformation of

$$\{\text{Loop}(x,z) \equiv G(z,z'),\ F(x,z) \equiv C(z')\} \qquad (5)$$

(cf. (4)) may lead to axioms for Loop when terms are substituted for x,z,z' as a result of applying F-axioms to the generator $F(x,z)\equiv C(z')$. In fact, transformation rules that constitute deduction-oriented program synthesis approaches such as *fold&unfold* (cf. [BD77]), *divide&conquer* (cf. [Smi85]) or *deductive tableaus* (cf. [MW 80,87]) can be derived from such expansions.

The variables x and z in (4) are called *input* variables, while z' is an *output* variable of (4). In the corresponding goal (5), x and z are universal(ly quantified) variables, while z' is an existential variable in which (5) is to be solved.

2.2 Generator matrices

Given a guarded clause c = $\gamma\Leftarrow\delta:\gamma'$ with output variable set X_{out}, expanding $\gamma\cup\gamma'$ into δ should be a correct method for proving c, provided that c is implied by the Gentzen clause $\exists X_{out}(\gamma\cup\gamma')\Leftarrow\delta$. c may fall into several clauses with different generators:

$$\gamma \Leftarrow \delta : \gamma_1'$$

$$\ldots$$

$$\gamma \Leftarrow \delta : \gamma_n'$$

Moreover, each generator γ_i' may imply another conclusion γ_i:

$$\gamma_1 \Leftarrow \delta : \gamma_1'$$

$$\ldots$$

$$\gamma_n \Leftarrow \delta : \gamma_n'$$

This is the most general form of a conjecture that can be treated by inductive expansion (cf. Sect. 5.3). If $\{\gamma_1',\ldots,\gamma_n'\}$ is minimal in the sense that two elements are not satisfiable simultaneously, we call $\{\gamma_1',\ldots,\gamma_n'\}$ a *minimal generator matrix*.

General Assumption Let us assume a set $X_{in} \subseteq X$ of *input variables* and call $X_{out} = X\text{-}X_{in}$ the set of *output variables.* In conjectures, X_{in} comprises variables to induce upon, while X_{out} represents the "unknowns" in which generators are to be solved. A term, atom or goal γ is called an *input term, input atom* or *input goal* if all variables of γ are input variables.

For all substitutions f, $f_{in} = f|X_{in}$ and $f_{out} = f|X_{out}$. For all $Z \subseteq X$, $Z_{in} = Z \cap X_{in}$ and $Z_{out} = Z \cap X_{out}$. ∎

Definition A Horn clause $\gamma \Leftarrow \delta \cup \gamma'$ is called a *guarded clause* with *guard* δ and *generator* γ' written as $\gamma \Leftarrow \delta : \gamma'$, if δ is an input goal and $var(\gamma) \subseteq X_{in} \cup var(\gamma')$. ∎

Definition Let δ be a goal and GM be a set of goals. GM is a *δ-minimal generator matrix* if for all $\gamma,\gamma' \in$ GM and all $f,g \in$ GS,

$$AX \vdash_{cut} (\delta \cup \gamma \cup \gamma'[g_{out}])[f] \text{ implies } \gamma = \gamma' \text{ and } fx \equiv_{AX} gx$$

$$\text{for all } x \in var(\gamma)_{out}.$$

GM = $\{\gamma_1,\ldots,\gamma_n\}$ is *δ-complete* if $\exists X_{out}\gamma_1 \vee \ldots \vee \exists X_{out}\gamma_n \Leftarrow \delta$ is inductively valid w.r.t. AX. ∎

Theorem 2.1 *A set CS = $\{\gamma_1 \Leftarrow \delta : \gamma_1',\ldots,\gamma_n \Leftarrow \delta : \gamma_n'\}$ of guarded clauses is inductively valid w.r.t. AX if the Gentzen clause*

$$c = \exists X_{out}(\gamma_1 \cup \gamma_1') \vee \ldots \vee \exists X_{out}(\gamma_n \cup \gamma_n') \Leftarrow \delta$$

is inductively valid w.r.t. AX and GM = $\{\gamma_1',\ldots,\gamma_n'\}$ is a δ-minimal generator matrix.

Conversely, c is inductively valid if CS is inductively valid and GM is δ-complete.

Proof. "if": Let $1 \le i \le n$ and f be a ground solution of $\delta \cup \gamma_i'$. Since c is inductively valid, there are $1 \le j \le n$ and $g \in GS$ such that $f_{in}+g_{out}$ solves $\gamma_j \cup \gamma_j'$. Since GM is a δ-minimal generator matrix, we have i = j and $fx \equiv_{AX} gx$ for all $x \in var(\gamma_i')_{out}$. Hence $f_{in}+g_{out}$ solves $\gamma_i \cup \gamma_i'$ and thus f solves γ_i. Therefore, $\gamma_i \Leftarrow \delta_i \cup \gamma_i'$ is inductively valid.

"only if": Let f be a ground solution of δ. Since GM is δ-complete, there are $1 \le i \le n$ and $g \in GS$ such that $\gamma_i'[f_{in}+g_{out}]$ is AX-valid. From $var(\delta) \subseteq X_{in}$ we conclude that $f_{in}+g_{out}$ solves $\delta \cup \gamma_i'$. Since CS is inductively valid, $f_{in}+g_{out}$ solves γ_i as well. Therefore, c is also inductively valid. ∎

For proving a set of Horn clauses by inductive expansion (cf. Sect. 5.3), the set must be presented as a set of guarded clauses with minimal generator matrix. Actually, inductive expansion proves c (cf. Thm. 2.1). For concluding CS from c, the generator matrix of CS must be minimal.

2.3 Constructor-based clauses

The minimality assumption is hardly tractable in its general form. In this section, we provide an effective criterion that uses the following notion of a set of constructor terms.

Definition Let C be a set of terms. C is a *set of constructors* if for all $c,d \in C$ and $f,g \in GS$ such that $c[f] \equiv_{AX} d[g]$, c and d are equal and $f|var(c)$ and $g|var(c)$ are AX-equivalent.

Let δ be a goal. C is *δ-complete for a term t* if for all ground solutions f of δ there are $c \in C$ and $g \in GS$ such that $t[f] \equiv_{AX} c[g]$. C is *complete for t* if C is ∅-complete for t. ∎

With respect to NSB (cf. Ex. 1.1), C = {0, x+1, (x,y), ε, x&s} is a set of constructors. This can be shown with the help of a constructor criterion, based on the fact that NSB is *ground confluent* (cf. Exs. 6.22 and 7.6). C∪{∅,add(x,b)} is complete for all ground terms of sort *nat, seq* or *bag,* but not for *nat×nat*-sorted ground terms of the form *div(x,0)*.

A semantic constructor characterization follows from Thm. 3.4 below: Given the initial (SIG,AX)-structure A, C is a set of constructors if and only if A interprets each $c \in C$ as an injective function c^A and if each two functions c^A and d^A, interpreting two different elements $c,d \in C$, have disjoint images.

Constructors allow us to confine our attention to *constructor-based* generator matrices, which consist of equational goals. More precisely, such a goal set has the form

$$\{\{t_1\equiv c_{11}, t_2\equiv c_{12}, \ldots, t_n\equiv c_{1n}\},$$
$$\ldots$$
$$\{t_1\equiv c_{k1}, t_2\equiv c_{k2}, \ldots, t_n\equiv c_{kn}\}\}$$

where each c_{ij} is a constructor. Certain conditions on the variables given below control the data flow from X_{in} and c_{ij-1} to t_j. In terms of *Concurrent Prolog* (cf. [Sha87], p. 287), the variable occurrences of t_j may be regarded as *read-only variables*, taken from X_{in} or c_{ij-1}.

Before presenting the exact definition of a constructor-based matrix and the proof that constructor-based matrices are generator matrices, let us illustrate this result using the following schema of two guarded clauses:

$$P(x,y) \Leftarrow Q(x) : F(x)\equiv c(y) \qquad \text{(CP)}$$

$$R(x,y) \Leftarrow Q(x) : F(x)\equiv d(y). \qquad \text{(CR)}$$

If {c(y),d(y)} is a set of constructors, then $\{F(x)\equiv c(y), F(x)\equiv d(y)\}$ is a minimal generator matrix:

Let f be a ground solution of Q(x) and g ∈ GS. If $\{F(fx)\equiv c(fy), F(fx)\equiv c(gy)\}$ is AX-valid, then c(fy) and c(gy) are AX-equivalent and thus fy and gy are AX-equivalent as well. If $\{F(fx)\equiv d(fy), F(fx)\equiv d(gy)\}$ is AX-valid, then d(fy) and d(gy) are AX-equivalent and thus again fy $\equiv_{AX}$ gy. But $\{F(fx)\equiv c(fy), F(fx)\equiv d(gy)\}$ or $\{F(fx)\equiv d(fy), F(fx)\equiv c(gy)\}$ cannot be AX-valid because c and d are different.

Hence $\{F(x)\equiv c(y), F(x)\equiv d(y)\}$ is a $\{Q(x)\}$-minimal generator matrix and thus, by Thm. 2.1, $F(x)\equiv c(y)$ and $F(x)\equiv d(y)$ are inductively valid if

$$\exists\{y\}\{P(x,y), F(x)\equiv c(y)\} \vee \exists\{y\}\{R(x,y), F(x)\equiv d(y)\} \Leftarrow Q(x)$$

is so.

The set of all constructor-based matrices is defined inductively as follows:

Definition

- For all $Z \subseteq X$, the singleton $\{\langle\emptyset,Z\rangle\}$ is a *(δ-complete) constructor-based matrix*.
- If for some k,n > 0 and all $1\le i\le k$ there are an equation $t\equiv c_i$ and a $((\delta\cup\{t\equiv c_i\})$-complete) constructor-based matrix

$$\{\langle\gamma_{ij}, X_{ij}\cup var(c_i)\rangle \mid 1\le j\le n\}$$

such that $\{c_1,...,c_k\}$ is a (δ-complete) set of constructors (for t), $var(t) \subseteq X_{ij}$ and $X_{ij} \cap var(c_i) = \emptyset$, then

$$\{\langle\{t\equiv c_i\}\cup\gamma_{ij}, X_{ij}\rangle \mid 1\le i\le k, 1\le j\le n\}$$

is a *(δ-complete) constructor-based matrix.* ∎

Note that, except for the constructor property and the completeness of term sets, the requirements for a constructor-based matrix are purely syntactic. δ-completeness can be reduced to the inductive validity of clauses involving *definedness predicates* (cf. Ex. 1.1). Criteria for the constructor property employ ground confluence (cf. Sect. 7.3) or the initial (SIG,AX)-structure (cf. Sect. 3.1).

Constructor-based matrices are minimal generator matrices:

Lemma 2.2 *Let CM be a constructor-based matrix such that for all* $\langle\gamma,Z\rangle \in$ *CM and* $t\equiv c \in \gamma$, c *is an output term and* $Z = X_{in}$.

GM = $\{\gamma \mid \langle\gamma,X_{in}\rangle \in CM\}$ *is a minimal generator matrix.*

Given an input goal δ, *GM is* δ*-complete if CM is* δ*-complete.*

Proof. Suppose there are $\langle\gamma,X_{in}\rangle,\langle\gamma',X_{in}\rangle \in CM$ and $f,g \in GS$ satisfying

$$AX \vdash_{cut} (\delta\cup\gamma)[f] \cup \gamma'[f'] \tag{1}$$

where $f' = f_{in}+g_{out}$. Let $\gamma = \{t_1\equiv c_1,...,t_n\equiv c_n\}$ and $\gamma' = \{t_1\equiv d_1,...,t_n\equiv d_n\}$ where, according to the inductive definition of CM, t_n is introduced first and t_1 last. (1) implies

$$t_k[f] \equiv_{AX} c_k[f] \quad \text{and} \quad t_k[f'] \equiv_{AX} d_k[f'] \tag{2}$$

for all $1\le k\le n$. We show by induction on k that for all $1\le i\le k$,

$$c_i = d_i \quad \text{and} \quad fx \equiv_{AX} f'x \ \text{ for all } x \in var(c_i) \tag{3}$$

If $k = 0$, then (3) holds trivially. Otherwise the induction hypothesis implies (3) for all $1\le i<k$. Moreover, $var(t_k) \subseteq var(\{c_1,...,c_{k-1}\}) \cup X_{in}$ and $var(t_k) \subseteq var(\{d_1,...,d_{k-1}\}) \cup X_{in}$. Hence by induction hypothesis, $fx \equiv_{AX} f'x$ for all $x \in var(t_k)$ and thus $t_k[f] \equiv_{AX} t_k[f']$. (2) implies $c_k[f] \equiv_{AX} d_k[f']$. Since c_k and d_k belong to a set of constructors, (3) also holds for $i = k$.

Since $var(\gamma) \subseteq var(\{c_1,...,c_n\}) \cup X_{in}$, we conclude $\gamma = \gamma'$ and $fx \equiv_{AX} f'x$ for all $x \in var(\gamma)$ from (3) for all $1\le i\le n$. Therefore, GM is a δ-minimal generator matrix.

Suppose that CM is δ-complete and for all $\langle\gamma,Z\rangle \in CM$, $card(\gamma) = n$. Let $f \in GS$ solve δ w.r.t. AX. To conclude that GM is δ-complete, we must find

$$\langle\gamma,Z\rangle \in CM \text{ and } g \in GS \text{ such that } AX \vdash_{cut} \gamma[f_{in}+g_{out}]. \tag{4}$$

Let AX $\vdash_{cut}$ $\delta[f]$. If CM = $\{\langle\emptyset,Z\rangle\}$ for some $Z \subseteq X$, then (4) holds trivially. Otherwise there are k,n > 0 and for all 1≤i≤k an equation $t\equiv c_i$ and a $(\delta\cup\{t\equiv c_i\})$-complete constructor-based matrix

$$\{\langle\gamma_{ij},\ X_{ij}\cup var(c_i)\rangle \mid 1\le j\le n\}$$

such that C = $\{c_1,...,c_k\}$ is a δ-complete set of constructors for t, $var(t) \subseteq X_{ij}$, $X_{ij}\cap var(c_i) = \emptyset$ and

$$CM = \{\langle\{t\equiv c_i\}\cup\gamma_{ij},\ X_{ij}\rangle \mid 1\le i\le k,\ 1\le j\le n\}.$$

Let $Y_i = var(c_i)$ and $Z_{ij} = X_{ij} \cup Y_i$. Since C is δ-complete for t, there are 1≤i≤s and $h \in GS$ such that $t[f] \equiv_{AX} c_i[h]$. Let $f' = f|(X-Y_i)+h|Y_i$. Since $var(\delta)\cap Y_i = \emptyset$, f' solves $\delta\cup\{t\equiv c_i\}$. By induction hypothesis, there are 1≤j≤n and $g' \in GS$ such that $f'|Z_{ij}+g'|(X-Z_{ij})$ solves γ_{ij}. Let

$$g = h|Y_i+g'|(X-Z_{ij}).$$

Since $(t\equiv c_i)[f|X_{ij}+g] = t[f]\equiv c_i[h]$ is AX-valid and

$$f|X_{ij}+g = f|X_{ij}+h|Y_i+g'|(X-Z_{ij}) = f'|Z_{ij}+g'|(X-Z_{ij})$$

solves γ_{ij}, $f|Z_{ij}+g$ solves $\{t\equiv c_i\}\cup\gamma_{ij} \in CM$. ∎

Lemma 2.2 suggests the following specialization of guarded clause sets.

Definition A set CS = $\{\gamma_1\Leftarrow\delta:\gamma_1',...,\gamma_n\Leftarrow\delta:\gamma_n'\}$ of guarded clauses is called a *(complete) constructor-based clause set* if CM = $\{\langle\gamma_1',X_{in}\rangle,...,\langle\gamma_n',X_{in}\rangle\}$ is a (δ-complete) constructor-based matrix such that for all 1≤i≤n and $t\equiv c \in \gamma_i'$, c is an output term. ∎

Thm. 2.1 and Lemma 2.2 yield

Theorem 2.3 *Let CS =* $\{\gamma_1\Leftarrow\delta:\gamma_1',...,\gamma_n\Leftarrow\delta:\gamma_n'\}$ *be a constructor-based clause set. CS is inductively valid if*

$$\exists X_{out}(\gamma_1\cup\gamma_1')\vee...\vee\exists X_{out}(\gamma_n\cup\gamma_n') \Leftarrow \delta$$

is inductively valid. If CS is complete, the converse holds true as well. ∎

Each clause of a constructor-based clause set has the form

$$\gamma \Leftarrow \delta : t_1\equiv c_1,\ t_2\equiv c_2,\ ...,\ t_n\equiv c_n.$$

The variables of γ are input variables or stem from a constructor c_i. Hence, in addition to the "data flow" from X_{in} and c_{i-1} to t_i, γ may contain output variables that occur in some c_i.

The fact that each goal in a constructor-based matrix has the same number of equations need not be a restriction. If two clauses $\gamma\Leftarrow\delta:\varphi$ and $\gamma'\Leftarrow\delta:\varphi'$ with

$\varphi \subseteq \varphi'$ are to be proved simultaneously, they should be transformed into $\gamma\cup\gamma' \Leftarrow \delta:\varphi'$ and $\gamma \Leftarrow \delta:\varphi\cup\varphi''$ where φ'' is the "negation" of $\varphi'-\varphi$.

Concerning the *conclusions* of constructor-based clause sets, we have added nothing to the definition of guarded clauses and thus obtain a much weaker notion than, e.g., the one given in [You88] where an equation of the form $F(c_1,...,c_n)\equiv t$ is called constructor-based if $c_1,...,c_n$ are constructors. Employing the decomposition principle discussed below, this equation can be translated into the inductively equivalent clause

$$F(x_1,...,x_n)\equiv t \quad \Leftarrow \quad x_1\equiv c_1,..., x_n\equiv c_n,$$

which might be an element of a constructor-based clause set.

Constructor-based clause sets provide the kernel of most functional or logic specifications as well as programming languages. For instance, the data flow from input to output variables reflects the operational semantics of logic programs. From list, tree and graph algorithms via interpreters and compilers up to *plan formation* and protocol specifications, the language of constructor-based clause sets seems to be powerful enough for bringing such tasks into a precise, comprehensible, verifiable *and* executable form.[1]

2.4 Sample constructor-based theorems

For illustrating the range of applications, we present a number of constructor-based clause sets, expressing requirements for concrete design specifications, most of which can be found in Chapter 8.

X_{out}	*conclusion*	*guards*	*generators*	
arithmetic (cf. Exs. 5.4, 5.9 - 5.11 and Sect. 8.2)				
	EvenOrOdd(x)	Def(x)		(EVOD)
q',r'	Loop(x,y,q,r) ≡ (q+q',r')	y > 0, Def(r), Def(y)	div(r,y) ≡ (q',r')	(DIVL)
	Def(div(x,y))	y > 0, Def(x), Def(y)		
	Loop(x,y,q,r) ≡ divS(x,y)	y > 0, x ≡ (y*q)+r		

[1]The translation of a sublanguage into PASCAL is described in [GHM87].

k	Loop(x,y) ≡ k*y		fact(x) ≡ k	
k	Loop(b,x,y) ≡ (x*k)+y		decode(b) ≡ k	(DL1)
r,s	Loop(c,r,s) ≡ ((r*s')+r',s*s')		decode(c) ≡ (r',s')	(DL2)
searching (cf. Sect. 8.3)				
y	y ∈ makeBag(x&s), y ≤ makeBag(x&s)		min(x&s) ≡ y	
	binsearch(x,s)	x ∈ makeBag(s), sorted(s)		
s',s"	conc(s',s") ≡ s	halve(s) ≡ (s',s")		
sorting (cf. Exs. 5.12 - 5.14 and Sect. 8.3)				
s'	sorted(s') makeBag(s') ≡ makeBag(s)	Def(s)	sort(s) ≡ s'	(SORT)
	sorted(insert(x,s))	sorted(s)		(cf. Ex. 5.13)
	makeBag(insert(x,s)) ≡ makeBag(x&s)			(cf. Ex. 5.14)
	sorted(merge(s,s'))	sorted(s), sorted(s')		
	makeBag(merge(s,s')) ≡ makeBag(s) ∪ makeBag(s')			
s',s"	makeBag(s) ≡ makeBag(s') ∪ makeBag(s")		halve(s) ≡ (s',s")	
	sorted(conc(s,s'))	sorted(s), sorted(s')		
	makeBag(conc(s,s')) ≡ makeBag(s) ∪ makeBag(s')			
s',s"	makeBag(s) ≡ makeBag(s') ∪ makeBag(s") makeBag(s') < x, x ≤ makeBag(s")		filter(x,s) ≡ (s',s")	
s	sorted(s)	Rep(T)	sort(heapify(T)) ≡ s	
tree manipulation (cf. Sects. 8.4 and 8.5)				
	balanced(insert(T,x))	balanced(T), Def(T)		(BAL)
T',i	height(T') ≡ height(T)+i	balanced(T), Def(T)	insertCrit(T,x) ≡ (T',i)	(HEI)

	ABminimize(a,x@Ts,b) ≡ max(a,min(minimize(x@Ts),b)) ABmaximize(a,x@Ts,b) ≡ max(a,min(maximize(x@Ts),b)) ABminimizeseq(a,Ts,b) ≡ max(a,min(minimizeseq(Ts),b)) ABmaximizeseq(a,Ts,b) ≡ max(a,min(maximizeseq(Ts),b))	a ≤ b	(ABMS)
graph marking (cf. Sect. 8.6)			
s'	DFLoop(g,k,s,w) ≡ DFLoop(g,k',s',w)	k ∈ nodes(g)	depthfirst(g,k,s) ≡ s' (DFL)
e,s',g'	depthfirst(g',k,s) ≡ s' e ≡ (g,k',k)	k ∈ nodes(g)	SchorrWaite((g,k,k'),s) ≡ (e,s') remove(g,s) ≡ g' (SWR)
e',s'	down(e,s,w) ≡ up(e',s',w)	Def(e)	SchorrWaite(e,s) ≡ (e',s') (SWL)
plan formation (cf. [Pad88b])			
plan	s:plan:isClear(z)		clear(z) ≡ plan
plan	isIn(s:plan,insert(e,k),k)		insertAct(e,k) ≡ plan
network properties (cf. Sect. 8.7)			
	net(ms,b,st,st')	fair(st), fair(st')	

Some of the arithmetic examples have been employed for illustrating *tableau proof methods* (cf. [MW80]) as well as for demonstrating how programs may be constructed by *completion* (cf. [Der83]; see also Sect. 7.4). Iterative division and insertion sort programs will be derived from the loop invariants DIVL and SORT in Exs. 5.9 and 5.12 respectively, according to the synthesis schema of Sect. 2.1. Declarative programs that decode rational binary numbers were used in [Knu68] for introducing *attributed grammars* (see also Sect. 8.1). The synthesis of corresponding iterative programs from the loop invariants DL1 and DL2 is worked out in [Pad88a,b] (cf. Sect. 2.1). For the joint construction and correctness proof of sorting algorithms, cf. [GB78] and [Smi85].

Previous algebraic versions of balanced-tree insertion can be found in [HO82], [O'D85] and [Pad88a,b]. In Sect. 8.4, we specify AVL tree as well as 2-3 tree insertion. The correctness condition BAL and its generalization HEI are each the same in both cases. In Sect. 8.5, inductive expansion, along with the program synthesis schema of Sect. 2.1, is used for the joint construction and correctness proof of *alpha-beta pruning* (cf. ABMS).

Section 8.6 on binary graphs includes an expansion of DFL, which states the correctness of iterative depth-first marking with respect to a corresponding recursive algorithm. SWR and SWL represent the correctness of respectively recursive and iterative *Schorr-Waite* graph marking (cf. [Gri79], [BP82]). Expansions of SWR and SWL are given in Sect. 8.6.

The plan formation examples *clear* and *insertAct* were inspired by the *blocks world* applications of [MW87]. For proofs by inductive expansion, see [Pad88b]. In Sect. 8.7, we show how to specify and reason about stream processing networks within Horn logic. An alternating bit protocol controlling a circular network is proved correct by inductive expansion.

2.5 Turning Gentzen into Horn clauses

EVOD and ABP are Horn clause simulations of Gentzen clauses. They follow a general schema for translating Gentzen clauses into inductively equivalent Horn clauses, using additional *conjecture predicates*. For instance, EVOD is equivalent to

$$\exists\{y\}\ x \equiv y*2 \ \vee\ \exists\{y\}\ x \equiv (y*2)+1 \ \Leftarrow\ \mathrm{Def}(x)$$

provided that the predicate *EvenOrOdd* is specified by

$$\mathrm{EvenOrOdd}(x) \ \Leftarrow\ x \equiv y*2 \qquad \text{(EVEN)}$$

$$\mathrm{EvenOrOdd}(x) \ \Leftarrow\ x \equiv (y*2)+1. \qquad \text{(ODD)}$$

ABP is inductively equivalent to

$$\exists\{bs,mbs,mbs',bs'\}\ \{send(ms,bs,b) \equiv mbs,\ channel(mbs,st) \equiv mbs',$$
$$receive(mbs',b) \equiv (ms,bs'),\ channel(bs',st') \equiv bs\} \Leftarrow fair(st),\ fair(st')$$

where the predicate *net* is specified by

$$net(ms,b,st,st') \ \Leftarrow\ send(ms,bs,b) \equiv mbs,\ channel(mbs,st) \equiv mbs',$$
$$receive(mbs',b) \equiv (ms,bs'),\ channel(bs',st') \equiv bs. \qquad \text{(NET)}$$

In general, let

$$c = \exists X_1\gamma_1 \vee \ldots \vee \exists X_n\gamma_n \Leftarrow \delta$$

be a Gentzen clause, $(z_1,\ldots,z_k)$ be a sequence of all universal variables of c, i.e.,

$$\{z_1,\ldots,z_k\} = X - (X_1 \cup \ldots \cup X_n).$$

Moreover, let $s_i = \text{sort}(z_i)$ for all $1 \le i \le k$. Add the predicate symbol $P_c : s_1,\ldots,s_k$ to SIG and the axioms

$$P_c(z_1,\ldots,z_k) \Leftarrow \gamma_1$$

$$\ldots$$

$$P_c(z_1,\ldots,z_k) \Leftarrow \gamma_n$$

to AX. By clause inversion (cf. Sect. 1.5), one obtains the inductive AX-theorem

$$\exists X_1\gamma_1 \vee \ldots \vee \exists X_n\gamma_n \Leftarrow P_c(z_1,\ldots,z_k). \qquad (AP_c)$$

Hence the proof of c can be reduced to a proof of the Horn clause

$$c' = P_c(z_1,\ldots,z_k) \Leftarrow \delta.$$

The translation suggests dispensing with Gentzen clauses and expressing every requirement for a design specification as a set of Horn clauses. However, c and c' have different sets of redices. c' need not be applicable to a goal to which c can be applied. Only a resolution step upon AP_c may turn a c-redex into a c'-redex. But AP_c is not a Horn clause. As we shall see later, a resolution step upon AP_c may be necessary when c' is proved inductively because the proof may proceed by case analysis, coming up with a proper *disjunction* $\varphi_1 \vee \ldots \vee \varphi_n$, but induction hypotheses are instances of the *Horn* clause c'. These are reachable from $\varphi_1 \vee \ldots \vee \varphi_n$ only by resolving upon AP_c.

Consequently, an inductive proof method for Horn clauses must admit the application of non-Horn lemmas as well, at least those that arise from clause inversion.

2.6 The decomposition principle

Using projection functions, the generator matrix of a constructor-based clause set may be shifted from the premise to the conclusion. Given the guarded clause

$$\gamma \Leftarrow \delta : t_1 \equiv c_1(x_1),\ldots,t_n \equiv c_n(x_n) \qquad (GC)$$

suppose that for all $1 \le i \le n$ and $x \in var(c_i)$, c_i has a "left inverse" c_i' that projects c_i on x, i.e. $c_i'(c_i(x)) \equiv x$ is an inductive theorem. Then GC is inductively equivalent to the generatorless clause

$$\gamma[c_1'(t_1)/x_1,\ldots,c_n'(t_n)/x_n] \Leftarrow \delta. \qquad (GC')$$

GC' has several drawbacks. First, left inverses must be specified. Second, *each* occurrence of x_i in γ must be replaced by $c_i'(t_i)$. Third, some $c_i(x_i)$ may denote an "error term" that is not in the domain of c_i'. For instance, the constructor-based matrix

$$\mathsf{div}(x,y) \equiv (q,r)$$
$$\mathsf{div}(x,y) \equiv \mathsf{div}(z,0)$$

contains the error term *div(z,0)*. Projections $p_1,p_2 : nat \times nat \longrightarrow nat$, which invert the pairing function, bring about further error terms, e.g., $p_1(div(x,0))$. Finally, the original clause GC is often much more comprehensible than GC'.

For all these reasons, we suggest proceeding conversely. Instead of removing premises, conclusions should be minimized by introducing variables for subterms and augmenting the generator with equations that relate these variables to the terms they stand for. In the extreme case, $\mathsf{P}t \Leftarrow \delta$ may be replaced by $\mathsf{P}x \Leftarrow \delta:\{x \equiv t\}$.

The impact of such modifications on expansion proofs is twofold. On the one hand, they may raise the number of atoms in a goal; on the other hand, they may reduce the size of an atom. Hence an expansion is broken up into smaller parts, which are more transparent and manageable than a small number of big formulas (cf. Chapter 8).

An alternative to modifying the axioms is to change the inference rules in a way such that applying $\mathsf{P}t \Leftarrow \delta$ has the same effect as applying $\mathsf{P}x \Leftarrow \delta:\{x \equiv t\}$ had with respect to the original rules. Calculi following this principle are usually called *lazy* or *demand-driven* (cf., e.g., [MMR86], [GS87], [Höl89]). Since lazy rules often create more subgoals than busy ones, they support the detection of failures (cf. Sect. 7.3 and [DH87], Sect. 5). In this sense, the rules of inductive expansion (cf. Chapter 5) are lazy because they generate equations of the form $x \equiv t$ instead of substituting t for the (input) variable x. Such equations are needed for subsequent applications of "case analysis lemmas" like

$$\exists X_1\, x \equiv t_1 \vee \ldots \vee \exists X_n\, x \equiv t_n \;\Leftarrow\; \gamma.$$

We could admit *non*-equational input atoms in the generator matrix of a constructor-based clause set. An extension of (SIG,AX) by Boolean functions allows us to translate such atoms into equations of the form $p \equiv true$. If the transformed generator matrix is to be complete, it must contain a further "row" involving $p \equiv false$. If it is to be minimal, *{true,false}* must be a set of constructors, i.e. *true* and *false* may not be AX-equivalent.

The simplest schema of a Boolean constructor-based clause set is given by

$$\varphi \;\Leftarrow\; p \equiv true \tag{C1}$$

$$\psi \Leftarrow p \equiv \textit{false}. \tag{C2}$$

{C1,C2} may define a function F, i.e., $\varphi = \{Fx \equiv t\}$ and $\psi = \{Fx \equiv t'\}$ for some t, t'.

Adding the conditional function *if_then_else_* : $bool, s, s \longrightarrow s$ permits turning {C1,C2} into the equation $Fx \equiv$ *if p then t else t'*.

However, when following the decomposition principle, we keep to {C1,C2}.

Not only logic programming languages but also functional ones support the use of guards and generators. For instance, in Standard ML (cf. [HMM86]), the axioms for div (cf. Ex. 1.1) can be implemented as follows:

fun div(x,y) = **if** x < y **then** (0,x)

                    else if y > 0 **then** **let** **val** (q,r) = div(x-y,y) **in** (q+1,r) **end**

                    else raise error

The **case** construct of SML allows us to encode constructor-based axioms that define a function F: the clause set

$$F(x) \equiv u_1 \Leftarrow t_1 \equiv c_{11}, t_2 \equiv c_{12}, ..., t_n \equiv c_{1n}$$

$$\cdots$$

$$F(x) \equiv u_k \Leftarrow t_1 \equiv c_{k1}, t_2 \equiv c_{k2}, ..., t_n \equiv c_{kn}$$

is translated into

    fun F(x) = **case** $(t_1, ..., t_n)$ **of**

                    $(c_{11}, c_{12}, ..., c_{1n})$ => u_1 |

                        $\cdots$

                    $(c_{k1}, c_{k2}, ..., c_{kn})$ => u_k |

                    _ => **raise** error

provided that for all $1 \leq i \leq k$ and $1 \leq j \leq n$, c_{ij} is built up from SML **datatype** constructors.

Hence deductive methods handling constructor-based axioms are directly applicable to verifying SML programs.

The distinction between input and output variables is well known from *imperative* programming. The former correspond to value parameters, the latter to variable parameters of procedures. This permits the translation of constructor-based axioms into an imperative language such as PASCAL (cf. [GHM87]). Input and output variables also correspond to respectively inherited and derived attributes of an attributed grammar (cf. Sect. 8.1).

3: Models and Correctness

This chapter on model-theoretic issues is a continuation of Section 1.3. In particular, we present and discuss *initial correctness* (Sect. 3.2) and *canonical term structures* (Sect. 3.3), which provide the link between given data type models and deductive methods for reasoning about them. Moreover, fundamental model- and proof-theoretic results about *conservative extensions* are presented (in Sects. 3.4 and 3.5). Later on, Cor. 6.19 provides a rewriting-oriented criterion for this property of specifications, which is also called *consistency* w.r.t. a given base specification.

Definition The congruence axioms for equality predicates ensure that $\equiv_{AX}$ is a SIG-congruence relation on the Herbrand structure DH = HS(T(SIG),D) where D is the set of all AX-valid atoms. The quotient of DH and $\equiv_{AX}$ is called the *free (SIG,AX)-structure, F(SIG,AX),* i.e., F(SIG,AX) = DH/$\equiv_{AX}$. ▮

Theorem 3.1 *For all atoms p,*

$$AX \vdash_{cut} p \quad \text{iff} \quad Mod(SIG,AX) \models p \quad \text{iff} \quad F(SIG,AX) \models p.$$

Proof. Let p be an AX-valid goal and A be a SIG-model of AX. A satisfies p if A satisfies the congruence axioms for all equality predicates of SIG and if the cut calculus is correct w.r.t. A. This amounts to checking that

(SUB-A) for all Horn clauses $p \Leftarrow \gamma$ and substitutions f,

$$A \models p \Leftarrow \gamma \quad \text{implies} \quad A \models p[f] \Leftarrow \gamma[f],$$

(CUT-A) for all atoms p,q and goals γ,δ,

$$A \models p \Leftarrow \gamma \cup \{q\} \quad \text{and} \quad A \models q \Leftarrow \delta \quad \text{imply} \quad A \models p \Leftarrow \gamma \cup \delta.$$

CUT-A is verified immediately. For SUB-A, one needs Prop. 1.2: Suppose that A satisfies $c = Pt \Leftarrow P_1t_1,\ldots,P_nt_n$. Let $b \in A^X$ such that for all $1 \le i \le n$, $b^*(t_i[f]) \in P_i^A$. Then by Prop. 1.2, $(b^* \circ f)^* t_i \in P_i^A$. Since A satisfies c, $(b^* \circ f)^* t \in P^A$ as well. Again by Prop. 1.2, $b^*(t[f]) \in P^A$. Hence A satisfies $c[f]$.

Secondly, we show that B = F(SIG,AX) is a SIG-model of AX. Let nat : DH⟶B be the natural mapping and A = DH. First, B is a SIG-structure with identity because for all $s \in S$, the relation $\equiv_s^B$ on B is given by all pairs <nat(t),nat(t')> such that t and t' are AX-equivalent. Moreover, B satisfies AX: Let $Pt \Leftarrow P_1t_1,\ldots,P_nt_n \in AX$ and $b \in B^X$ such that for all $1 \le i \le n$, $b^*t_i \in P_i^B$. Since $nat \circ f = b$ for some substitution f, we have $t_i[f] \in P_i^A$, i.e. for all $1 \le i \le n$, $P_it_i[f]$

is AX-valid. By SUB and CUT, Pt[f] is AX-valid. Hence $t[f] \in P^A$ and thus $b^*t \in P^B$.

Thirdly, let Pt be an atom satisfied by B = F(SIG,AX), i.e. for all $b \in B^X$, $b^*t \in P^B$, in particular: $(nat \circ id^X)^*t \in P^B$. Hence $nat(t) \in P^B$ and thus $t \in P^A$ where A = DH. We conclude that γ is AX-valid. ∎

The last paragraph of the previous proof does not hold if Pt is replaced by a conditional clause. For instance, all SIG-models of AX satisfy $p \Leftarrow p$, although $p \Leftarrow p$ is not derivable via the cut calculus. However, valid conditional clauses can be proved by "natural deduction":

Corollary 3.2 *Let $c = p \Leftarrow \gamma$ be a Horn clause and $x_1,\dots,x_n$ be the variables of γ. Fix new constants $k_1,\dots,k_n$ with $sort(k_i) = sort(x_i)$. Let SIG' = (S,OP∪{$k_1,\dots,k_n$},PR) and $f = \{k_1/x_1,\dots,k_n/x_n\}$. Then*

$$Mod(SIG,AX) \models c \quad \textit{iff} \quad AX \cup \gamma[f] \vdash_{cut} p[f].$$

Proof. By Thm. 3.1, it is sufficient to show that Mod(SIG,AX) satisfies c iff Mod(SIG',AX∪γ[f]) satisfies p[f].

Suppose that Mod(SIG,AX) satisfies c. Let A be a SIG'-model of AX∪γ[f] and $b \in A^X$ such that $bx_i = k_i^A$ for all $1 \le i \le n$. Since γ[f] is valid in A, b solves γ in A. Since A satisfies c, b solves p and thus p[f] in A. Hence A satisfies p[f].

Conversely, suppose that Mod(SIG',AX∪γ[f]) satisfies p[f] and let A be a SIG-model of AX. Furthermore, let b solve γ in A. A is extended to a SIG'-structure by defining $k_i^A = bx_i$ for all $1 \le i \le n$. Since b solves γ in A, A satisfies γ[f]. Hence A is a SIG'-model of AX∪γ[f] and thus by assumption, p[f] is valid in A. Therefore, b solves p in A, and we conclude that A satisfies c. ∎

The replacement of the variables of γ by constants prevents them from being instantiated during the derivation process. Only when Z = var(γ) is turned into a set of constants are we sure to prove $p \Leftarrow \gamma$. Otherwise substitutions of variables of Z yield a proof of the weaker proposition $\forall Zp \Leftarrow \forall Z\gamma$. For a complete calculus for conditional equations, cf. [Sel72], Sect. 5.

A further corollary of Thm. 3.1 states the connection between solutions w.r.t. AX (cf. Sect. 1.2) and solutions in models of AX (cf. Sect. 1.3).

Corollary 3.3 *A goal γ is solvable w.r.t. AX iff γ is solvable in all SIG-models of AX.*

Proof. Let γ[f] be AX-valid. By Thm. 3.1, γ[f] is valid in Mod(SIG,AX), i.e., for all SIG-models A of AX, $b \in A^X$ and $Pt \in \gamma$, $b^*(t[f]) \in P^A$. Hence by Prop. 1.2, $(b^*f)^*t \in P^A$, i.e., b^*f solves γ in A.

Conversely, if for all A $\in$ Mod(SIG,AX) some b solves γ in A, then in particular, some b = nat∘f solves γ in the free (SIG,AX)-structure. Hence γ[f] is AX-valid. ∎

3.1 Initial semantics

The following two sections deal with term-generated models and, in particular, with the *initial* structure Ini(SIG,AX), i.e. the *greatest* term-generated model of AX: each A $\in$ Gen(SIG,AX) is a quotient of Ini(SIG,AX). Initial semantics identifies data types with initial structures and presumes that equality relations have been specified explicitly, i.e., data are equal only if they are provably equal.

Viewed from the subset ordering of Herbrand interpretations, Ini(SIG,AX) is the *least* model of AX: ground goals are valid only if they are provably valid. It is easy to see that a specification including non-Horn clauses may lack a least model: Disjunctive axioms such as $p \vee q$ give rise to *several* minimal models; negated atoms entailing contradictions such as $p \wedge \neg p$ rule out any model.

A model-theoretic correctness notion and deduction-oriented correctness criteria will explicate the nature of initial semantics (cf. Sect. 3.2). First we establish the completeness result for initial semantics.

Definition The congruence axioms for equality predicates ensure that the restriction of $\equiv_{AX}$ to ground terms is a SIG-congruence relation on the Herbrand structure IH = HS(GT(SIG),GD) where GD is the set of all AX-valid ground atoms. The quotient of IH by $\equiv_{AX}$ is called the *initial (SIG,AX)-structure, Ini(SIG,AX)*, i.e., Ini(SIG,AX) = IH/$\equiv_{AX}$. ∎

Theorem 3.4 *For all atoms p,*

$$p \in ITh(AX) \quad \text{iff} \quad Gen(SIG,AX) \models p \quad \text{iff} \quad Ini(SIG,AX) \models p.$$

Proof. Let Pt $\in$ ITh(AX) and A be a term-generated SIG-model of AX. A satisfies all ground instances of Pt because A satisfies the congruence axioms for all predicates of SIG and because the cut calculus is correct w.r.t. A (see the proof of Thm. 3.1). Hence A satisfies Pt: Let $b \in A^X$. Since A is term-generated, there is f $\in$ GS such that $eval^A \circ f = b$. Since A $\models$ Pt[f], we obtain $b^*t \in P^A$ and thus A $\models$ Pt.

Secondly, we know that B = Ini(SIG,AX) is a SIG-model of AX. In fact, the proof that F(SIG,AX) is a SIG-model of AX (cf. Thm. 3.1) applies to B as well. Moreover, B is term-generated because the natural mapping nat : IH⟶ B agrees with $eval^B$.

Thirdly, let Pt be an atom satisfied by B = Ini(SIG,AX). Then for all b ∈ B^X, $b^*t \in P^B$; in particular for all f ∈ GS, $(nat \circ f)^*t \in P^B$. Hence nat(t[f]) ∈ P^B and thus t[f] ∈ P^A where A = IH. We conclude AX $\vdash_{cut}$ Pt[f] and thus Pt ∈ ITh(AX). ∎

When we are concerned with arbitrary Gentzen clauses, we have to distinguish between inductive validity and (the more restrictive) validity in Gen(SIG,AX). The construction of Ini(SIG,AX) as a quotient of IH immediately implies that each Gentzen clause c is inductively valid w.r.t. AX iff Ini(SIG,AX) satisfies c. However, a Horn (!) clause c is valid in Gen(SIG,AX) iff all ground instances of c are provable by "natural deduction" (cf. Cor. 3.2):

Corollary 3.5 *Given a Horn clause c = p⇐γ, Gen(SIG,AX) satisfies c iff for all f ∈ GS,*

$$AX \cup \gamma[f] \vdash_{cut} p[f]. \qquad (*)$$

Proof. Since γ[f] is ground, (*) holds true iff p[f] is inductively valid w.r.t. AX∪γ[f] and thus by Thm. 3.4 iff Gen(SIG,AX∪γ[f]) satisfies p[f]. Hence it remains to show that Gen(SIG,AX) satisfies c iff for all f ∈ GS, Gen(SIG,AX∪γ[f]) satisfies p[f].

Suppose that Gen(SIG,AX) satisfies c. Let f ∈ GS, A be a term-generated SIG-model of AX∪γ[f] and b ∈ A^X such that bx = $eval^A$(fx) for all x ∈ var(γ). Since A satisfies γ[f], b solves γ in A. Since A satisfies c, b solves p in A. Hence A satisfies p[f].

Conversely, suppose that for all f ∈ GS, Gen(SIG,AX∪γ[f]) satisfies p[f]. Let A be a term-generated SIG-model of AX and b a solution of γ in A. Then $eval^A \circ f$ = b for some f ∈ GS. Since b solves γ in A, A satisfies γ[f]. Hence by assumption, A satisfies p[f] and thus b solves p in A. We conclude that A satisfies c. ∎

3.2 Initial correctness

Given a SIG-structure A as the formal description of a data type on the one hand and a set AX of Horn clauses over SIG on the other hand, how can one check that AX is a correct axiomatization of A? The answer given by initial semantics is: show that A is isomorphic to Ini(SIG,AX). Initial correctness is characterized by a universal property that does not refer to the construction of Ini(SIG,AX) as a quotient of IH: for each SIG-model B of AX there is a unique *homomorphism* from Ini(SIG,AX) to B.

Definition Let A and B be two SIG-structures. An S-sorted function h : $A \longrightarrow B$ is *(SIG-) homomorphic* or a *(SIG-) homomorphism* if for all $F \in OP$ and $P \in PR$,

$$h \circ F^A = F^B \circ h \quad \text{and} \quad h(P^A) \subseteq P^B.$$

If, in addition, $P^B \subseteq h(P^A)$ and

- h is bijective or, equivalently,
- some function $g : B \longrightarrow A$ satisfies $g \circ h = id^A$ and $h \circ g = id^B$,

then h is a *(SIG-) isomorphism,* and A and B are called *(SIG-) isomorphic.*

Given a SIG-model A of AX, AX is *initially correct w.r.t. A* if for all SIG-models B of AX there is a unique homomorphism from A to B, called the *initial homomorphism* and denoted by ini^B. ∎

Lemma 3.6 *AX is initially correct w.r.t. Ini(SIG,AX).*

Proof. Let A = Ini(SIG,AX), B ∈ Mod(SIG,AX) and nat be the natural mapping from GT(SIG) to A. $ini^B : A \longrightarrow B$ is well-defined by $ini^B \circ nat = eval^B$. Moreover, ini^B is homomorphic: For all ground terms Ft,

$$ini^B \circ F^A \circ nat(t) = ini^B \circ nat(Ft) = eval^B(Ft) = F^B \circ eval^B(t) = F^B \circ ini^B \circ nat(t),$$

and for all ground atoms Pt, $nat(t) \in P^A$ implies $AX \vdash_{cut} Pt$. Hence B satisfies Pt, and thus

$$ini^B \circ nat(t) = eval^B(t) \in P^B.$$

Conversely, let $h : A \longrightarrow B$ be homomorphic. $h = ini^B$ follows by induction on the size of $Ft \in GT(SIG)$: By induction hypothesis, $h \circ F^A \circ nat(t) = F^B \circ h \circ nat(t)$. Hence

$$h \circ nat(Ft) = h \circ F^A \circ nat(t) = F^B \circ h \circ nat(t) = F^B \circ eval^B(t) = eval^B(Ft) = ini^B \circ nat(Ft).$$ ∎

The definition of initial correctness yields

Proposition 3.7 *Let AX be initially correct w.r.t. a SIG-structure A. AX is initially correct w.r.t. a SIG-structure B iff A and B are isomorphic.* ∎

Therefore Lemma 3.6 amounts to

Theorem 3.8 *Let A be a SIG-structure. A and Ini(SIG,AX) are isomorphic iff AX is initially correct w.r.t. A.* ∎

3.3 Canonical term structures

Thm. 3.8 gives rise to a proof method for initial correctness: Define a unique homorphism from A to an arbitrary model of AX. Since the concrete representation of A plays an important rôle in such a definition, purely deductive criteria to guide correctness proofs are not available. However, [GTW78], [Nou81], [Klä84] and [BV87] have investigated *canonical term structures* as particular data type models. Such structures do not only have a term carrier; their elements are *unique* representations of the elements of the given model A. Canonical term structures may either be defined directly or derived from a term representation function associated with A:

Definition Let A be a SIG-structure and nat be the natural mapping from GT(SIG) to Ini(SIG,AX). An S-sorted mapping $rep^A : A \longrightarrow GT(SIG)$ is called a *representation function for A* if

- $eval^A \circ rep^A = id^A$,
- rep^A satisfies the *representation condition,* i.e. $nat \circ rep^A$ is homomorphic or, equivalently, for all $w \in S^*$, $s \in S$, $F \in OP_{ws}$ and $a \in A_w$,

  $$F(rep^A(a)) \equiv_{AX} rep^A \circ F^A(a)$$

  and for all $P \in PR$ and $a \in P^A$, $AX \vdash_{cut} P(rep^A(a))$. ∎

Theorem 3.9 *Let A be a SIG-structure with identity. AX is initially correct w.r.t. A iff A satisfies AX and there is a representation function rep^A for A.*

Proof. Let AX be initially correct w.r.t. to A. Then AX is valid in A and there is a unique homomorphism ini^B from A to B = Ini(SIG,AX), which can be decomposed into a function $rep^A : A \longrightarrow GT(SIG)$ and the natural mapping nat from GT(SIG) to B. Moreover, id^A is the unique homomorphism from A to A. By Lemma 3.6, AX is initially correct w.r.t. B. Hence the unique homomorphism ini^A from B to A is defined by $ini^A \circ nat = eval^A$. Therefore

$$eval^A \circ rep^A = ini^A \circ nat \circ rep^A = ini^A \circ ini^B = id^A$$

and thus rep^A is an initial representation function for A.

Conversely, suppose that A satisfies AX and has a representation function rep^A. It is sufficient to show that the unique homomorphism ini^A from B = Ini(SIG,AX) to A is an isomorphism.

$nat \circ rep^A$ and thus $nat \circ rep^A \circ ini^A$ are homomorphic. Hence $nat \circ rep^A \circ ini^A = id^B$ because id^B is the unique homomorphism from B to B. Furthermore, $ini^A \circ nat \circ rep^A = eval^A \circ rep^A = id^A$. Thus ini^A is an isomorphism. ∎

The important deductive properties of A and rep^A are listed in the following corollary.

Corollary 3.10 *Let AX be initially correct w.r.t. a SIG-structure A with representation function* rep^A.

(1) For all ground terms t, $rep^A(eval^A(t)) \equiv_{AX} t$.

(2) For all ground terms t *there is a unique* $a \in A$ *such that* $t \equiv_{AX} rep^A(a)$.

(3) For all ground atoms Pt, $A \models Pt$ *implies* $AX \vdash_{cut} Pt$.

Proof. (1) Let B = Ini(SIG,AX) and ini^A be the unique homomorphism from B to A. Since $eval^A$ and id^B are unique homomorphisms from GT(SIG) to A and from B to B respectively, we obtain

$$nat \circ rep^A \circ eval^A = nat \circ rep^A \circ ini^A \circ nat = id^B \circ nat = nat.$$

Hence for all ground terms t, $rep^A(eval^A(t)) \equiv_{AX} t$.

(2) Let t be a ground term. By (1), there is $a \in A$ with $t \equiv_{AX} rep^A(a)$. Suppose that, in addition, $t \equiv_{AX} rep^A(b)$ for some $b \in A$. Since $rep^A(a) \equiv_{AX} rep^A(b)$, we conclude

$$a = eval^A(rep^A(a)) = eval^A(rep^A(b)) = b.$$

(3) Let A satisfy the ground atom Pt, i.e. $eval^A(t) \in P^A$. By the representation condition, $AX \vdash_{cut} Prep^A(eval^A(t))$. Hence (1) implies $AX \vdash_{cut} Pt$. ∎

Definition A set T of terms is *subterm closed* if all subterms of terms of T belong to T.

A SIG-structure B is a *canonical term structure* if the carrier of B is a subterm closed set of ground terms and if for all $t \in B$, $eval^B(t) = t$. ∎

If the image of a representation function for A is a subterm closed term set, A can be transformed into a canonical term structure:

Proposition 3.11 *Let AX be initially correct w.r.t. a SIG-structure A with representation function* rep^A *such that* $B = rep^A(A)$ *is subterm closed. Then B extends to a canonical term structure such that AX is initially correct w.r.t. B.*

Proof. Function and predicate symbols are interpreted in B as follows.

- For all $w \in S^*, s \in S, F \in OP_{ws}$ and $a \in A_w$, $F^B(rep^A(a)) = rep^A(F^A(a))$.
- For all $P \in PR$, $P^B = rep^A(P^A)$.

Since $eval^A \circ rep^A = id^A$, F^B is well-defined. Let $Ft \in B$. Then $Ft = rep^A(a)$ for some $a \in A$. Moreover, $t = rep^A(a')$ for some $a' \in A^*$ because B is subterm closed. Therefore

$$\begin{aligned} F^B(t) &= F^B(rep^A(a')) = rep^A(F^A(a')) = rep^A(F^A(eval^A(rep^A(a')))) \\ &= rep^A(F^A(eval^A(t))) = rep^A(eval^A(Ft)) = rep^A(eval^A(rep^A(a))) \\ &= rep^A(a) = Ft. \end{aligned}$$

Hence for all $t \in B$, $eval^B(t) = t$ and thus B is a canonical term structure. By the definition of B, the image restriction of rep^A is a surjective homomorphism from A to B. Since $eval^A \circ rep^A = id^A$, rep^A is injective. Since $P^B = rep^A(P^A)$, we conclude that A and B are isomorphic. Hence by Prop. 3.7, AX is initially correct w.r.t. B. ∎

Note that both Herbrand structures and canonical term structures have term carriers. However, the carrier of a Herbrand structure B is contextually closed (cf. Sect. 1.3) and has a fixed interpretation of function symbols, namely $F^B(t) = Ft$, while a canonical term structure B is only subterm closed and requires $F^B(t) = Ft$ only if $Ft \in B$.

If the data type is given as a canonical term structure A such that the inclusion of A into GT(SIG) is a representation function for A, then the representation condition can be simplified:

Theorem 3.12 *Let A be a canonical term structure. AX is initially correct w.r.t. A iff A satisfies AX and the* canonical representation condition:

- *for all $w \in S^*, s \in S, F \in OP_{ws}$ and $t \in A_w$, $Ft \equiv_{AX} F^A(t)$;*
- *for all $P \in PR$ and $t \in P^A$, $AX \vdash_{cut} Pt$.*

Proof. Let rep^A be the inclusion mapping from A to GT(SIG). Suppose that A satisfies AX and the canonical representation condition. Since $eval^A(t) = t$ for all $t \in A$, we have $eval^A \circ rep^A(t) = t$. Moreover, the canonical representation condition coincides with the representation condition of rep^A. Hence by Thm. 3.9, AX is initially correct w.r.t. A.

Conversely, suppose that AX is initially correct w.r.t. A. Then A satisfies AX and there is a unique homomorphism ini^B from A to B = Ini(SIG,AX), which can be decomposed into the inclusion mapping rep^A from A to GT(SIG) and the natural mapping nat from GT(SIG) to B. Hence for all $w \in S^*$, $s \in S$, $F \in OP_{ws}$ and $t \in A_w$,

$$nat(Ft) = F^B \circ nat(t) = F^B \circ nat \circ rep^A(t) = F^B \circ ini^B(t) = ini^B \circ F^A(t)$$
$$= nat \circ rep^A \circ F^A(t) = nat \circ F^A(t)$$

and thus $Ft \equiv_{AX} F^A(t)$. Moreover, for all $P \in PR$ and $t \in P^A$,

$$nat(t) = nat \circ rep^A(t) = ini^B(t) \in P^B,$$

i.e., Pt is AX-valid. ∎

Example 3.13 Let (SIG,AX) be the following specification of integer numbers:

```
INT
    sorts     int
              symbol   type
    functs    0        int
              succ     int⟶int
              pred     int⟶int
    vars      x        int
    axms  succ(pred(x)) ≡ x
              pred(succ(x)) ≡ x
```

The carrier of a canonical term structure A for INT is given by all ground terms constructed from 0 and either succ or pred:

$$A_{int} = GT(\{0,succ\}) \cup GT(\{0,pred\}).$$

OP is interpreted as follows:

$$0^A = 0$$

for all $t \in GT(\{0,succ\})$, $succ^A(t) = succ(t)$

for all $t \in GT(\{0,pred\})$, $succ^A(pred(t)) = t$

for all $t \in GT(\{0,succ\})$, $pred^A(succ(t)) = t$

for all $t \in GT(\{0,pred\})$, $pred^A(t) = pred(t)$

$$\equiv^A = \{(t,t) \mid t \in A_{int}\}.$$

Of course, A is subterm closed and satisfies $eval^A(t) = t$ for all $t \in A$. For most cases, the canonical representation condition follows immediately from the definition of A. The remaining proof obligations are:

for all $t \in GT(\{0,pred\})$, $succ^A(pred(t)) \equiv_{AX} succ(pred(t))$

for all $t \in GT(\{0,succ\})$, $pred^A(succ(t)) \equiv_{AX} pred(succ(t))$.

But these are immediate consequences of the two axioms of INT. ∎

Using Thm. 3.12, one may start a correctness proof before all necessary axioms have been established. For instance, the two remaining proof obligations of Ex. 3.13 enforce the axioms of INT.

Correctness proofs on the basis of Thm. 3.12 may also facilitate further inductive proofs.

Corollary 3.14 (Inductive theory criterion based on canonical term structures) *Suppose that AX is initially correct w.r.t. a canonical term structure A. A Horn clause* $p \Leftarrow \gamma$ *is inductively valid w.r.t. AX iff for all* $f \in GS$ *with* $f(X) \subseteq A$,

$$AX \vdash_{cut} \gamma[f] \text{ implies } AX \vdash_{cut} p[f].$$

Proof. Let $g \in GS$ such that $\gamma[g]$ is AX-valid. Since the inclusion of A into GT(SIG) is a representation function rep^A for A (cf. the proof of Thm. 3.12), Cor. 3.10(1) implies

$$AX \vdash_{cut} \gamma[rep^A \circ eval^A \circ g] = \gamma[eval^A \circ g].$$

Since $eval^A(g(X)) \subseteq A$, we conclude

$$AX \vdash_{cut} p[eval^A \circ g] = p[rep^A \circ eval^A \circ g]$$

from the assumption. Again by Cor. 3.10(1), $p[g]$ is AX-valid. ∎

3.4 Conservative extensions

Let (BSIG,BASE) be a subspecification of (SIG,AX).

Definition (SIG,AX) is *consistent* w.r.t. (BSIG,BASE) or a *conservative extension* of (BSIG,BASE) if all AX-valid ground atoms over BSIG (!) are BASE-valid. ∎

Corollary 3.15 (Consistency criterion based on canonical term structures) *Suppose that BASE is initially correct w.r.t. a canonical term BSIG-structure B.*

(SIG,AX) is consistent w.r.t. (BSIG,BASE) iff there is a SIG-model A of AX such that

(1) *for all sorts s of BSIG,* $A_s \subseteq GT(SIG)_s$,

(2) *for all predicates P of BSIG,* $P^A \cap B^* \subseteq P^B$,

(3) *for all* $t \in B$, $eval^A(t) = t$.

Proof. "if": Let Pt be an AX-valid ground atom over BSIG. By Cor. 3.10(1), $t \equiv_{BASE} t'$ for some $t' \in B^*$. Hence $AX \vdash_{cut} Pt'$. Since A satisfies AX, A satisfies Pt' as well, i.e. $eval^A(t') \in P^A$. By (3), $t' \in P^A$. By (2), $t' \in P^B$. Since B is canonical, $eval^B(t') = t' \in P^B$, i.e. B satisfies Pt'. By Cor. 3.10(3), Pt' and thus Pt are BASE-valid.

"only if": The construction of a SIG-model B of AX satisfying (1) and (2) is given by [Pad88a], Lemma 6.2.1. (3) is an immediate consequence of [Pad88a], Lemma 6.2.2.[1] ∎

Example 3.16 We extend (BSIG,BASE) = INT (cf. Ex. 3.13) to (SIG,AX) = INT' where

INT'

base	INT	
	symbol	*type*
functs	_+_	int,int⟶int
vars	x, y	int
axms	x+succ(y) ≡ succ(x+y)	
	x+pred(y) ≡ pred(x+y)	

Let A be defined as in Ex. 3.13 and B as follows:

$B_{int} = A_{int}$

for all $F \in \{0,succ,pred\}$, $F^B = F^A$

for all $t \in B_{int}$, $t +^B 0 = t$

for all $t \in B_{int}$ and $t' \in GT(\{0,succ\})$, $t +^B succ(t') = succ(t +^B t')$

for all $t \in B_{int}$ and $t' \in GT(\{0,pred\})$, $t +^B pred(t') = pred(t +^B t')$

$\equiv^B = \equiv^A$.

B satisfies the axioms of INT' as well as conditions 3.15(1)-(3). Hence by Cor. 3.15, INT' is consistent w.r.t. INT. ∎

INT' is consistent, but not complete w.r.t. INT:

Definition (SIG,AX) is *(sufficiently)* ***complete*** w.r.t. (BSIG,BASE) if for all sorts $s \in$ BSIG and $t \in GT(SIG)_s$ there is a ground term t' over BSIG such that $t \equiv_{AX} t'$. ∎

Completeness means that all functions of SIG-BSIG are specified as *total* functions. However, Cor. 3.15 is not restricted to complete extensions. This is important because many consistency criteria include completeness assumptions, ruling out the specification of proper partial functions.

---

[1]In fact, AX is initially correct w.r.t. the constructed model B (cf. [Pad88a], Thm. 6.2.3). Conversely, an arbitrary SIG-structure B satisfying AX and (1)-(3) is *not* sufficient for AX to be initially correct w.r.t. B.

From the model-theoretic viewpoint, completeness and consistency are complementary properties. Since (SIG,AX) includes (BSIG,BASE), the BSIG-restriction B of Ini(SIG,AX) satisfies BASE and thus there is an initial homomorphism ini^B. (SIG,AX) is complete w.r.t. (BSIG,BASE) iff ini^B is surjective. (SIG,AX) is consistent w.r.t. (BSIG,BASE) iff ini^B is injective.

For a deduction-oriented consistency criterion, cf. Cor. 6.19. A deduction-oriented completeness proof amounts to verifying that for all "non-base" functions F $\in$ SIG-BSIG, the atom *Def(F(x))* is inductively valid w.r.t. AX under the assumption that for all "base" functions G $\in$ BSIG, AX includes the axiom *Def(G(x))*$\Leftarrow$*Def(x)*.

As a general guideline for proving the correctness of a design specification, it is suggested that one proceeds in three steps:

- present the *sort building part* of a data type as a canonical term structure A over a base signature BSIG;
- derive an axiomatization BASE of A from an initial-correctness proof of A along the lines of Thm. 3.12 (cf. Ex. 3.13);
- define the *algorithmic part* of the data type on top of (BSIG,BASE) and show that the entire specification is consistent w.r.t. (BSIG,BASE) (cf. Ex. 3.16).

Axioms for the sort building part are rarely obvious. A proof of the canonical representation condition (cf. Thm. 3.12) may reveal them. The algorithmic part, however, is actually a set of function or predicate definitions. By Cor. 3.15, consistency w.r.t. the base specification ensures the existence of a model extension. This means that the "non-base" axioms define (partial) functions and predicates on the base model. Hence we do not gain anything from extending the base model to a SIG-structure explicitly. In particular, the non-base axioms of *design* specifications look nearly the same as the function or predicate definitions that build up the model extension (cf. Ex. 3.16).

3.5 Program equivalence

Given two specifications SP1 and SP2 with the same sorts, let β be a sort compatible bijection from the signature of SP1 to the signature of SP2. Moreover, let SP be a specification that includes SP1 and SP2 such that each function and predicate symbol F of SP1 is equivalent to βF with respect to ITh(SP), i.e., for a suitable tuple x of variables, the equation $F(x) \equiv \beta F(x)$ or the clauses $F(x) \Leftarrow \beta F(x)$ and $\beta F(x) \Leftarrow F(x)$ are inductively valid w.r.t. SP.

Theorem 3.17 (Criterion for program equivalence) *Let SP1, SP2 and SP be three specifications and* β *a bijection as above such that SP is consistent w.r.t. both SP1 and SP2. Then the inductive theories of SP1 and SP2 agree with each other "modulo"* β*, i.e.,*

$$ITh(\beta SP1) = ITh(SP2)$$

where β*SP1 denotes SP1 with all function and predicate symbols renamed according to* β.

Proof. Let $p \Leftarrow \gamma \in$ ITh(βSP1). We show that $p \Leftarrow \gamma$ is inductively valid w.r.t. SP2 as well. Then the converse follows from the fact that β is bijective.

At first, $p \Leftarrow \gamma = \beta q \Leftarrow \beta\delta$ for some clause $q \Leftarrow \delta$ over SP1. Let f be a ground substitution over SP2 such that $\gamma[f]$ is SP2-valid. Since SP2 ⊆ SP,

$$SP \vdash_{cut} \gamma[f]. \qquad (1)$$

Since β is a bijection, there is a ground substitution g over SP1 such that βg = f. Hence (1) implies

$$SP \vdash_{cut} \beta(\delta[g]).$$

By assumption,

$$SP \vdash_{cut} \delta[g]. \qquad (2)$$

Since $\delta[g]$ is a goal over SP1 and SP is consistent w.r.t. SP1, we conclude from (2) that $\delta[g]$ is SP1-valid. Since $q \Leftarrow \delta \in$ ITh(SP1),

$$SP1 \vdash_{cut} q[g].$$

SP1 ⊆ SP implies

$$SP \vdash_{cut} q[g]$$

and thus

$$SP \vdash_{cut} \beta(q[g]) \qquad (3)$$

by assumption. Since $\beta(q[g]) = p[f]$ is a goal over SP2 and SP is consistent w.r.t. SP2, (3) implies that $p[f]$ is SP2-valid.

Therefore, $p \Leftarrow \gamma \in$ ITh(SP2). ∎

Example 3.18 Let

SP1 = NSB ∪ {Loop,L2,L3},

SP2 = (NSB - {div,N6,N7}) ∪ {divL,L1,Loop,L2,L3}

(cf. Exs. 1.1, 5.8 and 5.9), βdiv = divL, βF = F for all function or predicate symbols F of SP1-{div} and

$$SP = SP1 \cup SP2 \cup \{\texttt{div(x,0)} \equiv \texttt{divL(x,0)}\}.$$

We will show in Ex. 5.8 that the clause

$$\texttt{div(x,y)} \equiv \texttt{divL(x,y)} \Leftarrow \texttt{y > 0, Def(x), Def(y)}$$

is inductively valid w.r.t. SP1 ∪ SP2 and thus w.r.t. SP. Since Def(x) ∈ ITh(SP), we conclude that the equation div(x,y)≡divL(x,y) is inductively valid w.r.t. SP.

Using Cor. 6.19, the consistency of SP w.r.t. both SP1 and SP2 can be proved easily. In fact, we had to use a generalization of Thm. 3.17 with a further specification SP' such that SP' is inductively equivalent to SP, SP is consistent w.r.t. SP1 and SP' is consistent w.r.t. SP2. SP' were given by

$$SP' = SP1 \cup SP2 \cup \{\texttt{divL(x,0)} \equiv \texttt{div(x,0)}\}.$$

The example works well because the error terms generated by *div* and *divL* respectively can be presented explicitly and thus the respective axioms

$$\texttt{div(x,0)} \equiv \texttt{divL(x,0)} \text{ and } \texttt{divL(x,0)} \equiv \texttt{div(x,0)},$$

can be added to SP1 ∪ SP2 without inducing reduction ambiguities (cf. Sect. 6.3). The situation is a little more difficult if *Def(x)* were not inductively valid. Then, for making *div* and *divL* equivalent w.r.t. all arguments, while avoiding reduction ambiguities, we had to add the axioms

$$\texttt{div(x,y)} \equiv \texttt{divL(x,y)} \Leftarrow \texttt{Undef(x)}$$
$$\texttt{div(x,y)} \equiv \texttt{divL(x,y)} \Leftarrow \texttt{Undef(y)}$$

and specify *Undef* as the negation of *Def.* ∎

4: Computing Goal Solutions

The cut calculus for Horn clauses is simple, but rather inefficient as the basis of a theorem prover. To prove a goal γ via this calculus means to derive γ from axioms (those of the specification and congruence axioms for equality predicates) using CUT and SUB (cf. Sect. 1.2). In contrast, the inference rules *resolution* (cf. [Rob65]) and *paramodulation* (cf. [RW69]) allow us to start out from γ and apply axioms for transforming γ into the empty goal $\emptyset$. The actual purpose of resolution and paramodulation is to compute goal solutions (cf. Sect. 1.2): If γ can be transformed into $\emptyset$, then γ is solvable. The derivation process involves constructing a solution f, and $\emptyset$ indicates the validity of γ[f].

A single derivation step from γ to δ via resolution or paramodulation proves the clause γ[g]$\Leftarrow\delta$ for some g. Since γ[g] is the conclusion of a Horn clause, which, if viewed as a logic program, is expanded (into δ), we call such derivations *expansions*. More precisely, the rules are *input* resolution and paramodulation where one of the two clauses to be transformed stems from an "input" set of axioms or, in the case of *inductive expansion* (cf. Chapter 5), arbitrary lemmas or induction hypotheses.

While input *resolution* is always "solution complete", input *paramodulation* has this property only if the input set includes all *functionally-reflexive* axioms, i.e., equations of the form Fx≡Fx (cf., e.g., [Höl89]). In [Pad88a], Sect. 5.3, we have shown that these axioms are only needed for establishing redices of other axioms. Hence, instead of adding them to the input set, we start out from the set of prefix extensions of AX:

Let CS be a set of Gentzen clauses.

Definition *CE(CS)* denotes the set of all conditional equations of CS. Given a term t, x ∈ var(t) and u≡u'$\Leftarrow\vartheta$ ∈ CE(CS), the conditional equation

$$t[u/x] \equiv t[u'/x] \Leftarrow \vartheta$$

is called a *prefix extension* of CS. *Pre(CS)* denotes the set of all prefix extensions of CS. ∎

General Assumption The set X_{goals} of variables occurring in goals of solving expansions upon AX (see below) is disjoint from var(Pre(AX)). ∎

Definition CS^{sym} denotes the set of all Gentzen clauses

$$c \;=\; \exists X_1\{t_1{\equiv}u_1\}\cup\vartheta_1 \vee\ldots\vee \exists X_n\{t_n{\equiv}u_n\}\cup\vartheta_n \Leftarrow \vartheta$$

such that $c \in CS$ or $\exists X_1\{u_1{\equiv}t_1\}\cup\vartheta_1\vee\ldots\vee\exists X_n\{u_n{\equiv}t_n\}\cup\vartheta_n\Leftarrow\vartheta \in CS$. ∎

Definition The *solving expansion calculus upon AX* consists of the following three inference rules, which transform pairs consisting of a goal and a substitution:

Resolution

$$\frac{\langle\gamma \cup \{p\},\, f\rangle}{\langle(\gamma \cup \vartheta)[g],\, f[g|X_{goals}]\rangle} \qquad \begin{array}{l} p[g] = q[g] \\ q\Leftarrow\vartheta \in \text{AX-CE(AX)} \end{array}$$

p is the *redex*, $(\gamma \cup \vartheta)[g]$ is the *resolvent* of $\gamma\cup\{p\}$ and $q\Leftarrow\vartheta$.

Paramodulation

$$\frac{\langle\delta[t/x],\, f\rangle}{\langle(\delta[u'/x] \cup \vartheta)[g],\, f[g|X_{goals}]\rangle} \qquad \begin{array}{l} t[g] = u[g] \\ u{\equiv}u'\Leftarrow\vartheta \in \text{Pre}(AX^{sym}) \end{array}$$

t is the *redex*, $(\delta[u'/x]\cup\vartheta)[g]$ is the *paramodulant* of $\delta[t/x]$ and $u{\equiv}u'\Leftarrow\vartheta$.

Unification

$$\frac{\langle\gamma \cup \{t{\equiv}t'\},\, f\rangle}{\langle\gamma[g],\, f[g]\rangle} \qquad t[g] = t'[g]$$

A *solving expansion of* $\langle\gamma_1,f_1\rangle$ *into* $\langle\gamma_n,f_n\rangle$ *upon AX* is a sequence $\langle\gamma_1,f_1\rangle,\ldots,\langle\gamma_n,f_n\rangle$ of goal-substitution pairs such that for all $1\le i<n$, $\langle\gamma_{i+1},f_{i+1}\rangle$ is obtained from $\langle\gamma_i,f_i\rangle$ by a single resolution, paramodulation or unification step. $\langle\gamma_1,f_1\rangle,\ldots,\langle\gamma_n,f_n\rangle$ is *successful* if $\gamma_n = \emptyset$. $\langle\gamma_1,f_1\rangle,\ldots,\langle\gamma_n,f_n\rangle$ is *failing* if γ_n is unsolvable.

As an element of a solving expansion, the pair $\langle\gamma,id\rangle$ is identified with the goal γ.

$\vdash^{sol}_{AX}$ denotes the corresponding inference relation. ∎

An expansion $\langle\gamma_1,f_1\rangle,\ldots,\langle\gamma_n,f_n\rangle$ starting with the identity substitution and ending with the empty goal returns a solution of γ_1, namely f_n. f_n is built up stepwise: for all $1\le i<n$ there is some g such that $f_{i+1} = f_i[g]$. Semantically, the pair $\langle\gamma,f\rangle$ agrees with the goal $\gamma\cup EQ(f)$ (cf. Sect. 1.2). By separating f from γ,

however, the modification of f caused by an expansion step on f is restricted to an *instantiation* of (the values of) f.

Proposition 4.1 *For all goals γ,δ and substitutions f,g,*

$$\gamma \vdash_{AX}^{sol} \langle\delta,f\rangle \quad \textit{implies} \quad \langle\gamma,g\rangle \vdash_{AX}^{sol} \langle\delta,g[f]\rangle \quad \textit{and} \quad \gamma[f] \vdash_{AX}^{sol} \delta. \blacksquare$$

Lemma 4.2 (Soundness of resolution and paramodulation) *If $\langle\delta,f\rangle$ is obtained from γ by a single resolution or paramodulation step, then all solutions of δ solve $\gamma[f]$ w.r.t. AX.*

Proof. In the case of resolution, we have $\gamma = \gamma'\cup\{p\}$, $p[g] = q[g]$, $\delta = (\gamma'\cup\vartheta)[g]$ and $f = g|X_{goals}$ for some γ',p,g and $q\Leftarrow\vartheta \in$ AX. If some h solves δ w.r.t. AX, we conclude that h solves $\gamma[g] = (\gamma'\cup\{p\})[g]$ as well. By the General Assumption, $var(\gamma) \subseteq X_{goals}$. Hence $\gamma[g] = \gamma[f]$. In case of paramodulation, the argument proceeds analogously. ∎

Theorem 4.3 (Soundness of solving expansions) *If $\gamma \vdash_{AX}^{sol} \langle\delta,f\rangle$, then all solutions of δ solve $\gamma[f]$ w.r.t. AX.*

In particular, if $\gamma \vdash_{AX}^{sol} \langle\emptyset,f\rangle$, then f solves γ w.r.t. AX.

In particular, if $\gamma \vdash_{AX}^{sol} \emptyset$, then γ is AX-valid.

Proof. By induction on the length of expansions, using Prop. 4.1 and Lemma 4.2. ∎

The expansion calculus is also complete, which is shown by successive transformations of a bottom-up proof via the cut calculus (cf. Sect. 1.2) into an expansion proof:

Theorem 4.4 (Completeness of successful solving expansions) *Let γ be a goal and f be a substitution. If f solves γ w.r.t. AX, then $\gamma \vdash_{AX}^{sol} \langle\emptyset,f|X_{goals}\rangle$.*

In particular, if γ is AX-valid, then $\gamma \vdash_{AX}^{sol} \emptyset$.

Proof sketch. Let EAX be the set of congruence axioms for all equality predicates of SIG, *sub(AX)* be the set of instances of AX, γ be a goal and f be a solution of γ w.r.t. AX.

We infer $\gamma \vdash_{AX}^{sol} \langle\emptyset,f|X_{goals}\rangle$ in four steps:

Step 1. All substitution steps in a cut calculus derivation of $\gamma[f]$ from AX∪EAX can be "shifted to the left", i.e., $\gamma[f]$ can be derived from sub(AX∪EAX) by a sequence of cuts (cf. [Pad88a], Prop. 4.9.1(2)).

Step 2. For all sets C of Horn clauses and all Horn clauses $c = \gamma\Leftarrow\delta$, if c is derivable from C by a sequence of cuts, then γ can be expanded into $\emptyset$ by resolving upon $C\cup\delta$ (cf. the proof of [Pad88a], Thm. 5.2.4(4)). Hence we conclude from Step 1 that $\gamma[f]$ can be expanded into $\emptyset$ by resolving upon sub(AX∪EAX).

Step 3. Resolution steps upon sub(CE(AX)∪(EAX-{x≡x})) are simulated as follows. A resolution step upon sub(CE(AX)) always splits into a paramodulation step and a subsequent unification step. A resolution step upon sub(EAX-{x≡x}) can be removed if it is part of a *successful* expansion, like the one of $\gamma[f]$ into $\emptyset$ (cf. Step 2). One argues by induction on the length of a shortest expansion of $\gamma[f]$ into $\emptyset$:

Let c = $p \Leftarrow \delta$ be the first clause of sub(EAX-{x≡x}) resolved upon in such an expansion. Then the expansion falls into three subexpansions:

$$\gamma[f] \vdash \ldots^{(1)} \ldots \vdash \varphi \cup \{p\} \vdash \varphi \cup \delta \vdash \ldots^{(2)} \ldots \vdash \emptyset. \quad (3)$$

(1) and, by induction on the length of (3), also (2) consist of resolution steps upon clauses from sub((AX-CE(AX))∪{x≡x}) and of paramodulation steps upon sub(CE(AX)), i.e.,

$$\gamma[f] \vdash^{sol}_{AX} \varphi \cup \{p\} \quad (4)$$

and

$$\varphi \cup \delta \vdash^{sol}_{AX} \emptyset. \quad (5)$$

Case 3.1. c is a symmetry axiom, i.e., c has the form $t' \equiv t \Leftarrow t \equiv t'$. Then (5) implies $t \equiv t' \vdash^{sol}_{AX} u \equiv u$ for some u and thus $p = t' \equiv t \vdash^{sol}_{AX} u \equiv u \vdash^{sol}_{AX} t \equiv t' \in \delta$.

Case 3.2. c is a transitivity axiom, i.e., c has the form $t \equiv t'' \Leftarrow \{t \equiv t', t' \equiv t''\}$. Then (5) implies $t' \equiv t'' \vdash^{sol}_{AX} u \equiv u$ for some u and thus $p = t \equiv t'' \vdash^{sol}_{AX} t \equiv u \vdash^{sol}_{AX} t \equiv t' \in \delta$.

Case 3.3. c is an OP-compatibility axiom, i.e., c has the form $Ft \equiv Ft' \Leftarrow t \equiv t'$. Then (5) implies $t \equiv t' \vdash^{sol}_{AX} u \equiv u$ for some u and thus $p = Ft \equiv Ft' \vdash^{sol}_{AX} Fu \equiv Fu \vdash^{sol}_{AX} \emptyset \subseteq \delta$.

Case 3.4. c is a PR-compatibility axiom, i.e., c has the form $Pt' \Leftarrow \{Pt, t \equiv t'\}$. Then (5) implies $t \equiv t' \vdash^{sol}_{AX} u \equiv u$ and thus $p = Pt' \vdash^{sol}_{AX} Pu \vdash^{sol}_{AX} Pt \in \delta$.

Hence in all four cases,

$$p \vdash^{sol}_{AX} \delta' \subseteq \delta \quad (6)$$

for some δ'. (4)-(6) imply $\gamma[f] \vdash^{sol}_{AX} \emptyset$.

Step 4. By Lemma 4.5, $\gamma[f] \vdash^{sol}_{AX} \emptyset$ implies $\gamma \vdash^{sol}_{AX} \langle \emptyset, f|X_{goals} \rangle$. ∎

Lemma 4.5 (Expansion lifting) *Let γ be a goal and f,g be substitutions. Then*

$$\gamma[f] \vdash^{sol}_{AX} \langle \delta, g \rangle \quad \textit{implies} \quad \gamma \vdash^{sol}_{AX} \langle \delta, f[g]|X_{goals} \rangle.$$

Moreover, each expansion of γ[f] *into* <δ,g> *is an instance of an expansion of* γ *into* <δ,f[g]/X_{goals}>.

Proof. [Pad88a], Lemma 5.3.2. ∎

Lifting may introduce paramodulation steps upon proper prefix extensions of AX into a given expansion. Suppose that an expansion of γ[f] into <δ,g> starts with a paramodulation step whose redex u[g] in γ[f] does not overlap γ, i.e., u[g] is a subterm of fx for some x ∈ var(γ), say fx = c[u[g]/z]. Then there is no corresponding redex in γ. Hence, applying the axiom u≡u'⇐ϑ to γ[f] corresponds to applying the prefix extension c[u/z]≡c[u'/z]⇐ϑ to γ.

The lifting lemma answers a question concerning the completeness of *computation rules*: Do different orders of selecting atoms or terms as expansion redices yield different results? By Prop. 4.1, an expansion of γ into <δ,f> can be transformed into a "substitutionless" expansion of γ[f] into δ, while lifting reverses the transformation. For substitutionless expansions, the order of selecting atoms (or *maximal terms;* see below) as redices is irrelevant. Hence the order is irrelevant for lifted expansions and thus for all expansions.

Irrelevance of maximal term selection means that, given an atom $P(t_1,...,t_n)$ with two paramodulation redices r_1 in t_i and r_2 in t_j, $i \neq j$, it does not matter whether r_1 is replaced first and r_2 second or r_2 first and r_1 second. If, however, both redices are located in t_i, the order of choosing r_1 and r_2 may make a difference. Only in the case that (SIG,AX) is *confluent,* one redex leading to a successful expansion is sufficient for deducing that all redices do so as well. But even confluence does not ensure that each two expansions of the same goal can be extended to expansions into a common goal. *This* notion of confluence was proposed by [FHS89]. It seems to generalize to goal transformations the notion of confluence used in term rewriting. However, it is too strong insofar as it does not take into account whether the axioms applied have solvable or unsolvable premises. For instance, paramodulating a goal with subterm *insert(x,y&s)* upon IN1 and IN2, respectively (cf. Ex. 1.1), leads to different paramodulants that cannot be expanded into a common goal. Nevertheless, NSB is (ground) confluent (cf. Ex. 6.22) because the premises of IN1 and IN2 have no common solution: only one of the two paramodulants may expand into the empty goal.

For turning the expansion calculus into a procedure for enumerating goal solutions, one requires that the unifier g occurring in rule applications be most general (cf. Sect. 1.1). Wayne Snyder pointed out an incorrect assumption in many completeness proofs, namely that a derived solution can be lifted to a most general one *in all variables*. In fact, this applies only to the variables of X_{goals}. Since the same mistake was made in our corresponding proof (cf. [Pad88a], Lemma 5.4.1), let us present here the corrected proof.

Theorem 4.6 (Completeness of most general solving expansions w.r.t. solving expansions) *If*

$$\gamma \vdash^{sol}_{AX} \langle \delta, f \rangle,$$

then there are a sequence $\langle \gamma_1, f_1 \rangle, \ldots, \langle \gamma_n, f_n \rangle$ *of goal-substitution pairs and a substitution h such that* $\gamma_1 = \gamma$, $f_1 = id$, $\gamma_n[h] = \delta$, $f_n[h]|X_{goals} = f|X_{goals}$ *and for all* $1 \le i < n$, $\langle \gamma_{i+1}, f_{i+1} \rangle$ *is obtained from* $\langle \gamma_i, f_i \rangle$ *by a single expansion step using a most general unifier* g.

Proof. Let $\langle \delta_1, f_1 \rangle, \ldots, \langle \delta_n, f_n \rangle$ be a shortest expansion of γ into $\langle \delta, f \rangle$.

Case 1: $n \le 2$. By inspecting the individual expansion rules, one obtains a goal δ' and a most general unifier g such that $\gamma \vdash^{sol}_{AX} \langle \delta', g \rangle$, $\delta'[h] = \delta$ and $g[h]|X_{goals} = f = f|X_{goals}$ for some h.

Case 2: $n > 2$. The induction hypothesis yields an expansion of γ with exclusively most general unifiers into some pair $\langle \delta', f' \rangle$ such that for some h, $\delta'[h] = \delta_{n-1}$, $f'[h]|X_{goals} = f_{n-1}|X_{goals}$ and w.l.o.g. $var(\delta') \cup var(f'(X_{goals})) \subseteq X_{goals}$.

Moreover, $\delta_{n-1} \vdash^{sol}_{AX} \langle \delta, g \rangle$ for some g with $f_{n-1}[g] = f$, and $\langle \delta, g \rangle$ is derived from δ_{n-1} by a single expansion step. Hence by Lemma 4.5, $\delta' \vdash^{sol}_{AX} \langle \delta, h[g]|X_{goals} \rangle$. Analogously to Case 1, one obtains a goal δ'' and a most general unifier g' such that $\delta' \vdash^{sol}_{AX} \langle \delta'', g' \rangle$, $\delta''[h'] = \delta$ and $g'[h']|X_{goals} = h[g]|X_{goals}$ for some h'. By Prop. 4.1, $\langle \delta', f' \rangle \vdash^{sol}_{AX} \langle \delta'', f'[g'] \rangle$. Hence an expansion only with most general unifiers leads from γ to $\langle \delta'', f'[g'] \rangle$:

$$\gamma \vdash^{sol}_{AX} \langle \delta', f' \rangle \vdash^{sol}_{AX} \langle \delta'', f'[g'] \rangle.$$

Finally, $\delta''[h'] = \delta$ and, since $var(f'(X_{goals})) \subseteq X_{goals}$,

$$f'[g'][h']|X_{goals} = f'[h][g]|X_{goals} = f_{n-1}[g]|X_{goals} = f|X_{goals}. \blacksquare$$

5: Inductive Expansion

An immediate consequence of Theorem 4.3 provides the starting point for inductive theorem *proving* by expansion: If γ expands into $\langle\delta,f\rangle$ such that the domain of f does not contain variables of γ, then $\gamma\Leftarrow\delta$ is inductively valid.

In Sect. 5.3, we generalize this idea to conjectures given as a set of guarded clauses, say

$$CS = \{\gamma_1\Leftarrow\delta:\gamma_1', \ldots, \gamma_n\Leftarrow\delta:\gamma_n'\},$$

with δ-minimal generator matrix $\{\gamma_1',\ldots,\gamma_n'\}$ (cf. Sect. 2.2). Usually, CS is constructor-based (cf. Sect. 2.3). By Thm. 2.1, CS is inductively valid if the Gentzen clause

$$\exists X_{out}(\gamma_1\cup\gamma_1') \vee\ldots\vee \exists X_{out}(\gamma_n\cup\gamma_n') \Leftarrow \delta$$

is inductively valid. Proving CS by inductive expansion means transforming the goal set

$$GM = \{\gamma_1\cup\gamma_1',\ldots,\gamma_n\cup\gamma_n'\}$$

into $\{\delta\}$. The inference rules to carry out the transformation are suitable variants of resolution and paramodulation (cf. Chapter 4). They comprise all the characteristics of inductive proofs, such as the application of lemmas, case analyses and induction steps.

Lemmas, i.e. inductive theorems presupposed or proved previously, are applied by *lemma resolution* or *lemma paramodulation* (cf. Sect. 5.1). We may have to apply a lemma L when its proof induces on other variables or with respect to an induction ordering other than the proof of the theorem where L is used. An infinite nesting of inductive arguments might result from applying only axioms. Hence resolution and paramodulation upon lemmas are vital for inductive proofs. Syntactically, a lemma may be an arbitrary Gentzen clause.

5.1 Case analyses

Usually, an inductive proof of $\gamma\Leftarrow\delta$ splits into subproofs, according to a case analysis that reflects a partition of GS. Some cases correspond to particular subgoals, others are given by particular substitutions for input variables of γ (cf. Sect. 2.2). For treating both case representations in a uniform way, such a substitution, say f, will be transformed into the set EQ(f) (cf. Sect. 1.2).

In forward proofs, the task of checking that a case analysis is complete is not part of the proof itself. Inductive expansion generates a case analysis whenever several lemmas are applied to the same goal. At such a *branching point* (an "or" node in the proof tree) we need not yet ensure that the case distinction is complete. This follows from later applying disjunctive lemmas like DN^{-1}, DS^{-1} or C3 (cf. Sect. 1.4). Resolving or paramodulating upon a disjunctive lemma establishes a *joining point* in the proof: several subexpansions are recombined into a single one.

Definition Let X_{in} be a given set of input variables (cf. Sect. 2.2). The *proving expansion calculus upon AX* consists of the following two inference rules, which transform a set of goals into a single goal.

Lemma resolution (upon an instance of a given lemma)

$$\frac{\{\lambda_1 \cup \varphi_1, \;\ldots,\; \lambda_n \cup \varphi_n\}}{(\lambda_1 \cup \ldots \cup \lambda_n)[g] \cup \vartheta \cup EQ(g_{in})} \qquad \begin{array}{l} \exists X_1\varphi_1[g] \vee \ldots \vee \exists X_n\varphi_n[g] \Leftarrow \vartheta \in ITh(AX), \\ \text{for all } 1 \le i \le n: \\ X_i \cap var(\lambda_i[g] \cup g(X_{in}) \cup X_{in}) = \emptyset \end{array}$$

Lemma paramodulation (upon an instance of a given lemma)

$$\frac{\{\lambda_1[t_1/x], \;\ldots,\; \lambda_n[t_n/x]\}}{(\lambda_1 \cup \ldots \cup \lambda_n)[g] \cup \vartheta \cup EQ(g_{in})} \qquad \begin{array}{l} \exists X_1(t_1 \equiv x)[g] \vee \ldots \vee \exists X_n(t_n \equiv x)[g] \Leftarrow \\ \vartheta \in ITh(AX), \text{ for all } 1 \le i \le n: \\ X_i \cap var(\lambda_i[g] \cup \vartheta \cup g(X_{in}) \cup X_{in}) = \emptyset \end{array}$$

A sequence $s_1,\ldots,s_n$ of goal sets is called a *proving expansion of s_1 into s_n upon AX* if for all $1 \le i < n$ and $\gamma \in s_{i+1} - s_i$ there is $s \subseteq s_i$ such that γ is obtained from s by a single lemma resolution or lemma paramodulation step.

The corresponding inference relation is denoted by $\vdash^{pro}_{AX}$. ∎

Lemma 5.1 (Soundness of lemma resolution and paramodulation) *If δ is obtained from $\{\gamma_1,\ldots,\gamma_n\}$ by a single lemma resolution or lemma paramodulation step, then*

$$\exists X_{out}\gamma_1 \vee \ldots \vee \exists X_{out}\gamma_n \Leftarrow \delta$$

is inductively valid w.r.t. AX.

Proof. Suppose that $f \in GS$ solves δ.

Case 1 (lemma resolution). Then $\delta = (\lambda_1 \cup \ldots \cup \lambda_n)[g] \cup \vartheta \cup EQ(g_{in})$ for some $\lambda_1,\ldots,\lambda_n,g,\vartheta$. From the conditions of lemma resolution we must infer

$$AX \vdash_{cut} (\lambda_j \cup \varphi_j)[f_{in}+h_{out}] \text{ for some } 1 \le j \le n \text{ and } h \in GS. \quad (1)$$

Since f solves ϑ and $\exists X_1\varphi_1[g] \vee ... \vee \exists X_n\varphi_n[g] \Leftarrow \vartheta$ is inductively valid, there are $1 \le j \le n$ and $h \in GS$ such that $g[h]$ solves φ_j and $h|(X-X_j) = f|(X-X_j)$.

$X_j \cap var(\lambda_j[g]) = \emptyset$ implies $\lambda_j[g][h] = \lambda_j[g][f]$, while $X_j \cap var(g(X_{in})) = \emptyset$ implies $g[h] = g[f]_{in}+g[h]_{out}$ and thus

$$AX \vdash_{cut} (\lambda_j \cup \varphi_j)[g][h] = (\lambda_j \cup \varphi_j)[g[f]_{in}+g[h]_{out}]. \quad (2)$$

Since f solves $EQ(g_{in})$, f_{in} and $g[f]_{in}$ are AX-equivalent. Hence (1) follows from (2).

Case 2 (lemma paramodulation). Then $\delta = (\lambda_1 \cup ... \cup \lambda_n)[g] \cup \vartheta \cup EQ(g_{in})$ for some $\lambda_1,...,\lambda_n$, g,ϑ. From the conditions of lemma paramodulation we must infer

$$AX \vdash_{cut} \lambda_j[t_j/x][f_{in}+h_{out}] \text{ for some } 1 \le i \le n \text{ and } h \in GS. \quad (3)$$

Since f solves ϑ and $\exists X_1(t_1 \equiv x)[g] \vee ... \vee \exists X_n(t_n \equiv x)[g] \Leftarrow \vartheta$ is inductively valid, there are $1 \le j \le n$ and $h \in GS$ such that $g[h]$ solves $t_j \equiv x$ and $h|(X-X_j) = f|(X-X_j)$.

$X_j \cap var(gx) = \emptyset$ implies $(gx)[h] = (gx)[f]$. Hence $t_j[g][h] \equiv (gx)[f]$ is AX-valid.

Let $g' = g[f]|(X-\{x\}) + \{t_j[g][h]/x\}$. Since $g[f]$ solves λ_j, g' also solves λ_j.

Since $X_j \cap var(\lambda_j[g]) \subseteq \emptyset$, we have $g'z = (gz)[f] = (gz)[h]$ for all $z \in var(\lambda_j)-\{x\}$.

$X_j \cap var(g(X_{in})) = \emptyset$ implies $g[h] = g[f]_{in}+g[h]_{out}$ and thus

$$AX \vdash_{cut} \lambda_j[g'] = \lambda_j[t_j/x][g][h] = \lambda_j[t_j/x][g[f]_{in}+g[h]_{out}]. \quad (4)$$

As f solves $EQ(g_{in})$, f_{in} and $g[f]_{in}$ are AX-equivalent. Hence (4) implies (3). ∎

Theorem 5.2 (Soundness of proving expansions) *A Gentzen clause* $\exists X_{out}\gamma_1 \vee ... \vee \exists X_{out}\gamma_n \Leftarrow \delta$ *is inductively valid w.r.t. AX if* $\{\gamma_1,...,\gamma_n\} \vdash^{pro}_{AX} \{\delta\}$.

Proof. We use induction on the length m of a shortest proving expansion of $\{\gamma_1,...,\gamma_n\}$ into $\{\delta\}$. If $m = 0$, then $\gamma_1 = ... = \gamma_n = \delta$, and the proof is complete. Otherwise, there are goal sets $s_1,...,s_k$ and goals $\delta_1,...,\delta_k$ such that $s_1 \cup ... \cup s_k = \{\gamma_1,...,\gamma_n\}$; for all $1 \le i \le k$ there is a proving expansion of s_i into $\{\delta_i\}$ with a length less than m. We obtain δ from $\{\delta_1,...,\delta_k\}$ by a single lemma resolution or paramodulation step.

By Lemma 5.1, $\exists X_{out}\delta_1 \vee ... \vee \exists X_{out}\delta_k \Leftarrow \delta$ is inductively valid. By the induction hypothesis, for all $1 \le i \le k$ and $s_i = \{\psi_1,...,\psi_j\}$, $\exists X_{out}\psi_1 \vee ... \vee \exists X_{out}\psi_j \Leftarrow \delta_i$ is inductively valid, thus so is $\exists X_{out}\gamma_1 \vee ... \vee \exists X_{out}\gamma_n \Leftarrow \delta$, since $s_1 \cup ... \cup s_k = \{\gamma_1,...,\gamma_n\}$. ∎

Lemma resolution and paramodulation each perform the joining of n expansions. The i-th expansion closes respectively with $\lambda_i \cup \varphi_i$ and $\lambda_i[t_i/x]$, by transforming all n goals into a single one. $EQ(g_{in})$ retains the actual substitution of all input variables as a set of equations, thus indicating a particular case to be joined later with other cases by resolving or paramodulating upon a disjunctive lemma. For instance, resolving upon DS^{-1} (cf. Sect. 1.4) joins two expansions: the first treating the case $s \equiv \varepsilon$, the second handling $s \equiv x \& s'$.

The existential variables of a lemma are restricted to occur only in

(1) redices, i.e., $X_i \cap var(\lambda_i[g]) = \emptyset$, or in

(2) instances of output variables, i.e., $X_i \cap var(g(X_{in})) = \emptyset$.

Trivial examples confirm that the two restrictions are essential. For instance, resolve any equation $t \equiv t'$ upon the transitivity axiom for $\equiv$, i.e., expand $t \equiv t'$ into $\{t \equiv x,\ x \equiv t'\}$. Disregarding (1), one can resolve $\{t \equiv x,\ x \equiv t'\}$ upon the valid lemma $\exists x{:}t \equiv x$ and come up with the resolvent $x \equiv t'$. Finally, resolving upon the reflexivity axiom $z \equiv z$ leads to the empty goal. So one would have shown that all equations are inductively valid!

Concerning lemma paramodulation, (1) involves the additional restriction that the right-hand side of the equation applied does not contain existential variables. Without this restriction, one can paramodulate $t \equiv t'$ upon $\exists x{:}t \equiv x$ and return the paramodulant $x \equiv t'$. Resolving upon $z \equiv z$ leads to $\emptyset$, and, again, one would have shown that all equations are inductively valid.

In general, if existential variables from the lemma instance c applied in a resolution step occur in $\lambda_i[g]$, we can no longer be sure that we are applying c. It could be the stronger clause

$$\exists X_1\varphi_1[g] \vee \ldots \vee \exists X_i(\lambda_i \cup \varphi_i)[g] \vee \ldots \vee \exists X_n\varphi_n[g] \Leftarrow \vartheta.$$

Moreover, an existential variable x in c is excluded from $g(X_{in})$ as it would contradict the universal quantification of X_{in}, or, in other words, instead of c, we are applying

$$\exists X_1\varphi_1[g] \vee \ldots \vee \exists(X_i - \{x\})\varphi_i[g] \vee \ldots \vee \exists X_n\varphi_n[g] \Leftarrow \vartheta\ .$$

Often the given lemmas do not apply directly to the current goal set, i.e., they need a preceding unification step. So let L be a set of inductive AX-theorems (which may be attached to the specification; cf. Sect. 9.2) and adapt the lemmas rules as follows:

Lemma resolution (upon a given lemma)

$$\frac{\{\lambda_1 \cup \varphi_1,\ \ldots,\ \lambda_n \cup \varphi_n\}}{(\lambda_1 \cup \ldots \cup \lambda_n \cup \vartheta)[g] \cup EQ(g_{in})} \qquad \begin{array}{l} \exists X_1\psi_1 \cup \vartheta_1 \vee \ldots \vee \exists X_n \psi_n \cup \vartheta_n \Leftarrow \vartheta \in L, \\ \text{for all } 1 \le i \le n\text{: } \varphi_i[g] = \psi_i[g], \\ g(X_i) \subseteq X,\ g \text{ is injective on } X_i, \\ g(X_i) \cap var(\lambda_i[g] \cup g(X_{in})) = \emptyset \end{array}$$

Lemma paramodulation (upon a given lemma)

$$\frac{\{\lambda_1[t_1/x],\ \ldots,\ \lambda_n[t_n/x]\}}{(\lambda_1[t/x] \cup \ldots \cup \lambda_n[t/x] \cup \vartheta)[g] \cup EQ(g_{in})} \qquad \begin{array}{l} \exists X_1\{u_1 \equiv t\} \cup \vartheta_1 \vee \ldots \vee \exists X_n\{u_n \equiv t\} \cup \vartheta_n \Leftarrow \\ \vartheta \in L^{sym} \text{ for all } 1 \le i \le n\text{: } t_i[g] = u_i[g], \\ g(X_i) \subseteq X,\ g \text{ is injective on } X_i, \\ g(X_i) \cap var(\lambda_i[t/x][g] \cup g(X_{in})) = \emptyset \end{array}$$

It is left to the reader to show that each expansion step obtained by this version of lemma resolution (paramodulation) can also be performed by the original. The lemma applied there is an instance of the lemma applied here.

Although the following rules can be simulated by lemma resolution or paramodulation steps, it is often more convenient to use them directly.

Factoring

$$\frac{\{\lambda \cup \{p,q\}\}}{(\lambda \cup \{p\})[g] \cup EQ(g_{in})} \qquad p[g] = q[g]$$

Unification

$$\frac{\{\lambda \cup \{t \equiv t'\}\}}{\lambda[g] \cup EQ(g_{in})} \qquad t[g] = t'[g]$$

Equational replacement

$$\frac{\{\lambda[t/x]\}}{\lambda[t'/x] \cup \{e\}} \qquad e = t \equiv t' \text{ or } e = t' \equiv t$$

Goal elimination

$$\frac{\{\lambda_1, \ldots, \lambda_n\}}{\lambda_1} \qquad n > 1$$

Factoring is resolution upon the lemma $p \Leftarrow p$. Unification is resolution upon the reflexivity axiom $x \equiv x$. Equational replacement is paramodulation respectively upon the lemma $e \Leftarrow e$ or upon the symmetry axiom $t \equiv t' \Leftarrow e$. Goal elimination is resolution upon $\lambda_1 \vee ... \vee \lambda_n \Leftarrow \lambda_1$.

Factoring is useful if there are two lemmas $p \Leftarrow \gamma$ and $p' \Leftarrow \gamma$ such that, say, $\{x\}$ = var(γ)-var(p) and $\{y\}$ = var(γ)-var(p'). If the lemmas are applied sequentially to a goal λ, we may obtain a subgoal with two instances of γ, say $\gamma[t/y]$ after applying $p \Leftarrow \gamma$ and $\gamma[t'/x]$ after applying $p' \Leftarrow \gamma$. In such a situation, one often aims at the "intersection" of both instances, namely $\gamma[t/y,t'/x]$, which can be achieved when applying $p \Leftarrow \gamma$ and, simultaneously, substituting t' for the "fresh" variable x. However, this requires foreseeing the instance of x that the subsequent application of $p' \Leftarrow \gamma$ will generate. But if fresh variables are not instantiated, then $\gamma[t/y]$ must be factored with $\gamma[t'/x]$ in order to accomplish $\gamma[t/y,t'/x]$.[1]

Equational replacement can be used for "folding" the premise δ of the conjecture $\gamma \Leftarrow \delta$. If an expansion of $\{\gamma\}$ leads to the goal set

$$\gamma[f_1] \cup \{x \equiv f_1 x \mid x \in X_{in}\}, ..., \gamma[f_n] \cup \{x \equiv f_n x \mid x \in X_{in}\},$$

reflecting a case analysis, we could proceed to corresponding instances of δ, say,

$$\delta[f_1] \cup \{x \equiv f_1 x \mid x \in X_{in}\}, ..., \delta[f_n] \cup \{x \equiv f_n x \mid x \in X_{in}\}. \qquad (1)$$

If $f_1,...,f_n$ represents a complete case analysis, a lemma of the form

$$\exists X_1 \{x \equiv f_1 x\} \vee ... \vee \exists X_n \{x \equiv f_n x\}. \qquad (2)$$

will result. However, (1) is cannot be resolved upon (2) unless we remove the X_i-occurrences from $\delta[f_i]$. For this purpose, the replacement rule is applied n times to (1). This yields the goal set

$$\delta \cup \{x \equiv f_1 x \mid x \in X_{in}\}, ..., \delta \cup \{x \equiv f_n x \mid x \in X_{in}\}. \qquad (3)$$

(3) can be resolved upon (2), and we come up with δ.[2]

An expansion E of γ is said to split into n subexpansions if E contains a subsequence of the form $\{\gamma,...\},\{\gamma,\gamma_1,...\},...,\{\gamma,\gamma_n,...\}$ such that for all $1 \le i \le n$, γ_i is obtained from $\{\gamma\}$ by a lemma resolution or paramodulation step. There are two possibilities for eliminating γ from the current goal set. Either one knows in advance the last step where γ is needed and discards γ immediately after it, or one removes γ in a separate step using the goal elimination rule. Soundness is guaranteed in both cases: if γ disappears after applying the lemma $\varphi \Leftarrow \delta$, then applying the "specialization" $\varphi \Leftarrow \delta \cup \gamma$ keeps γ in the goal set.

---

[1]For a concrete example of this kind, cf. Ex. 5.10.

[2]Cf. Ex. 5.4 and Sect. 5.5 for concrete examples of equational replacement.

5.2 Induction steps

Besides applying lemmas, we may resolve or paramodulate upon the conjecture whenever it comes as an induction hypothesis. This is guaranteed by adding a *descent condition* to the resolvent or paramodulant, whose expansion will succeed only if the present instance of the conjecture is "smaller" than the one just proved.

Given a set CS of Horn clauses, the descent condition is constructed from a *descent predicate* $>_{CS}$ *for CS*, which is a binary predicate on a product sort $s_1 \times ... \times s_k$ where $\{s_1,...,s_n\}$ is the multiset of sorts of all input variables. The descent predicate must be a Noetherian relation in *some* SIG-model of AX:

Definition A binary relation R on a set A is *Noetherian* or *well-founded* if there is no infinite sequence $a_1,a_2,a_3,...$ of elements of A such that for all i≥1, $\langle a_i,a_{i+1}\rangle \in R$. ▮

It is well known that a Noetherian relation R establishes the

Principle of Noetherian induction (w.r.t. R) If a predicate P on a set A satisfies the implication

$$(\forall\ (a,b) \in R : P(b))\ \text{ implies }\ P(a)$$

for all a ∈ A, then A satisfies P. (For the simple proof, cf. e.g., [Man74], p. 409.) ▮

If $>_{CS}$ is Noetherian in some SIG-model of AX, it is so in the initial (SIG,AX)-structure (cf. Sect. 3.1). In other words, the *CS-induction ordering* $>_{CS,AX}$ on ground terms, defined by

$$t >_{CS,AX} t' \quad \text{iff} \quad AX \vdash_{cut} t >_{CS} t',$$

is Noetherian.

Proposition 5.3 *The CS-induction ordering is well-founded iff there is a SIG-model A of AX such that* $>_{CS}{}^{A}$, *the interpretation of* $>_{CS}$ *in A, is well-founded.*

Proof. Let A be a SIG-model of AX with Noetherian relation $>_{CS}{}^{A}$. If $>_{CS,AX}$ would admit an infinite chain, then $>_{CS}{}^{A}$ would do so, too, because the cut calculus is correct w.r.t. A. Conversely, let $>_{CS,AX}$ be well-founded. A = Ini(SIG,AX) (cf. Sect. 3.1) interprets $>_{CS}$ as follows:

$$t^{A} >_{CS}{}^{A} t'^{A} \quad \text{iff} \quad t >_{CS,AX} t'.$$

If $>_{CS}{}^{A}$ would admit an infinite chain, then $>_{CS,GT}$ would do so as well. Hence $>_{CS}{}^{A}$ is Noetherian. The proof is complete because A is a SIG-model of AX. ▮

By definition, the CS-induction ordering is compatible with AX-equivalence: if $t >_{CS} t'$ is AX-valid, $t \equiv_{AX} u$ and $t' \equiv_{AX} u'$, then $u >_{CS} u'$ is also

AX-valid. In particular, AX $\vdash_{cut}$ {t $>_{CS}$ t', t≡t'} implies AX $\vdash_{cut}$ t' $>_{CS}$ t'. Hence, to be well-founded, $>_{CS,AX}$ must be *disjoint* from AX-equivalence. This distinguishes $>_{CS,AX}$ from an *AX-reduction ordering*, which includes the subrelation $\longrightarrow_{AX}$ of AX-equivalence (cf. Sect. 6.2).[1]

Let us take a closer look at the descent condition produced by an induction step. Think of a forward proof of a Horn clause c = p⇐γ. Each induction step replaces an instance of γ, say γ[f], by p[f] where c[f] is "smaller" than the instance just proved, say c[g]. More precisely: if X_{in} = $\{z_1,...,z_k\}$, then the atom

$$(gz_1,...,gz_k) >_{CS} (fz_1,...,fz_k) \qquad \text{(DC)}$$

is AX-valid. The induction step is a cut of c' = p[f]⇐γ[f]∪{DC} with γ[f]∪{DC}, which results in p[f]. In the corresponding top-down proof, p[f] is resolved upon c', yielding the resolvent γ[f]∪{DC}.

This view of induction steps underlies two further inference rules, which, together with the lemma rules of Sect. 5.1, yield the rules of inductive expansion, but which, in contrast with the lemma rules, depend on the conjecture set CS.

Definition Let CS be a set of Horn clauses, X_{in} = $\{z_1,...,z_k\}$ (cf. Sect. 2.2) and CS* be CS with $z_1,...,z_k$ renamed into disjoint variables $z_1^*,...,z_k^*$. The *inductive expansion calculus upon AX and CS* consists of lemma resolution, lemma paramodulation (cf. Sect. 5.1) and the following two inference rules, which transform single goals.

Inductive CS-resolution

$$\frac{\{\lambda \cup \varphi\}}{(\lambda \cup \vartheta \cup \{(t_1,...,t_k) >_{CS} (z_1^*,...,z_k^*)\})[g] \cup EQ(g_{in})}$$

φ[g] = ψ[g], ψ ⊆ γ
γ⇐ϑ ∈ CS*
for all 1≤i≤k: $t_i = z_i$ or $z_i \equiv t_i \in \lambda$

Inductive CS-paramodulation

$$\frac{\{\lambda[t/x]\}}{(\lambda[u'/x] \cup \vartheta \cup \{(t_1,...,t_k) >_{CS} (z_1^*,...,z_k^*)\})[g] \cup EQ(g_{in})}$$

t[g] = u[g],
u≡u' ∈ γ^{sym}
γ⇐ϑ ∈ CS*
for all 1≤i≤k:
$t_i = z_i$ or $z_i \equiv t_i \in \lambda$

[1]Nevertheless, reduction orderings are often constructed from induction orderings (cf. Sect. 6.2).

A sequence $s_1,\ldots,s_n$ of goal sets is called an *inductive expansion of* s_1 *into* s_n *upon AX and CS* if for all $1\le i<n$ and $\gamma \in s_{i+1}-s_i$ there is $s \subseteq s_i$ such that γ is obtained from s by a single lemma or inductive resolution or paramodulation step.

The corresponding inference relation is denoted by $\vdash^{ind}_{AX;CS}$. ∎

Since CS consists of Horn clauses, both inductive rules only apply to single goals and thus, in contrast to the lemma rules, these rules cannot rejoin several subexpansions.

5.3 Inductive expansion of guarded clauses

Let

$$CS = \{\gamma_1 \Leftarrow \delta:\gamma_1', \ldots, \gamma_n \Leftarrow \delta:\gamma_n'\}$$

be a set of guarded clauses with δ-minimal generator matrix $\{\gamma_1',\ldots,\gamma_n'\}$ (cf. Sect. 2.2). Theorem 2.1 tells us that CS is inductively valid if

$$c = \exists X_{out}(\gamma_1 \cup \gamma_1') \vee \ldots \vee \exists X_{out}(\gamma_n \cup \gamma_n') \Leftarrow \delta$$

is inductively valid. Below we show that inductive resolution and paramodulation are sound. Together with the correctness of lemma resolution and lemma paramodulation, one may then follow the proof of Thm. 5.2 and conclude that c is inductively valid if there is an inductive expansion of

$$GM = \{\gamma_1 \cup \gamma_1', \ldots, \gamma_n \cup \gamma_n'\}$$

into $\{\delta\}$ upon AX and c.

This procedure would only admit c as an induction hypothesis. But c can only be resolved or paramodulated upon after (the left-hand sides of) *all* summands of its conclusion have been established. One cannot apply *this* summand in one subexpansion and *that* summand in another subexpansion. Fortunately, c can be replaced by CS because CS is an inductive consequence of c. Since CS is a *set* of clauses, an expansion of GM into $\{\delta\}$ may use single elements of CS as induction hypotheses. The precise soundness result is given in Section 5.4.

An expansion splits into subexpansions when several lemmas or induction hypotheses are applied to the same goal. Conversely, several subexpansions are joined into a single one when a disjunctive lemma is resolved or paramodulated upon. Hence the essential part of an expansion of GM into $\{\delta\}$ may be regarded as a collapsed tree or an acyclic graph with goals at the nodes, in particular, with the elements of GM at the leaves and δ at the root. Paths starting out from a leaf, but not reaching δ, do not contribute to the proof and thus can be pruned (cf. Sect. 5.4). For instance, if n = 3, the expansion tree may look as shown in Fig. 5.1.

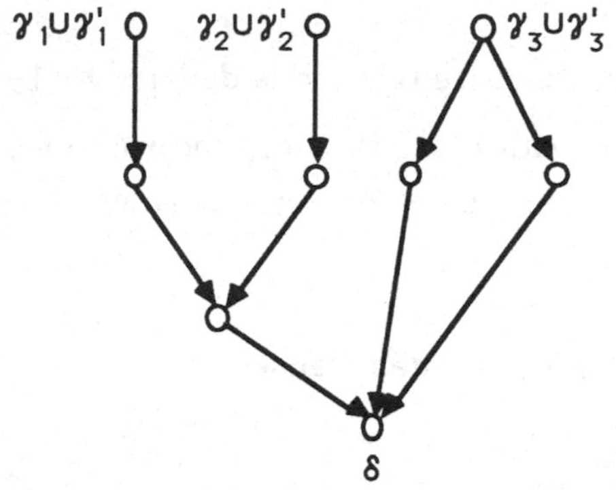

Figure 5.1 Schema of an expansion of a guarded clause set.

Example 5.4 Let (SIG,AX) = NSB (cf. Ex. 1.1). We turn the Gentzen clause

$$\exists\{y\}\ x \equiv y*2 \ \vee\ \exists\{y\}\ x \equiv (y*2)+1 \ \Leftarrow\ Def(x)$$

into a Horn clause according to Sect. 2.5:

$$EvenOrOdd(x) \ \Leftarrow\ Def(x). \qquad \text{(EVOD)}$$

The splitting lemmas applied in the following expansion of EVOD are the axioms

$$EvenOrOdd(x) \ \Leftarrow\ x \equiv y*2 \qquad \text{(EVEN)}$$
$$EvenOrOdd(x) \ \Leftarrow\ x \equiv (y*2)+1 \qquad \text{(ODD)}$$
$$0*2 \equiv 0 \qquad \text{(DB1)}$$
$$(x+1)*2 \equiv (x*2)+2. \qquad \text{(DB2)}$$

The joining lemmas are the inductive theorems

$$\exists\{y\}\ y*2 \equiv x \ \vee\ \exists\{y\}\ (y*2)+1 \equiv x \ \Leftarrow\ EvenOrOdd(x) \qquad \text{(L1)}$$
$$x \equiv 0 \ \vee\ x \equiv 0+1 \ \vee\ \exists\{y\}\ x \equiv y+2 \ \Leftarrow\ Def(x). \qquad \text{(L2)}$$

The expansion has the following collapsed tree structure where each set of edges with the same target is labelled with the lemma that causes the respective proof step:

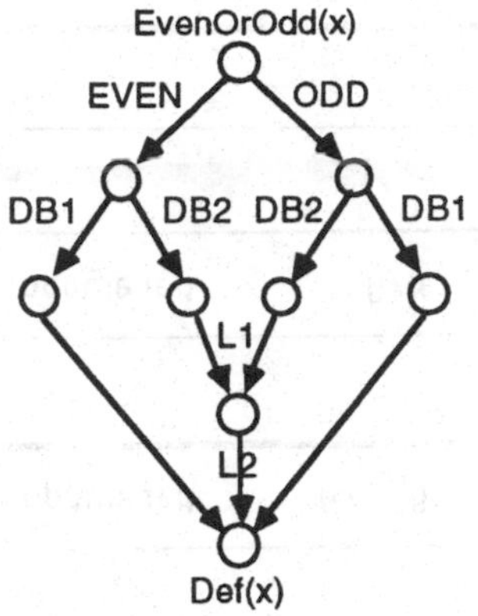

Figure 5.2 Schema of an expansion of EVOD.

The complete expansion $s_1,...,s_n$ reads as follows. The goals of s_i are separated from each other by thin lines. The entire goal set s_i is separated from the subsequent goal set s_{i+1} by a bold line.

goal name	*goal*	*substitution of X_{out}*	*rules applied*
	EvenOrOdd(x)		-- conclusion of EVOD
	EvenOrOdd(x)		
	x ≡ y*2		resolution upon EVEN
	EvenOrOdd(x)		
	x ≡ y*2		
	x ≡ 0	0/y	paramodulation upon DB1
	EvenOrOdd(x)		
G1	x ≡ (y'*2)+2	y'+1/y	paramodulation upon DB2
	x ≡ 0		
	x ≡ (y*2)+1		resolution upon ODD
	G1		
	x ≡ 0		

$x \equiv (y*2)+1$		
G1		
$x \equiv 0+1$	$0/y$	paramodulation upon DB1
$x \equiv 0$		
$x \equiv ((y'*2)+2)+1$	$y'+1/y$	paramodulation upon DB2
G1		
$x \equiv 0+1$		
$x \equiv 0$		
$x \equiv ((y'*2)+1)+2$		paramodulation upon $(z+2)+1 \equiv (z+1)+2$
G1		
$x \equiv 0+1$		
$x \equiv 0$		
EvenOrOdd(x') $x \equiv x'+2$		paramodulation upon L1
$x \equiv 0+1$		
$x \equiv 0$		
Def(x') $x'+2 >_{EVOD} x'$ $x \equiv x'+2$		inductive resolution
$x \equiv 0+1$		
$x \equiv 0$		
Def(x'+2) $x \equiv x'+2$		resolution upon $Def(x) \Leftarrow Def(x+2)$ and $x+2 >_{EVOD} x$
$x \equiv 0+1$		
$x \equiv 0$		

Def(x) x ≡ x'+2	equational replacement
x ≡ 0+1	
x ≡ 0	
Def(x)	resolution upon L2

5.4 The soundness proof

As the reader might expect, the correctness of inductive expansion is shown by induction, both on the length of an expansion and, along the CS-induction ordering, on the set GS of ground substitutions.

Theorem 5.5 (Soundness of inductive expansions) *Let*

$$CS = \{\gamma_1 \Leftarrow \delta:\gamma_1',\ldots,\gamma_n \Leftarrow \delta:\gamma_n'\}$$

be a set of guarded clauses with δ-minimal generator matrix $GM = \{\gamma_1',\ldots,\gamma_n'\}$, $X_{in} = \{z_1,\ldots,z_k\}$ *and let* $>_{CS}$ *be a descent predicate for CS such that the CS-induction ordering is well-founded. CS is inductively valid w.r.t. AX if*

$$\{\gamma_1\cup\gamma_1',\ldots,\gamma_n\cup\gamma_n'\} \vdash^{ind}_{AX;CS} \{\delta\}.$$

Proof. Let $f_1,\ldots,f_n \in GS$ such that for all $1\le i\le n$, f_i solves $\delta\cup\gamma_i'$. We show by Noetherian induction on the multiset $\{(f_iz_1,\ldots,f_iz_k) \mid 1\le i\le n\}$ along the extension of $>_{CS,AX}$ to multisets that f_i solves γ_i.

Let $1\le i\le n$ and $f = f_i$. Suppose there are $1\le j\le n$ and $h \in GS$ such that

$$AX \vdash_{cut} \delta[f] \text{ implies } AX \vdash_{cut} (\gamma_j\cup\gamma_j')[f_{in}+h_{out}]. \quad (1)$$

Since GM is δ-minimal and f solves $\delta\cup\gamma_i'$, we have i = j. Hence by (1), $f_{in}+h_{out}$ solves $\gamma_i\cup\gamma_i'$. Since $var(\gamma_i) \subseteq X_{in} \cup var(\gamma_i')$ and $fx \equiv_{AX} hx$ for all $x \in var(\gamma_i')_{out}$, we conclude that $\gamma_i[f]$ is AX-valid.

It remains to prove (1). We show that the following more general condition holds true:

(2) Let $\delta_1,\ldots,\delta_n$ and δ' be goals such that the expansion of $\{\gamma_1\cup\gamma_1',\ldots,\gamma_n\cup\gamma_n'\}$ into {δ} includes an inference step from $\delta_1,\ldots,\delta_n$ to δ'. Then for all $f' \in GS$ with $f'_{in} = f_{in}$ there are $1\le j\le n$ and $h \in GS$ such that

$$AX \vdash_{cut} \delta'[f'] \text{ implies } AX \vdash_{cut} \delta_j[f_{in}+h_{out}]. \quad (2)$$

The same inductive argument that leads from Lemma 5.1 to Thm. 5.2 can be used for deriving (1) from (2). It remains to prove (2) for each of the four inference rules defining $\vdash^{ind}_{AX;CS}$.

Suppose that $f' \in GS$ with $f'_{in} = f_{in}$ solves δ'.

Case 1. δ' is obtained from $\delta_1,\ldots,\delta_n$ by lemma resolution or lemma paramodulation. Then (2) follows from Lemma 5.1.

Case 2. $n = 1$ and δ' is obtained from δ_1 by inductive resolution. Then

$$\delta' = (\lambda \cup \vartheta \cup \{(t_1,\ldots,t_k) >_{CS} (z_1{}^*,\ldots,z_k{}^*)\})[g] \cup EQ(g_{in})$$

for some $\lambda, t_1,\ldots,t_k, g$ and $\gamma \Leftarrow \vartheta \in CS^*$. From the conditions of inductive resolution we must infer

$$AX \vdash_{cut} (\lambda \cup \varphi)[f_{in}+h_{out}] \text{ for some } h \in GS. \tag{3}$$

Since $g[f']$ solves λ, the definition of $t_1,\ldots,t_k$ implies that for all $1 \le j \le k$, $(gz_j)[f'] \equiv_{AX} t_j[g][f']$. Since f' solves $EQ(g_{in})$, f'_{in} and thus f_{in} are AX-equivalent to $g[f']_{in}$. Hence for all $1 \le j \le k$,

$$fz_j \equiv_{AX} t_j[g][f']. \tag{4}$$

Since $g[f']$ solves $(t_1,\ldots,t_k) >_{CS} (z_1{}^*,\ldots,z_k{}^*)$ and $AX \vdash_{cut} \delta[f']$, (4) implies

$$AX \vdash_{cut} (z_1,\ldots,z_k)[f] >_{CS} (z_1{}^*,\ldots,z_k{}^*)[g][f']. \tag{5}$$

Let $1 \le j \le n$ be the index of $\gamma \Leftarrow \vartheta$ in CS^*, i.e. $\gamma = \gamma_j{}^*$ and $\vartheta = (\delta \cup \gamma_j')^*$. Let $h = \{z_1/z_1{}^*,\ldots,z_k/z_k{}^*\}$, $g_j[h] = g[f']$ and $g_s = f_s$ for all $1 \le s \le n$ with $s \ne j$. Then (5) amounts to

$$(f_jz_1,\ldots,f_jz_k) >_{CS,AX} (g_jz_1,\ldots,g_jz_k)$$

and thus to

$$\{(f_sz_1,\ldots,f_sz_k) \mid 1 \le s \le n\} >^{multiset}_{CS;AX} \{(g_sz_1,\ldots,g_sz_k) \mid 1 \le s \le n\}. \tag{6}$$

Since $g_j[h] = g[f']$ solves $\vartheta = (\delta \cup \gamma_j')^*$, the assumption implies $AX \vdash_{cut} \delta \cup \gamma_s'[g_s]$ for all $1 \le s \le n$. Hence by (6) and the induction hypothesis, $AX \vdash_{cut} \gamma_s[g_s]$ for all $1 \le s \le n$.

Since $\psi \subseteq \gamma_j$, $g[f']$ solves ψ. Hence $g[f']$ solves φ because g unifies φ and ψ. Since $g[f']$ solves λ, we conclude

$$AX \vdash_{cut} (\lambda \cup \varphi)[g][f']. \tag{7}$$

Since f' solves $EQ(g_{in})$, $f'_{in} = f_{in}$ is AX-equivalent to $g[f']_{in}$. Thus by (7), $f_{in}+g[f']_{out}$ solves λ and φ. Hence (3) holds true.

Case 3. $n = 1$ and δ' is obtained from δ_1 by inductive paramodulation. Then

$$\delta' = (\lambda[t'/x] \cup \vartheta \cup \{(t_1,\ldots,t_k) >_{CS} (z_1{}^*,\ldots,z_k{}^*)\})[g] \cup EQ(g_{in})$$

for some $\lambda,\vartheta,t_1,\dots,t_k,g$ and $\gamma\Leftarrow\vartheta \in CS^*$. From the conditions of inductive paramodulation we must infer

$$AX \vdash_{cut} \lambda[u/x][f_{in}+h_{out}] \text{ for some } h \in GS. \tag{8}$$

With λ replaced by $\lambda[t'/x]$, the second paragraph of Case 2 also applies to this case.

Since $t\equiv t' \in \gamma_i^{sym}$, $g[f']$ solves $t\equiv t'$. Hence $g[f']$ is a solution of $\lambda[t/x]$ because $g[f']$ solves $\lambda[t'/x]$. Since g unifies u and t, we obtain

$$AX \vdash_{cut} \lambda[u/x][g][f']. \tag{9}$$

Since f' solves $EQ(g_{in})$, $f'_{in} = f_{in}$ is AX-equivalent to $g[f']_{in}$. Thus by (9), $f_{in}+g[f']_{out}$ solves $\lambda[u/x]$. Hence (8) holds true. ∎

For constructor-based clause sets (cf. Sect. 2.3), Thm. 5.5 amounts to

Corollary 5.6 *A constructor-based clause set* $CS = \{\gamma_1\Leftarrow\delta:\gamma_1',\dots,\gamma_n\Leftarrow\delta:\gamma_n'\}$ *is inductively valid w.r.t. AX if*

$$\{\gamma_1\cup\gamma_1',\dots,\gamma_n\cup\gamma_n'\} \vdash^{ind}_{AX;CS} \{\delta\}.$$

Proof. Lemma 2.2 and Thm. 5.5. ∎

Corollary 5.7 *A Horn clause* $c = \gamma\Leftarrow\delta$ *is inductively valid w.r.t. AX if*

$$\{\gamma\} \vdash^{ind}_{AX;c} \{\delta\}.$$

Proof. Let X_{in} = var(c). Then the conjecture follows from Cor. 5.6. ∎

Above we claimed that inductive proofs are not compositional insofar as replacing a lemma L within a proof of CS by a proof of L does not always yield a proof of CS. Nevertheless, inductive expansions are composed of inductive theorems: If the proof of CS *has been finished*, CS becomes a set of further lemmas and thus all induction steps of the proof can be regarded as applications of lemma resolution or lemma paramodulation. Each subexpansion of the proof of CS becomes a proving expansion upon AX (cf. Sect. 5.1), and we may conclude from Thm. 5.2 that a subexpansion of, say, $\{\varphi_1,\dots,\varphi_k\}$ into $\{\psi\}$ establishes the "subtheorem" $\exists X_{out}\varphi_1\vee \dots \vee\exists X_{out}\varphi_k\Leftarrow\psi$.

In particular, suppose we start a proof of CS by expanding $G = \{\gamma_1\cup\gamma_1',\dots,\gamma_n\cup\gamma_n'\}$ and stop the expansion when obtaining the goal set $G' = \{\varphi_1\cup\varphi_1',\dots,\varphi_k\cup\varphi_k'\}$. Suppose furthermore that the clause set $CS' = \{\varphi_1\Leftarrow\delta:\varphi_1',\dots,\varphi_k\Leftarrow\delta:\varphi_k'\}$ is constructor-based. Then the composition of

(1) $G \vdash^{ind}_{AX;CS} G'$ and (2) $G' \vdash^{ind}_{AX;CS'} \{\delta\}$

yields a proof of CS: Using the above argument, the Gentzen clause

$$c = \exists X_{out}\varphi_1 \cup \varphi_1' \vee \ldots \vee \exists X_{out}\varphi_k \cup \varphi_k' \Leftarrow \delta$$

is inductively valid. Hence by lemma resolution upon c, $G' \vdash^{pro}_{AX} \{\delta\}$.

(1) denotes a subproof of CS with remaining subconjecture CS'. EXPANDER provides the commands `fi` and `fid` for turning G' respectively into CS' or into c (cf. Sect. 9.2.5). Roughly stated, CS' *implies* CS. But this means that (2) possibly uses a stronger induction hypothesis than (1). Hence an inductive expansion of CS upon AX and CS into $\{\delta\}$ is not always decomposable into (1) and (2).

A subexpansion of $G \vdash^{ind}_{AX;CS} \{\delta\}$ that contains an unsolvable goal δ_1 does not contribute to a proof of CS. W.l.o.g., the associated collapsed tree (cf. Sect. 5.3) would include a path from δ_1 to δ, which either consists of unsolvable goals or can be divided into a first subpath $\delta_1,\ldots,\delta_k$ of unsolvable goals and a second subpath $\delta_{k+1},\ldots,\delta$ of solvable goals. In the first case, CS is trivially valid. In the second case there are goals $\varphi_1,\ldots,\varphi_s$ and a lemma resolution or paramodulation step from $\{\delta_k,\varphi_1,\ldots,\varphi_s\}$ to δ_{k+1}. By Lemma 5.1, the clause

$$\exists X_{out}\delta_k \vee \exists X_{out}\varphi_1 \vee \ldots \vee \exists X_{out}\varphi_s \Leftarrow \delta_{k+1} \tag{3}$$

is inductively valid. Since δ_{k+1} is solvable, but δ_k is unsolvable, the clause

$$\exists X_{out}\varphi_1 \vee \ldots \vee \exists X_{out}\varphi_s \Leftarrow \delta_{k+1} \tag{4}$$

is also inductively valid. Hence we may apply (4) instead of (3) and obtain δ_{k+1} without referring to the path $\delta_1,\ldots,\delta_k$, which thus becomes irrelevant for the proof of CS.

The question remains of how we can detect an unsolvable goal. By Thm. 4.4, δ_1 is unsolvable if neither resolution nor paramodulation nor unification applies to δ_1. This does not help much because each goal has infinitely many paramodulants. However, if the specification is *ground confluent* and has finitely many axioms, we need to consider only finitely many paramodulants and hence obtain an effective criterion for unsolvability (cf. Cor. 7.3).

5.5 Sample expansions

The examples of this section employ inductive expansion for deriving programs from their correctness conditions (cf. Sect. 2.1). Example 5.8 leads to an iterative program for natural number division. Example 5.12 aims at *sort by insertion*. Examples 5.9, 5.10, 5.13 and 5.14 prove invariants used in Examples 5.8 and 5.12, respectively. All examples start out from (SIG,AX) = NSB (cf. Ex. 1.1).

As pointed out in Sect. 2.1, program synthesis by inductive expansion reflects the *fold-unfold* approach of [BD77]. It would be worthwhile to investigate other program transformation principles, such as *tupling* (cf. [BD77], Sect. 4), *continuation* (cf. [Rea89], Sect. 9.4.2; [KS85], p. 138) or *higher order generalization* (cf. [PS87]; see also Ex. 6.24) in this context.

Example 5.8 (iterative division) A recursive program for natural number division, which returns quotient and remainder, is given by

```
div(x,y) ≡ (0,x)    ⇐   x < y                                  (N6)

div(x,y) ≡ (q+1,r)  ⇐   x ≥ y,  y > 0,  div(x-y,y) ≡ (q,r).    (N7)
```

Let us infer axioms for the function

```
divL : nat,nat ⟶ nat×nat
```

representing an *iterative* division program, which calls the *loop function*

```
Loop : nat,nat,nat,nat ⟶ nat×nat
```

that accumulates the quotient and remainder of the first two arguments in the last two arguments. divL calls Loop with initial accumulator values t and u:

```
divL(x,y) ≡ Loop(x,y,q,r)  ⇐   q ≡ t,  r ≡ u.                  (L1)
```

t and u are regarded as additional constants of NSB. Terms over NSB that are respectively equivalent to t and to u will be derived from a proof that divL and div are equivalent functions:

```
divL(x,y) ≡ div(x,y)  ⇐   y > 0, Def(x), Def(y).               (DIVL0)
```

We prove DIVL0 by expanding the conclusion of DIVL0 into the premise of DIVL0:

goal	*substitution of* X_{out}	*rules applied*
divL(x,y) ≡ div(x,y)		-- conclusion of DIVL0
Loop(x,y,q,r) ≡ div(x,y) q ≡ t, r ≡ u		paramodulation upon L1
(q+q',r') ≡ div(x,y) y > 0, Def(r), Def(y) div(r,y) ≡ (q',r') q ≡ t, r ≡ u		paramodulation upon DIVL (see below)
(q',r') ≡ div(x,y) y > 0, Def(r), Def(y) div(r,y) ≡ (q',r') 0 ≡ t, r ≡ u	0/q	paramodulation upon 0+x ≡ x

div(x,y) ≡ (q',r') y > 0, Def(r), Def(y) div(r,y) ≡ (q',r') 0 ≡ t, r ≡ u		resolution upon a symmetry axiom
div(x,y) ≡ (q',r') y > 0, Def(x), Def(y) 0 ≡ t, x ≡ u	x/r	factoring
y > 0, Def(x), Def(y) 0 ≡ t, x ≡ u		resolution upon DDIV (see below)

If we set t = 0 and u = x in L1:

$$\text{divL}(x,y) \equiv \text{Loop}(x,y,q,r) \;\Leftarrow\; q \equiv 0,\; r \equiv x \qquad \text{(L1)}$$

the expansion can be continued:

y > 0, Def(x), Def(y) 0 ≡ 0, x ≡ x	resolution upon DDIV (see below)
y > 0, Def(x), Def(y)	unification

We have applied the lemmas

$$\text{Loop}(x,y,q,r) \equiv (q{+}q',r') \;\Leftarrow\; y > 0,\ \text{Def}(r),\ \text{Def}(y) : \text{div}(r,y) \equiv (q',r') \qquad \text{(DIVL)}$$

$$\exists\{q,r\}\ \text{div}(x,y) \equiv (q,r) \;\Leftarrow\; y > 0,\ \text{Def}(x),\ \text{Def}(y). \qquad \text{(DDIV)}$$

DIVL is proved in the following examples. The proof of DDIV is left to the reader. ∎

Example 5.9 (invariant of iterative division; first version) DIVL is a typical generalization of an actual conjecture (DIVL0). Following [BD77], we may call the step from DIVL0 to DIVL an *eureka* step because DIVL is a *loop invariant* (cf. Sect. 2.1) that cannot be derived automatically, but must be guessed from attempts to prove DIVL0. If the recursive program to be transformed adopts a schema that corresponds to a particular invariant schema, the transformation must be carried out only for the schema and not for each of its instances. In this way, inductive expansion supports the development of program transformation rules in the sense of [BW82].

As program transformation is not restricted to recursion removal, so inductive expansion may realize other "optimizations" as well, as far as they "result from considering a program fragment in its context of use. The *fold-unfold* methodology is effective because it captures just this idea. By unfolding the definition of a function, its body can interact with its context by the application of algebraic laws or abstraction" ([Gol86], p. 758). In fact, unfolding is lemma paramodulation, while folding is inductive paramodulation.

Since {(q',r')} is a set of constructors, {DIVL} is a constructor-based clause set with input variables x,y,q,r, guard {y > 0, Def(r), Def(y)} and generator matrix {div(r,y) ≡ (q',r')}. Following Cor. 5.6, we prove DIVL by expanding the conclusion and the generator matrix upon AX and DIVL into the guard. A direct proof using Cor. 5.7 is not reasonable because the starting goal would only consist of the conclusion of DIVL. We would need axioms for Loop in order to start the proof, while the expansion of conclusion *and* generators allows to derive such axioms from the proof (cf. Sect. 2.1).

goal name	*goal*	*substitution of X_{out}*	*rules applied*
G1	Loop(x,y,q,r) ≡ (q+q',r') div(r,y) ≡ (q',r')		-- conclusion of DIVL -- generator of DIVL
	G1		
	Loop(x,y,q,r) ≡ (q+0,r) r < y	0/q' r/r'	resolution upon N6
	G1		
(i)	Loop(x,y,q,r) ≡ (q,r) r < y		paramodulation upon N1
	G1		
	r < y		resolution upon L2 (see below)
	Loop(x,y,q,r) ≡ (q+(k+1),r') y > 0, r ≥ y div(r-y,y) ≡ (k,r')	k+1/q'	resolution upon N7
	r < y		
(ii)	Loop(x,y,q,r) ≡ ((q+1)+k,r') r ≥ y div(r-y,y) ≡ (k,r')		paramodulation upon x+(y+1) ≡ (x+1)+y
	r < y		

Goal	Rule
(iii) $Loop(x,y,q,r) \equiv Loop(x,y,q+1,r-y)$ $(x,y,q,r) >_{DIVL} (x,y,q+1,r-y)$ $y > 0,\ Def(r-y),\ Def(y)$ $r \geq y$ $div(r-y,y) \equiv (k,r')$	inductive paramodulation
$r < y$	
$Loop(x,y,q,r) \equiv Loop(x,y,q+1,r-y)$ $r > r-y$ $y > 0,\ Def(r-y),\ Def(y)$ $r \geq y$ $div(r-y,y) \equiv (k,r')$	resolution upon GR_{DIVL} (see below)
$r < y$	
$Loop(x,y,q,r) \equiv Loop(x,y,q+1,r-y)$ $y > 0,\ Def(r-y),\ Def(y)$ $r \geq y$ $div(r-y,y) \equiv (k,r')$	resolution upon $r > r-y \Leftarrow y > 0, r \geq y$
$r < y$	
(iv) $Loop(x,y,q,r) \equiv Loop(x,y,q+1,r-y)$ $y > 0,\ Def(r-y),\ Def(y)$ $r \geq y$	resolution upon DDIV
$r < y$	
$y > 0,\ Def(r-y),\ Def(y)$ $r \geq y$	resolution upon L3 (see below)
$r < y$	
$y > 0,\ Def(r),\ Def(y)$ $r \geq y$	resolution upon DSUB (see below)
$r < y$	
$y > 0,\ Def(r),\ Def(y)$	resolution upon $r < y \vee r \geq y \Leftarrow Def(r), Def(y)$

Subgoals (i) and (iv) suggest the axioms for Loop, which, together with L1, form the intended iterative division program:

$$Loop(x,y,q,r) \equiv (q,r) \Leftarrow r < y \quad \text{(L2)}$$
$$Loop(x,y,q,r) \equiv Loop(x,y,q+1,r-y) \Leftarrow r \geq y,\ y > 0. \quad \text{(L3)}$$

Note that the inductive paramodulation rule applied to subgoal (ii) replaces the *right*-hand side of the conclusion of DIVL by the *left*-hand side. The resulting paramodulant contains the conclusion of L3, which illustrates the coincidence of an induction step and an actual program synthesis (*folding*) step. Subgoal (iii) suggests the descent predicate for DIVL:

$$(x,y,q,r) >_{DIVL} (x',y',q',r') \Leftarrow r > r'. \qquad (GR_{DIVL})$$

A proof of the lemma

$$Def(x-y) \Leftarrow Def(x), Def(y) \qquad (DSUB)$$

is left to the reader.

We conclude from Cor. 5.6 that DIVL is inductively valid w.r.t. NSB ∪ {L1,L2,L3}. Simultaneously, we have derived the iterative program {L1,L2,L3}. For its *equivalence* to the recursive program {N6,N7}, cf. Ex. 3.18.

Example 5.10 (invariant of iterative division; second version) There is an alternative proof of DIVL (cf. Ex. 5.8), which starts out from the Gentzen clause

$$\exists \{q',r'\} \{Loop(x,y,q,r) \equiv (q+q',r'), div(r,y) \equiv (q',r')\} \Leftarrow y > 0, Def(r), Def(y) \quad (DIVL1)$$

and does not use the totality of div (cf. DDIV in Ex. 5.9). By Thm. 2.3, DIVL is inductively valid if DIVL1 is so. For proving DIVL1, we follow Sect. 2.5, specify a predicate P_{DIVL1} by

$$P_{DIVL1}(x,y,q,r) \Leftarrow Loop(x,y,q,r) \equiv (q+q',r'), div(r,y) \equiv (q',r') \qquad (PDIV)$$

and turn DIVL1 into the inductively equivalent Horn clause

$$P_{DIVL1}(x,y,q,r) \Leftarrow y > 0, Def(r), Def(y). \qquad (DIVL2)$$

For establishing an induction hypothesis, we have to apply the inverse of PDIV:

$$\exists \{q',r'\} \{Loop(x,y,q,r) \equiv (q+q',r'), div(r,y) \equiv (q',r')\} \Leftarrow P_{DIVL1}(x,y,q,r). \qquad (PDIV^{-1})$$

somewhere in the proof of DIVL2. In fact, we want to resolve upon the second equation and then to paramodulate upon the first one. Hence we separate $PDIV^{-1}$ into two clauses:

$$\{Loop(x,y,q,r) \equiv (q+q',r'), div(r,y) \equiv (q',r')\}$$
$$\Leftarrow P_{DIVL1}(x,y,q,r), Loop(x,y,q,r) \equiv (q+q',r') \qquad (PDIV1^{-1})$$

$$\exists \{q',r'\} \{Loop(x,y,q,r) \equiv (q+q',r')\} \Leftarrow P_{DIVL1}(x,y,q,r). \qquad (PDIV2^{-1})$$

Otherwise a conflict with the conditions on applying lemmas with existential variables would result (cf. Sect. 5.1).

Here is the inductive expansion of DIVL2:

goal name	*goal*	*substitution of X_{out}*	*rules applied*
	P_{DIVL1}(x,y,q,r)		
G1	Loop(x,y,q,r) ≡ (q+q',r') div(r,y) ≡ (q',r')		resolution upon PDIV
	G1		
	Loop(x,y,q,r) ≡ (q+0,r) r < y	0/q' r/r'	resolution upon N6
	G1		
	Loop(x,y,q,r) ≡ (q,r) r < y		paramodulation upon N1
	G1		
	r < y		resolution upon L2
	Loop(x,y,q,r) ≡ (q+(k+1),r') y > 0, r ≥ y div(r−y,y) ≡ (k,r')	k+1/q'	resolution upon N7
	r < y		
	Loop(x,y,q,r) ≡ ((q+1)+k,r') y > 0, r ≥ y div(r−y,y) ≡ (k,r')		paramodulation upon x+(y+1) ≡ (x+1)+y
	r < y		
	Loop(x,y,q,r) ≡ ((q+1)+k,r') P_{DIVL1}(x,y,q+1,r−y) y > 0, r ≥ y		resolution upon $PDIV1^{-1}$
	r < y		
	Loop(x,y,q,r) ≡ Loop(x,y,q+1,r−y) P_{DIVL1}(x,y,q+1,r−y) y > 0, r ≥ y		paramodulation upon $PDIV2^{-1}$
	r < y		
	Loop(x,y,q,r) ≡ Loop(x,y,q+1,r−y) Def(r−y), Def(y)		inductive resolution

```
(x,y,q,r) >DIVL (x,y,q+1,r-y)
y > 0, r ≥ y
-----------------------------------------------------------------------
r < y
=======================================================================
Loop(x,y,q,r) ≡ Loop(x,y,q+1,r-y)        resolution upon GRDIVL
Def(r-y), Def(y)
r > r-y
y > 0, r ≥ y
-----------------------------------------------------------------------
r < y
=======================================================================
Loop(x,y,q,r) ≡ Loop(x,y,q+1,r-y)        resolution upon
Def(r-y), Def(y)                         r > r-y  ⇐  y > 0, r ≥ y
y > 0, r ≥ y
-----------------------------------------------------------------------
r < y
=======================================================================
Def(r-y), Def(y)                         resolution upon L3
y > 0, r ≥ y
-----------------------------------------------------------------------
r < y
=======================================================================
Def(r), Def(y)                           resolution upon DSUB
y > 0, r ≥ y                             (cf. Ex. 5.9)
-----------------------------------------------------------------------
r < y
=======================================================================
Def(r), Def(y)                           resolution upon
y > 0                                    r < y ∨ r ≥ y  ⇐  Def(r), Def(y)
=======================================================================
```

By Thm. 2.3, DIVL1 implies DIVL (cf. Ex. 5.8). Conversely, Thm. 2.3 tells us that DIVL implies DIVL1 if the generator matrix of DIVL is complete, i.e., if DDIV (cf. Ex. 5.8) is inductively valid. Hence we need the validity of DDIV for concluding the equivalence between DIVL and DIVL1 (and thus DIVL2). This observation complies with the direct proof of DIVL, given by Ex. 5.9, where DDIV was applied explicitly. ∎

Exercise 5.11 Starting out from the specification

```
divS(x,y) ≡ (q,r)  ⇐  x ≡ (q*y)+r, r < y                     (DIVS)
```

of natural number division, infer the iterative program {L1,L2,L3} (cf. Exs. 5.8 and 5.9) from proofs of

```
divL(x,y) ≡ divS(x,y)  ⇐  y > 0, Def(x), Def(y)
```

and

Loop(x,y,q,r) ≡ divS(x,y) ⇐ y > 0, x ≡ (q*y)+r.

Show the correctness of div (cf. Ex. 1.1) with respect to divS by expanding

div(x,y) ≡ divS(x,y) ⇐ y > 0, Def(x), Def(y)

and compare the expansion with other proofs of this example, such as [MW80], pp. 105ff, or [Der83], Sect. 4.2. ∎

Example 5.12 (sort by insertion) Two clauses over NSB (cf. Ex. 1.1) capture the correctness of a sorting algorithm sort : seq⟶seq:

sorted(sort(s)) ⇐ Def(s)

makeBag(sort(s)) ≡ makeBag(s) ⇐ Def(s).

The first clause states that sort returns a sorted sequence. The second clause ensures that the sorted sequence is a permutation of the original one. Following the decomposition principle (cf. Sect. 2.6), we replace both clauses by a single one:

{sorted(s'), makeBag(s') ≡ makeBag(s)} ⇐ Def(s) : sort(s) ≡ s'. (SORT)

Let us infer a sorting algorithm, i.e., axioms for sort, from an expansion of SORT. Since NSB provides the auxiliary function insert, the program will realize sort-by-insertion.

Many sorting algorithms follow a divide-and-conquer schema for which [GB78] and [Smi85] have worked out synthesis rules. Sort-by-insertion as well as quicksort and mergesort are built up of two auxiliary functions, a split operation that divides a sequence s into subsequences to be sorted individually, and a join operation that combines the sorted subsequences into a sorted permutation of s. The split operations of mergesort and quicksort are halve and filter respectively. The join operations are merge and conc respectively (cf. Sect. 8.3).

Sort-by-insertion has no explicit split operation, but the join operation is given by insert. The expansion of SORT will reach a point where the fact that insert respects sorted and makeBag must be employed in order to continue:

sorted(insert(x,s)) ⇐ sorted(s), Def(x), Def(s) (LEM1)

makeBag(insert(x,s)) ≡ add(x,makeBag(s)) ⇐ Def(x), Def(s). (LEM2)

LEM1 and LEM2 are proved in Exs. 5.13 and 5.14, respectively.

Following Cor. 5.6, we prove SORT by expanding the conclusion and the generator {sort(s) ≡ s'} into the guard {Def(s)}. Let X_{in} = {s}.

goal name	*goal*	*substitution of* X_{out}	*rules applied*
G1	sorted(s') makeBag(s') ≡ makeBag(s) sort(s) ≡ s'		-- conclusion of SORT -- generator of SORT
	G1 makeBag(ε) ≡ makeBag(s) sort(s) ≡ ε	 ε/s'	 resolution upon SO1
(i)	G1 sort(ε) ≡ ε s ≡ ε		 unification
	G1 s ≡ ε		 resolution upon IS1 (see below)
	sorted(s') makeBag(s') ≡ add(x,makeBag(s")) sort(x&s") ≡ s' s ≡ x&s" s ≡ ε		 paramodulation upon BA2
	sorted(s_1) makeBag(insert(x,s_1)) ≡ add(x,makeBag(s")) sort(x&s") ≡ insert(x,s_1) s ≡ x&s" s ≡ ε	insert(x,s_1)/s'	resolution upon LEM1
	sorted(s_1) add(x,makeBag(s_1)) ≡ add(x,makeBag(s")) sort(x&s") ≡ insert(x,s_1) s ≡ x&s" s ≡ ε		 paramodulation upon LEM2
	Def(s"), sort(s") ≡ s_1 x&s" $>_{SORT}$ s" add(x,makeBag(s_1)) ≡ add(x,makeBag(s")) sort(x&s") ≡ insert(x,s_1) s ≡ x&s"		inductive resolution

	s ≡ ε		
(ii)	Def(s"), x&s" $>_{SORT}$ s" add(x,makeBag(s")) ≡ add(x,makeBag(s")) sort(x&s") ≡ insert(x,s_1) s ≡ x&s"	sort(s") ≡ s_1	inductive paramodulation
	s ≡ ε		
(iii)	Def(s") sort(x&s") ≡ insert(x,sort(s")) s ≡ x&s"	sort(s")/s_1	resolution upon GR_{SORT} (see below) and unification
	s ≡ ε		
	Def(s") s ≡ x&s"		resolution upon IS2 (see below)
	s ≡ ε		
	Def(x&s") s ≡ x&s"		resolution upon Def(s') ⇐ Def(x&s')
	s ≡ ε		
	Def(s) s ≡ x&s"		equational replacement
	s ≡ ε		
	Def(s)		resolution upon s≡ε ∨ ∃ {x,s'} s≡x&s' ⇐ Def(s)

In contrast with Examples 5.8-5.10, the case distinction involved in the previous expansion is due to the instantiation of an input variable: lemma resolution upon SO1 creates the subgoal s≡ε, lemma paramodulation upon BA2 produces s≡x&s'.

Subgoals (i) and (iii) suggest the axioms for sort, which form the intended program for sort-by-insertion:

sort(ε) ≡ ε (IS1)

sort(x&s) ≡ insert(x,sort(s)). (IS2)

Subgoal (ii) suggests the descent predicate for SORT:

x&s $>_{SORT}$ s. (GR_{SORT})

We conclude from Cor. 5.6 that SORT is inductively valid w.r.t. NSB ∪ {IS1,IS2}. Simultaneously, we have derived the sort algorithm {IS1,IS2}. ∎

Example 5.13 (insert respects sorted) Following Cor. 5.7, we prove LEM1 by expanding the conclusion of LEM1 into the premise of LEM1:

goal name	*goal*	*substitution of X_{out}*	*rules applied*
	sorted(insert(x,s))		-- conclusion of LEM1
	sorted(insert(x,s))		
	sorted(x&ε) s ≡ ε		paramodulation upon IN1
	sorted(insert(x,s))		
	s ≡ ε		resolution upon SO2
	sorted(insert(x,s))		
	sorted(x&y&s') x ≤ y s ≡ y&s'		paramodulation upon IN2
	s ≡ ε		
	sorted(insert(x,s))		
	sorted(y&s') x ≤ y s ≡ y&s'		resolution upon SO3
	s ≡ ε		
	sorted(insert(x,s))		
G1	sorted(s) x ≤ y s ≡ y&s'		equational replacement
	s ≡ ε		
G2	sorted(y&insert(x,s')) x > y s ≡ y&s'		paramodulation upon IN3
	G1		

	s ≡ ε		
	G2		
	sorted(y&x&ε) x > y s ≡ y&ε	ε/s'	paramodulation upon IN1
	G1		
	s ≡ ε		
	G2		
	sorted(x&ε) y ≤ x x > y s ≡ y&ε		resolution upon SO2
	G1		
	s ≡ ε		
	G2		
	y ≤ x x > y s ≡ y&ε		resolution upon SO1
	G1		
	s ≡ ε		
	G2		
G3	x > y s ≡ y&ε		resolution upon y ≤ x ⇐ x > y
	G1		
	s ≡ ε		
	G2		
	sorted(y&x&z&s") x ≤ z x > y s ≡ y&z&s"	z&s"/s'	paramodulation upon IN2

	G3	
	G1	
	s ≡ ε	
	G2	
	sorted(x&z&s") y ≤ x, x ≤ z, x > y s ≡ y&z&s"	resolution upon SO3
	G3	
	G1	
	s ≡ ε	
	G2	
	sorted(x&z&s") x ≤ z, x > y s ≡ y&z&s"	resolution upon y ≤ x ⇐ x > y
	G3	
	G1	
	s ≡ ε	
	G2	
	sorted(z&s") x ≤ z, x > y s ≡ y&z&s"	resolution upon SO3
	G3	
	G1	
	s ≡ ε	
	G2	
G4	sorted(y&z&s") x ≤ z, x > y s ≡ y&z&s"	resolution upon $SO3^{-1}$ (see below)

	G3		
	G1		
	s ≡ ε		
	sorted(y&z&insert(x,s")) x > z, x > y s ≡ y&z&s"	z&s"/s'	paramodulation upon IN3
	G4		
	G3		
	G1		
	s ≡ ε		
(i)	sorted(z&insert(x,s")) y ≤ z, x > z, x > y s ≡ y&z&s"		resolution upon SO3
	G4		
	G3		
	G1		
	s ≡ ε		
	sorted(insert(x,z&s")) y ≤ z, x > z, x > y s ≡ y&z&s"		paramodulation upon $IN3^{-1}$ (see below)
	G4		
	G3		
	G1		
	s ≡ ε		
(ii)	sorted(z&s"), Def(x), Def(z&s") (x,y&z&s") $>_{LEM}$ (x,z&s") y ≤ z, x > z, x > y s ≡ y&z&s"		inductive resolution
	G4		

G3	
G1	
s ≡ ε	
sorted(z&s"), Def(x), Def(z&s") y ≤ z, x > z, x > y s ≡ y&z&s"	resolution upon GR_{LEM} (see below)
G4	
G3	
G1	
s ≡ ε	
sorted(y&z&s"), Def(x), Def(z&s") x > z, x > y s ≡ y&z&s"	resolution upon $SO3^{-1}$ (see below)
G4	
G3	
G1	
s ≡ ε	
sorted(y&z&s"), Def(z&s") Def(x), Def(z) x > y s ≡ y&z&s"	resolution upon x ≤ z ∨ x > z ⇐ Def(x), Def(z)
G3	
G1	
s ≡ ε	
sorted(y&z&s"), Def(z&s") Def(x), x > y s ≡ y&z&s"	resolution upon Def(z) ⇐ Def(z&s')
G3	
G1	

s ≡ ε	
sorted(y&z&s"), Def(y&z&s") Def(x), x > y s ≡ y&z&s"	resolution upon Def(z&s') ⇐ Def(y&z&s')
G3	
G1	
s ≡ ε	
sorted(s), Def(s) Def(x), x > y s ≡ y&z&s"	equational replacement
G3	
G1	
s ≡ ε	
sorted(s), Def(s) Def(x), x > y s ≡ y&s' Def(s')	paramodulation upon s≡ε ∨ ∃ {x,s'} s≡x&s' ⇐ Def(s)
G1	
s ≡ ε	
sorted(s), Def(s) Def(x), Def(y) s ≡ y&s' Def(s')	resolution upon x ≤ y ∨ x > y ⇐ Def(x), Def(y)
s ≡ ε	
sorted(s), Def(s) Def(x) s ≡ y&s' Def(y&s')	resolution upon {Def(y), Def(s')} ⇐ Def(y&s')
s ≡ ε	
sorted(s), Def(s) Def(x) s ≡ y&s'	equational replacement

s ≡ ε	
sorted(s), Def(s) Def(x)	resolution upon s≡ε ∨ ∃ {x,s'} s≡x&s' ⇐ Def(s)

Paramodulation of (i) upon

$$\text{y\&insert(x,s)} \equiv \text{insert(x,y\&s)} \;\Leftarrow\; x > y \qquad (\text{IN3}^{-1})$$

is necessary for achieving sorted(insert(x,z&s")), the redex for inductive resolution.

Subgoal (ii) suggests the descent predicate for LEM1 (and LEM2; cf. Ex. 5.14):

$$(x,y\&s) >_{LEM} (x,s). \qquad (\text{GR}_{\text{LEM}})$$

The lemma

$$\{x \le y,\ \text{sorted(y\&s)}\} \;\Leftarrow\; \text{sorted(x\&y\&s)} \qquad (\text{SO3}^{-1})$$

has been applied for accomplishing the guard of SORT. ▮

Example 5.14 (insert respects makeBag) Following Cor. 5.7, we prove LEM2 by expanding the conclusion of LEM2 into the premise of LEM2:

goal name	*goal*	*rules applied*
	makeBag(insert(x,s)) ≡ add(x,makeBag(s))	-- conclusion of LEM2
	makeBag(insert(x,s)) ≡ add(x,makeBag(s))	
	makeBag(x&ε) ≡ add(x,makeBag(ε)) s ≡ ε	paramodulation upon IN1
	makeBag(insert(x,s)) ≡ add(x,makeBag(s))	
	s ≡ ε	resolution upon BA2
	makeBag(insert(x,s)) ≡ add(x,makeBag(s))	
	makeBag(x&y&s') ≡ add(x,makeBag(y&s')) x ≤ y s ≡ y&s'	paramodulation upon IN2
	s ≡ ε	
	makeBag(insert(x,s)) ≡ add(x,makeBag(s))	
G1	x ≤ y s ≡ y&s'	resolution upon BA2

$s \equiv \varepsilon$	
makeBag(y&insert(x,s')) ≡ add(x,makeBag(y&s')) x > y s ≡ y&s'	paramodulation upon IN3
G1	
$s \equiv \varepsilon$	
add(y,makeBag(insert(x,s'))) ≡ add(x,makeBag(y&s')) x > y s ≡ y&s'	paramodulation upon BA2
G1	
$s \equiv \varepsilon$	
add(y,add(x,makeBag(s'))) ≡ add(x,makeBag(y&s')) (x,y&s') $>_{LEM}$ (x,s') Def(x), Def(s'), x > y s ≡ y&s'	inductive paramodulation
G1	
$s \equiv \varepsilon$	
add(y,add(x,makeBag(s'))) ≡ add(x,add(y,makeBag(s'))) Def(x), Def(y&s'), x > y s ≡ y&s'	paramodulation upon BA2 resolution upon GR_{LEM} and Def(s') ⇐ Def(y&s')
G1	
$s \equiv \varepsilon$	
Def(x), Def(s), x > y s ≡ y&s'	resolution upon BA3 and equational replacement
G1	
$s \equiv \varepsilon$	
Def(x), Def(s), Def(y) s ≡ y&s'	resolution upon x ≤ y ∨ x > y ⇐ Def(x), Def(y)
$s \equiv \varepsilon$	

Def(x), Def(s), Def(y&s') s ≡ y&s'	resolution upon Def(y) ⇐ Def(y&s')
s ≡ ε	
Def(x), Def(s) s ≡ y&s'	equational replacement
s ≡ ε	
Def(x), Def(s)	resolution upon DS^{-1}

Since NSB contains fewer axioms defining makeBag than axioms defining sorted, the expansion of LEM2 is much shorter than the expansion of LEM1 (cf. Ex. 5.13). ∎

6: Directed Expansion and Reduction

Chapters 6 and 7 deal with expansion calculi that exploit the fact that a design specification is *ground confluent*. First, *directed expansion* restricts paramodulation to left-to-right applications of prefix extensions of equational axioms (cf. Chapter 4). *Narrowing* (cf. Sect. 7.2) goes a step further and confines the input of expansion rules to pure axioms. *Reductive expansion* provides an alternative to inductive expansion, which originates from the idea of proving inductive validity by proving consistency (cf. Sect. 3.4) and reducing consistency to ground confluence (cf. Sects. 7.4 and 7.5).

Variables of a Horn clause occurring in its premise, but not in (the left-hand side of) its conclusion, called *fresh variables*, are usually banished as soon as one turns to a reduction calculus. This restriction cannot be maintained when arbitrary declarative programs are to be treated: if one follows the decomposition principle (cf Sect. 2.6), then fresh variables are created automatically. They are then forbidden because they violate the usual condition that there is a Noetherian *reduction ordering*, i.e., that a reduction calculus admits only finite derivations. We shall see in Sect. 6.2 that other conditions on a reduction ordering can be weakened so as to often preserve the Noetherian property even if fresh variables are permitted.

Definition (cf. Chapter 4) The *directed (solving) expansion calculus upon AX* consists of the following three inference rules, which transform pairs consisting of a goal and a substitution:

Resolution

$$\frac{\langle \varphi \cup \{p\}, f\rangle}{\langle (\varphi \cup \vartheta)[g], f[g|X_{goals}]\rangle} \qquad \begin{array}{l} p[g] = q[g] \\ q \Leftarrow \vartheta \in \text{AX-CE(AX)} \end{array}$$

Directed Paramodulation

$$\frac{\langle \delta[t/x], f\rangle}{\langle (\delta[u'/x] \cup \vartheta)[g], f[g|X_{goals}]\rangle} \qquad \begin{array}{l} t[g] = u[g] \\ u \equiv u' \Leftarrow \vartheta \in \text{Pre(AX)} \end{array}$$

Unification	
$\dfrac{\langle \gamma \cup \{t\equiv t'\}, f\rangle}{\langle \gamma[g], f[g]\rangle}$	$t[g] = t'[g]$

A *directed expansion of* $\langle \gamma_1, f_1\rangle$ *into* $\langle \gamma_n, f_n\rangle$ *upon* AX is a sequence $\langle \gamma_1, f_1\rangle, \ldots, \langle \gamma_n, f_n\rangle$ of goal-substitution pairs such that for all $1 \le i < n$, $\langle \gamma_{i+1}, f_{i+1}\rangle$ is obtained from $\langle \gamma_i, f_i\rangle$ by a single resolution, directed paramodulation or unification step.

$\vdash_{AX}$ denotes the corresponding inference relation.

A directed expansion of the form $\gamma_1, \ldots, \gamma_n$ is called a *goal reduction*. Hence, goal reductions are generated by the following "substitutionless" variants of the above rules:

Resolution	
$\dfrac{\gamma \cup \{q[g]\}}{\gamma \cup \vartheta[g]}$	$q \Leftarrow \vartheta \in AX\text{-}CE(AX)$
Reduction	
$\dfrac{\delta[u[g]/x]}{\delta[u'[g]/x] \cup \vartheta[g]}$	$u \equiv u' \Leftarrow \vartheta \in AX$
Reflection	
$\dfrac{\gamma \cup \{t \equiv t\}}{\gamma}$	

A goal γ is *AX-convergent* if $\gamma \vdash_{AX} \emptyset$, i.e., if γ is reducible into the empty goal via the previous rules. ▮

Definition Given a term or atom v, $x \in var(v)$, a substitution g and $u \equiv u' \Leftarrow \vartheta \in AX$, the expression

$$v[u[g]/x] \longrightarrow_{AX} v[u'[g]/x] \Leftarrow \vartheta[g]$$

is called a *conditional term reduction*.

Let t, t' be terms or atoms and γ be a goal. Expressions of the form $t \longrightarrow_{AX}^{+} t' \Leftarrow \gamma$ are generated by the following rules:

- $t \longrightarrow_{AX} t' \Leftarrow \gamma$ implies $t \longrightarrow_{AX}^{+} t' \Leftarrow \gamma$.

- If $t \longrightarrow_{AX}^{+} t' \Leftarrow \gamma$ and $t' \longrightarrow_{AX}^{+} t'' \Leftarrow \gamma'$, then $t \longrightarrow_{AX}^{+} t'' \Leftarrow \gamma \cup \gamma'$.

The *term reduction relation* $\longrightarrow_{AX}$ consists of all pairs (t,t') such that for some AX-convergent γ, $t \longrightarrow_{AX} t' \Leftarrow \gamma$ is a conditional term reduction. For substitutions f and g, $f \longrightarrow_{AX}^{*} g$ stands for the set $\{fx \longrightarrow_{AX}^{*} gx \mid x \in X\}$.

A term (atom, substitution) u is an *AX-reduct* of a term (atom, substitution) t if $t \longrightarrow_{AX}^{*} u$. A goal δ is an AX-reduct of a goal γ if for all $q \in \delta - \gamma$ there is $p \in \gamma$ such that $p \longrightarrow_{AX}^{*} q$. ∎

If fresh variables and non-equality predicates are forbidden, this definition of term reduction is equivalent to Kaplan's (cf. [Kap84]) who, instead of referring to goal reduction, presents $\longrightarrow_{AX}$ as the limit of approximating relations $\longrightarrow_{AX,i}$, $i \geq 0$:

$t \longrightarrow_{AX} t'$ iff $t \longrightarrow_{AX,i} t'$ for some $i \geq 0$ where

- $t \longrightarrow_{AX,0} t'$ iff $t = t'$,
- $t \longrightarrow_{AX,i+1} t'$ iff there are v,f,x and $u \equiv u' \Leftarrow \{u_1 \equiv u_1', \ldots, u_n \equiv u_n'\} \in$ AX such that $t = v[u[f]/x]$, $t' = v[u'[f]/x]$ and for all $1 \leq j \leq n$, $u_j[f] \longrightarrow^{*}_{AX,i} v_j$ and $u_j'[f] \longrightarrow^{*}_{AX,i} v_j$ for some v_j.

Goal reduction generalizes from equational logic to Horn logic with equality the notion of a *rewrite proof* (cf. [BDH86]) or a *reductional proof* (cf. [Küc89]). AX-convergence generalizes *joinability* (cf. [DOS88]).

The following proposition is an immediate consequence of Thm. 4.3 and the previous definitions.

Proposition 6.1

(1) *AX-convergent goals are AX-valid.*

(2) *For all terms t,t', $\{t \equiv t'\}$ is AX-convergent iff t and t' have a common AX-reduct.*

(3) *For all atoms p and term reductions $p \longrightarrow_{AX} p'$, $\{p\}$ is AX-convergent if $\{p'\}$ is AX-convergent.* ∎

6.1 Ground confluence

Let us return to our discussion of computation rules in Chapter 4 where we mentioned that a reasonable notion of confluence should consider only *successful* expansions. Or, with regard to goal reduction, confluence refers to *convergent* goals:

Definition A goal γ is *strongly AX-convergent*, written as $\gamma \longrightarrow\vdash_{AX} \emptyset$, if all AX-reducts of γ are AX-convergent. (SIG,AX) is *ground confluent* if all AX-convergent ground goals are strongly AX-convergent. ▮

Definition Given a term or atom t, AX is *confluent at t* if for all term reductions $t \longrightarrow_{AX}^* v$ and $t \longrightarrow_{AX}^* v'$, $\{v \equiv v'\}$ is AX-convergent. ▮

Traditionally, (SIG,AX) is called *ground confluent* if AX is confluent at all ground terms. So, how do we benefit from the new notion?

The difference is related to the difference between goal and term reduction. If atoms are regarded as terms, then predicates become Boolean functions (cf. Sect. 2.6), an atom p becomes the equation $p \equiv true$, a successful goal reduction $\{p\} \vdash_{AX} \emptyset$ becomes the term reduction $p \longrightarrow_{AX}^* true$, and ground confluence becomes confluence at atoms.

However, predicates are particular Boolean functions. A predicate is a partial Boolean function into *{true}*, while Boolean functions in general map into *{true,false}*. Accordingly, an atom is a Boolean term confined to the context $\_ \equiv true$. Predicates make this restriction implicit; it need not always be mentioned. If one does not distinguish between terms and atoms, the notion of confluence must be more specific: (SIG,AX) is ground confluent iff

(1) AX is confluent at all non-Boolean ground terms t,

(2) for all ground term reductions $p \longrightarrow_{AX}^* true$ and $p \longrightarrow_{AX}^* q$, $\{q \equiv true\}$ is AX-convergent.

But this equivalence becomes invalid as soon as some Boolean term may occur in a context different from $\_ \equiv true$. Hence we need a syntactical distinction between "atom terms" p used only in the context $\_ \equiv true$ and associated with confluence notion (2) and "proper" Boolean terms at which AX must be confluent because they occur in other contexts as well. The distinction is accomplished easily by turning the leftmost symbol of atom terms into predicates.[1]

A notion of confluence tailored to goal reduction was also defined in [FHS89]. However, it is much stronger than ours (cf. Chapter 4). Without restricting the goals to convergent ones, it only replaces term reduction by goal reduction: If $\gamma \vdash_{AX} \delta$ and $\gamma \vdash_{AX} \delta'$, then $\delta \vdash_{AX} \varphi$ and $\delta' \vdash_{AX} \varphi$ for some φ.

[1]Unfortunately, rewriting hardliners tend to ignore the advantage that mathematicians draw from distinguishing between functions and predicates since the invention of formal logic.

We proceed with some facts about convergence, subconvergence and confluence at terms.

Lemma 6.2 (Confluence at terms and strong convergence of equations)[1]

(1) An AX-convergent equation $t \equiv t'$ *is strongly AX-convergent if AX is confluent at all AX-reducts of* t *and* t'.

(2) AX is confluent at a term t *iff* $t \equiv t$ *is strongly AX-convergent.*

Proof. (1) Let $t \equiv t' \vdash_{AX} \emptyset$ and $t \equiv t' \longrightarrow_{AX}{}^* p$. Then t and t' have a common AX-reduct, say t''. Moreover, $p = v \equiv v'$ for some v,v' with $t \longrightarrow_{AX}{}^* v$ and $t' \longrightarrow_{AX}{}^* v'$. Hence by assumption, t'' and v as well as t'' and v' have a common reduct, say u and u', respectively. Since $t \longrightarrow_{AX}{}^* t''$, the assumption also implies that $u \equiv u'$ and thus p are AX-convergent.

(2) Let $t \longrightarrow_{AX}{}^* v$ and $t \longrightarrow_{AX}{}^* v'$. If $t \equiv t$ is strongly AX-convergent, $v \equiv t$ and thus $v \equiv v'$ are AX-convergent. Conversely, let $t \equiv t \longrightarrow_{AX}{}^* p$. Then $p = v \equiv v'$ for some v,v' with $t \longrightarrow_{AX}{}^* v$ and $t \longrightarrow_{AX}{}^* v'$. If AX is confluent at t, then p is AX-convergent. ∎

Proposition 6.1(2), (3) immediately yields

Lemma 6.3 *For all atoms* p *and terms* t,t',

$$p[t/x] \longrightarrow\vdash_{AX} \emptyset \text{ and } t \equiv t' \vdash_{AX} \emptyset \text{ imply } p[t'/x] \vdash_{AX} \emptyset. \blacksquare$$

Lemma 6.4 *Let* $c = q \Leftarrow \vartheta \in AX$ *and* $f \in GS$. *If* $\vartheta[f]$ *is AX-convergent, then* $q[f]^{sym}$ *(cf. Chapt. 4) is AX-convergent.*

Proof. Let $\vartheta[f]$ be AX-convergent. If c is not a conditional equation, we obtain $q[f] \vdash_{AX} \vartheta[f]$ by resolution. Hence $q[f] \vdash_{AX} \emptyset$. Otherwise $q = u \equiv u'$ for some u,u'. By the definition of $\longrightarrow_{AX}$, $u[f] \longrightarrow_{AX} u'[f]$. Hence $q[f]^{sym}$ is AX-convergent. ∎

Definition A Gentzen clause $c = \exists X_1 \gamma_1 \vee \ldots \vee \exists X_n \gamma_n \Leftarrow \delta$ is *reductively valid w.r.t. AX* or a *reductive AX-theorem* if for all $f \in GS$,

$$\delta[f] \longrightarrow\vdash_{AX} \emptyset \quad \text{implies} \quad \gamma_i[g] \longrightarrow\vdash_{AX} \emptyset$$

for some $1 \le i \le n$ and $g \in GS$ with $g|(X-X_i) = f|(X-X_i)$. *RTh(AX)* denotes the set of reductive AX-theorems.

Let BASE $\subseteq$ AX. c is *reductively valid w.r.t. (BASE,AX)* or a *reductive (BASE,AX)-theorem* if for all $f \in GS_{NF}$,

$$\delta[f] \vdash_{BASE} \emptyset \text{ and } \delta[f] \longrightarrow\vdash_{AX} \emptyset$$

[1]From now on we identify, in goal reductions, the atom p with the goal {p}.

imply

$$\gamma_i[g] \vdash_{BASE} \emptyset \text{ and } \gamma_i[g] \rightarrow\vdash_{AX} \emptyset$$

for some $1 \le i \le n$ and $g \in GS$ with $g|(X-X_i) = f|(X-X_i)$. *RTh(BASE,AX)* denotes the set of reductive (BASE,AX)-theorems. ∎

Theorem 6.5 (Completeness of directed expansions and goal reductions)

(1) Let γ be a ground goal and $\gamma_1,\ldots,\gamma_n$ be a successful solving expansion of γ (cf. Chapter 4) such that for all $1 \le i \le n$, $\gamma_i \vdash_{AX} \emptyset$ implies $\gamma_i \rightarrow\vdash_{AX} \emptyset$. Then γ is AX-convergent. Consequently, if (SIG,AX) is ground confluent, then all AX-valid ground goals are AX-convergent.

(2) (SIG,AX) is ground confluent iff all AX-valid ground goals are AX-convergent.

(3) (SIG,AX) is ground confluent iff $ITh(AX) = RTh(AX)$.

(4) (SIG,AX) is ground confluent iff for all goals γ and substitutions f such that $f(X_{goals}) \subseteq GT(SIG)$,

$$AX \vdash_{cut} \gamma[f] \quad \text{implies} \quad \gamma \vdash_{AX} \langle\emptyset, f|X_{goals}\rangle.$$

Proof. (1) Let $AX \vdash_{cut} \gamma$. Since the solving expansion calculus is complete (cf. Thm. 4.4), there is a shortest (not necessarily directed) successful expansion $\gamma,\gamma_2,\ldots,\gamma_n$ upon AX. We show $\gamma \vdash_{AX} \emptyset$ by induction on n. If n = 0, then $\gamma = \emptyset$, and the proof is complete.

Let n > 0. The induction hypothesis implies $\gamma_2 \vdash_{AX} \emptyset$.

Case 1. γ_2 is obtained from γ by reflection. Then $\gamma \vdash_{AX} \gamma_2$ and thus $\gamma \vdash_{AX} \emptyset$.

Case 2. γ_2 is obtained from γ by resolution upon AX and $q \Leftarrow \vartheta$ is the axiom applied. Then there are p,q,f,x,ψ such that $\gamma = \psi\cup\{p\}$, $p = q[f]$ and $\gamma_2 = \psi\cup\vartheta[f]$. Since $\vartheta[f] \vdash_{AX} \emptyset$, Lemma 6.4 implies that p is AX-convergent. Hence $\psi \vdash_{AX} \emptyset$ implies $\gamma \vdash_{AX} \emptyset$.

Case 3. γ_2 is obtained from γ by paramodulation upon AX^{sym} and $u \equiv u' \Leftarrow \vartheta$ is the conditional equation applied. Then we have one of two subcases:

Case 3.1. The atom selected from γ for being paramodulated upon $u \equiv u' \Leftarrow \vartheta$ is an equation, say $t \equiv t'$. Then there are c,u,f,x,ψ such that w.l.o.g.[1] $\gamma = \psi\cup\{t \equiv t'\}$, $t = c[u'[f]/x]$ and

$$\gamma_2 = \psi \cup \{c[u[f]/x] \equiv t'\} \cup \vartheta[f].$$

---

[1] t and t' might be exchanged

By Prop. 6.1(2), $c[u[f]/x]\equiv t' \vdash_{AX} \emptyset$ implies $c[u[f]/x]\longrightarrow_{AX}{}^{*}v$ and $t'\longrightarrow_{AX}{}^{*}v$ for some v. Since $\vartheta[f] \vdash_{AX} \emptyset$, Lemma 6.4 implies that $(u\equiv u')[f]$ and thus $c[u[f]/x]\equiv t$ are also AX-convergent. Again by Prop. 6.1(2), $c[u[f]/x]\longrightarrow_{AX}{}^{*}v'$ and $t\longrightarrow_{AX}{}^{*}v'$ for some v'. Since $c[u[f]/x]\equiv t' \longrightarrow\vdash_{AX} \emptyset$, $v'\equiv v$ and thus $t\equiv t'$ are AX-convergent. Hence $\psi \vdash_{AX} \emptyset$ implies $\gamma \vdash_{AX} \emptyset$.

Case 3.2. The atom p selected from γ for being paramodulated upon $u\equiv u'\Leftarrow\vartheta$ is not an equation. Then there are q,u,f,x,ψ such that $\gamma = \psi\cup\{p\}$, $p = q[u'[f]/x]$ and

$$\gamma_2 = \psi \cup \{q[u[f]/x]\} \cup \vartheta[f].$$

Since $\vartheta[f] \vdash_{AX} \emptyset$, Lemma 6.4 implies that $(u\equiv u')[f]$ is also AX-convergent. By Prop. 6.1 (2), $u[f]\longrightarrow_{AX}{}^{*}v$ and $u'[f]\longrightarrow_{AX}{}^{*}v$ for some v. Since $q[u[f]/x] \longrightarrow\vdash_{AX} \emptyset$, $q[v/x]$ and thus p are AX-convergent. Hence $\psi \vdash_{AX} \emptyset$ implies $\gamma \vdash_{AX} \emptyset$.

This finishes the proof of (1).

(2) The "only if" part follows from (1). Let all AX-valid ground goals be AX-convergent. We show that all AX-convergent ground atoms p are strongly AX-convergent.

Let $p \vdash_{AX} \emptyset$ and $p\longrightarrow_{AX}{}^{*}p'$. Then there are an atom q, $x \in var(q)$ and a term reduction $t\longrightarrow_{AX}{}^{*}t'$ such that $p = q[t/x]$ and $p' = q[t'/x]$. By Prop. 6.1(2), $t\equiv t' \vdash_{AX} \emptyset$. Hence Prop. 6.1 (1) implies $AX \vdash_{cut} \{p,t\equiv t'\}$ and thus $AX \vdash_{cut} p'$. By (1), p' is AX-convergent.

(3) "only if": Let (SIG,AX) be ground confluent, $c = \exists X_1\gamma_1\vee\ldots\vee\exists X_n\gamma_n\Leftarrow\delta \in$ ITh(AX) and $f \in$ GS such that $\delta[f]$ is strongly AX-convergent. Then by 6.1(1), f solves δ. Hence there are $1\le i\le n$ and $g \in$ GS such that $f|(X-X_i)+g|X_i$ solves γ_i. By (2), $\gamma_i[f|(X-X_i)+g|X_i]$ is AX-convergent and thus strongly AX-convergent because (SIG,AX) is ground confluent. Hence c is reductively valid.

Suppose that c is reductively valid and f solves δ. Then by (2), $\delta[f]$ is AX-convergent and thus strongly AX-convergent because (SIG,AX) is ground confluent. Hence there are $1\le i\le n$ and $g \in$ GS such that $\gamma_i[f|(X-X_i)+g|X_i]$ is strongly AX-convergent. By 6.1(1), $f|(X-X_i)+g|X_i$ solves γ_i. Therefore c is inductively valid.

"if": Suppose that all inductive theorems are reductively valid. Then, in particular, for all ground goals γ, $AX \vdash_{cut} \gamma$ implies $\gamma \vdash_{AX} \emptyset$. Hence by (2), (SIG,AX) is ground confluent.

(4) By Prop. 4.1 and Lemma 4.5 (which holds for $\vdash_{AX}$ as well as for $\vdash^{sol}_{AX}$, $\gamma[f]$ is AX-convergent iff $\gamma \vdash_{AX} \langle\emptyset, f|X_{goals}\rangle$. Hence the conjecture follows from (2). ∎

The completeness result for most general solving expansions (cf. Thm. 4.6) holds true for $\vdash_{AX}$ as well as for $\vdash^{sol}_{AX}$.

6.2 Strong termination

The Knuth-Bendix superposition theorem (cf. [KB70]) reduces confluence to the convergence of *critical clauses* (called *critical pairs* in the case of equations). It employs an inductive argument based on a *reduction ordering* with respect to which reducts of a term t are smaller than t. In the case of *conditional* axioms, premises must also be smaller than conclusions. Let us list out all the properties a reduction ordering > must satisfy.

First of all, > must be defined on terms and atoms simultaneously. Hence, in the context of >, an equation $t \equiv t'$ is identified with the multiset $\{t, t'\}$ of its two sides, while all other atoms are regarded as terms. Then > extends to multisets M and M' of terms and atoms as follows:

$M > M'$ iff $M \neq M'$ and for all $t' \in M'-M$ there is $t \in M-M'$ such that $t > t'$.

For the simple proof that a Noetherian ordering > extends to a Noetherian multiset ordering, cf. [DM79]. We use the multiset extension without a particular index of >, but denote the *lexicographic* extension of > to finite term sequences by $>_{lex}$.

General Assumption When dealing with terms and atoms simultaneously, it is sometimes convenient to extend SIG by a "bottom" constant $\bot$ and to regard each Horn clause as a conditional equation over

$$SIG^{\bot} = SIG \cup \{\bot\}.$$

Given a set CS of Horn clauses, let

$$CS^{\bot} = CE(CS) \cup \{p \equiv \bot \Leftarrow \vartheta \mid p \Leftarrow \vartheta \in CS\text{-}CE(CS)\}.$$

$p \equiv \bot$ reminds one of the equation $p \equiv true$ (cf. Sect. 6.1). Nevertheless, we shall keep to the distinction between atoms and terms. Given an atom p, the equation $p \equiv \bot$ is only another notation for p. ∎

Definition An *AX-reduction ordering* > is a transitive and Noetherian relation on $GT(SIG^{\bot}) \cup GAt(SIG^{\bot})$ satisfying the following conditions:

AX-reduction property:

- There is GS' $\subseteq$ GS such that for all $t \equiv t' \Leftarrow \delta \in AX^{\perp}$, terms and non-equational atoms c, x $\in$ var(c) and f $\in$ GS with f | (var({t'}$\cup\delta$)−var(t)) $\in$ GS', δ[f] $\vdash_{AX}$ $\emptyset$ implies c[t[f]/x] > c[t'[f]/x] and t[f] > δ[f].

Subterm property:

- For each ground term or atom p and all proper subterms t of p, p > t.

(SIG,AX) is *strongly terminating* if there is an AX-reduction ordering. ∎

At first sight, an AX-reduction ordering seems to be confined to a syntactic relation that only depends on the actual terms and atoms in the clauses of AX. Indeed, it must not be confused with the induction ordering defined by a descent predicate for an inductive expansion (cf. Sect. 5.2). Nevertheless, one may bring such semantic orderings into agreement with the conditions on a reduction ordering. But this must be done with great care. For instance, from a semantic point of view, a ground term t representing a positive number should satisfy t > t−1. However, the subterm property (see above) implies t−1 > t. Hence t > t by transitivity, and this conflicts with the requirement that > be Noetherian.

In fact, the situation is more subtle. The AX-reduction property suggests that > is monotone, i.e., for all terms u,u',v and x $\in$ var(v), if u > u', then v[u/x] > v[u'/x]. But monotonicity is also incompatible with t > t−1: u = t, u' = t−1 and v $\in$ {x(−1)^n | n $\geq$ 1} yields the infinite sequence

$$t > t-1 > t-1-1 > t-1-1-1 > \ldots$$

A solution of this problem is provided by *semantic path orderings,* which are syntactic *and* semantic because they both satisfy the properties of a reduction ordering and are defined from (descent) predicates of (SIG,AX). Originally, semantic path orderings were introduced for *unconditional* rewrite systems (cf. [KL80], [Hue86], [Der87]) where they are only needed for proving the termination of rather tricky examples. For the *conditional* case, however, they are extremely important. Let us follow the notions of [KL80] and derive a *path calculus* for proving descent conditions $\gamma \gg \delta$ where >> is interpreted as an AX-reduction ordering constructed in a uniform way from predicates of (SIG,AX).

Definition A pair ($>_S$,$\approx$) of two relations on GT(SIG$^{\perp}$) $\cup$ GAt(SIG$^{\perp}$) is called a *semantic ordering for AX* if $>_S$ is transitive and Noetherian, $>_S \circ \approx$ and $\approx \circ >_S$ are subrelations of $>_S$ and $\approx$ is *AX-reduction compatible,* i.e.,

- for all ground term reductions $t \longrightarrow_{AX} t'$ and each term or atom p with var(p) = {x}, p[t/x] $\approx$ p[t'/x]. ∎

Definition Given a pair $(>_s,\approx)$ of two relations on $GT(SIG^\perp) \cup GAt(SIG^\perp)$, the *path ordering > based on* $(>_s,\approx)$ is inductively defined as follows. Let $t = F(t_1,\ldots,t_k)$ and $t' = G(u_1,\ldots,u_n)$ be ground terms or atoms.

Subterm rule:

- If $t_i \geq t'$ for some $1 \leq i \leq k$, then $t > t'$.

Semantic rule:

- If $t >_s t'$ and $t > \{u_1,\ldots,u_n\}$, then $t > t'$.

Multiset rule:

- If $t \approx t'$ and $\{t_1,\ldots,t_k\} > \{u_1,\ldots,u_n\}$, then $t > t'$.

Least element rule:

- $t > \perp$. ∎

The multiset rule may be replaced by a lexicographic variant, which, for preserving the transitivity of >, needs a further applicability condition.

Lexicographic rule:

- If $t \approx t'$, $(t_1,\ldots,t_k) >_{lex} (u_1,\ldots,u_n)$ and $t > \{u_1,\ldots,u_n\}$, then $t > t'$.

In fact, the lexicographic rule can mostly be avoided if the "semantic" relation $>_s$ is a lexicographic ordering on term tuples (cf. the semantic rule). For instance, equations such as those defining the Ackermann function:

$$Ack(0,x) \equiv x+1 \quad \text{(ACK1)}$$

$$Ack(x+1,0) \equiv Ack(x,1) \quad \text{(ACK2)}$$

$$Ack(x+1,y+1) \equiv Ack(x,Ack(x+1,y)), \quad \text{(ACK3)}$$

which cannot be handled with a non-semantic multiset path ordering (cf. [KL80]), are nonetheless decreasing with respect to the path ordering (with multiset rule) if $>_s$ is lexicographic (cf. Ex. 6.9).

Definition Let BASE ⊆ AX and > be a relation on $GT(SIG^\perp) \cup GAt(SIG^\perp)$. BASE is *decreasing w.r.t.* > if there is GS' ⊆ GS such that, for all $t \equiv t' \Leftarrow \delta \in BASE^\perp$ and $f \in GS$, with $f \mid (var(\{t'\} \cup \delta) - var(t)) \in GS'$,

- $\delta[f] \vdash_{AX} \emptyset$ implies $t[f] > t'[f]$ and $t[f] > \delta[f]$ ∎

Lemma 6.6 *Let > be the path ordering based on a pair* $(>_s,\approx)$ *of two relations on* $GT(SIG^\perp) \cup GAt(SIG^\perp)$.

(1) > is transitive and Noetherian if $>_s$ *is transitive and Noetherian and* $>_s \circ \approx$ *and* $\approx \circ >_s$ *are subrelations of* $>_s$.

(2) $>$ is an AX-reduction ordering if $(>_S, \approx)$ is a semantic ordering for AX and AX is decreasing w.r.t. $>$.

Proof. (1) Given terms or atoms $p = F(t_1,...,t_k)$, q and r with $p > q > r$, $p > r$ can be shown by induction on size(p)+size(q)+size(r) (cf. [Hue86], Sect. 4.4). The proof is straightforward but tedious because, according to the four rules defining $>$, one has to consider sixteen cases generating the triple $p > q > r$. For instance, if $p > q$ and $q > r$ are obtained by the semantic rule and the subterm rule, resp., then $p >_S q' > r$ for some proper subterm q' of q. Since $p > q''$ for all proper subterm q' of q'' of q and thus of q', we have $p > q'$. Hence the induction hypothesis implies $p > r$.

Now suppose that $>$ is not well-founded. We follow [KL80], p.16: there is a minimal counterexample $p_1 > p_2 > p_3 > ...$ in the sense that for all $n \geq 1$, p_n has minimal size among all counterexamples starting with $p_1 > ... > p_n$. Assume that $p_1 > p_2 > p_3 > ...$ includes a pair $p_i > p_{i+1}$ obtained by applying the subterm rule to a proper subterm t of p_i and $t \geq p_{i+1}$. Then $p_i > t$ by the subterm rule and $p_{i-1} > t$ since $>$ is transitive. So $p_1 > ... > p_{i-1} > t \geq p_{i+1} > ...$ is a smaller counterexample than $p_1 > p_2 > p_3 > ...$, which we claimed to be minimal.

Hence for all $i \geq 1$, $p_i > p_{i+1}$ is obtained by applying the semantic rule or the multiset rule. Since $>_S$ is well-founded, there is $r \geq 1$ such that for all $i \geq r$, $p_i > p_{i+1}$ is derived by applying the multiset rule. Hence there is an infinite sequence of numbers $k_1,k_2,k_3,...$ and proper subterms t_{k_j} of p_{k_j} such that $r \leq k_1 < k_2 < k_3 < ...$, $p_r > t_{k_1}$ and for all $j \geq 1$, $t_{k_j} > t_{k_{j+1}}$. Since $>$ is transitive, $p_{r-1} > t_{k_1}$. But then $p_1 > ... > p_{r-1} > t_{k_1} > t_{k_2} > t_{k_3} > ...$ is a smaller counterexample than $p_1 > p_2 > p_3 > ...$, and, again, the latter is not minimal.

For the lexicographic rule, the existence of an infinite sequence $k_1,k_2,k_3,...$ with the above properties is proved as follows. For all $i \geq r$, let $h(i)$ be the minimal $1 \leq j \leq n_i$ with $u_{ij} > u_{i+1,j}$ where $p_i = F_i(u_{i1},...,u_{in_i})$. Let $M = \{h(i) \mid i \geq r\}$. $k_1,k_2,k_3,...$ exists by induction on card(M). Let $J = \{i \geq r \mid h(i) = \min(M)\}$. If J is infinite, set $\{k_1,k_2,k_3,...\} = J$ and $t_{k_i} = u_{k_i,\min(M)}$. Otherwise let $r' = \max(J)+1$. By induction hypothesis, there are an infinite sequence $k_1,k_2,k_3,...$ and proper subterms t_{k_j} of p_{k_j} such that $r' \leq k_1 < k_2 < k_3 < ...$, $p_{r'} > t_{k_1}$ and for all $j \geq 1$, $t_{k_j} > t_{k_{j+1}}$. Since $>$ is transitive, $p_r > t_{k_1}$.

Therefore, $>$ is well-founded.

(2) By (1), $>$ is transitive and Noetherian. The subterm property follows from one or several applications of the subterm rule. For $>$ to be an AX-reduction ordering, it remains to show that $>$ satisfies the AX-reduction property.

Let $t \equiv t' \Leftarrow \delta \in AX^{\perp}$, c be a term or a non-equational atom, $x \in var(c)$ and $f \in GS$ with $f|(var(\{t'\} \cup \delta) - var(t)) \in GS'$, such that $\delta[f] \vdash_{AX} \emptyset$. Since AX is decreasing w.r.t. >, $t[f] > t'[f]$ and $t[f] > \delta[f]$. We infer

$$u = c[t[f]/x] > c[t'[f]/x] = u'$$

by induction on size(c). If $c = \{x\}$, the proof is complete. Otherwise $c = c'[F(...,x,...)/z]$ for some c',F,z. Since $t[f] \longrightarrow_{AX} t'[f]$ and ≈ is AX-reduction compatible, we have, by the multiset or the lexicographic rule, $F(...,t[f],...) \approx F(...,t'[f],...)$. Hence $F(...,t[f],...) > F(...,t'[f],...)$. Since $F(...,t[f],...) \longrightarrow_{AX} F(...,t'[f],...)$, we conclude $u > u'$ from the induction hypothesis. ∎

Semantic orderings $(>_s,\approx)$ are constructed from a finite reflexive and transitive relation $\geq_{SIG}$ on the set of function and predicate symbols, which reflects the order of their axiomatization. $>_s$ combines $\geq_{SIG}$ with descent predicates of (SIG,AX) and thus becomes compatible with AX-equivalence.

Definition Let SIG be finite and $\geq_{SIG}$ be a reflexive and transitive relation on the set of function and non-equality predicate symbols of SIG. Moreover, let $>_d$ be a (set of) binary predicate symbol(s) of SIG such that the relation $>_{AX}$ on ground terms, defined by

$$t >_{AX} t' \quad \text{iff} \quad AX \vdash_{cut} t >_d t',$$

is transitive and Noetherian. Let GS' ⊆ GS.

The *path calculus for* $(\geq_{SIG}, >_d, GS')$ consists of the following inference rules, transforming *extended goals*, i.e., sets of goals and expressions of the form $\gamma \approx \delta$ or $\gamma >> \delta$ where γ and δ are goals, atoms or terms. Let $>_{SIG}$ and $\approx_{SIG}$ denote respectively the strict part and the equivalence kernel of $\geq_{SIG}$, i.e.

$$>_{SIG} = \geq_{SIG} - \leq_{SIG} \quad \text{and} \quad \approx_{SIG} = \geq_{SIG} \cap \leq_{SIG}.$$

Multiset rules

$$\frac{\varphi \cup \{p\} >> \psi \cup \{q\}}{p >> q,\ \varphi \cup \{p\} >> \psi} \qquad \frac{\varphi >> \psi \cup \{\perp\}}{\varphi >> \psi}$$

$$\frac{\varphi \cup \{p\} >> \psi \cup \{p\}}{\varphi >> \psi} \qquad \frac{\varphi \cup \{p\} >> \emptyset}{\emptyset}$$

Subterm rules

$$\frac{F(t_1,...,t_k) >> \varphi}{t_i >> \varphi} \quad 1 \leq i \leq k \quad \frac{F(t_1,...,t_k) >> t_i}{\emptyset}$$

$$\frac{F(t_1,...,t_k) >> G(u_1,...,u_n)}{F(t_1,...,t_k) \approx G(u_1,...,u_n),\ \{t_1,...,t_k\} >> \{u_1,...,u_n\}}$$

Signature ordering rules	
$\dfrac{F(t_1,\ldots,t_k) >> G(u_1,\ldots,u_n)}{F(t_1,\ldots,t_k) >> \{u_1,\ldots,u_n\}}$	$F >_{SIG} G$
$\dfrac{F(t_1,\ldots,t_k) >> G(u_1,\ldots,u_n)}{\{(t_1,\ldots,t_k) >_d (u_1,\ldots,u_n)\},\ F(t_1,\ldots,t_k) >> \{u_1,\ldots,u_n\}}$	$F \approx_{SIG} G$
$\dfrac{F(t_1,\ldots,t_k) \approx G(u_1,\ldots,u_n)}{\{t_{i1} \equiv u_1, \ldots, t_{in} \equiv u_n\}}$	$F \approx_{SIG} G$ $1 < i_1 < \ldots < i_n < k$
Fresh variable rule	
$\dfrac{\varphi >> x}{\varphi\ fx \mid f \in GS'\}}$	$x \in X - var(\varphi)$

$\vdash_{path}$ denotes the corresponding inference relation.

Let > be the path ordering based on $(>_s, \approx)$ where $>_s$ and $\approx$ are defined as follows. For all ground terms or atoms $t = F(t_1 \ldots, t_k)$ and $t' = G(u_1,\ldots,u_n)$,

- $t >_s t'$ iff $F >_{SIG} G$ or $F \approx_{SIG} G$ and $(t_1,\ldots,t_k) >_{AX} (u_1,\ldots,u_n)$.
- $t \approx t'$ iff $F \approx_{SIG} G$ and there are $1 \le i_1 < \ldots < i_n \le k$ such that

  $t_{i1} \equiv_{AX} u_1, \ldots, t_{in} \equiv_{AX} u_n$.

> is called the *AX-path ordering for* $(GS', \ge_{SIG}, >_d)$. ∎

One immediately concludes from the definitions of the path calculus on the one hand and the AX-path ordering on the other hand that for extended goals $\gamma >> \gamma'$ and goals φ,

$\gamma >> \gamma' \vdash_{path} \varphi$ implies $\gamma[f] > \gamma'[f]$

for all AX-solutions $f \in GS$ of φ such that $f \mid (var(\{\gamma'\}) - var(\gamma)) \in GS'$. (*)

Thus we obtain the following method for proving boundary conditions:

Theorem 6.7 *Let $GS' \subseteq GS$, $BASE \subseteq AX$ and > be the AX-path ordering for $(GS', \ge_{SIG}, >_d)$.*

(1) *BASE is decreasing w.r.t. > if for all $t \equiv t' \Leftarrow \delta \in BASE^{\perp}$ there is a clause c = $\varphi \Leftarrow \delta$ such that*

$$t >> \{t'\} \cup \delta \vdash_{path} \varphi \vdash^{ind}_{AX;c} \delta.$$

(2) *(SIG,AX) is strongly terminating if AX is decreasing w.r.t. >.*

Proof. (1) follows from (*) and the soundness of inductive expansion (cf. Cor. 5.7). For (2), we claim that > is an AX-reduction ordering. By Lemma 6.6, it remains to show that ($>_s$,≈) as defined above is a semantic ordering.

Since $\geq_{SIG}$ is finite and $>_{AX}$ is transitive and Noetherian, $>_{SIG}$ and thus $>_s$ are transitive and Noetherian as well. Since $>_{SIG} \circ \approx_{SIG} \cup \approx_{SIG} \circ >_{SIG} \subseteq >_{SIG}$ and $>_{AX}$ is compatible with AX-equivalence, $>_s \circ \approx$ and $\approx \circ >_s$ are subrelations of $>_s$. Since $t \longrightarrow_{AX} t'$ implies $t \equiv_{AX} t'$, ≈ is AX-reduction compatible. ∎

Before applying Thm. 6.7 to examples, let us compare the above notion of a reduction ordering to the one given in [DOS88] and [DJ90][1]. There the corresponding AX-reduction property neither includes the convergence assumption ($\delta[f] \vdash_{AX} \emptyset$) nor the restriction of fresh variable substitutions that is necessary for maintaining strong termination in the presence of fresh variables (see the end of this section). The situation is different if one aims at a decision procedure for AX-convergence:

Proposition 6.8 *Let AX be finite and > be an AX-reduction ordering such that the following condition holds true.*

AX-premise property: *For all $t \equiv t' \Leftarrow \delta \in AX^{\perp}$ and $f \in GS$, $t[f] > \delta[f]$.*

Then the set of AX-convergent ground goals is decidable and thus, if (SIG,AX) is ground confluent, the set of AX-valid ground goals is decidable as well.

Proof. Let γ be a ground goal and Prem(γ) be the set of premises of all axiom instances that have redices in γ. Since for all $\delta \in$ Prem(γ), $\gamma > \delta$, Noetherian induction along > implies that convergence is decidable for each $\delta \in$ Prem(γ). Hence we can construct the set CPrem(γ) of all AX-convergent elements of Prem(γ).

Let Red(γ) be the set of all goals obtained from γ by applying an axiom instance whose premise belongs to CPrem(γ). Since for all $\varphi \in$ Red(γ), $\gamma > \varphi$, Noetherian induction along > implies that convergence is decidable for each $\varphi \in$ Red(γ). Hence we can construct the set CRed(γ) of all AX-convergent elements of Red(γ).

γ is AX-convergent iff either γ is empty or CRed(γ) is not empty. ∎

In practice, one does not benefit much from Prop. 6.8. The validity of a single *ground* goal is a rare proof obligation. Other uses of reduction orderings, such as establishing confluence and proving reductive validity, are much more

---

[1]These papers summarize several approaches to conditional term rewriting.

important. For these purposes, the AX-premise property must be changed into the AX-reduction property. Otherwise one will hardly find reduction orderings for "real" data type specifications, particularly if these include logic programs with recursive calls in the premise (cf. Sect. 0.2).

The transitivity axiom for a binary relation seems to violate every termination property. For example, look at the following specification of integers:

INT

sorts	int	
	symbol	*type*
functs	s	int ⟶ int
	p	int ⟶ int
	_-_	int,int ⟶ int
	-_	int ⟶ int
preds	_>_	int , int
	$\_>_d\_$	int×int, int×int
vars	x,y,z,x',y' ; int	
axms	p(s(x)) = x	
	s(p(x)) = x	
	x-0 = x	
	x-s(y) = p(x-y)	
	x-p(y) = s(x-y)	
	-x = 0 -x	
	s(x) > x	
	x > p(x)	
	x > z ⇐ x > y, y > z (TRANS)	
	$(x,y) >_d (x',y')$ ⇐ x > x'	
	$(x,y) >_d (x,y')$ ⇐ x ≥ y', y' > y	

Let

$$R_{AX} = \{(F,G) \mid \exists\, Ft \equiv t' \Leftarrow \vartheta \in AX^{\perp} : G \in op(\{t'\} \cup \vartheta)\} \cup \{(>,G) \mid G \in SIG-\{>_d\}\}$$

and $\geq_{SIG}$ be the reflexive and transitive closure of R_{AX}. Following Thm. 6.7, we show that INT is decreasing w.r.t. the path ordering for (GS, $\geq_{SIG}$, $>_d$). The crucial axiom is TRANS. We have to find a clause $c = \varphi \Leftarrow \delta$ such that

$$(x > z) >> \{x > y, y > z\} \;\vdash_{path}\; \varphi \;\vdash^{ind}_{AX;c}\; \delta$$

and $\delta \subseteq \{x > y, y > z\}$. A suitable expansion reads as follows:

$$\begin{aligned}(x > z) >> \{x > y, y > z\} \;&\vdash_{path}\; \{(x,z) >_d (x,y), (x,z) >_d (y,z)\},\; (x > z) >> \{x,y,z\}\\ &\vdash_{path}\; \{(x,z) >_d (x,y), (x,z) >_d (y,z)\},\; (x > z) >> \{y\}\\ &\vdash_{path}\; \{(x,z) >_d (x,y), (x,z) >_d (y,z)\}\end{aligned}$$

by the fresh variable rule because $> \notin op(fy)$

$$\begin{aligned}&\vdash^{pro}_{AX}\; \{x \geq y, y > z, x > y\}\\ &\vdash^{pro}_{AX}\; \{x > y, y > z\}. \qquad \text{(EXP)}\end{aligned}$$

Example 6.9 To show that NSB is decreasing we augment NSB with well-founded relations on pairs:

NSB'

base	NSB	
	symbol	*type*
preds	$>_d$	nat×nat,nat×nat
	$>_d$	nat×bag,nat×bag
vars	x,y,x',y' : nat; b,b' : bag	
axms	$(x,y) >_d (x',y') \Leftarrow x > x'$	
	$(x,b) >_d (x',b') \Leftarrow x > x'$	
	$(x,b) >_d (x,b') \Leftarrow b > b'$	
	$add(x,b) > \emptyset$	
	$add(x,b) > add(y,b') \Leftarrow b > b'$	

Let $R_{AX} = \{(F,G) \mid \exists\, Ft \equiv t' \Leftarrow \vartheta \in AX^{\perp}: G \in op(\{t'\} \cup \vartheta)\} \cup \{\langle div,G\rangle \mid G \in SIG\}$ and $\geq_{SIG}$ be the reflexive and transitive closure of R_{AX}. Following Thm. 6.7, we show that NSB' is decreasing w.r.t. the path ordering for (GS, $\geq_{SIG}$, $>_d$). The crucial axioms are N7 and BA3:

$$div(x,y) \equiv (q+1,r) \;\Leftarrow\; x \geq y,\; y > 0,\; div(x-y,y) \equiv (q,r) \qquad \text{(N7)}$$

$$add(x,add(y,b)) \equiv add(y,add(x,b)) \;\Leftarrow\; x > y. \qquad \text{(BA3)}$$

For N7, we have to find a clause $c = \varphi \Leftarrow \delta$ such that

$$div(x,y) >> \{(q+1,r)\} \cup \gamma \ \vdash_{path} \ \varphi \ \vdash^{ind}_{AX;c} \ \delta$$

and $\delta \subseteq \gamma = \{x \geq y, y > 0, div(x-y,y), (q,r)\}$. A suitable expansion reads as follows:

$$\begin{aligned} div(x,y) >> \{(q+1,r)\} \cup \gamma \ &\vdash_{path} \ div(x,y) >> \{q, r, div(x-y,y)\} \\ &\vdash_{path} \ div(x,y) >> div(x-y,y) \end{aligned}$$

by the fresh variable rule because div $\notin$ op({fq,fr})

$$\begin{aligned} &\vdash_{path} \ \{(x,y) >_d (x-y,y)\}, \ div(x,y) >> (x-y,y) \\ &\vdash_{path} \ \{(x,y) >_d (x-y,y)\}, \ div(x,y) >> (x,y) \\ &\vdash_{path} \ \{(x,y) >_d (x-y,y)\} \\ &\vdash^{pro}_{AX} \ \{x > x-y\} \\ &\vdash^{pro}_{AX} \ \{x \geq y, y > 0\}. \end{aligned}$$

The proving-expansion part of EXP1 consists of resolution steps upon the lemmas

$$(x,y) >_d (x',y') \ \Leftarrow \ x > x'$$
$$x > x-y \ \Leftarrow \ x \geq y, \ y > 0.$$

For BA3, an expansion reads as follows:

$$\begin{aligned} &add(x,add(y,b)) >> \{add(y,add(x,b)), x > y\} \\ &\quad \vdash_{path} \ \{(x,add(y,b)) >_d (y,add(x,b))\}, \ add(x,add(y,b)) >> (y,add(x,b)) \\ &\quad \vdash_{path} \ \{(x,add(y,b)) >_d (y,add(x,b))\}, \ add(x,add(y,b)) >> add(x,b) \\ &\quad \vdash_{path} \ \{(x,add(y,b)) >_d (y,add(x,b)), (x,add(y,b))) >_d (x,b)\} \\ &\quad \vdash^{pro}_{AX} \ \{x > y, \ add(y,b) > b\} \\ &\quad \vdash^{pro}_{AX} \ \{x > y\}. \end{aligned} \qquad \text{(EXP2)}$$

The proving-expansion part of EXP2 consists of resolution steps upon axioms and the lemma $add(x,b) >_d b$. ∎

It is essential that $t \longrightarrow_{AX} t'$ does not imply $t > t'$. For instance, an axiom of the form

$$F(x) \equiv c(z) \ \Leftarrow \ \gamma(x,z) \qquad (1)$$

leads to infinite term reductions if there is a *left inverse* c' of c in the sense that z is an AX-reduct of c'(c(z)). Let u,v be ground terms such that $\gamma(u,v)$ is AX-convergent. Then (1) implies $F(u) \longrightarrow_{AX} c(v)$, while $c'(c(v)) \longrightarrow_{AX}^{*} v$ yields $\gamma(u,c'(c(v))) \vdash_{AX} \emptyset$. Hence $F(u) \longrightarrow_{AX} c(v)$ implies $\gamma(u,c'(F(u))) \vdash_{AX} \emptyset$ and thus, again by (1),

$$F(u) \longrightarrow_{AX} c(c'(F(u))) \longrightarrow_{AX} c(c'(c(c'(F(u))))) \longrightarrow_{AX} \ldots \qquad (2)$$

Nevertheless, (1) may be decreasing. For instance, Ex. 6.9 contains the derivation step

$$\mathrm{div}(x,y) \gg \{q, r\} \vdash_{path} \mathrm{div}(x,y) \gg \emptyset \tag{3}$$

via the fresh variable rule. (4) starts with

$$\mathrm{div}(x,y) \gg \{q,r\} \vdash_{path} \mathrm{div}(fx,fy) \gg \{fq,fr \mid f \in GS'\} \tag{4}$$

where GS' = GS. Since div ∉ op({fq,fr}), (4) implies (3). However, this is no longer true if NSB were to include the projections p_1, p_2 : nat×nat⟶nat, which yield the left inverse of the pairing operator (_,_). Then we might have (5) for f with

$$fq = p_1(\mathrm{div}(fx-fy,fy)) \quad \text{and} \quad fr = p_2(\mathrm{div}(fx-fy,fy))$$

and thus div ∈ op({fq,fr}). Nevertheless, div $>_{SIG}$ $\{p_1, p_2\}$ and

$$((x,y) >_d (x-y,y)) \vdash^{pro}_{AX} \{x \geq y, y > 0\}$$

(cf. EXP1) imply

$$\mathrm{div}(fx,fy) \gg \{fq,fr\} \vdash_{path} \mathrm{div}(x,y) \gg \emptyset. \tag{5}$$

However, there are other ground substitutions f, which satisfy the premise

$$x \geq y,\ y > 0,\ \mathrm{div}(x-y,y) \equiv (q,r)$$

of N7, but violate (5). For instance, let

$$fq = p_1(\mathrm{div}(fx,fy))-1.$$

Here GS' must be confined to ground substitutions that do not map into terms containing subterms that are equivalent to terms of the form div(t,u+1). The conditions on GS' required by Thm. 6.7 still hold true: each ground term of the form div(t,u+1) has a reduct not containing div!

An axiom of the form (1) is decreasing w.r.t. the AX-path ordering for a triple (GS', $\geq_{SIG}$, $>_d$) if for all f ∈ GS and f' ∈ GS' such that $\gamma(fx,f'z) \vdash_{AX} \emptyset$, each subterm G(t) of c(f'z) or γ(fx,f'z) satisfies either F $>_{SIG}$ G or F $\approx_{SIG}$ G and AX $\vdash_{cut}$ fx $>_d$ t.

Another approach to cope with termination proofs is to avoid inverse functions. Using the decomposition principle (cf. Sect. 2.6), we can often dispense with them. Suppose we want to prove a goal of the form δ(c'(F(u))) with c' being a left inverse of some function c. Then there is the equivalent c'-free clause

$$\exists \{x\}\ \delta(x) \cup \{c(x) \equiv F(u)\} \tag{6}$$

and the proof of δ(c'(F(u))) can be transformed into a proof of (6) where each application of an axiom of the form p(x,c'(d(x)))⟸ϑ is replaced by an application of the equivalent c'-free clause

$$p(x,z) \Leftarrow \{d(x)\equiv c(z)\} \cup \vartheta.$$

Inverse functions are often not *uniform* and thus, when occurring as contexts of recursive calls, may complicate proofs of partial correctness (cf. [Pad90], Sect. 8).

Reduction modulo equations (cf. [JKi86]; the *congruence class approach* of [Pad88a]) and *unfailing completion* (cf. [HR87]) extend the classical rewriting approach to "non-terminating" axioms, which are separated from those that respect a reduction ordering. As an alternative to these concepts, we propose to equip usually non-terminating axioms with an "orienting" premise:

$$add(x,add(y,b)) \equiv add(y,add(x,b)) \Leftarrow x > y. \qquad \textbf{(BA3)}$$

The premise $x > y$ ensures the termination of reductions upon BA3. This complies with the theory of NSB: reduction steps upon BA3 "approximate" elements of the canonical term structure that represents bags as sorted number sequences and with respect to which NSB is initially correct (cf. Sect. 3.3).

To sum up, strong termination as defined here is not at all restrictive. Even proper partial-recursive functions fulfil this requirement as soon as they are specified by means of step functions (cf. [Pad90], Sect. 8). A number of examples suggests that most design specifications can be proved to be strongly terminating with the help of Thm. 6.7.

Before presenting confluence criteria based on a reduction ordering, let us show that strong termination is indispensible for proving the confluence of a specification with *conditional* axioms.

Let $t\equiv t' \Leftarrow \gamma \in$ AX and $f,g \in$ GS such that $f \longrightarrow_{AX}{}^* g$ and $\gamma[f]$ is AX-convergent. Then

$$t[f]\equiv t[f] \longrightarrow_{AX}{}^* t'[f]\equiv t[g]. \qquad (*)$$

For (SIG,AX) to be ground confluent, $t[f]\equiv t[f]$ must be strongly AX-convergent, in particular, $t'[f]\equiv t[g]$ must be AX-convergent. Of course,

$$t'[f]\equiv t[g] \vdash_{AX} \{t'[g]\equiv t'[g]\} \cup \gamma[g] \vdash_{AX} \gamma[g].$$

But how shall we prove that $\gamma[g]$ is AX-convergent? If there is an AX-reduction ordering >, we have $t[f] > \gamma[f]$, and the well-foundedness of >

allows us to conclude $\gamma[f] \rightarrow\vdash_{AX} \emptyset$ by induction along >. Hence in particular, $\gamma[g] \vdash_{AX} \emptyset$.[1]

6.3 Critical clauses

Let > be an AX-reduction ordering.

Under this assumption, [WB83] and [Küc89] reduce the confluence at a term t (cf. Sect. 6.1) to "subconnectedness" or "pseudo-confluence" at t. In terms of goal reduction, pseudo-confluence at p means that for all reductions $p \rightarrow_{AX} q$ there is a successful solving expansion $\gamma_1,\ldots,\gamma_n$ of q such that $p > \gamma_i$ for all $1 \le i \le n$. In fact, Noetherian induction along > allows us to conclude confluence from pseudo-confluence:

Let p be convergent. By induction hypothesis, $\gamma_i \rightarrow\vdash_{AX} \emptyset$ for all AX-convergent γ_i. Hence by Thm. 6.5(1), q is AX-convergent.

In other words, the induction hypothesis implies that AX is *subconfluent* at p:

Definition AX is *subconfluent* at a term or goal γ if for all goals δ with $\gamma > \delta$,

$$\delta \vdash_{AX} \emptyset \text{ implies } \delta \rightarrow\vdash_{AX} \emptyset.$$

Let BASE $\subseteq$ AX. (BASE,AX) is *subconfluent* at a goal γ if for all goals δ with $\gamma > \delta$,

$$\delta \vdash_{AX} \emptyset \text{ implies } \delta \vdash_{BASE} \emptyset \text{ and } \delta \rightarrow\vdash_{AX} \emptyset. \blacksquare$$

For coping with full Horn logic we abstract from the equation-oriented notion of a critical pair by turning to *critical clauses*. The general situation reads as follows. (We assume that the reader is familiar with the notion of a symbol occurrence in a term or an atom.)

Definition Let $c = t \equiv t' \Leftarrow \gamma \in AX^{\perp}$, $d = u \equiv u' \Leftarrow \delta \in AX$, $f,g \in GS$, v be a term or an atom and x be a variable occurring exactly once in v such that

---

[1] [Pad88a], Thm. 9.6.1, presents a criterion for *strong confluence*, which does not require strong termination, but which was designed for another notion of goal reduction where the reflection rule only applies to equations $t \equiv t$ with AX-reduced t (cf. Sect. 6.4). This allows one to induce on the length of a rewrite proof that generates (*) and not on $t[f]$ along >. [DOS87], Thm. 2, provides a criterion for *shallow-joinability*, which is similar to strong confluence. Here the induction weight is not the proof length, but the proof depth, i.e., the least i such that $t \rightarrow_{AX,i} t'$ (cf. Kaplan's definition of $\rightarrow_{AX}$ given above). However, this criterion only works for ***normal*** axioms, whose premises are equations with AX-reduced and ground right-hand sides.

- $t[f] = v[u[g]/x]$,
- *u overlaps t at x*, i.e., the occurrence of x in v is a function symbol occurrence in t.

Let $\varphi = \gamma[f] \cup \delta[g]$. Let $p = v[u'[g]/x] \equiv t'[f]$ if v is a term and $p = v[u'[g]/x]$ otherwise. $p \Leftarrow \varphi$ is called a *critical clause of (SIG,AX)*. The pair $<t[f],cc>$ is called a *(ground) reduction ambiguity of (SIG,AX) induced by <c,d>*. ▮

In the unconditional equational case, reduction ambiguities have the form $<t,u \equiv u'>$. By the above argument, we have to consider only those terms t such that AX is subconfluent at t. This leads us to a weakening of the notion of reductive validity (cf. Sect. 6.1):

Definition Let p be a term or an atom and $c = \exists X_1\gamma_1 \vee ... \vee \exists X_n\gamma_n \Leftarrow \delta$ be a Gentzen clause.

c is *sub-p-reductively valid w.r.t. AX* or a *sub-p-reductive AX-theorem* if for all $f \in GS$ such that AX is subconfluent at $p[f]$,

$$\delta[f] \longrightarrow\vdash_{AX} \emptyset \quad \text{implies} \quad \gamma_i[g] \longrightarrow\vdash_{AX} \emptyset$$

for some $1 \le i \le n$ and $g \in GS$ with $f|(X-X_i) = g|(X-X_i)$. *p-RTh(AX)* denotes the set of sub-p-reductive AX-theorems.

Let BASE $\subseteq$ AX. c is *sub-p-reductively valid w.r.t. (BASE,AX)* or a *sub-p-reductive (BASE,AX)-theorem* if for all $f \in GS$ such that (BASE,AX) is subconfluent at $p[f]$,

$$\delta[f] \vdash_{BASE} \emptyset \text{ and } \delta[f] \longrightarrow\vdash_{AX} \emptyset$$

imply

$$\gamma_i[g] \vdash_{BASE} \emptyset \text{ and } \gamma_i[g] \longrightarrow\vdash_{AX} \emptyset$$

for some $1 \le i \le n$ and $g \in GS$ with $f|(X-X_i) = g|(X-X_i)$. *p-RTh(BASE,AX)* denotes the set of sub-p-reductive (BASE,AX)-theorems. ▮

Definition (SIG,AX) is *critical clause convergent* if for each reduction ambiguity <p,c> of (SIG,AX), c is sub-p-reductively valid w.r.t. AX . ▮

The well-known Superposition Theorem for unconditional equations (cf. [KB70]) can now be generalized to Horn logic with equality:

Theorem 6.10 (Superposition Theorem for Horn clauses) *Let (SIG,AX) be strongly terminating. (SIG,AX) is ground confluent iff (SIG,AX) is critical clause convergent.*

Now we get into trouble with our weak notion of strong termination. Since $\longrightarrow_{AX}$ is not a subrelation of >, we cannot conclude the strong convergence of a goal γ from its convergence by inducing on γ along >. But the existence of fresh variables does not allow us to strengthen strong termination. Many important applications would not work in the AX-reduction property or if we set GS' = GS in the path calculus (cf. Sect. 6.2). The alternative is to restrict $\longrightarrow_{AX}$ to a subrelation of >, of course in a way that preserves all reduction properties obtained so far. Hence we introduce the following

General Assumption There is a fixed set NF $\subseteq$ T(SIG) of *normal forms* with X $\subseteq$ NF such that, when the rules of directed expansion, goal reduction or term reduction are applied, only normal forms are substituted for fresh variables. Let GS_{NF} be the set of ground substitutions into normal forms. Instances of NF by GS_{NF} must be normal forms, too, and each ground term must have an AX-reduct in NF (where the notion of AX-reduct is also adapted to the normal form restriction of term reduction). GS_{NF} is supposed to agree with GS' (cf. Sect. 6.2). ∎

GS_{NF} is supposed to contain all the AX-reducts f' used in the AX-reduction property. If strong termination is proved via the path calculus for a triple (GS', $\geq_{SIG}$, $>_d$), then GS_{NF} is supposed to agree with GS' (cf. Sect. 6.2).

Now $\longrightarrow_{AX}$ is a subrelation of >. The reader should review the results of Sect. 6.1 and check whether they remain valid under the new definition of $\vdash_{AX}$ and $\longrightarrow_{AX}$. Of course, only the places where the inference rules of $\vdash_{AX}$ and $\longrightarrow_{AX}$ are applied explicitly must be taken into account. In fact, this is only Lemma 6.4, which must be modified as follows:

Lemma 6.4 (revised) *Let* $c = q \Leftarrow \vartheta \in AX$ *and* $f \in GS$. *If* $\vartheta[f]$ *is strongly AX-convergent, then* $q[f]^{sym}$ *is AX-convergent.*

Proof. If $\vartheta[f]$ is strongly AX-convergent, then for some AX-reduct g of f, $\vartheta[g]$ is AX-convergent and we can conclude $q[g]^{sym} \vdash_{AX} \emptyset$ as in Lemma 6.4. Hence q[f] is AX-convergent as well. ∎

Lemma 6.4 was only applied in the proof of Thm. 6.5 (1) where ground confluence is assumed. Hence convergence can be replaced by strong convergence.

Proof of Theorem 6.10. "only if": Let $<p,q \Leftarrow \gamma>$ be a reduction ambiguity of (SIG,AX) such that γ is strongly AX-convergent. Then there is a goal $\delta \subseteq \gamma$ such that $p \Leftarrow \delta$ is the instance of an axiom and $p \longrightarrow_{AX} q$. Hence δ is AX-convergent and we conclude $p \vdash_{AX} \emptyset$ and thus $q \longrightarrow \vdash_{AX} \emptyset$ from Lemma 6.4 and the ground confluence of (SIG,AX).

"if": Suppose that (SIG,AX) is critical clause convergent. Let p be an AX-convergent ground atom. We show by induction on p along the given AX-reduction ordering > that p is strongly AX-convergent. Let $p \longrightarrow_{AX} q \longrightarrow_{AX}^{*} p'$ be a term reduction. Then

$$p = d[v_0[g]/x] \quad \text{and} \quad q = d[v_1[g]/x]$$

for some d,x,g and $v_0 \equiv v_1 \Leftarrow \vartheta \in AX$, $\vartheta[g] \vdash_{AX} \emptyset$ and $p > \{q\} \cup \vartheta[g]$. Suppose that q is AX-convergent. Then by induction hypothesis, $p' \vdash_{AX} \emptyset$. Hence it remains to show that q is AX-convergent.

By induction hypothesis, $\vartheta[g]$ is strongly AX-convergent. Since $p \vdash_{AX} \emptyset$, there is a successful goal reduction $\gamma_1,\dots,\gamma_n$ of p.

Case 1. γ_2 is obtained from p by resolution. Then $p = p_0[f]$ and $\gamma_2 = \gamma[f] \vdash_{AX} \emptyset$ for some f and $p_0 \Leftarrow \gamma \in AX$. Since $p > \gamma_2$, the induction hypothesis implies that γ_2 is strongly AX-convergent. Let $\varphi = \gamma_2 \cup \vartheta[g]$.

Critical case 1.1. The occurrence of x in d is a function symbol occurrence in p_0. Since $p = p_0[f] = d[v_0[g]/x]$, $q = d[v_1[g]/x]$, $p_0 \Leftarrow \gamma$, $v_0 \equiv v_1 \Leftarrow \vartheta \in AX$ and $\varphi = \gamma[f] \cup \vartheta[g]$, $\langle p, q \Leftarrow \varphi \rangle$ is a reduction ambiguity of (SIG,AX). Since (SIG,AX) is critical clause convergent, $q \Leftarrow \varphi \in p\text{-RTh}(AX)$. By induction hypothesis, AX is subconfluent at p . Therefore, $q \Leftarrow \varphi \in p\text{-RTh}(AX)$ implies $q \vdash_{AX} \emptyset$ because φ is strongly AX-convergent.

Case 1.2. The occurrence of x in d is not a function symbol occurrence in p_0.

Case 1.2.1. p_0 is linear, i.e. each variable occurs at most once in p_0. Then $p_0[f] = d[v_0[g]/x]$ and $q = d[v_1[g]/x]$ imply $q = p_0[f']$ for some f' with $f \longrightarrow_{AX}^{*} f'$. Since $\gamma[f]$ is strongly AX-convergent, $\gamma[f']$ is also AX-convergent. Hence by Lemma 6.4, $q = p_0[f']$ is AX-convergent.

Case 1.2.2. p_0 is not linear. Then there are a linear atom p_1, a function h : $var(p_1) \longrightarrow var(p_0)$ and a substitution f' such that $p_0 = p_1[h]$, $fhz \longrightarrow_{AX}^{*} f'z$ for all $z \in var(p_1)$ and $p_1[f'] = q$.

Let $x \in var(p_0)$ and $h^{-1}x = \{z_1,\dots,z_n\}$. Then for all $1 \le i \le n$, $fx = fhz_i$, and thus $fx \longrightarrow_{AX}^{*} f'z_i$. Since $p > fx$, we conclude from the induction hypothesis that $fx \equiv fx$ is strongly AX-convergent. By Lemma 6.2(2), (SIG,AX) is confluent at fx. Hence a straightforward induction on n yields a common reduct t_x of $f'z_1,\dots,f'z_n$. Let

$$f'' = \{t_x/x \mid x \in var(p_0)\} + f|(X - var(p_0)).$$

Then $q = p_1[f'] \longrightarrow_{AX}{}^* p_1[h][f"] = p_o[f"]$, $f \longrightarrow_{AX}{}^* f"$ and thus $p = p_o[f] \longrightarrow_{AX}{}^* p_o[f"]$. Since $\gamma[f]$ is strongly AX-convergent, $\gamma[f"]$ is AX-convergent. Hence by Lemma 6.4, $p_o[f"]$ and thus q are AX-convergent.

Case 2. γ_2 is obtained from p by reduction. Then there is an AX-convergent atom q' such that $p \longrightarrow_{AX} q' \vdash_{AX} \emptyset$,

$$p = c[u_o[f]/x] \quad \text{and} \quad q' = c[u_1[f]/x]$$

for some c,x,f and $u_o \equiv u_1 \Leftarrow \gamma \in AX$, $\gamma[f] \vdash_{AX} \emptyset$ and $p > \{q'\} \cup \gamma[f]$. By induction hypothesis, $\{q'\} \cup \gamma[f]$ is strongly AX-convergent. Let $t = u_o[f]$ and $t' = u_1[f]$.

Case 2.1. There are a linear atom r and terms u,u' such that

$$p = r[t/x,u/y], \quad q = r[t/x,u'/y], \quad q' = r[t'/x,u/y]$$

where $u = v_o[g]$ and $u' = v_1[g]$. Since q' is strongly AX-convergent and $u \longrightarrow_{AX} u'$, $r[t'/x,u'/y]$ is AX-convergent. Hence q is AX-convergent, too.

Case 2.2. W.l.o.g. there are a linear atom r and a term $t"$ such that

$$p = r[t/x], \quad q = r[t"/x], \quad q' = r[t'/x]$$

and $t = d[v_o[g]/z] \longrightarrow_{AX} t" = d[v_1[g]/z]$ for some d. Suppose that $t' \equiv t"$ is AX-convergent. Since q' is strongly AX-convergent, Lemma 6.3 implies $q \vdash_{AX} \emptyset$. Hence it remains to show that $t' \equiv t"$ is AX-convergent.

Case 2.2.1. r is not an equation or the side of r that contains x is not a variable. Then $p = r[t/x] > \{t,t\}$ and thus by induction hypothesis, $t \equiv t$ is strongly AX-convergent. Hence $t' \equiv t"$ is AX-convergent.

Case 2.2.2. r is an equation and the side of r that contains x is equal to x. Let $\varphi = \gamma[f] \cup \vartheta[g]$. We have $u_o[f] = t = d[v_o[g]/z]$.

Critical case 2.2.2.1. The occurrence of z in d is a function symbol occurrence in u_o. Hence $<t \equiv t', \; t" \equiv t' \Leftarrow \varphi>$ is a reduction ambiguity of (SIG,AX). Since (SIG,AX) is critical clause convergent, $t" \equiv t' \Leftarrow \varphi \in$ t-RTh(AX). Since $p = r[t/x] \geq \{t\}$, the induction hypothesis implies that AX is subconfluent at t. Therefore, $t" \equiv t' \Leftarrow \varphi \in$ t-RTh(AX) implies $t" \equiv t' \vdash_{AX} \emptyset$ because φ is strongly AX-convergent.

Case 2.2.2.2. The occurrence of z in d is not a function symbol occurrence in u_o.

Case 2.2.2.2.1. u_o is linear, i.e. each variable occurs at most once in u_o. Then $u_o[f] = d[v_o[g]/z]$ and $t" = d[v_1[g]/z]$ imply $t" = u_o[f']$ for some f' with $f \longrightarrow_{AX}{}^* f'$. Since $\gamma[f]$ is strongly AX-convergent, $\gamma[f']$ is AX-convergent, too.

Hence by Lemma 6.4, $(u_0 \equiv u_1)[f']$ is AX-convergent and thus $t'' \equiv t' = u_0[f'] \equiv u_1[f]$ is AX-convergent as well.

Case 2.2.2.2.2. u_0 is not linear. Then u_0 cannot be a variable and thus for all $x \in var(u_0)$, fx is a proper subterm of t. Moreover, there are a linear term v, a function $h : var(v) \longrightarrow var(u_0)$ and a substitution f' such that $u_0 = v[h]$, $fhz \longrightarrow_{AX}{}^{*} f'z$ for all $z \in var(v)$ and $v[f'] = t''$.

Let $x \in var(u_0)$ and $h^{-1}x = \{z_1,...,z_n\}$. Then for all $1 \le i \le n$, $fx = fhz_i$, and thus $fx \longrightarrow_{AX}{}^{*} f'z_i$. Since $t > fx$, we conclude from the induction hypothesis that $fx \equiv fx$ is strongly AX-convergent. By Lemma 6.2(2), (SIG,AX) is confluent at fx. Hence a straightforward induction on n yields a common reduct t_x of $f'z_1,...,f'z_n$. Let

$$f'' = \{t_x/x \mid x \in var(u_0)\} + f|(X - var(u_0)).$$

Then $t'' = v[f'] \longrightarrow_{AX}{}^{*} v[h][f''] = u_0[f'']$, $f \longrightarrow_{AX}{}^{*} f''$ and thus $t' = u_1[f] \longrightarrow_{AX}{}^{*} u_1[f'']$. Since $\gamma[f]$ is strongly AX-convergent, $\gamma[f'']$ is AX-convergent. Hence by Lemma 6.4, $(u_0 \equiv u_1)[f'']$ is AX-convergent and thus $t'' \equiv t' = v[f'] \equiv u_1[f]$ is AX-convergent as well.

Case 3. γ_2 is obtained from p by reflection. Then $p = t \equiv t$ for some t. Hence w.l.o.g. $q = t \equiv t'$ and $t \longrightarrow_{AX} t'$ for some t'. Thus q is AX-convergent. ∎

Strong termination of (SIG,AX) is crucial for the inductive argument of the preceding proof: the induction hypothesis ensures that certain subgoals are strongly convergent. In Cases 1.1 and 2.2.2.2.1, this allows us to apply the assumption that critical clauses are convergent, while in Cases 1.2 and 2.2.2.2.2, Lemma 6.4 became applicable.

The strong-convergence assumption in the definition of (sub)reductive validity makes critical clause convergence a weaker condition than *critical pair joinability* (cf. [DOS88]). The following examples show that strong convergence of critical clause premises is essential for preserving confluence under clause decomposition (cf. Sect. 2.6).

Example 6.11 Suppose we have a ground confluent specification (SIG,AX) that is to be extended by a function symbol F and a single axiom for F without fresh variables, say

$$Fx \equiv v(Ft) \Leftarrow \vartheta. \qquad \text{(FP)}$$

Since for no $c \in AX$, <FP,c> or <c,FP> induces a reduction ambiguity and the only reduction ambiguities induced by <FP,FP> are reflexive equations, the extended specification (SIG∪{F},AX∪{FP}) is also ground confluent, provided that it is strongly terminating. However, turning FP into

$$Fx\equiv v(y) \Leftarrow \vartheta \cup \{Ft\equiv y\} \qquad \text{(LP)}$$

violates the ground confluence unless the ground instances of $Ft\equiv y$ are strongly convergent:

For ground terms u,u' and $f \in$ GS, <LP,LP> induces the reduction ambiguity <Fx[f],cc> where the critical clause cc is given by

$$v(u')\equiv v(u) \Leftarrow \vartheta[f] \cup \{Ft[f]\equiv u, Ft[f]\equiv u'\}.$$

Is cc reductively valid?

The assumption that the premise of cc is convergent, in particular, that Ft[f] and u as well as Ft[f] and u' have common reducts t' and t" respectively, does not suffice for concluding that $v(u')\equiv v(u)$ is also convergent. Only if $Ft[f]\equiv u$ is strongly convergent and thus the reduct $t''\equiv t'$ of $Ft[f]\equiv u$ is convergent, do t' and t" have a common reduct v' and do we obtain a successful reduction of the conclusion of cc:

$$v(u')\equiv v(u) \vdash_{AX\cup\{LP\}} v(t'')\equiv v(t') \vdash_{AX\cup\{LP\}} v(v')\equiv v(v') \vdash_{\emptyset} \emptyset. \blacksquare$$

Example 6.12 The reduction ambiguities of NSB are induced by <N6,N7>, <N7,N6>, <N7,N7> and <BA3,BA3> (cf. Ex. 1.1).

Reduction ambiguities <t1,cc1> induced by <N6,N7> (analogously: <N7,N6>) have the form

div(v,v') (t1)

$$(t+1,u) \equiv (0,v) \Leftarrow v < v',\ v' > 0,\ v \ge v',\ div(v-v',v') \equiv (t,u). \qquad \text{(cc1)}$$

If the premise of cc1 were NSB-convergent, both $v < v'$ and $v \ge v'$ would be NSB-convergent, which is impossible (cf. Ex. 7.4). Hence cc1 is reductively valid w.r.t. NSB.

Reduction ambiguities <t2,cc2> induced by <N7,N7> have the form

div(v,v') (t2)

$$(t'+1,u') \equiv (t+1,u) \Leftarrow v \ge v',\ v' > 0,\ div(v-v',v') \equiv (t,u),\ div(v-v',v') \equiv (t',u'). \qquad \text{(cc2)}$$

The convergence proof follows the schema of Ex. 6.11:

Suppose that the premise of cc2 is strongly convergent. First, div(v-v',v') and (t,u) as well as div(v-v',v') and (t',u') have common reducts r and r' respectively. Since $r\equiv r'$ is a reduct of $(t,u)\equiv(t',u')$, there are reducts $r_0\equiv r_0'$ of $t\equiv t'$ and $r_1\equiv r_1'$ of $u\equiv u'$ such that $r = (r_0,r_1)$ and $r' = (r_0',r_1')$. As a reduct of $div(v-v',v')\equiv(t,u)$, $r'\equiv r$ is convergent. Hence r_0' and r_0 as well as r_1' and r_1 have common reducts s_0 and s_1 respectively. Therefore, the conclusion of cc2 is convergent:

$$(t'+1,u') \equiv (t+1,u) \vdash_{NSB} (r_0'+1,r_1') \equiv (r_0+1,r_1) \vdash_{NSB} (s_0+1,s_1) \equiv (s_0+1,s_1) \vdash_{\emptyset} \emptyset.$$

Hence cc2 is reductively valid w.r.t. NSB.

Reduction ambiguities <t3,cc3> induced by <BA3,BA3> have the form

$$\text{add}(t,\text{add}(t',\text{add}(t'',u))) \qquad \text{(t3)}$$

$$\text{add}(t,\text{add}(t'',\text{add}(t',u))) \equiv \text{add}(t',\text{add}(t,\text{add}(t'',u))) \Leftarrow t > t',\ t' > t''. \qquad \text{(cc3)}$$

The conclusion of cc3 can be reduced into $t > t''$:

$$\text{add}(t,\text{add}(t'',\text{add}(t',u))) \equiv \text{add}(t',\text{add}(t,\text{add}(t'',u)))$$

$$\vdash_{\{BA3\}} \{\text{add}(t'',\text{add}(t,\text{add}(t',u))) \equiv \text{add}(t',\text{add}(t'',\text{add}(t,u))),\ t > t''\}$$

$$\vdash_{\{BA3\}} \{\text{add}(t'',\text{add}(t',\text{add}(t,u))) \equiv \text{add}(t'',\text{add}(t',\text{add}(t,u))),\ t > t',\ t' > t'', t > t''\}$$

$$\vdash_{AX} \{t > t''\}.$$

For cc3 to be reductively valid, $t > t''$ must be convergent. This can only be concluded from results of the next section (cf. Ex. 6.22). ∎

Ex. 6.12 illustrates that, in practice, proofs of critical clause convergence are not carried out for each reduction ambiguity individually. Instead, the established goal reductions provide a reduction *schema* that applies to an infinite number of reduction ambiguities. Hence we extend the above notion as follows:

Definition A pair consisting of an atom and a clause that subsumes a ground reduction ambiguity is also called a *reduction ambiguity*. A set RA of reduction ambiguities is *AX-complete* if each ground reduction ambiguity of (SIG,AX) is subsumed by an element of RA. ∎

Lemma 6.13 (Criterion for critical clause convergence) *Given an AX-complete set RA of reduction ambiguities, (SIG,AX) is critical clause convergent if for all <p,cc> ∈ RA, cc ∈ p-RTh(AX).*

Proof. Let $\langle p,q \Leftarrow \gamma \rangle$ be a ground reduction ambiguity of (SIG,AX). By assumption, $p = p'[f]$ and $q \Leftarrow \gamma = (q' \Leftarrow \gamma')[f]$ for some $\langle p',q' \Leftarrow \gamma' \rangle \in RA$ and $f \in GS$. Suppose that AX is subconfluent at p and γ is strongly AX-convergent. Since $q' \Leftarrow \gamma' \in$ p-RTh(AX), $q = q'[f]$ is AX-convergent.

Hence $q \Leftarrow \gamma$ is a sub-p-reductive AX-theorem. ∎

6.4 Proving reductive validity

The convergence proof for reduction ambiguities induced by <BA3,BA3> (cf. Ex. 6.12) would succeed if we could infer the convergence of $t > t''$ from the convergence of $t > t'$ and $t' > t''$. In general, lemmas such as

$$x > z \Leftarrow x > y,\ y > z$$

must be *reductively* valid if they are used in a proof of the reductive validity of, say, $p \Leftarrow \gamma$. The proof may start with several goal reductions $p \vdash_{AX} \gamma_1, \dots, p \vdash_{AX} \gamma_n$. Then it remains to show that $\gamma_1 \vee \dots \vee \gamma_n \Leftarrow \gamma$ is reductively valid.

This suggests the question for proving reductive validity in a hierarchical way, using a calculus such as inductive expansion. Inductive and reductive validity are not very different. Both notions are concerned with ground instances, and AX-validity corresponds to AX-convergence. So we may ask whether *inductive* expansion upon *reductively* valid lemmas is sound for proving *reductive* theorems? We take the weaker notion of sub-p-reductive validity because it is sufficient for critical clause convergence and of sub-p-reductive lemmas are rather available than reductive ones (cf. Thm. 6.21).

Definition Let X_{in} be a given set of input variables (cf. Sect. 2.2), BASE $\subseteq$ AX and p be a term or an atom. The *sub-p-reductive expansion calculus upon (BASE,AX)* consists of the following two inference rules, which transform a set of goals into a single goal.

Sub-p-reductive resolution

$$\frac{\{\lambda_1 \cup \varphi_1,\ \dots,\ \lambda_n \cup \varphi_n\}}{(\lambda_1 \cup \dots \cup \lambda_n)[g] \cup \vartheta \cup EQ(g_{in})}$$

$\exists X_1\varphi_1[g] \vee \dots \vee \exists X_n\varphi_n[g] \Leftarrow \vartheta \in$ p-RTh(BASE,AX), for all $1 \le i \le n$: $X_i \cap var(\lambda_i[g] \cup g(X_{in})) = \emptyset$

Sub-p-reductive paramodulation

$$\frac{\{\lambda_1[t_1/x],\ \dots,\ \lambda_n[t_n/x]\}}{(\lambda_1 \cup \dots \cup \lambda_n)[g] \cup \vartheta \cup EQ(g_{in})}$$

$\exists X_1(t_1 \equiv x)[g] \vee \dots \vee \exists X_n(t_n \equiv x)[g] \Leftarrow \vartheta \in$ p-RTh(BASE,AX), for all $1 \le i \le n$: $X_i \cap var(\lambda_i[g] \cup g(X_{in})) = \emptyset$

A sequence $s_1, \dots, s_n$ of goal sets is called a *sub-p-reductive expansion of* s_1 *into* s_n *upon (BASE,AX)* if for all $1 \le i < n$ and $\delta \in s_{i+1} - s_i$ there is $s \subseteq s_i$ such that δ is obtained from s by a single sub-p-reductive resolution or paramodulation step and each $\gamma \in s$ is *p-bounded* w.r.t. (δ,BASE) (see below).

The corresponding inference relation is denoted by $\vdash^{p}_{BASE;AX}$ ($\vdash^{p}_{AX}$ if BASE = AX). ∎

Definition Let BASE $\subseteq$ AX. Given a term or an atom p and goals γ,δ, γ is *p-bounded w.r.t. (δ,BASE)* if for all f $\in$ GS,

$$\delta[f] \vdash_{BASE} \emptyset \quad \text{implies} \quad p[f] > \gamma[f]. \ ∎$$

As for proofs that axioms are decreasing we employ the path calculus for a suitable triple ($\geq_{SIG}$, $>_d$, GS') and use the following criterion (cf. Sect. 6.2):

- γ is p-bounded w.r.t. (δ,BASE) if there is a clause $c = \varphi \Leftarrow \delta$ such that

$$p >> \gamma \ \vdash_{path} \ \varphi \ \vdash^{ind}_{AX;c} \ \delta$$

where GS' = $\{f \in GS \mid \delta[f] \vdash_{BASE} \emptyset\}$.

Subreductive expansions are proved correct against subreductive validity the same as inductive expansions were proved correct against inductive validity (cf. Lemma 5.1 and Thm. 5.2):

Lemma 6.14 (Soundness of sub-p-reductive resolution and paramodulation) *Let BASE $\subseteq$ AX and p be an input term or atom. If δ is obtained from $\{\gamma_1,\dots,\gamma_n\}$ by a single sub-p-reductive resolution or paramodulation step, then $\exists X_{out}\gamma_1 \vee \dots \vee \exists X_{out}\gamma_n \Leftarrow \delta$ is sub-p-reductively valid w.r.t. (BASE,AX).*

Proof. Let f $\in$ GS such that (BASE,AX) is subconfluent at p[f] and δ[f] is BASE-convergent and strongly AX-convergent.

Case 1 (resolution). Let $\delta = (\lambda_1 \cup \dots \cup \lambda_n)[g] \cup \vartheta \cup EQ(g_{in})$. From the conditions of sub-p-reductive resolution we must infer

$$(\lambda_j \cup \varphi_j)[f_{in}+h_{out}] \vdash_{BASE} \emptyset \quad \text{and} \quad (\lambda_j \cup \varphi_j)[f_{in}+h_{out}] \longrightarrow\!\vdash_{AX} \emptyset \tag{1}$$

for some $1 \leq j \leq n$ and h $\in$ GS.

Since ϑ[f] is BASE-convergent and strongly AX-convergent and $\exists X_1\varphi_1[g] \vee \dots \vee \exists X_n\varphi_n[g] \Leftarrow \vartheta$ is a sub-p-reductive (BASE,AX)-theorem, there are $1 \leq j \leq n$ and h $\in$ GS such that $\varphi_j[g][h]$ is BASE-convergent and strongly AX-convergent and $h|(X-X_j) = f|(X-X_j)$.

$X_j \cap var(g(X_{in})) = \emptyset$ implies $g[h] = g[f]_{in}+g[h]_{out}$ and thus

$$\varphi_j[g[f]_{in}+g[h]_{out}] \longrightarrow\!\vdash_{AX} \emptyset. \tag{2}$$

$X_j \cap var(\lambda_j[g]) = \emptyset$ implies $\lambda_j[g][h] = \lambda_j[g][f]$. Since $\lambda_j[g] \subseteq \delta$ and δ[f] is strongly AX-convergent, we obtain

$$\lambda_j[g[f]_{in}+g[h]_{out}] = \lambda_j[g][f] \longrightarrow\vdash_{AX} \emptyset. \quad (3)$$

Moreover, $EQ(g_{in})[f]$ is AX-convergent. Hence by (2), (3) and Lemma 6.3,

$$(\lambda_j \cup \varphi_j)[f_{in}+g[h]_{out}] \vdash_{AX} \emptyset. \quad (4)$$

Since $\lambda_j \cup \varphi_j$ is p-bounded w.r.t. (δ,BASE) and $\delta[f]$ is BASE-convergent,

$$p[f] > (\lambda_j \cup \varphi_j)[f_{in}+g[h]_{out}]. \quad (5)$$

Since (BASE,AX) is subconfluent at $p[f]$, (4) and (5) imply (1).

Case 2 (paramodulation). Let $\delta = (\lambda_1 \cup ... \cup \lambda_n)[g] \cup \vartheta \cup EQ(g_{in})$. From the conditions of sub-p-reductive paramodulation we must infer

$$\lambda_j[t_j/x][f_{in}+h_{out}] \vdash_{BASE} \emptyset \text{ and } \lambda_j[t_j/x][f_{in}+h_{out}] \longrightarrow\vdash_{AX} \emptyset \quad (6)$$

for some $1 \le j \le n$ and $h \in GS$.

Since $\vartheta[f]$ is BASE-convergent and strongly AX-convergent and

$$\exists X_1(t_1 \equiv x)[g] \vee ... \vee \exists X_n(t_n \equiv x)[g] \Leftarrow \vartheta$$

is a sub-p-reductive (BASE,AX)-theorem, there are $1 \le j \le n$ and $h \in GS_{NF}$ such that $(t_j \equiv x)[g][h]$ is BASE-convergent and strongly AX-convergent and $h|(X-X_j) = f|(X-X_j)$.

$X_j \cap var(g(X_{in})) = \emptyset$ implies $g[h] = g[f]_{in}+g[h]_{out}$ and $X_j \cap var(\lambda_j[g]) = \emptyset$ implies $\lambda_j[g][h] = \lambda_j[g][f]$. Since $\lambda_j[g] \subseteq \delta$ and $\delta[f]$ is strongly AX-convergent, we obtain

$$\lambda_j[(g[f]_{in}+g[h]_{out})|(X-\{x\}) + g[h]|\{x\}] = \lambda_j[g][f] \longrightarrow\vdash_{AX} \emptyset. \quad (7)$$

Since $g[h] = g[f]_{in}+g[h]_{out}$, $(t_j \equiv x)[g][h]$ is strongly AX-convergent and $EQ(g_{in})[f]$ is AX-convergent, Lemma 6.3 implies

$$t_j[f_{in}+g[h]_{out}] \equiv (gx)[h] \vdash_{AX} \emptyset. \quad (8)$$

Since $EQ(g_{in})[f]$ is AX-convergent, f_{in} and $g[f]_{in}$ have a common reduct f'. Hence by (7),

$$\lambda_j[(f'+g[h]_{out})|(X-\{x\}) + g[h]|\{x\}] \longrightarrow\vdash_{AX} \emptyset. \quad (9)$$

By (8), (9) and Lemma 6.3,

$$\lambda_j[(f'+g[h]_{out})|(X-\{x\}) + \{t_j[f_{in}+g[h]_{out}]/x\}] \vdash_{AX} \emptyset. \quad (10)$$

We conclude from (10) and $f_{in} \longrightarrow_{AX}{}^* f'$ that

$$\lambda_j[t_j/x][f_{in}+g[h]_{out}] = \lambda_j[(f_{in}+g[h]_{out})|(X-\{x\}) + \{t_j[f_{in}+g[h]_{out}]/x\}]$$

is AX-convergent. (11)

Since $\lambda_j[t_j/x]$ is p-bounded w.r.t. (δ,BASE) and $\delta[f]$ is BASE-convergent,

$$p[f] > \lambda_j[t_j/x][f_{in}+g[h]_{out}]. \qquad (12)$$

Since (BASE,AX) is subconfluent at p[f], (11) and (12) imply (6). ∎

Theorem 6.15 (Soundness of sub-p-reductive expansions) *Given BASE ⊆ AX and an input term or atom p, a Gentzen clause* $\exists X_{out}\gamma_1 \vee \ldots \vee \exists X_{out}\gamma_n \Leftarrow \delta$ *is sub-p-reductively valid w.r.t. (BASE,AX) if* $\{\gamma_1,\ldots,\gamma_n\} \vdash^{p}_{BASE;AX} \{\delta\}$.

Proof. This follows analogously to Thm. 5.2. ∎

Corollary 6.16 (Refined criterion for critical clause convergence) *Given an AX-complete set RA of reduction ambiguities, (SIG,AX) is critical clause convergent if for all* $\langle p,q \Leftarrow \gamma\rangle \in RA$,

$$\{\{q\}\} \vdash^{p}_{AX} \{\gamma\}.$$

Proof. Let X_{in} = var(TH) and <p,cc> ∈ RA. By Thm. 6.15, cc ∈ p-RTh(AX). Hence by Lemma 6.13, (SIG,AX) is critical clause convergent. ∎

The subreductive expansion calculus allows us to prove subreductive theorems by applying subreductively valid lemmas. This yields a hierarchical procedure, which needs a starting point, i.e., lemmas that are known to be subreductively valid. Theorem 6.5(3) suggests beginning with *inductive* theorems because inductive validity coincides with reductive validity iff (SIG,AX) is ground confluent. However, the purpose of establishing subreductive theorems is to *prove* ground confluence (via critical clause convergence). Hence we would run into a circular argument when presuming the equivalence of inductive and reductive validity. If inductively valid lemmas were to be applied in a subreductive expansion, they would have to be valid on a "lower level", which is usually given by a *base specification*:

General Assumption Let (BSIG,BASE) be a subspecification of (SIG,AX), called the *base specification.* Terms, atoms, goals and clauses over BSIG are called *base terms, base atoms, base goals* and *base clauses.* The clauses of BASE are called *base axioms.* Base clauses that are inductively valid w.r.t. BASE are called *inductive base theorems.* ∎

A base specification may serve several purposes. In Section 3.4, when aiming at a structured correctness proof, we have used (BSIG,BASE) for establishing the sort building part of (SIG,AX) and reserved the extension AX-BASE for "algorithmic" function and predicate definitions: First, BASE is proved initially correct w.r.t. a (canonical) base structure; second, the entire specification (SIG,AX) is proved consistent w.r.t. (BSIG,BASE). Theorem 3.12 provides a deduction-oriented criterion for the first part. Likewise, one obtains such a criterion for consistency (Cor. 6.19), which involves ground confluence and *reductive* consistency:

Definition (SIG,AX) is *reductively consistent w.r.t. (BSIG,BASE)* if all AX-convergent ground base goals are BASE-convergent. Given a term or atom p, (SIG,AX) is *sub-p-reductively consistent w.r.t. (BSIG,BASE)* if all ground base goals γ, which are p-bounded w.r.t. (γ,AX), are BASE-convergent. ∎

Lemma 6.17 (Consistency and reductive consistency)

(1) If (SIG,AX) is ground confluent and reductively consistent w.r.t. (BSIG,BASE), then (SIG,AX) is consistent w.r.t. (BSIG,BASE).

(2) Suppose that (BSIG,BASE) is ground confluent and the set of base normal forms is reductively complete w.r.t. (BSIG,BASE). If (SIG,AX) is consistent w.r.t. (BSIG,BASE), then (SIG,AX) is reductively consistent w.r.t. (BSIG,BASE).

Proof. (1) Let γ be an AX-valid ground base goal. Since (SIG,AX) is ground confluent, Thm. 6.5(2) implies that γ is AX-convergent. Hence by assumption, γ is BASE-convergent and thus BASE-valid.

(2) Let γ be an AX-convergent ground base goal. Then γ is AX-valid and thus BASE-valid by assumption. Since the base specification is ground confluent, Thm. 6.5(2) implies that γ is BASE-convergent. ∎

For avoiding the above-mentioned circularity that arises from identifying inductive and reductive theorems when proving confluence let us find out sufficient conditions under which inductive *base* theorems are subreductively valid.

At first, (SIG,AX) must be reductively consistent w.r.t. the base specification. In particular, AX-convergent ground instances of BASE-premises must be BASE-convergent. The check can be confined to instances by AX-reduced substitutions, provided that (SIG,AX) is *weakly terminating*.

Definition Let BASE ⊆ AX. A term t is *BASE-reduced w.r.t. AX* if there is no conditional term reduction $t \longrightarrow_{BASE} t' \Leftarrow \gamma$ such that γ is AX-convergent. A substitution f is BASE-reduced w.r.t. AX if all elements of f(dom(f)) are BASE-reduced w.r.t. AX.

An atom p is *BASE-reduced w.r.t. AX* if there is no AX-convergent goal γ such that $p \vdash_{BASE} \gamma$.

A term, substitution or atom is *AX-reduced* if BASE = AX.

An AX-reduced term t' is an *AX-reduced form* of a term t if $t \longrightarrow_{AX}{}^{*} t'$. (SIG,AX) is *weakly terminating* if each ground term over SIG has an AX-reduced form. ∎

Since > includes $\longrightarrow_{AX}{}^{+}$, strong termination implies weak termination.

Secondly, the base specification must be ground confluent so that, by Thm. 6.5(3), every *inductive* BASE-theorem becomes a *reductive* BASE-theorem. For this purpose, the set of base axioms should be kept small.

Thirdly, AX-convergent ground instances of BASE-premises, at least those by AX-reduced substitutions, must be base goals. This is a rather weak completeness condition on SIG w.r.t. BSIG. Actually, it says that AX-reduced ground terms, which can be substituted for BASE-premise variables, are base terms. Hence, together with weak termination of (SIG,AX), it implies that the functions in terms that can be substituted for BASE-premise variables comprise a complete specification w.r.t. (BSIG,BASE) (cf. Sect. 3.4).

The crucial assumption is reductive consistency. Let us give a criterion for this property.

Definition A set CS of Horn clauses is *ground reducible w.r.t. (BSIG,BASE)* if for all $t \equiv t' \Leftarrow \gamma \in CS^{\perp}$ (cf. Sect. 6.2) and $f \in GS$ such that $\gamma[f]$ is AX-convergent,

- $t[f]$ contains a symbol from SIG-BSIG or
- $t[f]$ is not BASE-reduced w.r.t. AX. ∎

Definition A set CS of Horn clauses *respects BSIG* if for all $p \Leftarrow \gamma \in CS$ and $f \in GS$ such that $\gamma[f]$ is strongly AX-convergent, the following condition holds true:

- If $p = t \equiv t'$ for some t,t', then for all base atoms q such that $q[t'[f]/x]$ is strongly AX-convergent, $q[t[f]/x] \vdash_{BASE} \varphi$ for some AX-convergent base goal φ;
- otherwise $p[f] \vdash_{BASE} \varphi$ for some AX-convergent base goal φ. ∎

Each base clause $p \Leftarrow \gamma$ without fresh variables respects BSIG because $\varphi = q[t'[f]/x]$ ($\varphi = \gamma[f]$, resp.) is an AX-convergent base goal with $q[t[f]/x] \vdash_{BASE} \varphi$ ($p[f] \vdash_{BASE} \varphi$, resp.).

In general, let Z be the set of fresh variables of $p \Leftarrow \gamma$ and $f \in GS$ such that $\gamma[f]$ and $q[t'[f]/x]$ are strongly AX-convergent. *If all terms of f(Z) have a base AX-reduct*, then there is $g \in GS$ such that $f \longrightarrow_{AX}{}^{*} g$, $g|(X\text{-}Z) = f|(X\text{-}Z)$, and $\varphi = q[t'[g]/x]$, $\varphi = \gamma[g]$ are base goals with $q[t[f]/x] \vdash_{BASE} \varphi$, $p[f]$

$\vdash_{\mathsf{BASE}} \varphi$ respectively. By assumption, φ is AX-convergent. Hence $p \Leftarrow \gamma$ respects BSIG.

Lemma 6.18 (Criterion for subreductive consistency) *Suppose that*

(1) (SIG,AX) is strongly terminating,

(2) AX-BASE is ground reducible w.r.t. (BSIG,BASE),

(3) BASE respects BSIG.

Given a term or atom p, (SIG,AX) is sub-p-reductively consistent w.r.t. (BSIG,BASE) if AX is subconfluent at p.

Proof. Let γ be an AX-convergent ground base goal with $p > \gamma$. We will show $\gamma \vdash_{\mathsf{BASE}} \emptyset$ by Noetherian induction on γ along $>$. If $\gamma = \emptyset$, the proof is complete. Otherwise $\gamma \vdash_{\mathsf{AX}} \varphi$ and $\gamma > \varphi$ for some AX-convergent goal φ obtained from γ by reflection, resolution or reduction. In the first case, $\gamma = \varphi \cup \{t \equiv t\}$ for some t. Since $\gamma > \varphi$ and φ is a base goal, the induction hypothesis implies $\varphi \vdash_{\mathsf{BASE}} \emptyset$ and thus $\gamma \vdash_{\mathsf{BASE}} \emptyset$. For the remaining cases we proceed as follows.

Since $p > \gamma > \varphi$, since γ and φ are AX-convergent and since AX is subconfluent at p, γ and φ are strongly AX-convergent.

Case 1. φ is obtained from γ by resolution or reduction upon BASE. Since BASE respects BSIG and φ is strongly AX-convergent, there is an AX-convergent base goal γ' with $\gamma \vdash_{\mathsf{BASE}} \gamma'$. Since $\gamma > \gamma'$, the induction hypothesis implies $\gamma' \vdash_{\mathsf{BASE}} \emptyset$ and thus $\gamma \vdash_{\mathsf{BASE}} \emptyset$.

Case 2. φ is obtained from γ by resolution or reduction upon AX-BASE. Since AX-BASE is ground reducible and φ is AX-convergent, we have $\gamma \vdash_{\mathsf{BASE}} \varphi'$ for some goal φ'. Since γ is strongly AX-convergent, φ' is AX-convergent. $p > \gamma > \varphi'$ implies $\varphi' \rightarrow\!\vdash_{\mathsf{AX}} \emptyset$ because AX is subconfluent at p. Hence $\gamma \vdash_{\mathsf{BASE}} \gamma'$ for some AX-convergent base goal γ' because BASE respects BSIG. Since $\gamma > \gamma'$, the induction hypothesis implies $\gamma' \vdash_{\mathsf{BASE}} \emptyset$ and thus $\gamma \vdash_{\mathsf{BASE}} \emptyset$. ∎

Lemmata 6.17(1) and 6.18 provide the following consistency criterion, which, in contrast with Cor. 3.15, does not require the building of a SIG-structure.

Corollary 6.19 (Reduction-oriented consistency criterion) *Suppose that*

(1) (SIG,AX) is ground confluent and strongly terminating,

(2) AX-BASE is ground reducible w.r.t. (BSIG,BASE),

(3) BASE respects BSIG.

Then (SIG,AX) is consistent w.r.t. (BSIG,BASE). ∎

The following lemma presents two criteria for subreductive validity the first of which is used in *reductive expansions* (cf. Sect. 7.4), while the second is tailored to proofs of critical clause convergence with the help of Cor. 6.16. Both criteria establish basic lemmas to be applied in subreductive expansions.

Lemma 6.20 (From base inductive validity to subreductive validity) *Let p be a term or an atom and* $L = \exists X_1\gamma_1 \vee \ldots \vee \exists X_n\gamma_n \Leftarrow \delta$ *be an inductive base theorem such that for all* $1 \le i \le n$, γ_i *is p-bounded w.r.t.* (δ,AX).

(1) *L is sub-p-reductively valid w.r.t. (BASE,AX) if SIG = BSIG and the base specification is ground confluent.*

(2) *L is sub-p-reductively valid w.r.t. AX if*

- *the base specification is ground confluent,*
- δ *is p-bounded w.r.t.* (δ,AX),
- *all AX-convergent instances of* δ *by AX-reduced ground substitutions are base goals,*
- *(SIG,AX) is strongly terminating,*
- *AX-BASE is ground reducible w.r.t. (BSIG,BASE),*
- *BASE respects BSIG.*

Proof. (1) Let $f \in GS$ such that (BASE,AX) is subconfluent at $p[f]$ and $\delta[f]$ is BASE-convergent and strongly AX-convergent. Then BASE $\vdash_{cut} \delta[f]$. Since SIG = BSIG and L is an inductive base theorem, there is $1 \le i \le n$ such that BASE $\vdash_{cut} \gamma_i[g]$ for some g with $g|(X-X_i) = f|(X-X_i)$. Since (SIG,BASE) is ground confluent, Thm. 6.5(2) implies that $\gamma_i[g]$ is BASE-convergent and thus AX-convergent. Since γ_i is p-bounded w.r.t. (δ,AX), we have $p[f] > \gamma_i[g]$. Hence $\gamma_i[g]$ is strongly AX-convergent. Therefore, $L \in$ p-RTh(BASE,AX).

(2) Let $f \in GS$ such that AX is subconfluent at $p[f]$ and $\delta[f]$ is strongly AX-convergent. Then $\delta[f'] \vdash_{AX} \emptyset$ for some AX-reduced base substitution f' with $f' \rightarrow_{AX}{}^{*} f$ because (SIG,AX) is strongly terminating. By assumption, $\delta[f']$ is a base goal. By assumption and Lemma 6.18, (SIG,AX) is sub-$p[f']$-reductively consistent w.r.t. (BSIG,BASE) because AX is subconfluent at $p[f']$. Since δ is p-bounded w.r.t. (δ,AX) and $\delta[f']$ is AX-convergent, we have and $p[f] \ge p[f'] > \delta[f']$. Hence $\delta[f'] \vdash_{BASE} \emptyset$ and thus BASE $\vdash_{cut} \delta[f']$.

Since L is an inductive base theorem, there is $1 \le i \le n$ such that BASE $\vdash_{cut} \gamma_i[g]$ for some g with $g|(X-X_i) = f'|(X-X_i)$. We conclude from Thm. 6.5(2) that $\gamma_i[g]$ is BASE-convergent. Hence $f \rightarrow_{AX}{}^{*} f'$ and $f'|(X-X_i) = g|(X-X_i)$ imply $\gamma_i[f|(X-X_i)+g|X_i] \vdash_{AX} \emptyset$. Since γ_i is p-bounded w.r.t. (δ,AX), we have $p[f] >$

$\gamma_i[f|(X-X_i)+g|X_i]$. Hence $\gamma_i[f|(X-X_i)+g|X_i]$ is strongly AX-convergent. Therefore, L ∈ p-RTh(AX). ∎

Without referring to a base specification we have the following criteria for subreductive theorems:

Lemma 6.21 (Basic criteria for subreductive validity w.r.t. AX) *Let p be a term or an atom and γ,δ be goals such that γ is p-bounded w.r.t. (δ,AX). $\gamma \Leftarrow \delta$ is sub-p-reductively valid w.r.t. AX if*

(1) $\gamma \Leftarrow \delta \in AX^{sym}$ *or*

(2) $\gamma \vdash_{AX} \delta$.

Proof. Let f ∈ GS such that AX is subconfluent at p[f] and δ[f] is strongly AX-convergent.

(1) Let $\gamma \Leftarrow \delta \in AX^{sym}$. By Lemma 6.4, $\gamma[f] \vdash_{AX} \emptyset$. By assumption, p[f] > γ[f]. Hence γ[f] is strongly AX-convergent.

(2) Let $\gamma \vdash_{AX} \delta$. Then $\gamma[f] \vdash_{AX} \delta[g]$ for some AX-reduct g of f. Hence δ[g] and thus γ[f] are AX-convergent. By assumption, p[f] > γ[f]. Hence γ[f] is strongly AX-convergent. ∎

6.5 Sample confluence proofs

Example 6.22 (cf. Ex. 6.9) The ground reduction ambiguities of NSB' are induced by <N7,N7> and <BA3,BA3>. They are subsumed by the pairs $<t_1, p_1 \Leftarrow \delta_1>$ and $<t_2, p_2 \Leftarrow \delta_2>$ respectively, where

$$t_1 = \text{div}(x,y)$$

$$t_2 = \text{add}(x,\text{add}(y,\text{add}(z,b)))$$

$$p_1 \Leftarrow \delta_1 = (q'+1,r') \equiv (q+1,r) \Leftarrow \{\text{div}(x-y,y) \equiv (q,r),\ \text{div}(x-y,y) \equiv (q',r'),\ x \ge y,\ y > 0\}$$

$$p_2 \Leftarrow \delta_2 = \text{add}(x,\text{add}(z,\text{add}(y,b))) \equiv \text{add}(y,\text{add}(x,\text{add}(z,b))) \Leftarrow \{x > y,\ y > z.\}.$$

By Lemma 6.13, (SIG,AX) is critical clause convergent if for i=1,2, $p_i \Leftarrow \delta_i \in t_i$-RTh(NSB'). Following Lemma 6.21(2), we look for goal reductions of p_i. Unfortunately, reductions of p_1 do not exist and reductions of p_2 do not lead to δ_2:

$$\begin{aligned} p_2 &\vdash_{(BA3)} \{\text{add}(z,\text{add}(x,\text{add}(y,b))) \equiv \text{add}(y,\text{add}(z,\text{add}(x,b))),\ x > z\} \\ &\vdash_{(BA3)} \{\text{add}(z,\text{add}(y,\text{add}(x,b))) \equiv \text{add}(z,\text{add}(y,\text{add}(x,b))),\ x > y,\ y > z,\ x > z\} \\ &\vdash_{\emptyset} \{x > y,\ y > z,\ x > z\}. \qquad (R_2) \end{aligned}$$

Since a direct proof of $p_i \Leftarrow \delta_i$ does not succeed, we turn to Cor. 6.16 and expand $\{\{p_i\}\}$ into $\{\delta_i\}$:

$$\{\{p_1\}\} \vdash^{t1}_{AX} \{\delta_1\} \quad \text{(EXP1)}$$

$$\{\{p_2\}\} \vdash^{t2}_{AX} \{\delta_2 \cup \{x > z\}\} \vdash^{t2}_{AX} \{\delta_2\} \qquad \text{(EXP2)}$$

where we have applied the lemmas $L_1 = p_1 \Leftarrow \psi_1$, $L_2 = p_2 \Leftarrow \delta_2 \cup \{x>z\}$ and $L_3 = \{x>z\} \Leftarrow \delta_2$ where

$$\psi_1 = \{pair \equiv (q,r),\ pair \equiv (q',r'),\ x \geq y,\ y > 0\},$$

By Lemma 6.21(2), R_2 implies $L_2 \in t_2$-RTh(NSB'). Morever, let

$$BSIG = \{0,\ \_+1,\ (\_,\_),\ >,\ <,\ \leq\},$$

$$BASE = \{LE1, LE2, LT, GT\}$$

(cf. Ex. 1.1). L_1 and L_3 are inductive base theorems. By Ex. 6.9, (SIG,AX) is strongly terminating. Since (BSIG,BASE) is critical clause convergent and strongly terminating, we conclude from Thm. 6.10 that (BSIG,BASE) is ground confluent. Moreover, ψ_1 is t_1-bounded w.r.t. (ψ_1, AX) and δ_2 is t_2-bounded w.r.t. (δ_2, AX). All AX-reduced non-base ground terms have the form div(t,0) and thus do not occur in AX-convergent instances of ψ_1 or δ_2. Hence by Lemma 6.20 (2), $L_i \in t_i$-RTh(NSB') for i=1,3.

EXPi, i=1,2, is a sub-t_i-reductive expansion. Hence by Cor. 6.16, NSB' is critical clause convergent and thus by Thm. 6.10, NSB' is ground confluent. ∎

Example 6.23 We extend NSB' into NSB" by the inequality on natural numbers and by a deletion operator for bags:

$$x \not\equiv y \Leftarrow x > y \qquad \text{(NEQ1)}$$

$$x \not\equiv y \Leftarrow x < y \qquad \text{(NEQ2)}$$

$$del(x,add(x,b)) \equiv b \qquad \text{(DEL1)}$$

$$del(x,add(y,b)) \equiv add(y,del(x,b)) \Leftarrow x \not\equiv y. \qquad \text{(DEL2)}$$

There are additional reduction ambiguities, induced by <DEL1,BA3> and <DEL2,BA3> and subsumed by $<t_1, p_1 \Leftarrow \delta_1>$ and $<t_2, p_2 \Leftarrow \delta_2>$ respectively, where

$$t_1 = del(x,add(x,add(y,b)))$$

$$t_2 = del(x,add(y,add(z,b)))$$

$$p_1 \Leftarrow \delta_1 = del(x,add(y,add(x,b))) \equiv add(y,b) \Leftarrow \{x > y\}$$

$$p_2 \Leftarrow \delta_2 = del(x,add(z,add(y,b))) \equiv add(y,del(x,add(z,b))) \Leftarrow \{x \not\equiv y,\ y > z\}.$$

We obtain the following goal reductions:

$$
\begin{array}{lll}
p_1 \vdash_{(DEL2)} & \{add(y,del(x,add(x,b))) \equiv add(y,b),\ x \not\equiv y\} & \\
\vdash_{(DEL1)} & \{add(y,b) \equiv add(y,b),\ x \not\equiv y\} & \\
\vdash_{\emptyset} & x \not\equiv y. & (R_1) \\
p_2[z/x] = & del(z,add(z,add(y,b))) \equiv add(y,del(z,add(z,b))) & \\
\vdash_{(DEL1)} & add(y,b) \equiv add(y,b) & \\
\vdash_{\emptyset} & \emptyset. & (R_2) \\
p_2 \vdash_{(DEL2)} & \{add(z,del(x,add(y,b))) \equiv add(y,add(z,del(x,b))),\ x \not\equiv z\} & \\
\vdash_{(DEL2)} & \{add(z,add(y,del(x,b))) \equiv add(y,add(z,del(x,b))),\ x \not\equiv z,\ x \not\equiv y\} & \\
\vdash_{(BA3)} & add(z,add(y,del(x,b))) \equiv add(z,add(y,del(x,b))),\ x \not\equiv z,\ x \not\equiv y,\ y > z\} & \\
\vdash_{\emptyset} & \{x \not\equiv z,\ x \not\equiv y,\ y > z\}. & (R_3)
\end{array}
$$

The reductions do not lead to the premises δ_i, i=1,2. So we turn to Cor. 6.16 and expand $\{\{p_i\}\}$ into $\{\delta_i\}$:

$$\{\{p_1\}\} \vdash^{t1}_{AX} \{\gamma_1 \cup \delta_1\} \vdash^{t1}_{AX} \{\delta_1\} \qquad \text{(EXP1)}$$

$$\{\{p_2\}\} \vdash^{t2}_{AX} \{p_2[z/x]\} \cup \varphi,\ \delta_2 \cup \varphi'\} \vdash^{t2}_{AX} \{\delta_2 \cup \varphi,\ \delta_2 \cup \varphi'\} \vdash^{t2}_{AX} \{\delta_2\}. \qquad \text{(EXP2)}$$

The lemmas applied in EXP1 and EXP2 are respectively $L_1 = p_1 \Leftarrow \gamma_1 \cup \delta_1$, $L_2 = \gamma_1 \Leftarrow \delta_1$, $L_3 = \varphi \Leftarrow \varphi$ and $L_4 = p_2 \Leftarrow \delta_2 \cup \varphi'$, $L_5 = p_2[z/x] \Leftarrow \delta_2 \cup \varphi$ and $L_6 = \varphi \vee \varphi'$ where

$$\gamma_1 = \{x \not\equiv y\},\ \ \varphi = \{x \equiv z\}\ \text{ and }\ \varphi' = \{x \not\equiv z\}.$$

By Lemma 6.21(2), R_1, R_2 and R_3 imply $L_1 \in t_1$-RTh(NSB") and $L_4, L_5 \in t_2$-RTh(NSB"). Moreover, let

$$\text{BSIG}' = \text{BSIG} \cup \{\not\equiv\},$$

$$\text{BASE}' = \text{BASE} \cup \{\text{NEQ1},\text{NEQ2}\}$$

(cf. Ex. 6.22). L_2, L_3 and L_6 are inductive base theorems. Moreover, δ_1 is t_1-bounded w.r.t. (δ_1,AX) and φ is t_2-bounded w.r.t. (φ,AX). All AX-reduced non-base ground terms have the form div(t,0) and thus do not occur in AX-convergent instances of δ_1 or φ. Hence by Lemma 6.20(2), $L_2 \in t_1$-RTh(NSB") and $L_3, L_6 \in t_2$-RTh(NSB").

EXPi, i=1,2, is a sub-t_i-reductive expansion. Hence by Cor. 6.16, NSB" is critical clause convergent and thus by Thm. 6.10 and a straightforward extension of Ex. 6.9 to NSB", NSB" is ground confluent. ∎

In the following example, the function repByMin is defined by means of a guarded clause (RBM) that is not constructor-based: its premise includes an equation $t \equiv c$ with a "feedback" variable that occurs on *both* sides of $t \equiv c$.

Example 6.24 (cf. [Bir84])

TREE

base	NSB' (cf. Ex. 6.9)		
sorts	tree		
	symbol	*type*	
functs	<_>	nat ⟶ tree	
	_•_	tree,tree ⟶ tree	
	repByMin	tree ⟶ tree	
	rep&min	tree,nat ⟶ tree×nat	
	min	nat,nat ⟶ nat	
vars	x,y,y' : nat; z,z',l,l',r,r' : tree		
axms	repByMin(z) ≡ z' ⇐ rep&min(z,x) ≡ (z',x)		(RBM)
	rep&min(<x>,y) ≡ (<y>,x)		(RM1)
	rep&min(l•r,x) ≡ (l'•r',min(y,y')) ⇐ rep&min(l,x) ≡ (l',y), rep&min(r,x) ≡ (r',y')		(RM2)
	min(x,y) ≡ x ⇐ x ≤ y		(MIN1)
	min(x,y) ≡ y ⇐ y ≤ x		(MIN2)

rep&min(t,x) carries out two operations simultaneously: replacing all entries of t by x and computing the least entry of t. repByMin(t) replaces all entries of t within a single tree traversal. The premise of the defining equation RBM represents a circular network (cf. Sect. 8.7). According to input, output and feedback channels of such a network, the variables of RBM fall into input, output and feedback variables: z, z', x are input, output, feedback variables respectively.

Given R_{AX} as in Ex. 6.9, let $\geq_{SIG}$ be the reflexive and transitive closure of

$$R_{AX} \cup \{(\text{repByMin},G) \mid G \in SIG\} \cup \{(\text{rep\&min},G) \mid G \in SIG-\{\text{repByMin}\}\}.$$

Of course, RM1, MIN1 and MIN2 are decreasing. Concerning RBM and RM2, one may proceed analogously to N7 (cf. Ex. 6.9). The crucial path expansion steps read as follows:

$$\text{repByMin(z)} >> \{z,z',x\} \ \vdash_{path} \ \emptyset \quad (1)$$
$$\text{rep\&min(l•r,x)} >> \{l',y,r',y'\} \ \vdash_{path} \ \emptyset. \quad (2)$$

Both steps are applications of the fresh variable rule (cf Sect. 6.2). (1) and (2) follow from the definition of $\geq_{SIG}$ and the fact that tree- and nat-terms do not contain the symbol rep&min, provided that NF is confined to the set of TREE-terms that do not contain repByMin (cf. Sect. 6.3). Indeed, since repByMin is specified as a total function, each ground TREE-term has a reduct in NF!

We conclude from Thm. 6.7 and Ex. 6.9 that all axioms of TREE are decreasing w.r.t. the path ordering for $(GS_{NF}, \geq_{SIG}, >_d)$.

The ground reduction ambiguities of TREE are induced by <N7,N7>, <BA3,BA3>, <MIN1,MIN2> and <RBM,RBM>. That those induced by <N7,N7> and <BA3,BA3> are subreductive NSB'- and thus TREE-theorems has been shown in Ex. 6.22. The others are subsumed by $\langle t_1, p_1 \Leftarrow \delta_1 \rangle$ and $\langle t_2, p_2 \Leftarrow \delta_2 \rangle$ respectively, where

$$t_1 = \mathtt{min(x,y)}$$

$$t_2 = \mathtt{repByMin(z)}$$

$$L_1 = p_1 \Leftarrow \delta_1 = \mathtt{y} \equiv \mathtt{x} \Leftarrow \{\mathtt{x} \le \mathtt{y},\ \mathtt{y} \le \mathtt{x}\}$$

$$L_2 = p_2 \Leftarrow \delta_2 = \mathtt{z''} \equiv \mathtt{z'} \Leftarrow \{\mathtt{rep\&min(z,x)} \equiv \mathtt{(z',x)},\ \mathtt{rep\&min(z,y)} \equiv \mathtt{(z'',y)}\}.$$

Let

$$\text{BSIG'} = \text{BSIG} \cup \{\mathtt{min}, \mathtt{rep\&min}, \_\!\circ\!\_\},$$

$$\text{BASE'} = \text{BASE} \cup \{\text{MIN1,MIN2,RM1,RM2}\}$$

(cf. Ex. 6.22). L_1 and L_2 are inductive base theorems. Moreover, δ_i is t_i-bounded w.r.t. (δ_i, AX) and all TREE-reduced non-base ground terms have the form div(t,0) and thus do not occur in AX-convergent instances of δ_1 or δ_2. Hence by Lemma 6.20(2), $L_i \in t_i$-RTh(TREE) for i=1,2. We conclude from Lemma 6.13 that TREE is critical clause convergent and thus from Thm. 6.10 that TREE is ground confluent.

As a circular program, RBM cannot be translated directly into a functional program. The circle is cut open if a tree is mapped to a function when it is traversed to find its least entry (cf. [PS87]; see [Rea89], Sect. 8.4.2, for an SML version). This can be expressed axiomatically by introducing the functional sort nat⟶tree.

The general schema for constructing terms over a signature SIG with functional sorts reads as follows:

- Variables and constants of SIG are terms over SIG.
- A function symbol f : s1...sn⟶s ∈ SIG is a constant with (functional) sort s1...sn⟶s.
- If t is a term of sort s1...sn⟶s and t1,...,tn are terms of sort s1,...,sn, resp., then t(t1,...,tn) is a term of sort s.

The cut calculus for Horn clauses over SIG (cf. Sect. 1.2) is extended by the following axioms:

- $F(x1,...,xn) = G(y1,...,yn) \Leftarrow F = G,\ x1 = y1, ..., xn = yn$
- $F = G \Leftarrow \forall \{x1,...,xn\}\ F(x1,...,xn) = G(x1,...,xn)$ (extensionality axiom)

where x1,...,xn,y1,...,yn,F,G are variables of suitable sorts. Based on the corresponding extension of AX-validity and AX-equivalence, the initial (SIG,AX)-structure is constructed as in Sect. 3.1. Initial homomorphisms, however, need only exist for term-generated SIG-models of AX because the extensionality axiom may imply ground equations that do not hold in other models (cf. [MTW88]).

Functional sorts may be given names, such as fun for nat⟶tree:

```
FUNTREE
    base   NSB'  (cf. Ex. 6.9)
    sorts  tree, fun = nat⟶tree
           symbol        type
    functs <_>           nat ⟶ tree
           _∘_           tree,tree ⟶ tree
           repByMin      tree ⟶ tree
           rep&min       tree ⟶ fun×nat
           leaf          fun
           _•_           fun,fun ⟶ fun
    vars   x,y : nat;  z,l,r : tree;  f,f' : fun
    axms   repByMin(z) ≡ f(x)  ⇐  rep&min(z) ≡ (f,x)
           rep&min(<x>) ≡ (leaf,x)
           rep&min(l∘r) ≡ (f•f',min(x,y)) ⇐ rep&min(l) ≡ (f,x), rep&min(r) ≡ (f',y)
           leaf(x) ≡ <x>
           (f•f')(x) ≡ f(x)∘f'(x)
```

By applying f to x, x is entered simultaneously into all leaves of the tree represented by f. ∎

6.6 On rewriting logics

In the previous sections, we were concerned with rewriting-oriented calculi: goal reduction for proving goals, directed expansion for solving goals, term reduction for computing reduced forms, and subreductive expansion for proving ground confluence. The corresponding inference relations are sound w.r.t. AX-validity or AX-equivalence. They are *means* for special proof purposes. They do not stand for themselves and thus should not be confused with a *rewriting logic* for transition systems for modelling concurrent, object-oriented or other imperative language features (cf., e.g., [Jor87], [GM87], [GM88], [Huß88], [SL89]).

A transition relation TR can be axiomatized as part of a Horn clause specification, but the requirements to TR often do not comply with properties such as termination or confluence. If TR is added as a binary predicate to a specification of states to be rewritten, TR becomes *compatible* with the equivalence relation $\equiv_{AX}$. It is perhaps a conceptual mistake to introduce TR as a presentation of AX-equivalence. $\equiv_{AX}$ defines the *static* identity of objects, TR provides a *dynamic* system for manipulating objects and changing states.

For instance, TR may be generated by a set RR of conditional rewrite rules of the form

$$t \longrightarrow t' \text{ if } u_1 \longrightarrow v_1 \wedge \ldots \wedge u_k \longrightarrow v_k$$

where $t, t', u_1, v_1, \ldots, u_k, u_k$ are terms over a state specification STATE. Following the rewriting logic presented in [Mes90], Sect. 2.4, TR may be specified as an extension of STATE:

TRANSITION

base STATE

preds $\_\longrightarrow\_ : s,s$ for all sorts s of STATE

vars $x, x_1, \ldots, x_n, y, y_1, \ldots, y_n, z : s$

axms $x \longrightarrow x$

$x \longrightarrow z \Leftarrow x \longrightarrow y,\ y \longrightarrow z$

$F(x_1, \ldots, x_n) \longrightarrow F(y_1, \ldots, y_n) \Leftarrow x_1 \longrightarrow y_1, \ldots, x_n \longrightarrow y_n$

for all function symbols F of STATE

$t \longrightarrow t'[y_1/x_1, \ldots, y_n/x_n] \Leftarrow u_1 \longrightarrow v_1, \ldots, u_k \longrightarrow v_k, x_1 \longrightarrow y_1, \ldots, x_n \longrightarrow y_n$

for all $r = (t \longrightarrow t' \text{ if } u_1 \longrightarrow v_1 \wedge \ldots \wedge u_k \longrightarrow v_k) \in$ RR such that

$var(r) = \{x_1, \ldots, x_n\}$.

7: Implications of Ground Confluence

How do we benefit from ground confluent specifications? Most of the advantages follow from Thm. 6.5: If (SIG,AX) is ground confluent, then and only then directed expansions yield all ground AX-solutions. Sects. 7.1 and 7.2 deal with refinements of directed expansion: *strategic expansion* and *narrowing*. Sect. 7.3 presents syntactic criteria for a set of terms to be a set of constructors (cf. Sect. 2.3). The results obtained in Sects. 7.2 and 7.3 provide the *failure rule* and the *clash rule* that check goals for unsolvability and thus help to shorten every kind of expansion proof (see the final remarks of Sect. 5.4).

Sect. 7.4 deals with the proof of a set CS of inductive theorems by showing that (SIG,AX∪CS) is consistent w.r.t. (SIG,AX) (cf. Sect. 3.4). Using consequences of the basic equivalence between consistency and inductive validity (Lemma 7.9) we come up with *reductive expansion*, which combines goal reduction and subreductive expansion (cf. Sect. 6.4) into a method for proving inductive theorems. While inductive expansion is always sound, the correctness of reductive expansion depends on ground confluence and strong termination of (SIG,AX). Under these conditions, an *inductive* expansion can always be turned into a reductive expansion (Thm 7.18). Conversely, a reductive expansion can be transformed in such a way that most of its "boundary conditions" hold true automatically (Thm. 7.19).

The chapter will close with a deduction-oriented concept for specification refinements, or *algebraic implementations*. Both the implementing level and the implemented level of a refinement admit an extension, the former by *abstraction functions*, the latter by *representation predicates*, such that the union of both extensions is consistent w.r.t. each of them. Hence, for proving refinements correct, one of the consistency criteria, Cors. 3.15 and 6.19, may be used. Several examples illustrate the concept and an associated proof method based on the reduction-oriented criterion Cor. 6.19.

7.1 Strategic expansion

Srong termination is not only crucial for confluence proofs (cf. Thm. 6.10) and the decidability of AX-convergence (cf. Prop 6.8). It also allows us to prefer term reductions to other directed-expansion steps. Within such expansions, one may modify subgoals according to a *reduction strategy* before performing deduction steps that change the current substitution.

Definition (cf. Chapter 4) A function RS : At(SIG)⟶At(SIG) is called an *AX-reduction strategy* if for all atoms p and $f \in$ GS, RS(p)$[f]$ is an AX-reduct of $p[f]$. Given an AX-reduction strategy RS, the *strategic (solving) expansion calculus upon AX and R* consists of the following three inference rules, which transform goal-substitution pairs:

Strategic resolution $$\frac{\langle \varphi \cup \{p\}, f\rangle}{\langle RS((\varphi \cup \vartheta)[g]), f[g \mid X_{goals}]\rangle}$$	$p[g] = q[g]$ $q \Leftarrow \vartheta \in$ AX-CE(AX)
Strategic paramodulation $$\frac{\langle \delta[t/x], f\rangle}{\langle RS((\delta[u'/x] \cup \vartheta)[g]), f[g \mid X_{goals}]\rangle}$$	$t[g] = u[g]$ $u \equiv u' \Leftarrow \vartheta \in$ Pre(AX)
Unification $$\frac{\langle \gamma \cup \{t \equiv t'\}, f\rangle}{\langle \gamma[g], f[g]\rangle}$$	$t[g] = t'[g]$

A *strategic expansion of* $\langle\gamma_1,f_1\rangle$ *into* $\langle\gamma_n,f_n\rangle$ *upon AX and RS* is a sequence $\langle\gamma_1,f_1\rangle,\dots,\langle\gamma_n,f_n\rangle$ of goal-substitution pairs such that for all $1 \le i < n$, $\langle\gamma_{i+1},f_{i+1}\rangle$ is obtained from $\langle\gamma_i,f_i\rangle$ by a single strategic resolution, strategic paramodulation or unification step.

$\vdash_{AX}^{RS}$ denotes the corresponding inference relation. ∎

Corollary 7.1 (Completeness of strategic expansion) *Suppose that (SIG,AX) is ground confluent and strongly terminating. Let* γ *be a goal and* f *be a substitution such that* $f(X_{goals}) \subseteq GT(SIG)$*. Then*

$$AX \vdash_{cut} \gamma[f] \quad \text{implies} \quad \gamma \vdash_{AX}^{RS} \langle \emptyset, f \mid X_{goals}\rangle. \qquad (*)$$

Proof. Suppose that f solves γ w.r.t. AX. Theorem 6.5(4) implies $\gamma \vdash_{AX} \langle\emptyset, f \mid X_{goals}\rangle$. We will show (*) by induction on $\gamma[f]$ along the given AX-reduction ordering >. If γ is empty, the proof is complete. Otherwise

$$\gamma \vdash_{AX} \langle\delta, g\rangle \vdash_{AX} \langle\emptyset, g[h \mid X_{goals}]\rangle$$

for some $\delta \neq \gamma$ and g,h such that $g[h|X_{goals}] = f|X_{goals}$ and $\langle\delta,g\rangle$ is obtained from γ by applying a rule of the directed expansion calculus. Hence $\gamma[f] = \gamma[g][h] \vdash_{AX} \delta[h] \vdash_{AX} \emptyset$ and thus $RS(\delta)[h] \vdash_{AX} \emptyset$ because $\delta[h] \longrightarrow_{AX}^{*} RS(\delta)[h]$ and (SIG,AX) is ground confluent. By expansion lifting (cf. Lemma 4.5), $RS(\delta) \vdash_{AX} \langle\emptyset,h|X_{goals}\rangle$. Since $\gamma[f] > \delta[h] > RS(\delta)[h]$, the induction hypothesis implies

$$RS(\delta) \vdash^{RS}_{AX} \langle\emptyset,h|X_{goals}\rangle.$$

Hence

$$\gamma \vdash^{RS}_{AX} \langle RS(\delta),g\rangle \vdash^{RS}_{AX} \langle\emptyset,g[h|X_{goals}]\rangle = \langle\emptyset,f|X_{goals}\rangle. \blacksquare$$

7.2 Narrowing

In directed expansions, conditional equations are always applied from left to right. Do (most general) solving expansions become enumerable under this restriction? No. Even if AX is finite, there are infinitely many prefix extensions of a single axiom each of which yields a redex of the current goal. Hence paramodulation must be confined to "pure" axiom applications. This leads to a further restriction of the solving expansion calculus, which resembles the narrowing procedure invented by Slagle (cf. [Sla74]) and Lankford (cf. [Lan75]):[1]

Definition (cf. Chapter 4) The *narrowing (solving) calculus upon AX* consists of the following three inference rules, which transform goal-substitution pairs:

Rule	Inference	Condition
Resolution	$\dfrac{\langle\varphi \cup \{p\}, f\rangle}{\langle(\varphi \cup \vartheta)[g], f[g\|X_{goals}]\rangle}$	$p[g] = q[g]$, $q \Leftarrow \vartheta \in$ AX-CE(AX)
Narrowing	$\dfrac{\langle\delta[t/x], f\rangle}{\langle(\delta[u'/x] \cup \vartheta)[g], f[g\|X_{goals}]\rangle}$	$t \notin X$, $t[g] = u[g]$, $u \equiv u' \Leftarrow \vartheta \in$ AX
Unification	$\dfrac{\langle\gamma \cup \{t \equiv t'\}, f\rangle}{\langle\gamma[g], f[g]\rangle}$	$t[g] = t'[g]$

[1]For recent results and references concerning the underlying calculus, cf. [Pad88a].

A *narrowing expansion of* $\langle\gamma_1,f_1\rangle$ *into* $\langle\gamma_n,f_n\rangle$ *upon AX* is a sequence $\langle\gamma_1,f_1\rangle,\ldots,\langle\gamma_n,f_n\rangle$ of goal-substitution pairs such that for all $1\le i<n$, $\langle\gamma_{i+1},f_{i+1}\rangle$ is obtained from $\langle\gamma_i,f_i\rangle$ by a single resolution, narrowing or unification step.

$\vdash^{nar}_{AX}$ denotes the corresponding inference relation. ∎

The narrowing rule does not only avoid prefix extensions, it also forbids a redex t that is only a variable. Both conditions make the set of narrowing redices of a finite goal a finite set, provided that CE(AX) is also finite.

The completeness result for directed expansions (Thm. 6.5(4)) is retained, but only for *AX-reduced* solutions (cf. Sect. 6.4):

Theorem 7.2 (Completeness of narrowing) *(SIG,AX) is ground confluent iff for all goals and AX-reduced substitutions* f *such that* $f(X_{goals}) \subseteq GT(SIG)$,

$$AX \vdash_{cut} \gamma[f] \quad \textit{implies} \quad \gamma \vdash^{nar}_{AX} \langle\emptyset,f|X_{goals}\rangle. \qquad (*)$$

Proof. "only if": Suppose that f solves γ w.r.t. AX. Theorem 6.5(4) implies $\gamma \vdash_{AX} \langle\emptyset,f|X_{goals}\rangle$. We will show (*) by induction on the minimal number n of paramodulation steps in a directed expansion of γ into $\langle\emptyset,f|X_{goals}\rangle$. If n = 0, then (*) follows immediately.

Otherwise $\gamma \vdash_{AX} \langle\emptyset,f|X_{goals}\rangle$ can be decomposed as follows. First, $\gamma \vdash^{nar}_{AX} \langle\varphi,h\rangle$ for some φ,h. Second, a directed paramodulation step expands φ into some $\langle\psi,h'\rangle$. Third, $\psi \vdash_{AX} \langle\emptyset,h''\rangle$ for some h'' such that $h[h'][h''] = f|X_{goals}$. By induction hypothesis,

$$\psi \vdash^{nar}_{AX} \langle\emptyset,h''\rangle.$$

If the directed paramodulation step from φ to $\langle\psi,h'\rangle$ were not a narrowing step, then

$$\psi = \varphi'[c[u'[g]/x]/y] \cup \vartheta[g] \quad \text{and} \quad h' = \{c[u[g]/x]/y\}$$

for some φ' with $\varphi'[z/y] = \varphi$, $u \equiv u' \Leftarrow \vartheta \in$ AX and some c,g,x,y,z. By Prop. 4.1, $\psi \vdash_{AX} \langle\emptyset,h''\rangle$ implies $\vartheta[g][h''] \subseteq \psi[h''] \vdash_{AX} \emptyset$. Hence $u[g][h''] \longrightarrow_{AX} u'[g][h'']$, in contrast to the assumption that f and thus $h'[h'']$ are AX-reduced.

Therefore, the step from φ to $\langle\psi,h'\rangle$ must be a narrowing step, and we conclude

$$\gamma \vdash^{nar}_{AX} \langle\varphi,h\rangle \vdash^{nar}_{AX} \langle\psi,h[h']\rangle \vdash^{nar}_{AX} \langle\emptyset,h[h'][h'']\rangle = \langle\emptyset,f|X_{goals}\rangle.$$

"if": Since narrowing expansions are directed expansions, the conjecture follows from Thm. 6.5(4). ∎

The completeness result for most general solving expansions (cf. Thm. 6.4) holds true for $\vdash^{nar}_{AX}$ as well as for $\vdash^{sol}_{AX}$.

Several refinements of the narrowing rule have been proposed: *normal* or *reduced narrowing* ([Fay79]), which combines narrowing with strategic expansion (cf. Sect. 7.1); *basic narrowing* ([Hul80]), which avoids unnecessary redices; *lazy narrowing* ([Red85], [You88]), which applies the rule only to decomposed axioms (cf. Sect. 2.6); narrowing strategies based on redex selection functions ([Pad87], [Ech88]); and *optimized narrowing*, which combines narrowing with other rules for speeding up the expansion process ([Huß85]). Conditions for their completeness are given in [Pad88a].

Let us now answer the question asked at the end of Sect. 5.4: how can unsolvable goals be detected and deleted from inductive expansions? By the previous theorem, a goal γ can be removed if neither unification nor resolution nor narrowing *upon AX* is applicable to γ, provided that (SIG,AX) is ground confluent and weakly terminating (cf. Sect. 6.4).

Corollary 7.3 *Let (SIG,AX) be ground confluent and weakly terminating and let γ be a nonempty goal that is solvable w.r.t. AX. Then there is a narrowing expansion of γ into $\langle\emptyset,g\rangle$ for some g.*

Proof. Suppose that some $f \in GS$ solves γ w.r.t. AX. By assumption, there is an AX-reduced form g of f. Since g is AX-equivalent to f, g solves γ as well. Hence by Thm. 7.2, $\gamma \vdash^{nar}_{AX} \langle\emptyset, g|X_{goals}\rangle$. ∎

Hence, if the assumptions of Cor. 7.3 are satisfied, the calculus of inductive expansion (cf. Sect. 5.2) can be extended by the following inference rule, which deletes an unsolvable goal:

Failure rule

$$\frac{\{\gamma \cup \varphi\}}{\text{FAIL}} \qquad \text{there is no successful narrowing expansion of } \varphi$$

Example 7.4 Using the failure rule, we show that $\gamma = \{x<y,\ x\geq y\}$ is unsolvable w.r.t. NSB (cf. Ex. 1.1). Up to a renaming of variables and the selected computation rule (cf. Chapter 4), each most general narrowing expansion of γ begins with

$$\gamma \vdash^{nar}_{\{LT;GE\}} \{x+1\leq y,\ y\leq x\} \vdash^{nar}_{\{LE2\}} \langle\{x\leq z,\ z+1\leq x\},\ z+1/y\rangle \qquad \text{(NAR1)}$$

or with

$$\gamma \vdash^{nar}_{\{LT;GE\}} \{x+1 \le y,\ y \le x\} \vdash^{nar}_{\{LE1\}} \langle\{x+1 \le 0\},\ 0/y\rangle \qquad \text{(NAR2)}$$

or with

$$\gamma \vdash^{nar}_{\{LT;GE\}} \{x+1 \le y,\ y \le x\} \vdash^{nar}_{\{LE2\}} \langle\{x'+1+1 \le z+1,\ z \le x'\},\ z+1/y\rangle$$

$$\vdash^{nar}_{\{LE2\}} \langle\{x'+1 \le z,\ z \le x'\},\ z+1/y\rangle. \qquad \text{(NAR3)}$$

NAR1 and NAR3 lead to circular expansions: the second and the third or, respectively the fourth, goal agree up to a renaming of variables. NAR2 has no further narrowing redices. Hence there is no successful narrowing expansion.

Look at the proof of Thm. 7.2: a successful directed expansion is a narrowing expansion if the computed solution is AX-reduced. Since NSB' is strongly terminating, each ground solution has an AX-reduced form. Hence there is no successful directed expansion of γ because, as shown above, there is no successful narrowing expansion of γ. Therefore, ground instances of γ are not NSB'-convergent (cf. Ex. 6.12). In Exs. 6.9 and 6.22 we have shown that NSB' is strongly terminating and ground confluent. Thus by Cor. 7.3, γ is unsolvable w.r.t. NSB'. ∎

The failure rule serves for *refuting* a goal. For *proving* a conjecture by inductive expansion, however, it would be totally ineffective to restrict the inference rules to resolution and narrowing upon axioms. In general, this may lead to infinitely many subexpansions because essential induction hypotheses are no longer generated (cf. Ex. 5.13) or applied (cf. Ex. 5.9). Moreover, proving $\gamma \Leftarrow \delta$ means expanding γ into δ, but for achieving δ, we may have to apply inverses of axioms even if δ is only a small guard (cf. Sects. 5.3 and 5.5). And not only inverses of axioms but also a number of further lemmas may be convenient for obtaining a hierarchical and thus *comprehensible* proof.

7.3 Constructor criteria

A ground confluent specification entails two criteria for a set of terms to be a set of constructors (cf. Sect. 2.3).

Definition A set C of terms is *ground distinguishable* if for all $c,d \in C$ and $f,g \in GS$, $c[f] = d[g]$ implies $c = d$. C is *linear* if for all $c \in C$, each variable occurs at most once in c. ∎

Corollary 7.5 (Constructor criteria based on ground confluence) *Let (SIG,AX) be ground confluent and C be a ground distinguishable set of terms such that for all* c $\in$ C *and* $t \equiv t' \Leftarrow \gamma \in$ *AX,* t *does not overlap* c.

C is a set of constructors if C is linear or if (SIG,AX) is weakly terminating (cf. Sect. 6.4).

Proof. Let c,d $\in$ C and f,g $\in$ GS such that c[f] and d[g] are AX-equivalent. By Thm. 6.5(1) and Prop. 6.1(2), c[f] and d[g] have a common AX-reduct t. Since left-hand sides of conditional equations of AX do not overlap elements of C, there are linear terms c',d' and f',g' $\in$ GS such that for some h : $X \longrightarrow X$, c'[h] = c, d'[h] = d, $h[f] \longrightarrow_{AX}^{*} f'$, $h[g] \longrightarrow_{AX}^{*} g'$ and c'[f'] = t = d'[g'].

If C is linear, then, w.l.o.g., h = id^X and thus c[f'] = t = d[g']. Hence c = d because C is ground distinguishable. But then f'|var(c) = g'|var(c) and thus f'|var(c) is a common AX-reduct of f|var(c) and g|var(c). Therefore, fx $\equiv_{AX}$ gx for all x $\in$ var(c).

If (SIG,AX) is weakly terminating, then f and g have AX-reduced forms f" and g" respectively. Ground confluence implies $f' \longrightarrow_{AX}^{*} h[f"]$ and $g' \longrightarrow_{AX}^{*} h[g"]$. Hence

$$t \longrightarrow_{AX}^{*} c'[h][f"] = c[f"] \quad \text{and} \quad t \longrightarrow_{AX}^{*} d'[h][g"] = d[g"].$$

Again, ground confluence implies $c[f"] \longrightarrow_{AX}^{*} t'$ and $d[g"] \longrightarrow_{AX}^{*} t'$ for some t'. Since f" and g" are AX-reduced and left-hand sides of conditional equations of AX do not overlap elements of C, c[f"] = d[g"]. Hence c = d because C is ground distinguishable. Therefore, f"|var(c) = g"|var(c) and thus f"|var(c) is a common AX-reduct of f|var(c) and g|var(c). Again, fx $\equiv_{AX}$ gx for all x $\in$ var(c). ∎

Example 7.6 Let (SIG,AX) = NSB' (cf. Ex. 6.9). By Ex. 6.22, (SIG,AX) is ground confluent. Of course, C = {0, x+1, (x,y), ε, x&s} is linear and ground distinguishable. Since left-hand sides of conditional equations of NSB' do not overlap elements of C, we conclude from Cor. 7.5 that C is a set of constructors. ∎

Corollary 7.5 provides a simple criterion for *Boolean consistency*. If (SIG,AX) includes constants *true* and *false* together with Boolean functions, the question arises whether *true* and *false* are AX-inequivalent, in other words, whether *{true,false}* is a set of constructors.

Corollary 7.7 *Suppose that (SIG,AX) is ground confluent and for all* $t \equiv t' \Leftarrow \gamma \in$ *AX,* t $\notin$ {true,false}. *Then* true *and* false *are not AX-equivalent.*

Proof. Let C = {*true,false*}. Since C is a set of ground terms, C is, trivially, ground distinguishable and linear, and $c \in C$ can be overlapped by a term t only if t = c. Hence by Cor. 7.5, C is a set of constructors. ∎

Corollary 7.5 allows us to identify constructor-based clause sets (cf. Sect. 2.3). Moreover, it is useful for recognizing unsolvable goals in cases where the failure rule does not apply. Since equations between instances of different constructors are unsolvable, the inductive expansion calculus can be extended by a further rule that deletes unsolvable goals:

Clash rule

$$\frac{\gamma \cup \{c[f] \equiv d[g]\}}{\text{FAIL}} \qquad c \text{ and } d \text{ belong to a set of constructors, } c \neq d$$

Of course, the clash rule is applicable only if previous expansion steps have generated equations between constructor instances. This is a further argument for decomposing lemmas by adding equations to their premises (cf. Sect. 2.6).

It may consume a lot of time to check every subgoal for the applicability of the failure rule or the clash rule. These costs can be reduced considerably by taking into account that some subexpansions are more "failure-prone" than others. For instance, if two lemmas $q \Leftarrow \delta$ and $q' \Leftarrow \delta'$ are applicable to a solvable atom p, then δ and δ' often contradict each other, i.e., $\delta \cup \delta'$ is unsolvable. Moreover, if p is part of a goal γ that already contains δ, then the assumption that γ is solvable implies that δ' is unsolvable. Consequently, the application of $q' \Leftarrow \delta'$ to γ is useless because it leads to an unsolvable goal.

Hence, among several lemmas that are applicable to p, those where not only the conclusion but also (part of) the premise is unifiable with p should be preferred . Only if no premise matches, must the first lemma to be applied be guessed. Then it is in fact reasonable to check the resulting goal immediately for unsolvability by means of the failure rule or the clash rule.

7.4 Proof by consistency

While inductive expansion employs induction rules and thus follows traditional theorem proving, *inductive completion* (cf., e.g., [HH82], [JKo86], [KM87], [Fri89], [Küc89]) avoids explicit induction steps by following a procedure that turns the original conjecture into a consistency statement (cf.

Sect. 3.4). This means that a clause set CS is proved by adding CS to the axioms of (SIG,AX) and checking the consistency of (SIG,AX∪CS) w.r.t. (SIG,AX). Whenever this cannot be proved directly, inductive completion starts a stepwise transformation of AX∪CS into a sequence of inductively equivalent axiom sets $R_1,R_2,...$ until, hopefully, some R_n satisfies the given consistency criteria.

Hence the basic fact behind *proof by consistency* is the equivalence between inductive validity of CS w.r.t. AX and consistency of (SIG,AX∪CS) w.r.t. (SIG,AX). This is an immediate consequence of the following model-theoretic characterization of inductive validity.

Let CS be a set of Horn clauses.

Lemma 7.8 (cf. Sect. 3.1) *CS is inductively valid w.r.t. AX iff Ini(SIG,AX) is isomorphic to Ini(SIG,AX∪CS).*

Proof. "only if": Let A = Ini(SIG,AX) and CS ⊆ ITh(AX). Then A satisfies AX∪CS. Let B be a SIG-model of AX∪CS. By Thm. 3.8, applied to AX, there is a unique homomorphism ini^B from A to B. Hence by Thm. 3.8, applied to AX∪CS, A is isomorphic to the initial (SIG,AX∪CS)-structure.

"if": Suppose that A = Ini(SIG,AX) is isomorphic to Ini(SIG,AX∪CS). Then A satisfies CS. Hence CS ⊆ ITh(AX). ∎

Lemma 7.9 (Proof by consistency) *CS is inductively valid w.r.t. AX iff (SIG,AX∪CS) is consistent w.r.t. (SIG,AX).*

Proof. "if": Let p⇐γ ∈ CS and f ∈ GS solve γ w.r.t. AX. Then p[f] is AX∪CS-valid and thus AX-valid because (SIG,AX∪CS) is consistent w.r.t. (SIG,AX).

"only if": Let γ be an AX∪CS-valid ground goal. In particular, γ is inductively valid w.r.t. AX∪CS and thus valid in B = Ini(SIG,AX∪CS). By Lemma 7.8, B is isomorphic to A = Ini(SIG,AX). Hence A satisfies γ as well. Therefore, γ is an inductive AX-theorem and thus AX-valid. ∎

In terms of the General Assumption in Sect. 6.4, the base specification (BSIG,BASE) is now given by (SIG,AX), while the whole specification is (SIG,AX∪CS). Since both specifications have the same signature, we may specialize the definition of reductive consistency (cf. Sect. 6.4) as follows:

Definition AX∪CS is *reductively consistent w.r.t. AX* if all AX∪CS-convergent ground goals are AX-convergent. ∎

Lemma 6.17 yields the following refinement of Lemma 7.9:

Lemma 7.10 (Inductive validity and reductive consistency)

(1) Let (SIG,AX∪CS) be ground confluent. If AX∪CS is reductively consistent w.r.t. AX, then CS ⊆ ITh(AX).

(2) Let (SIG,AX) be ground confluent. If CS ⊆ ITh(AX), then (SIG,AX∪CS) is reductively consistent w.r.t. AX. ▮

Following the way Lemma 6.17 is turned into a reduction-oriented consistency criterion (Cor. 6.19), we infer an inductive validity criterion from Lemma 7.10. For this purpose, the notion of ground reducibility (cf. Sect. 6.4) is specialized to the case *SIG* = *BSIG*:

Definition CS is *ground reducible w.r.t. AX* if for all $t \equiv t' \Leftarrow \gamma \in CS^{\perp}$ and $f \in$ GS such that $\gamma[f]$ is AX∪CS-convergent, $t[f]$ is not AX-reduced w.r.t. AX∪CS. ▮

Lemma 7.11 (Inductive validity and ground reducibility)[1]

(1) Suppose that (SIG,AX∪CS) is strongly terminating and ground confluent. If CS is ground reducible w.r.t. AX, then CS ⊆ ITh(AX).

(2) Suppose that (SIG,AX∪CS) is strongly terminating and (SIG,AX) is ground confluent. If CS ⊆ ITh(AX), then CS is ground reducible w.r.t. AX.

Proof. (1) In the terms of Section 6.4, let the base specification (BSIG,BASE) be given by (SIG,AX) and the extension by (SIG,AX∪CS). Then conditions 6.19(1), (2) are assumed here as well, while 6.19(3) holds trivially. Hence by Cor. 6.19, (SIG,AX∪CS) is consistent w.r.t. AX and thus by Lemma 7.9, CS ⊆ ITh(AX).

(2) Assume that CS ⊆ ITh(AX) is not ground reducible w.r.t. AX. Then for some $t \equiv t' \Leftarrow \gamma \in CS^{\perp}$ and $f \in$ GS, $\gamma[f]$ is AX∪CS-convergent, but $t[f]$ is AX-reduced w.r.t. AX∪CS. By Lemma 7.10(2), (SIG,AX∪CS) is reductively consistent w.r.t. AX. Hence $\gamma[f] \vdash_{AX \cup CS} \emptyset$ implies $\gamma[f] \vdash_{AX} \emptyset$. Since (SIG,AX) is ground confluent, $\gamma[f]$ is strongly AX-convergent.

By Thm. 6.5(3), $t \equiv t' \Leftarrow \gamma$ and $t \Leftarrow \gamma$ respectively are reductively valid w.r.t. AX. Hence $(t \equiv t')[f]$ and $t[f]$ respectively are AX-convergent. If $t' = \perp$, then t is an atom and $t[f] \vdash_{AX} \emptyset$ contradicts the AX-reducedness of $t[f]$. Otherwise $t[f]$ and $t'[f]$ would have a common AX-reduct. Hence $t'[f] \longrightarrow_{AX}^{*} t[f]$ because $t[f]$ is AX-reduced. But $\gamma[f] \vdash_{AX \cup CS} \emptyset$ implies $t[f] \longrightarrow_{AX \cup CS} t'[f]$ and thus $t[f] \longrightarrow_{AX \cup CS}^{+} t[f]$, in contrast to the assumption that (SIG,AX∪CS) is strongly terminating. ▮

[1]For unconditional equational specifications, this result agrees with [JKo86], Thm. 1.

Lemma 7.11(1) justifies inductive completion: starting out from an AX-reduction ordering, let us try to prove that

(1) CS is decreasing w.r.t. that ordering (cf. Sect. 6.2),

(2) for all elements <p,cc> of an (AX∪CS)-complete set of reduction ambiguities, cc is sub-p-reductively valid w.r.t. AX∪CS (cf. Sect. 6.3),

(3) CS is ground reducible w.r.t. AX.

This procedure is rather naive because, in step (2), it does not consider the difference between AX and CS. While AX consists of more or less abstract algorithms and thus tends to be terminating and confluent, CS comprises requirements to the data type specified by AX. In contrast to AX, CS may induce a great number of reduction ambiguities and need not be decreasing w.r.t. the AX-reduction ordering. Hence inductive completion attempts to achieve (1)-(3) by transforming (SIG,AX∪CS) stepwise into a strongly terminating and ground confluent specification (SIG,AX'∪CS') such that CS' includes CS and is ground reducible w.r.t. AX', while AX' is a set of inductive AX-theorems. By Lemma 7.11(1), CS' ⊆ ITh(AX') and thus CS ⊆ ITh(AX).

Besides neglecting the difference between axioms and theorems, two concerns are mixed up in the above procedure: proving theorems on the one hand and checking conditions such as (1)-(3), which ensure that the proof procedure works correctly. This often leads to incomprehensible proofs because a simultaneous transformation of AX and CS according to (1)-(3) is less goal-directed than an expansion of CS upon AX.

Let us keep to Lemma 7.11, but derive from it a more sophisticated proof procedure that retains the goal-directedness of inductive expansion. More precisely, we aim at a characterization of (1)-(3) that is established automatically when CS is expanded. The main idea is to combine and simplify (2) and (3).

Definition CS is *inductively convergent w.r.t. AX* if for all $t \equiv t' \Leftarrow \gamma \in CS^{\perp}$ and $f \in GS$ such that $\gamma[f]$ is AX-convergent and strongly AX∪CS-convergent and (AX,AX∪CS) is subconfluent at $t[f]$ (cf. Sect. 6.3), the following conditions hold true:

- If $t' \neq \perp$, then there is a term reduction $t[f] \longrightarrow_{AX}{}^{+} u$ such that $u \equiv t'[f]$ is AX∪CS-convergent.
- If $t' = \perp$, then $t[f]$ is not AX-reduced w.r.t. AX∪CS. ∎

In fact, inductive convergence allows us to infer the ground confluence of (SIG,AX∪CS) from that of (SIG,AX):

Theorem 7.12 (Confluence and inductive convergence) *Suppose that (SIG,AX) is ground confluent and (SIG,AX∪CS) is strongly terminating.*

(1) If CS is inductively convergent w.r.t. AX, then (SIG,AX∪CS) is ground confluent and AX∪CS is reductively consistent w.r.t. AX.

(2) If CS is inductively valid and ground reducible w.r.t. AX, then CS is inductively convergent w.r.t. AX.

Proof. (1) Suppose that CS is inductively convergent w.r.t. AX. Let p be an AX∪CS-convergent ground atom. We will show $p \vdash_{AX} \emptyset$ and $p \longrightarrow \vdash_{AX\cup CS} \emptyset$ by induction on p along the given AX∪CS-reduction ordering >.

Let $p \longrightarrow_{AX\cup CS} q \longrightarrow_{AX\cup CS}{}^{*} p'$ be a term reduction. Then

$$p = d[v_0[g]/x] \quad \text{and} \quad q = d[v_1[g]/x]$$

for some d,x,g and $v_0 \equiv v_1 \Leftarrow \vartheta \in$ AX∪CS, $\vartheta[g] \vdash_{AX\cup CS} \emptyset$ and $p > \vartheta[g]$. Suppose that q is strongly AX∪CS-convergent. Then by induction hypothesis, $p' \vdash_{AX} \emptyset$. Hence it remains to prove $p \vdash_{AX} \emptyset$ and $q \vdash_{AX\cup CS} \emptyset$.

Since $p \vdash_{AX\cup CS} \emptyset$, there is a successful goal reduction $\gamma_1,\ldots,\gamma_n$ of p. By induction hypothesis, $\vartheta[g] \cup \gamma_2$ is AX-convergent and strongly AX∪CS-convergent and (AX,AX∪CS) is subconfluent at $v_0[g]$.

Case 1. $p \vdash_{AX} \gamma_2$. Then $\gamma_2 \vdash_{AX} \emptyset$ implies $p \vdash_{AX} \emptyset$.

Case 1.1. $v_0 \equiv v_1 \Leftarrow \vartheta \in$ AX. Then $p \longrightarrow_{AX} q$ and thus $q \vdash_{AX} \emptyset$ because $p \vdash_{AX} \emptyset$ and (SIG,AX) is ground confluent.

Case 1.2. $v_0 \equiv v_1 \Leftarrow \vartheta \in$ CS. Since CS is inductively convergent w.r.t. AX, there is a term reduction $v_0[g] \longrightarrow_{AX}{}^{+} u$ such that $u \equiv v_1[g]$ is AX∪CS-convergent. Since (SIG,AX) is ground confluent, $p \vdash_{AX} \emptyset$ implies $d[u/x] \vdash_{AX} \emptyset$. Since $p > d[u/x]$, the induction hypothesis implies $d[u/x] \longrightarrow \vdash_{AX\cup CS} \emptyset$ and thus, by Lemma 6.3, $q = d[v_1[g]/x]$ is AX∪CS-convergent.

Case 2. $p \vdash_{CS} \gamma_2$.

Case 2.1. γ_2 is obtained from p by resolution. Then $p = p_0[f]$ and $\gamma_2 = \gamma[f] \vdash_{AX\cup CS} \emptyset$ for some f and $p_0 \Leftarrow \gamma \in$ CS. By induction hypothesis, γ_2 is AX-convergent and strongly AX∪CS-convergent and $v_0[g]$ is subconfluent at p. Since CS is inductively convergent w.r.t. AX, there is a goal reduction $p_0[g] \vdash_{AX} \delta$ such that δ is AX∪CS-convergent. $p > \delta$ implies $\delta \vdash_{AX} \emptyset$ and thus $p \vdash_{AX} \emptyset$.

Case 2.1.1. $v_0 \equiv v_1 \Leftarrow \vartheta \in$ AX. Then $p \longrightarrow_{AX} q$ and thus $q \vdash_{AX} \emptyset$ because $p \vdash_{AX} \emptyset$ and (SIG,AX) is ground confluent.

Case 2.1.2. $v_0 \equiv v_1 \Leftarrow \vartheta \in$ CS. As in Case 1.2 we obtain $q \vdash_{AX\cup CS} \emptyset$.

Case 2.2. γ_2 is obtained from p by reduction. Then there is an AX∪CS-convergent atom q' such that $p \longrightarrow_{AX\cup CS} q' \vdash_{AX\cup CS} \emptyset$,

$$p = c[u_0[f]/x] \quad \text{and} \quad q' = c[u_1[f]/x]$$

for some c,x,f and $u_0 \equiv u_1 \Leftarrow \gamma \in$ CS, $\gamma[f] \vdash_{AX\cup CS} \emptyset$ and $p > \{q'\} \cup \gamma[f]$. By induction hypothesis, $\{q'\} \cup \gamma[f]$ is AX-convergent and strongly AX∪CS-convergent and (AX,AX∪CS) is subconfluent at $u_0[f]$. Since CS is inductively convergent w.r.t. AX, there is a term reduction $u_0[f] \longrightarrow_{AX}{}^{+} u$ such that $u \equiv u_1[f]$ is AX∪CS-convergent.

By Lemma 6.3, $c[u/x]$ is AX∪CS-convergent. Since $p > c[u/x]$, the induction hypothesis implies $c[u/x] \vdash_{AX} \emptyset$ and $c[u/x] \longrightarrow\vdash_{AX\cup CS} \emptyset$. Hence $p \longrightarrow_{AX}{}^{+} c[u/x] \vdash_{AX} \emptyset$ implies $p \vdash_{AX} \emptyset$.

Case 2.2.1. $v_0 \equiv v_1 \Leftarrow \vartheta \in$ AX. Then $p \longrightarrow_{AX} q$. Since $p \longrightarrow_{AX}{}^{+} c[u/x]$ and (SIG,AX) is ground confluent, there are term reductions $q \longrightarrow_{AX}{}^{*} r$ and $c[u/x] \longrightarrow_{AX}{}^{*} r$. Hence $r \vdash_{AX\cup CS} \emptyset$ and thus $q \vdash_{AX\cup CS} \emptyset$.

Case 2.2.2. $v_0 \equiv v_1 \Leftarrow \vartheta \in$ CS. Since CS is inductively convergent w.r.t. AX, there is a term reduction $v_0[g] \longrightarrow_{AX}{}^{+} u'$ such that $u' \equiv v_1[g]$ is AX∪CS-convergent.

Since (SIG,AX) is ground confluent, there are term reductions $c[u/x] \longrightarrow_{AX}{}^{*} r$ and $d[u'/x] \longrightarrow_{AX}{}^{*} r$. Hence $r \vdash_{AX\cup CS} \emptyset$ and thus $d[u'/x] \vdash_{AX\cup CS} \emptyset$. Since $p > d[u'/x]$, the induction hypothesis implies $d[u'/x] \longrightarrow\vdash_{AX\cup CS} \emptyset$. Hence by Lemma 6.3, $q = d[v_1[g]/x]$ is AX∪CS-convergent.

(2) Suppose that CS is inductively valid and ground reducible w.r.t. AX. Let $t \equiv t' \Leftarrow \gamma \in$ CS and $f \in$ GS such that $\gamma[f]$ is AX-convergent and strongly AX∪CS-convergent and (AX,AX∪CS) is subconfluent at $t[f]$.

Since CS is ground reducible w.r.t. AX, there is a conditional term reduction $t[f] \longrightarrow_{AX} u \Leftarrow \psi$ such that ψ is AX∪CS-convergent. Since (AX,AX∪CS) is subconfluent at $t[f]$, $t[f] > \psi$ implies $\psi \vdash_{AX} \emptyset$. Hence $t[f] \longrightarrow_{AX} u$. Moreover, $\gamma[f]$ is strongly AX-convergent because (SIG,AX) is ground confluent. Hence by Thm. 6.5(3), $t[f] \equiv t'[f]$ is strongly AX-convergent as well. Therefore $u \equiv t'[f]$ is AX-convergent and we conclude that $t \equiv t' \Leftarrow \gamma$ is inductively convergent w.r.t. AX. ∎

Theorem 7.12 can be strengthened as follows.

Theorem 7.13 (Inductive validity and inductive convergence) *Suppose that (SIG,AX) is ground confluent and (SIG,AX∪CS) is strongly terminating.*

CS ⊆ ITh(AX) iff CS is inductively convergent w.r.t. AX.

Proof. "if": By Thm. 7.12(1), (SIG,AX∪CS) is ground confluent and AX∪CS is reductively consistent w.r.t. AX. Hence AX∪CS-convergent ground goals are AX-convergent and strongly AX∪CS-convergent. In particular, (AX,AX∪CS) is subconfluent at all ground goals. Therefore, CS is ground reducible because CS is inductively convergent. Hence by Lemma 7.11(1), CS ⊆ ITh(AX).

"only if": By Lemma 7.11(2), CS is ground reducible. Hence by Thm. 7.12(2), CS is inductively convergent. ∎

Inductive convergence is equivalent to inductive validity under the assumptions that (SIG,AX) is ground confluent and, using Thm. 6.7(2), that AX∪CS is decreasing w.r.t. an AX∪CS-reduction ordering. So what do we benefit from the characterization of inductive validity given by Thm. 7.13? A proof of CS by inductive convergence may involve applications of AX *and* CS, while a proof of inductive (or reductive) validity uses only AX.

Let us proceed as in the case of critical clause convergence (cf. Sect. 6.3) and reduce the infinite set of conjectures associated with a proof by inductive convergence to a finite set. In contrast with the set of reduction ambiguities, this set of conjectures varies according to the initial AX-reductions $t[f] \longrightarrow_{AX} u$ ($t[f] \vdash_{AX} \varphi$, resp.).

The set can be restricted to AX-reduced substitutions:

Let $t \equiv t' \Leftarrow \gamma \in CS^{\perp}$ such that $\gamma[f]$ is strongly AX∪CS-convergent and fx is not AX-reduced for some $x \in var(t)$. Then $fx \longrightarrow_{AX} v$ for some v. Let $g = \{v/x\}+f|(X-\{x\})$. Hence $\gamma[g]$ is AX∪CS-convergent and thus by Lemma 6.4, $t[g] \equiv t'[g]$ is AX∪CS-convergent. Therefore,

- $t[f] \longrightarrow_{AX} t[g]$ and $t[g] \equiv t'[f] \vdash_{AX\cup CS} \emptyset$ if $t' \neq \perp$,
- $t[f] \vdash_{AX} t[g] \vdash_{AX\cup CS} \emptyset$ if $t' = \perp$.

If, on the other hand, f is AX-reduced, then $t \equiv t' \Leftarrow \gamma \in CS^{\perp}$ and a term reduction $t[f] \longrightarrow_{AX} u$ induce the reduction ambiguity $<t[f], u \equiv t'[f] \Leftarrow \gamma[f]>$. In the equational case, sets of critical clauses $u \equiv t'[f]$ whose convergence is sufficient for proving the inductive validity of $t \equiv t'$ have been characterized by *complete superposition occurrences* (cf. [Fri89]) or *inductively complete sets of term positions* (cf. [Küc89]). The Horn clause approach admits a more general criterion:

Lemma 7.14 (Criterion for inductive convergence) *CS is inductively convergent w.r.t. AX if for each* $t \equiv t' \Leftarrow \gamma \in CS^{\perp}$ *there is a term set (goal set, resp.) GS =* $\{u_1,\ldots,u_n\}$ *such that*

(1) *for all* $1 \le i \le n$, $t \longrightarrow_{AX}{}^{+} u_i$ *if* $t' \neq \bot$, $t \vdash_{AX} u_i$ *if* $t' = \bot$,

(2) $\{u_1 \equiv t', \ldots, u_n \equiv t'\} \vdash^{t}_{AX;AX \cup CS} \{\gamma\}$.

Proof. Let $c = t \equiv t' \Leftarrow \gamma \in CS^{\bot}$ and $f \in GS$ such that $\gamma[f]$ is AX-convergent and strongly AX∪CS-convergent and (AX,AX∪CS) is subconfluent at $t[f]$. Let X_{in} = var(c). By (2) and Thm. 6.15, $\exists X_{out} u_1 \equiv t' \vee \ldots \vee \exists X_{out} u_n \equiv t' \Leftarrow \gamma \in$ t-RTh(AX,AX∪CS). Hence there are $1 \le i \le n$ and $g \in GS$ such that $(u_i \equiv t')[g]$ is AX-convergent and strongly AX∪CS-convergent and $g_{in} = f_{in}$.

If $t' \neq \bot$, then by (1), $t[f] = t[g] \longrightarrow_{AX}{}^{+} u_i[h]$ for some AX-reduct h of g.

If $t' = \bot$, then by (1), $t[f] = t[g] \vdash_{AX} u_i[h]$ for some AX-reduct h of g.

Since $u_i[g] \equiv t'[f]$ is strongly AX∪CS-convergent, $u_i[h] \equiv t'[f]$ is AX∪CS-convergent. ∎

Definition A proof of $c = t \equiv t' \Leftarrow \gamma \in CS^{\bot}$ that establishes (1) and (2) is called a *reductive expansion of c upon (AX,CS).* ∎

Theorem 7.15 (Soundness of reductive expansions) *Suppose that (SIG,AX) is ground confluent and (SIG,AX∪CS) is strongly terminating.*

CS ⊆ ITh(AX) and (SIG,AX∪CS) is ground confluent if there is a reductive expansion of each c ∈ CS upon (AX,CS).

Proof. Combine Theorems 7.12(1) and 7.13 with Lemma 7.14. ∎

The following criteria for subreductive theorems yield lemmas that may be applied in part (2) of a reductive expansion.

Lemma 7.16 (Basic criteria for subreductive validity w.r.t. (AX,AX∪CS)) *Let p be a term or an atom and* $L = \exists X_1 \gamma_1 \vee \ldots \vee \exists X_n \gamma_n \Leftarrow \delta$ *such that for all* $1 \le i \le n$, γ_i *is p-bounded w.r.t. (δ,AX). L is sub-p-reductively valid w.r.t. (AX,AX∪CS) if*

(1) $L \in (AX \cup CS[h])^{sym}$ *for some substitution h or*

(2) $\gamma_1 \vdash_{AX \cup CS} \delta$ *or*

(3) *L is inductively valid w.r.t. AX and (SIG,AX) is ground confluent.*

Proof. Let $f \in GS$ such that (AX,AX∪CS) is subconfluent at $p[f]$ and $\delta[f]$ is AX-convergent and strongly AX∪CS-convergent.

(1) Let $L \in (AX \cup CS[h])^{sym}$ for some h. By Lemma 6.4, $\gamma_1[f] \vdash_{AX \cup CS} \emptyset$. By assumption, $p[f] > \gamma_1[f]$. Hence $\gamma_1[f]$ is AX-convergent and strongly AX∪CS-convergent.

(2) Let $\gamma_1 \vdash_{AX \cup CS} \delta$. Then $\gamma_1[f] \vdash_{AX \cup CS} \delta[g]$ for some AX-reduct g of f. Hence $\delta[g]$ and thus $\gamma_1[f]$ are AX∪CS-convergent. By assumption, $p[f] > \gamma_1[f]$. Hence $\gamma_1[f]$ is AX-convergent and strongly AX∪CS-convergent.

If (3) holds true, then by Lemma 6.20(1), L ∈ p-RTh(AX,AX∪CS). ∎

In particular, Thm. 7.16(3) allows us to use arbitrary inductive AX-theorems as lemmas in part (2) of a reductive expansion.

Example 7.17 (Associativity) Let (SIG,AX) = NSB' (cf. Ex. 6.9) and

$$c \;=\; (x+y)+z \equiv x+(y+z).$$

Let us check the assumptions of Thm. 7.15. By Ex. 6.22, (SIG,AX) is ground confluent. By Ex. 6.9, (SIG,AX) is strongly terminating. Since (SIG,AX∪{c}) must also be strongly terminating, let us use Thm. 6.7 and look for an expansion of the form

$$(x+y)+z >> x+(y+z) \;\vdash_{path}\; \varphi \;\vdash^{ind}_{AX;\varphi}\; \emptyset.$$

Unfortunately, such an expansion does not exist because the rules of the path calculus (cf. Sect. 6.2) only admit $\varphi = \{x+y \equiv x,\ z \equiv y+z\}$ or $\varphi = \{(x+y,z) >_d (x,y+z)\}$, which is not inductively valid. Hence we add the function symbol $F : nat,nat \longrightarrow nat$ to SIG and the axiom $F(x,y) \equiv x+y$ to AX and modify the conjecture c into the inductively equivalent equation

$$c' \;=\; F(x+y,z) \equiv x+(y+z).$$

Extend $\geq_{SIG}$ by {(F,G) | G ∈ SIG-{F}} and let GS' be the set of all substitutions into ground terms over SIG-{F}.

Let $t = F(x+y,z)$. Then AX∪{c'} is decreasing w.r.t. the path ordering for (GS', $\geq_{SIG}$, $>_d$) and all atoms of the form $p[F(x+y,k)/x]$ with p ∈ GAt(SIG-{F}) are t-bounded w.r.t. ($z \equiv k+1$,AX):

$$\begin{array}{lll} t >> p[F(x+y,k)/x] & \vdash_{path} & F(x+y,z) >> F(x+y,k) \\ & \vdash_{path} & \{(x+y,z) >_d (x+y,k)\},\ F(x+y,z) >> \{x+y,\ k\} \\ & \vdash_{path} & \{(x+y,z) >_d (x+y,k)\},\ F(x+y,z) >> k \\ & \vdash_{path} & \{(x+y,z) >_d (x+y,k)\} \\ & \vdash^{pro}_{AX} & \{z > k\} \;\;\vdash^{pro}_{AX}\;\; \{z \equiv k+1\}. \end{array} \qquad \text{(PATH)}$$

Hence we obtain the following reductive expansion of c':

(1) $F(x+y,z) \longrightarrow_{AX} (x+y)+z$

(2) $(x+y)+z \equiv x+(y+z) \vdash^{t}_{AX} \qquad \{\{x+y \equiv x+(y+0),\ z \equiv 0\},$

$$
\begin{array}{ll}
& \{((x+y)+k)+1 \equiv x+(y+(k+1)),\ z \equiv k+1\}\} \\
\vdash^{t}_{AX} & \{\{x+y \equiv x+y,\ z \equiv 0\}, \\
& \{((x+y)+k)+1 \equiv x+((y+k)+1),\ z \equiv k+1\}\} \\
\vdash^{t}_{AX} & \{\{z \equiv 0\},\ \{((x+y)+k)+1 \equiv (x+(y+k))+1,\ z \equiv k+1\}\} \\
\vdash^{t}_{AX} & \{\{z \equiv 0\},\ \{F(x+y,k)+1 \equiv (x+(y+k))+1,\ z \equiv k+1\}\} \\
\vdash^{t}_{AX;AX\cup\{c'\}} & \{\{z \equiv 0\},\ \{(x+(y+k))+1 \equiv (x+(y+k))+1,\ z \equiv k+1\}\} \\
\vdash^{t}_{AX} & \{\{z \equiv 0\},\ \{z \equiv k+1\}\} \\
\vdash^{t}_{AX} & \emptyset. \qquad\qquad (EXP)
\end{array}
$$

By Lemma 7.16, the lemmas

$$
\begin{array}{l}
(x+y)+k \equiv F(x+y,k) \ \Leftarrow\ z \equiv k+1 \\
F(x+y,k) \equiv x+(y+k) \ \Leftarrow\ z \equiv k+1 \\
z \equiv 0 \ \vee\ \exists\{k\}\ z \equiv k+1.
\end{array}
$$

used in EXP are sub-t-reductively valid w.r.t. (AX,AX∪{c'}). By PATH, all goals of EXP are t-bounded w.r.t. ($z \equiv k+1$,AX). Hence EXP is a sub-t-reductive expansion upon (AX,AX∪{c'}).

We conclude from Thm. 7.15 that c' and thus c are inductive AX-theorems.

∎

7.5 Reductive versus inductive expansion

Example 7.17 suggests that constructing a reductive expansion amounts to constructing a subreductive expansion like EXP, while the initial term or goal reduction is generated automatically by applying an axiom for an auxiliary function or predicate like F. Moreover, if F is defined as the greatest element of SIG w.r.t. $\geq_{SIG}$, then the modified conjecture c' is automatically decreasing and most of the goals of EXP are automatically bounded.

So far, methods using explicit induction were difficult to compare with approaches to inductive completion because of their different theoretical foundations. With inductive expansion on the one hand and reductive expansion on the other hand, we hope to bring these concepts close enough to admit a comparison. Let us recapitulate the essentials of both calculi.

Both of them use resolution and paramodulation as basic inference rules. Inductive expansion generates a descent condition when applying a conjecture, which is built up from Noetherian orderings on the initial (SIG,AX)-structure Ini(SIG,AX). Reductive expansion assumes that (SIG,AX) is ground confluent and strongly terminating. Instead of generating a descent condition when applying a conjecture $c = t \equiv t' \Leftarrow \gamma$, each subgoal of a reductive expansion is t-bounded w.r.t. an AX-path ordering, which is also constructed from Noetherian orderings on Ini(SIG,AX). As Ex. 7.17 has shown, a slight modification of (SIG,AX) is sufficient for ensuring the t-boundedness of all subgoals except those where the c is applied. But they are exactly those goals δ, which inductive expansions augment with a descent condition of the form

$$\{(t_1,\ldots,t_k) >_c (u_1,\ldots,u_k)\} \qquad (*)$$

(cf. Sect. 5.2). Remember that the t_i and u_i are instances of input variables of c. Hence, in contrast with the corresponding boundary condition $t > \delta$, (*) does not take into account the structure of t and δ. It is this structural aspect of boundary conditions that may admit a reductive expansion in cases where inductive expansions fail.

Conversely, each inductive expansion of c corresponds to a reductive expansion of some $c' = t_0 \equiv t' \Leftarrow \gamma$ with $t_0 \longrightarrow_{AX} t$ ($t_0 \vdash_{AX} t$, resp.). Let us illustrate the transformation for

$$c \;=\; (x+y)+z \equiv x+(y+z).$$

An inductive expansion of c that uses the lexicographic ordering on $\mathbb{N}^3$ as a descent predicate (cf. Sect. 5.2) reads as follows:

$$
\begin{array}{lll}
\{\{c\}\} \vdash^{pro}_{AX} & \{\{x+y \equiv x+(y+0),\ z \equiv 0\},\ \{((x+y)+k)+1 \equiv x+(y+(k+1)),\ z \equiv k+1\}\} & \\
\vdash^{pro}_{AX} & \{\{x+y \equiv x+y,\ z \equiv 0\},\ \{((x+y)+k)+1 \equiv x+((y+k)+1),\ z \equiv k+1\}\} & \\
\vdash^{pro}_{AX} & \{\{z \equiv 0\},\ \{((x+y)+k)+1 \equiv (x+(y+k))+1,\ z \equiv k+1\}\} & \\
\vdash^{pro}_{AX} & \{\{z \equiv 0\},\ \{(x+y)+k \equiv x+(y+k),\ z \equiv k+1\}\} & \\
\vdash^{ind}_{AX;\{c\}} & \{\{z\equiv 0\},\ \{(x,y,z) >_c (x,y,k),\ z\equiv k+1\}\} & (1) \\
\vdash^{pro}_{AX} & \{\{z\equiv 0\},\ \{z > k,\ z\equiv k+1\}\} & (2) \\
\vdash^{pro}_{AX} & \{\{z\equiv 0\},\ \{z\equiv k+1\}\} & \\
\vdash^{pro}_{AX} & \emptyset. & \text{(Ind-EXP)}
\end{array}
$$

Add the predicate symbol P : nat,nat,nat and the axiom $P(x,y,z) \Leftarrow c$ to NSB' and prove $c' = P(x,y,z)$. To this end P is turned into the greatest element of SIG w.r.t. $\geq_{SIG}$ and $>_d$ is extended by $>_c$. A reductive expansion that corresponds to

Ind-EXP starts with the goal reduction $c' \vdash_{AX} p$, proceeds with Ind-EXP and replaces (1) and (2) by resolution steps upon $AX \cup \{c'\}$:

$$\{\{z \equiv 0\}, \{(x+y)+k \equiv x+(y+k), z \equiv k+1\}\}$$
$$\vdash^{c'}_{AX} \{\{z\equiv 0\}, \{P(x,y,k), z\equiv k+1\}\} \vdash^{c'}_{AX;AX\cup\{c'\}} \{\{z\equiv 0\}, \{z\equiv k+1\}\}.$$

It remains to show that $P(x,y,k)$ is c'-bounded w.r.t. $(z\equiv k+1,AX)$. Indeed,

$P(x,y,k)$ is c'-bounded w.r.t. $(z\equiv k+1,AX)$

if $P(fx,fy,fz) > P(fx,fy,fk)$ for all ground solutions f of $z\equiv k+1$

if $(fx,fy,fz) >_{c,AX} (fx,fy,fk)$ for all ground solutions f of $z\equiv k+1$

if all ground solutions of $z\equiv k+1$ solve $(x,y,z) >_c (x,y,k)$.

Theorem 7.18 (From inductive to reductive expansions) *Suppose that (SIG,AX) is ground confluent and > is the AX-path ordering for a triple (GS', $\geq_{SIG}$, $>_d$).*

Let $c = p \Leftarrow \gamma$, $var(c) = \{z_1,\ldots,z_k\}$, $p' = P(z_1,\ldots,z_k)$, $c' = p' \Leftarrow \gamma$ and $p' \Leftarrow p \in AX$. Then

$$\{\gamma\} \vdash^{ind}_{AX;c} \{\delta\} \quad \text{implies} \quad \{\gamma\} \vdash^{p'}_{AX;AX\cup\{c'\}} \{\delta\}.$$

Proof. Let $>_c$ be the descent predicate for c. > is extended as follows. For all ground terms and atoms $q = P(t_1,\ldots,t_k)$ and $t = F(u_1,\ldots,u_n)$,

$$q > t \text{ iff } F \neq P \text{ or } F = P \text{ and } (t_1,\ldots,t_k) >_{c,AX} (u_1,\ldots,u_n).$$

Of course, c' and $p' \Leftarrow p$ are decreasing w.r.t. > and all goals that do not contain P are p'-bounded w.r.t. AX. Hence each goal of an inductive expansion Ind-EXP of c upon AX and c is p'-bounded and, by Lemma 7.16(3), all lemmas applied in Ind-EXP are sub-p'-reductive $(AX,AX\cup\{c'\})$-theorems. It remains to transform each induction step of Ind-EXP into a sub-p'-reductive expansion upon $(AX,AX\cup\{c'\})$. W.l.o.g., we consider only resolution steps:

Inductive c-Resolution

$$\frac{\{\lambda \cup \{q\}\}}{\delta = (\lambda \cup \gamma^* \cup \{(t_1,\ldots,t_k) >_c (z_1^*,\ldots,z_k^*)\})[g] \cup EQ(g_{in})}$$

$q[g] = p^*[g]$, for all $1\leq i\leq k$: $t_i = z_i$ or $z_i \equiv t_i \in \lambda$

We simulate the induction step as follows:

$$\{\lambda \cup \{q\}\} \quad \vdash^{p'}_{AX} \quad \{\lambda[g] \cup \{p'^*[g]\} \cup EQ(g_{in})\}$$
$$\vdash^{p'}_{AX;AX\cup\{c'\}} \quad \{\lambda[g] \cup \gamma^*[g] \cup EQ(g_{in})\}$$
$$\vdash^{p'}_{AX} \quad \{\delta\}. \qquad \text{(Ind-STEP)}$$

The derivation is obtained by applying three lemmas:

- the inverse $p^*[g] \Leftarrow p'^*[g]$ of the axiom instance $p'^*[g] \Leftarrow p^*[g]$;
- the instance $p'^*[g] \Leftarrow \gamma^*[g]$ of c';
- the tautology $\lambda[g] \Leftarrow \delta$ (because $\lambda[g] \subseteq \delta$).

By Lemma 7.16(1), (3), they are sub-p'-reductively valid w.r.t. (AX∪{c'},AX) provided that $p'^*[g]$ is p'-bounded w.r.t. (AX,δ). Indeed, if $f \in GS$ solves δ w.r.t. AX, then f solves

- $EQ(g_{in})$, i.e. for all $1 \le i \le k$, $fz_i \equiv_{AX} (gz_i)[f]$,
- $\lambda[g]$ and thus for all $1 \le i \le k$, $(gz_i)[f] \equiv_{AX} t_i[g][f]$,
- $\{(t_1,...,t_k) >_c (z_1{}^*,...,z_k{}^*)\}[g]$.

Hence

$$(fz_1,...,fz_k) >_{c,AX} (gz_1{}^*,...,gz_k{}^*)[f]$$

and thus

$$p'[f] = P(fz_1,...,fz_k) > P(gz_1{}^*,...,gz_k{}^*)[f] = p'^*[g][f].$$

Therefore, Ind-STEP is a sub-p'-reductive expansion upon (AX,AX∪{c'}). ∎

In particular, the previous proof shows how a conjecture $c = p \Leftarrow \gamma$ is turned into an inductively equivalent one, $c' = p' \Leftarrow \gamma$, which is decreasing. One should note, however, that c' is usually less structured than c that could be taken into account for verifying a boundary condition. In Ex. 7.17, c has been changed in a less rigorous way. The term structure of p is preserved, but the leftmost function symbol of p has been renamed. This transformation can be generalized as follows:

Theorem 7.19 (Soundness of reductive expansion with renaming) *Suppose that (SIG,AX) is ground confluent and > is the AX-path ordering for a triple* $(GS', \ge_{SIG}, >_d)$.

Let $SIG' = \{F' \mid F \in SIG\}$. *Extend* $\ge_{SIG}$ *to* SIG∪SIG' *by defining: for all* $F,G \in SIG$ *and* $F',G' \in SIG'$:

- $F' \ge_{SIG} G$,
- $F' \ge_{SIG} G'$ *iff* $F \ge_{SIG} G$.

Moreover, let

- $AXE = AX \cup \{F'x \equiv Fx \mid F \in OP\} \cup \{P'x \Leftarrow Px \mid P \in PR-\{\equiv\}\}$,
- *for all* $t = Fu$, $t' = F'u$,
- *for all* $c = Ft \equiv u \Leftarrow \gamma$, $c' = F't \equiv u \Leftarrow \gamma$,
- *for all* $c = Pt \Leftarrow \gamma$ *with* $P \neq \equiv$, $c' = P't \Leftarrow \gamma$,
- $CS' = \{c' \mid c \in CS\}$.

CS $\subseteq$ *ITh(AX) and (SIG,AX*$\cup$*CS) is ground confluent if for all* $t \equiv u \Leftarrow \gamma \in CS^{\perp}$,

$$\{\{t \equiv u\}\} \vdash^{t'}_{AXE;AXE \cup CS'} \{\gamma\}.$$

Proof. Of course, AXE$\cup$CS' is decreasing w.r.t. the extension of > to terms and atoms over SIG$\cup$SIG'. With the help of Thm. 6.10, one immediately concludes from the ground confluence of (SIG,AX) that (SIG$\cup$SIG',AXE) is ground confluent as well. Hence by Thm. 7.15, CS' $\subseteq$ ITh(AXE) and (SIG$\cup$SIG',AXE$\cup$CS') is ground confluent if for all $t' \equiv u \Leftarrow \gamma \in CS'^{\perp}$ there is a term set, goal set respectively, GS = $\{u_1,\ldots,u_n\}$ such that

(1) for all $1 \le i \le n$, $t' \longrightarrow_{AXE}{}^{+} u_i$ if $u \neq \perp$, $t' \vdash_{AXE} u_i$ if $u = \perp$,

(2) $\{u_1 \equiv u,\ldots,u_n \equiv u\} \vdash^{t'}_{AXE;AXE \cup CS'} \{\gamma\}$.

Let n = 1 and $u_1 = \{t\}$. Then (1) holds true because $t' \longrightarrow_{AXE}{}^{+} t$ ($t' \vdash_{AXE} t$, resp.). (2) is assumed. CS' $\subseteq$ ITh(AXE) implies CS $\subseteq$ ITh(AX). Since AXE$\cup$CS'-convergent goals over SIG are AX$\cup$CS-convergent, (SIG,AX$\cup$CS) is ground confluent because (SIG$\cup$SIG',AXE$\cup$CS') is ground confluent. ∎

When using Theorem 7.19, one avoids considering part (1) of a reductive expansion. Part (2) gets easier because all goals over SIG in a sub-t'-reductive expansion upon (AXE,AXE$\cup$CS') are automatically t'-bounded (cf. Ex. 7.17). The remaining boundary conditions b have the form

$$t' \gg p[t'[f]/x]$$

for some atom p and substitution f over SIG and reduce to the atom

$$(z_1,\ldots,z_k) >_d (fz_1,\ldots,fz_k)$$

where $\{z_1,\ldots,z_k\}$ = var(t'). Hence, although t' has more structure than $P(z_1,\ldots,z_k)$ (cf. Thm. 7.18), this structure does not affect the validity of b. The situation may be different if several conjectures are proved simultaneously. Then boundary conditions

$$t_1' \gg p[t_2'[f]/x] \text{ and } t_2' \gg q[t_1'[g]/x]$$

with $t_1 \neq t_2$ may arise where the structures of t_1 and t_2 play a certain role.[1]

Implementations of *proof by consistency* tend to automate the whole proof process. They try to overcome the necessity of user interaction for choosing the "right" lemmas, generalizations, axioms (program synthesis!) and descent predicates, which is involved in explicit induction proofs. But experiments with reductive expansion lead us to claim that a fairly general proof-by-consistency method cannot relieve us from interaction either. Of course, single derivation steps can and should be carried out mechanically by the theorem prover. The global control, however, must be left to the user. And the prover must inform him about the proof process that helps him to comprehend the proof and hence to proceed successfully.

Provers based on inductive or reductive expansion can achieve this goal because both methods are compositional: subexpansions are proofs of subtheorems; proved conjectures can be used as lemmas in subsequent proofs. Comprehensibility is not only needed for controlling a proof, it is also essential for developing *learning* and *reuse* capabilities, such as the recognition of proof schemata, which provide advanced deduction rules.

An overview of currently used theorem provers is given in [Lin88].

7.6 Specification refinement

The research on abstract data types has brought about a number of formal concepts for specification refinement, usually called *algebraic* or *abstract implementation* (cf., e.g., [Hoa72], [Gut77], [EKMP82], [ST88]). Most of the work has been concerned with model theory and only a little research has been devoted to deductive methods for proving the associated correctness conditions.

Let (SIG,AX) be the *abstract* specification to be implemented and (SIG',AX') be the *concrete* specification to implement (SIG,AX).

Implementation concepts not only are different with respect to the associated correctness conditions, they also propose different schemata for extending the concrete specification to an implementation of the abstract one, i.e., to a specification IMPLA, which maps concrete objects onto abstract objects and which defines SIG in terms of SIG'. On the other hand, a suitable modification IMPLR of (SIG,AX) should restrict AX to those abstract objects that are to be implemented.

Subsequent examples suggest the following syntactical requirements:

---

[1]This conjecture should be confirmed by examples!

Definition A pair of specifications (IMPLA,IMPLR) is an *implementation* of (SIG,AX) by (SIG',AX') if IMPLA = (SIGA,AXA) and IMPLR = (SIGR,AXR) satisfy the following syntactical requirements:

- SIG ∪ SIG' ⊆ SIGA, SIG ⊆ SIGR and AX' ⊆ AXA.
- For certain sorts $s_1,\dots,s_n$ ∈ SIG' and s ∈ SIG, SIGA includes an *abstraction function* $abs_s : s_1,\dots,s_n \rightarrow s$.
- For certain sorts s ∈ SIG, SIGR includes a *representation predicate* $Rep_s : s$.
- For each c = $p \Leftarrow \gamma$ ∈ AX, AXR contains a clause

$$p \Leftarrow \gamma \cup \{Rep_{s1}(x_1),\dots,Rep_{sn}(x_n)\}$$

  where $\{x_1,\dots,x_n\} \subseteq var(c) \cap \{x \in X \mid Rep_{sort(x)} \in SIGR\}$. ▮

Definition A *polymorphic specification* PSPEC is a specification with *sort variables, parameterized sorts* and *constraints*. Parameterized sorts, such as seq(S) or fun(S,S'), are names taking sort variables as parameters. *Sort terms* over sorts, sort variables and parameterized sorts yield new sorts and new parameterized sorts. Semantically, we identify PSPEC with an *arbitrary* inhabited specification ESPEC (cf. Sect. 1.1) such that

- sorts of ESPEC are substituted for the sort variables of PSPEC,
- Ini(ESPEC) satisfies the constraints of PSPEC (cf. Sect. 3.1),
- the rest of PSPEC is part of ESPEC.

Given sort variables S1,...,Sn and sorts s1,...,sn, the specification *PSPEC(S1←s1,..., Sn←sn)* results from PSPEC by substituting s1,...,sn for all occurrences in PSPEC of S1,...,Sn, resp. ▮

Admittedly, this is a rough definition of polymorphic specifications. But for our proof-theoretical purposes and the subsequent examples, it is sufficient. Other applications may enforce a further assumption on ESPEC, based on a *parameterized specification* (cf. [EM85]), which is derived from PSPEC:

Let (PAR,PSPEC') be a pair of specifications such that

- PSPEC' is PSPEC with all sort variables regarded as sorts,
- PAR is a subspecification of PSPEC' whose sorts are exactly the sort variables of PSPEC.

Let (S,OP,PR) be the signature of PAR and A be a model of PAR. Then the *free extension PSPEC'(A)* is PSPEC' together with A as a set of constants and

- for all $w \in S^*$, $s \in S$, $F \in OP_{ws}$ and $a \in A_w$, $F^A(a) \equiv F(a)$,
- for all $P \in PR$ and $a \in P^A$, $P(a)$

as additional axioms.

With regard to the parameterized specification (PAR,PSPEC'), the initial structure of an inhabited specification ESPEC representing the semantics of PSPEC should agree with Ini(PSPEC(A)) for some model A of PAR satisfying the constraints of PSPEC.[1]

Example 7.20 (ARRAY implements STACK) The following specifications ARRAY and STACK are polymorphic.

ARRAY

base	NSB' (cf. Ex. 6.9)		
sort vars	index, entry		
sorts	array		
	symbol	*type*	
functs	ω	array	
	put	array,index,entry ⟶ array	
	_[_]	array,index ⟶ entry	
preds	_ ≢ _	index,index	
	_ >> _	index,index	
vars	a : array; m,n : index; x,y : entry		
axms	put(put(a,n,x),n,y) ≡ put(a,n,y)		(PP1)
	put(put(a,m,x),n,y) ≡ put(put(a,n,y),m,x) ⇐ m >> n		(PP2)
	put(a,n,x)[n] ≡ x		(PA1)
	put(a,m,x)[n] ≡ a[n] ⇐ m ≢ n		(PA2)
constrs	∀ n : ¬ n ≢ n		
	∀ m,n : m >> n ∨ m ≡ n ∨ n >> m		
	>> is Noetherian		

STACK

sort vars	entry	
sorts	stack	
	symbol	*type*
functs	ε	stack
	push	entry,stack ⟶ stack
	pop	stack ⟶ stack

[1] Consequently, the constraints of PSPEC should only involve symbols from the signature of PAR.

	top stack ⟶ entry	
vars	x : entry; s : stack	
axms	pop(push(x,s)) ≡ s	(ST1)
	top(push(x,s)) ≡ x	(ST2)
IMPLA		
base	ARRAY(index←nat)	
	... *signature of STACK* ...	
functs	abs : array,nat ⟶ stack	
vars	a : array; m,n : nat; x : entry	
axms	abs(put(a,m,x),n) ≡ abs(a,n) ⇐ m ≥ n	(A0)
	ε ≡ abs(a,0)	(A1)
	push(x,abs(a,n)) ≡ abs(put(a,n,x),n+1)	(A2)
	pop(abs(a,n+1)) ≡ abs(a,n)	(A3)
	top(abs(a,n+1)) ≡ a[n]	(A4)
	m >> n ⇐ m > n	
IMPLR		
	... *signature of STACK* ...	
preds	Rep : stack	
vars	x : entry; s : stack	
axms	Rep(ε)	(R1)
	Rep(push(x,s)) ⇐ Rep(s)	(R2)
	pop(push(x,s)) ≡ s ⇐ Rep(s)	
	top(push(x,s)) ≡ x ⇐ Rep(s) ∎	

Definition An implementation (IMPLA,IMPLR) of (SIG,AX) by (SIG',AX') is *correct* if IMPL = IMPLA ∪ IMPLR is consistent w.r.t. both IMPLA and IMPLR (cf. Sect. 3.4). ∎

For proving that **IMPL is consistent w.r.t. IMPLA,** the extension IMPLR may be decomposed into

(1) a specification *REP* of the representation predicates and
(2) the set *Rep(AX)* of modified axioms specifying the functions and predicates of SIG.

Hence the consistency of IMPL w.r.t. IMPLA falls into

(1) the consistency of IMPL' = IMPLA ∪ REP w.r.t. IMPLA and
(2) the consistency of IMPL = IMPL' ∪ Rep(AX) w.r.t. IMPL'.

Since IMPL' and IMPL = IMPL' ∪ Rep(AX) have the same signature, we conclude from Lemma 7.9 that (2) holds true iff

(a) Rep(AX) is inductively valid w.r.t. IMPL'.

This means that IMPLA satisfies AX on all abstract objects selected by representation predicates, i.e., all abstract objects to be implemented. For (1), one may apply the following syntactical consistency criterion:

Lemma 7.21 A specification (SIG,AX) is consistent w.r.t. a subspecification (BSIG,BASE) if the following conditions hold true:

(*) For all $P(t_1,...,t_n) \Leftarrow \delta \in$ AX-BASE, P ∈ SIG-BSIG[1] or P is an equality predicate and both t_1 and t_2 contain a function symbol of SIG-BSIG.

(**) If there is a fresh variable in $BASE^{sym}$ (cf. Chapt. 6), then the range sorts of all function symbols of SIG-BSIG are sorts in SIG-BSIG.

Proof. Let γ be an AX-valid ground goal over BSIG. By Thm. 4.4, there is a shortest successful solving expansion $\gamma,\gamma_2,...,\gamma_n$ upon AX, consisting of ground goals. We show BASE $\vdash_{cut} \gamma$ by induction on n. If n = 0, then $\gamma = \emptyset$, and the proof is complete.

Let n > 0. From (*), γ gives γ_2 by a resolution, paramodulation or unification step upon BASE. Since γ is a goal over BSIG, (**) implies that γ_2 is also a goal over BSIG. Hence by induction hypothesis, γ_2 and thus γ are BASE-valid. ∎

Since REP does not add function symbols to IMPLA, the conditions of Lemma 7.21 hold true for (BSIG,BASE) = IMPLA and (SIG,AX) = IMPL' if

(b) all axioms of REP have the form $Rep(t) \Leftarrow \delta$.

For proving that **IMPL is consistent w.r.t. IMPLR**, the extension IMPLA may be decomposed into

(3) a specification *ABS* consisting of the concrete specification (SIG',AX') together with the definition of SIG in terms of SIG' and

(4) a set *EQA* of axioms defining equivalence relations induced by abstraction functions.

Hence the consistency of IMPL w.r.t. IMPLR, which means that IMPL does not identify different abstract objects, falls into

(3) the consistency of IMPL" = IMPLR ∪ ABS w.r.t. IMPLR and

(4) the consistency of IMPL = IMPL" ∪ EQA w.r.t. IMPL".

---

[1] If P is the equality predicate for a sort *s*, the condition implies that *s* is a sort in SIG-BSIG.

Since IMPL" and IMPL = IMPL" ∪ EQA have the same signature, (4) follows immediately from Lemma 7.9 if

(c) EQA is inductively valid w.r.t. IMPL",

while Cor. 6.19 provides the following sufficient conditions for (3):

(5) the axioms of ABS are ground reducible w.r.t. IMPLR,
(6) AXR respects SIGR,
(7) IMPL" is ground confluent and strongly terminating.

Using Thm. 6.10 and results from Sect. 6.4 we reduce (5)-(6) to the following requirements:

(d) for all $t \equiv t' \Leftarrow \gamma \in ABS^{\perp}$, t contains a function from SIG or an abstraction function;

(e) all ground instances of fresh variables of IMPLR have IMPL"-reducts over SIGR;

(f) IMPL" is critical clause convergent and strongly terminating.

Since (d)-(f) are reduction-oriented conditions, the direction of an equational axiom may be essential. For instance, in Ex. 7.20, (e) does not hold for A1. Hence we invert A1:

$$\text{abs(a,0)} \equiv \varepsilon. \qquad (A1^{-1})$$

However, <A2,A1^{-1}> induces the new reduction ambiguity <t,cc> with

$$\begin{aligned} t &= \text{push(x,abs(a,0))} \\ cc &= \text{push}(x,\varepsilon) \equiv \text{abs(put(a,0,x),0+1)}. \end{aligned}$$

Since cc is not convergent, we also invert A2:

$$\text{abs(put(a,n,x),n+1)} \equiv \text{push(x,abs(a,n))} \qquad (A2^{-1})$$

and obtain reduction ambiguities induced by A2^{-1} and ARRAY-axioms that are convergent (cf. Ex. 7.23 below). Note that we introduced a Noetherian relation >> into ARRAY in order to make IMPL" strongly terminating (cf. Sect. 6.2).

Theorem 7.22 (Criterion for implementation correctness) Given two specifications IMPLA = (SIGA,AXA) and IMPLR = (SIGR,AXR) satisfying the above syntactical requirements, the pair (IMPLA,IMPLR) is a correct implementation of (SIG,AX) by (SIG',AX') if conditions (a)-(f) hold true. ∎

Example 7.23 (ARRAY implements STACK; cf. Ex. 7.20) Let

$$ABS = ARRAY \cup \{A1^{-1}, A2^{-1}, A3, A4\}, \; EQA = \{A0\}.$$

The proof of conditions (a)-(e) is left to the reader. For making IMPL" = IMPLR ∪ ABS strongly terminating we attached the premise m >> n to PP2. Note that a suitable signature ordering > must satisfy pop > abs > push.

It remains to show that IMPL" is ground confluent. To apply Cor. 6.16, we present a complete set RA of reduction ambiguities <t,p⇐γ> of IMPL". All elements of RA are listed below except those induced only by ARRAY-axioms.

t	*p*⇐*γ*	*induced by*
pop(abs(put(a,n,x),n+1))	pop(push(x,abs(a,n))) ≡ abs(put(a,n,x),n)	<A3,A2⁻¹>
top(abs(put(a,n,x),n+1))	top(push(x,abs(a,n))) ≡ put(a,n,x)[n]	<A4,A2⁻¹>
abs(put(put(a,n,x),n,y),n+1)	abs(put(a,n,y),n+1) ≡ push(y,abs(put(a,n,x),n))	<A2⁻¹,PP1>
abs(put(put(a,m,x),n,y),n+1)	abs(put(put(a,n,y),m,x),n+1) ≡ push(y,abs(put(a,m,x),n)) ⇐ m >> n	<A2⁻¹,PP2>

For each <t,p⇐γ> ∈ RA, there is a straightforward sub-t-reductive expansion of {{p}} into {γ} upon AXR∪ABS[1]. Hence by Cor. 6.16, IMPL" is critical clause convergent. ▮

Example 7.24 (BINSEARCH implements SET)

SET

base	NSB'	
sort vars	entry	
sorts	set	
	symbol	*type*
functs	∅	set
	insert	entry,set ⟶ set
preds	_ ∈ _	entry,set
	_ >> _	entry,entry
vars	x : entry; s : set	
axms	insert(x,insert(x,s)) ≡ insert(x,s)	
	insert(x,insert(y,s)) ≡ insert(y,insert(x,s)) ⇐ x >> y	
	x ∈ insert(x,s)	

[1]Note that the expansions of some <t,p⇐γ> ∈ RA include applications of axiom A0, which is sub-t-reductively valid w.r.t. AXR∪ABS.

	x ∈ insert(y,s) ⇐ x ∈ s	
constrs	∀ x,y : x >> y ∨ x ≡ y ∨ y >> x	
	>> is Noetherian	

IMPLA

base	BINSEARCH (cf. Sect. 8.3)	
	... *signature of SET(entry←nat)* ...	
functs	abs : seq ⟶ set	
vars	x,y : nat; s : seq	
axms	abs(x&x&s) ≡ abs(x&s)	
	abs(x&y&s) ≡ abs(y&x&s)	
	∅ ≡ abs(ε)	(A1)
	insert(x,abs(s)) ≡ abs(x&s)	(A2)
	x ∈ abs(s) ⇐ binsearch(x,s)	(A3)

IMPLR

	... *signature of SET(entry←nat)* ...	
preds	Rep : set	
vars	x : nat; s : set	
axms	Rep(∅)	(R1)
	Rep(insert(x,s)) ⇐ Rep(s)	(R2)
	p ⇐ γ ∪ {Rep(s)}	*for all axioms p⇐γ of SET*
	x >> y ⇐ x > y	

As in the previous example, most conditions of Thm. 7.22 are easy to verify. The proof of ground confluence may again follow Cor. 6.16 provided that A1 and A2 were inverted. ▮

Further (multi)set implementations can be found in [Pad81] and [EKMP82].

Example 7.25 (STACK implements SYMTAB; cf. [Gut77])

SYMTAB

sort vars

id, attrs

sorts	symtab	
	symbol	*type*
functs	init	symtab
	enter	symtab ⟶ symtab
	add	symtab,id,attrs ⟶ symtab
	leave	symtab ⟶ symtab

	retrieve	symtab,id ⟶ attrs
preds	_ ≢ _	id,id
	inblock	symtab,id

vars st : symtab; i,j : id; at : attrs

axms

```
leave(enter(st)) ≡ st                                          (SYM1)
leave(add(st,i,at)) ≡ leave(st)
retrieve(enter(st),i) ≡ retrieve(st)
retrieve(add(st,i,at),i) ≡ at
retrieve(add(st,i,at),j) ≡ retrieve(st,j)  ⇐  i ≢ j            (SYM2)
inblock(add(st,i,at),i)
inblock(add(st,i,at),j)  ⇐  i ≢ j, inblock(st,j)
```

constrs ∀ i : ¬ i ≢ i

IMPLA

base STACK(entry←array), ARRAY(index←id, entry←attrs) (cf. Ex. 7.20)

... *signature of SYMTAB* ...

sorts bool

	symbol	*type*
functs	true	bool
	false	bool
	abs	stack ⟶ symtab
	inarray	array,id ⟶ bool

vars s,s' : stack; x : array; i,j : id; at : attrs

axms

```
init ≡ abs(push(ω,ε))                                          (A1)
enter(abs(s)) ≡ abs(push(ω,s))                                 (A2)
add(abs(push(x,s)),i,at) ≡ abs(push(put(x,i,at),s))            (A3)
leave(abs(s)) ≡ abs(pop(s))  ⇐  pop(s) ≡ push(x,s')            (A4)
retrieve(abs(push(x,s)),i) ≡ x[i]  ⇐  inarray(x,i) ≡ true      (A5)
retrieve(abs(push(x,s)),i) ≡ retrieve(abs(s),i)⇐inarray(x,i) ≡ lse  (A6)
inblock(abs(push(x,s)),i)  ⇐  inarray(x,i) ≡ true              (A7)
inarray(ω,i) ≡ false                                           (A8)
```

inarray(put(x,i,at),i) ≡ true (A9)

inarray(put(x,i,at),j) ≡ inarray(x,j) ⇐ i ≢ j (A10)

IMPLR

... *signature of SYMTAB* ...

preds Rep : symtab

vars st : symtab; i : id; at : attrs

axms Rep(init) (R1)

Rep(enter(st)) ⇐ Rep(st) (R2)

Rep(add(st,i,at)) ⇐ Rep(st) (R3)

p ⇐ γ ∪ {Rep(st)} *for all axioms p⇐γ of SYMTAB*

As in Ex. 7.23, most conditions of Thm. 7.22 are easy to verify. The proof of ground confluence may again follow Cor. 6.16 provided that A1, A2 and A3 were inverted.

As a part of 7.22(a) let us show by inductive expansion that SYM1⇐Rep(st) and SYM2⇐Rep(st) are inductively valid w.r.t. IMPL'. At the end of the proofs we apply the lemma

st ≡ abs(push(x,s)) ⇐ Rep(st). (L)

L follows from R1-R3 and A1-A3.

goal	*rules applied*
leave(enter(st)) ≡ st	-- SYM1
st ≡ abs(s), leave(abs(push(ω,s))) ≡ abs(s)	paramodulation upon A2
st ≡ abs(s), abs(pop(push(ω,s))) ≡ abs(s) pop(push(ω,s)) ≡ push(x,s')	paramodulation upon A4
st ≡ abs(s), abs(s) ≡ abs(s) s ≡ push(x,s')	paramodulation upon ST1 (cf. Ex. 7.20)
st ≡ abs(s), s ≡ push(x,s')	resolution upon x≡x
st ≡ abs(push(x,s'))	unification
Rep(st)	resolution upon L

goal	*rules applied*

```
retrieve(add(st,i,at),j) ≡ retrieve(st,j)            -- conclusion of SYM2
=========================================================================
st ≡ abs(push(x,s))                                   paramodulation upon A3
retrieve(abs(push(put(x,i,at),s)),j) ≡ retrieve(abs(push(x,s)),j)
=========================================================================
st ≡ abs(push(x,s))
put(x,i,at)[j] ≡ retrieve(abs(push(x,s)),j)           paramodulation upon A5
inarray(put(x,i,at),j) ≡ true
-------------------------------------------------------------------------
st ≡ abs(push(x,s))
retrieve(abs(s),j) ≡ retrieve(abs(push(x,s)),j)       paramodulation upon A6
inarray(put(x,i,at),j) ≡ false
=========================================================================
st ≡ abs(push(x,s))
put(x,i,at)[j] ≡ retrieve(abs(push(x,s)),j)           paramodulation upon A10
inarray(x,j) ≡ true
i ≢ j
-------------------------------------------------------------------------
st ≡ abs(push(x,s))
retrieve(abs(s),j) ≡ retrieve(abs(push(x,s)),j)       paramodulation upon A10
inarray(x,j) ≡ false
i ≢ j
=========================================================================
st ≡ abs(push(x,s))
put(x,i,at)[j] ≡ x[j]                                 paramodulation upon A5
inarray(x,j) ≡ true
i ≢ j
-------------------------------------------------------------------------
st ≡ abs(push(x,s))
retrieve(abs(s),j) ≡ retrieve(abs(s),j)               paramodulation upon A6
inarray(x,j) ≡ false
i ≢ j
=========================================================================
st ≡ abs(push(x,s))
inarray(x,j) ≡ true                                   resolution upon PA1
i ≢ j                                                 (cf. Ex. 7.20)
-------------------------------------------------------------------------
st ≡ abs(push(x,s))
inarray(x,j) ≡ false                                  unification
i ≢ j
=========================================================================
st ≡ abs(push(x,s))                                   resolution upon
i ≢ j                                                 b≡true ∨ b≡false
=========================================================================
Rep(st)                                               resolution upon L
i ≢ j
=========================================================================
```

8: Examples

By presenting a number of design and requirement specifications, this chapter illustrates the range of applications captured by Horn logic with equality. Besides a signature and axioms, many of these specifications include a list of *theorems* and a list of *conjectures*. The former are lemmas used in proofs of the latter, which express correctness conditions on declarative programs specified by the axioms. Some of these axioms are translated into SML programs (cf. Sect. 2.6). Some proofs are carried out by inductive or subreductive expansion.

8.1 Attributed grammars

A well-known way of defining an interpreter or a compiler for a language L is to *attribute* or *decorate* a context-free grammar G for L with semantic information (cf. [Knu68]). If this information is attached to the *abstract syntax* derived from G and not to G itself, an attributed grammar becomes a particular set of guarded clauses. For example, the following grammar G, written in Backus-Naur form, generates strings with a two-dimensional layout:

text ::= string	(START)
string ::= string box	(SEQ)
string ::= string *up* box	(UP)
string ::= string *down* box	(DOWN)
string ::= ε	(EMPTY)
box ::= (string)	(BLOCK)
box ::= *read*	(READ)

The abstract syntax derived from G is given by the following signature:

ABS-G

sorts	text, string, box	
functs	*symbol*	*type*
	START	string ⟶ text
	SEQ	string,box ⟶ string
	UP	string,box ⟶ string
	DOWN	string,box ⟶ string
	EMPTY	string
	BLOCK	string ⟶ box
	READ	box

Terms over ABS-G, also called *abstract syntax trees,* will be compiled into sequences of print commands that establish the desired text layout. For this purpose, ABS-G is extended by an appropriate target language and a compile function *compN* for each nonterminal N of G (or sort N of ABS-G).

```
COMPILE-G
   base     ABS-G, NSB
   sorts    code
   functs   symbol        type
            read          code
            print         nat,nat ⟶ code
            ε             code
            _ ; _         code,code ⟶ code
            compText      text ⟶ code
            compString    string,nat,nat ⟶ code×nat×nat×nat
            compBox       box,nat,nat ⟶ code×nat×nat×nat
            max           nat,nat ⟶ nat
   vars     s : string;  b : box;  c,c' : code;  x,y,l,h,t,l',h',t' : nat
   axms     compText(START(s)) ≡ c   ⇐   compString(s,0,0) ≡ (c,l,h,t)
            compString(SEQ(s,b),x,y) ≡ (c;c',l+l',max(h,h'),max(t,t'))
                    ⇐   compString(s,x,y) ≡ (c,l,h,t),
                        compBox(b,x+l,y) ≡ (c',l',h',t')
            compString(UP(s,b),x,y) ≡ (c;c',l+l',h+h'-1,max(t,t'-h+1))
                    ⇐   compString(s,x,y) ≡ (c,l,h,t),
                        compBox(b,x+l,y+h-1) ≡ (c',l',h',t')
            compString(DOWN(s,b),x,y) ≡ (c;c',l+l',max(h,h'-t-1),t+t'+1)
                    ⇐   compString(s,x,y) ≡ (c,l,h,t),
                        compBox(b,x+l,y-t-1) ≡ (c',l',h',t')
            compString(EMPTY,x,y) ≡ (ε,0,0,0)
            compBox(BLOCK(s),x,y) ≡ compString(s,x,y)
            compBox(READ,x,y) ≡ (read;print(x,y),1,2,0)
            max(x,y) ≡ y   ⇐   x ≤ y
            max(x,y) ≡ x   ⇐   x > y
```

A string or a box has two *inherited* attributes: the two coordinates of its bottom-left edge. As the example illustrates, inherited attributes of a nonterminal N are *arguments* of the compile function *compN* for N. A string or a box has three *derived* attributes: the length, the height (above the baseline) and the depth (below the baseline). Derived attributes of a nonterminal N are *values* of *compN* .

8.2 More arithmetic

As in Exs. 5.8-5.10, the following extensions of NSB (cf. Ex. 1.1) relate recursive to iterative programs of arithmetic functions.

```
FACTORIAL
    base       NSB
               symbol     type
    functs     fact       nat ⟶ nat
               factL      nat ⟶ nat
               Loop       nat,nat ⟶ nat
    vars       x,y : nat
    axms       fact(0) ≡ 1
               fact(x+1) ≡ (x+1)*fact(x)
               factL(x) ≡ Loop(x,1)
               Loop(0,y) ≡ y
               Loop(x+1,y) ≡ Loop(x,y*(x+1))
    conjects   factL(x) ≡ fact(x)
               Loop(x,y) ≡ fact(x)*y
```

Binary numbers, represented as sequences over {0,L}, are translated into unary numbers both recursively and iteratively:

```
BIN-TO-NAT
    base       NSB
    sorts      bin
               symbol     type
    functs     0          bin
               L          bin
               _0         bin ⟶ bin
               _L         bin ⟶ bin
               decode     bin ⟶ nat
               decodeL    bin ⟶ nat
               Loop       bin,nat,nat ⟶ nat
    vars       b : bin;  x,y : nat
    axms       00 ≡ 0
               0L ≡ L
               decode(0) ≡ 0
               decode(L) ≡ 1
               decode(b0) ≡ decode(b)*2
               decode(b0) ≡ decode(b)*2+1
               decodeL(b) ≡ Loop(b,1,0)
               Loop(0,x,y) ≡ y
               Loop(L,x,y) ≡ x+y
               Loop(b0,x,y) ≡ Loop(b,x*2,y)
```

```
            Loop(bL,x,y) ≡ Loop(b,x*2,x+y)
conjects    decodeL(b) ≡ decode(b)
            Loop(b,x,y) ≡ (decode(b)*x)+y
```

Next, this translation is extended from natural to rational numbers. A binary rational number $x_1 \ldots x_k \bullet y_1 \ldots y_n$ is compiled into a fraction whose denominator is a power of 2. For instance, LOLO•LOLL becomes 10 + 1/2 + 1/8 + 1/16 = (160 + 8 + 2 + 1)/16 = 171/16.

```
BIN-TO-RAT
  base      BIN-TO-NAT
  sorts     rat, binrat
            symbol     type
  functs    _          nat ⟶ rat
            _/2        rat ⟶ rat
            _+_        rat,rat ⟶ rat
            _*_        rat,rat ⟶ rat
            _•         bin ⟶ binrat
            _0         binrat ⟶ binrat
            _L         binrat ⟶ binrat
            decode     binrat ⟶ rat×rat
            decodeL    binrat ⟶ rat×rat
            Loop       binrat,rat,rat ⟶ rat×rat
  vars      x,y : nat;  r,s,r',s' : rat;  b : bin;  c : binrat
  axms      0/2 ≡ 0
            (1+1)/2 ≡ 1
            x + r/2 ≡ (x*2+r)/2
            r/2 + x ≡ (r+x*2)/2
            r/2 + s/2 ≡ (r+s)/2
            x * r/2 ≡ (x*r)/2
            r/2 * x ≡ (r*x)/2
            r/2 * s/2 ≡ (r*s)/2/2
            decode(b•) ≡ (decode(b),1)
            decode(c0) ≡ (r,s/2)   ⇐   decode(c) ≡ (r,s)
            decode(cL) ≡ (r+s/2,s/2)   ⇐   decode(c) ≡ (r,s)
            decodeL(c) ≡ Loop(c,0,1)
            Loop(b•,r,s) ≡ (decode(b)+r,s)
            Loop(c0,r,s) ≡ Loop(c,r/2,s/2)
            Loop(cL,r,s) ≡ Loop(c,(r+1)/2,s/2)
  conjects  decodeL(c) ≡ decode(c)
            Loop(c,r,s) ≡ ((r*s')+r',s*s')   ⇐   decode(c) ≡ (r',s')
```

8.3 Searching and sorting

We first define the minimum of a sequence and some auxiliary functions and predicates on bags (cf. Ex. 1.1).

SEQ-MINIMUM

base	NSB	
	symbol	*type*
functs	min	seq ⟶ nat
	_∪_	bag,bag ⟶ bag
preds	_∈_	nat,bag
	_≤_	nat,bag
	_≤_	bag,nat
vars	x,y,z : nat; s : seq; b,b' : bag	
axms	min(x&ε) ≡ x	
	min(x&y&s) ≡ z ⇐ min(y&s) ≡ z, z ≤ x	
	min(x&y&s) ≡ x ⇐ min(y&s) ≡ z, z > x	
	∅ ∪ b ≡ b	
	add(x,b) ∪ b' ≡ add(x,b ∪ b')	
	x ∈ add(x,b)	
	x ∈ add(y,b) ⇐ x ∈ b	
	x ≤ ∅	
	x ≤ add(y,b) ⇐ x ≤ y, x ≤ b	
	∅ ≤ x	
	add(x,b) ≤ y ⇐ x ≤ y, b ≤ y	
conjects	min(x&s) ∈ makeBag(x&s)	
	min(x&s) ≤ makeBag(x&s)	

Secondly, we implement *binary search* by a logic program for the predicate binsearch. Conjecture C1 given below is a precondition on this program: binsearch(x,s) is valid if x occurs in s and s is sorted. Note that the program uses two *append* operators for sequences, that of NSB and a second one, also denoted by _&_, which adds an element at the right of a sequence.

BINSEARCH

base	SEQ-MINIMUM	
	symbol	*type*
functs	halve	seq ⟶ seq×seq
	_&_	seq,nat ⟶ seq
	_•_	seq,seq ⟶ seq
preds	binsearch	nat,seq
vars	x,y,z : nat; s,s',s",t,t' : seq	

axms	binsearch(x,s) ⇐ halve(s) ≡ (s',x&s")	
	binsearch(x,s) ⇐ halve(s) ≡ (s',y&s"), x < y, binsearch(x,s')	
	binsearch(x,s) ⇐ halve(s) ≡ (s',y&s"), x ≥ y, binsearch(x,s")	
	halve(ε) ≡ (ε,ε)	
	halve(x&ε) ≡ (x&ε,ε)	
	halve(x&y&s) ≡ (x&t,t'&z) ⇐ y&s ≡ s'&z, halve(s') ≡ (t,t')	(A1)
	ε&x ≡ x&ε	(A2)
	(x&s)&y ≡ x&(s&y)	(A3)
	ε•s ≡ s	
	(x&s)•s' ≡ x&(s•s')	
thms	s'•s" ≡ s ⇐ halve(s) ≡ (s',s")	(T1)
conjects	binsearch(x,s) ⇐ x ∈ makeBag(s), sorted(s)	(C1)

Note that {ε, x&s} as well as {ε, s&x} are sets of constructors (cf. Sect. 2.3 and Ex. 7.6). Only C = {ε, x&s, s'&y} is not such a set because axioms A2 and A3 entail equivalences between ground instances of C. Hence {A1} is constructor-based. T1 states a correctness condition on halve and is needed as a lemma for C1.

8.3.1 Bubble-, merge- and quicksort

Using the terminology for divide- and -conquer algorithms, halve is a *split* operation for binsearch just as insert is a *join* operation for sort-by-insertion (cf. Ex. 5.12). Analogously, correctness conditions on suitable split and join operations are crucial for verifying bubblesort, mergesort and quicksort:

BUBBLESORT

base	BINSEARCH	
	symbol *type*	
functs	bubblesort seq ⟶ seq	
	bubble seq ⟶ seq	
vars	x,y : nat; s,s' : seq	
axms	bubblesort(ε) ≡ ε	
	bubblesort(x&s) ≡ bubblesort(s')&y ⇐ bubble(x&s) ≡ s'&y	
	bubble(x&ε) ≡ x&ε	
	bubble(x&y&s) ≡ x&bubble(y&s) ⇐ x ≤ y	
	bubble(x&y&s) ≡ y&bubble(x&s) ⇐ x > y	
thms	sorted(s&x) ⇐ sorted(s), bubble(y&s) ≡ s'&x	(T)
conjects	sorted(bubblesort(s))	(C)
	makeBag(bubblesort(s)) ≡ makeBag(s)	

An inductive expansion of C is given in Ex. 9.2.4. T translates the recursive definition of `bubblesort` into an inductive property of `sorted`: substitute `bubblesort(s')` for s in T. For a proof of T, cf. Ex. 9.4.

```
MERGESORT
 base     BINSEARCH
          symbol         type
 functs   mergesort      seq ⟶ seq
          merge          seq,seq ⟶ seq
 vars     x,y : nat;  s,s',s" : seq
 axms     mergesort(s) ≡ merge(mergesort(s'),mergesort(s")) ⇐ halve(s) ≡ (s',s")
          merge(ε,s) ≡ s
          merge(s,ε) ≡ s
          merge(x&s,y&s') ≡ x&merge(s,y&s')   ⇐   x ≤ y
          merge(x&s,y&s') ≡ y&merge(x&s,s')   ⇐   x > y
 thms     sorted(merge(s,s'))  ⇐  sorted(s), sorted(s')
          makeBag(merge(s,s')) ≡ makeBag(s) ∪ makeBag(s')
          makeBag(s) ≡ makeBag(s') ∪ makeBag(s")  ⇐   halve(s) ≡ (s',s")
 conjects sorted(mergesort(s))
          makeBag(mergesort(s)) ≡ makeBag(s)
```

```
QUICKSORT
 base     BINSEARCH
          symbol            type
 functs   quicksort         seq ⟶ seq
          filter            nat,seq ⟶ seq
 vars     x,y : nat;  s,s',s" : seq;  b : bag
 axms     quicksort(ε) ≡ ε
          quicksort(x&s) ≡ quicksort(s')∘(x&quicksort(s"))  ⇐  filter(x,s) ≡ (s',s")
          filter(x,ε) ≡ (ε,ε)
          filter(x,y&s) ≡ (s',y&s")   ⇐   x ≤ y,  filter(x,s) ≡ (s',s")
          filter(x,y&s) ≡ (y&s',s")   ⇐   x > y,  filter(x,s) ≡ (s',s")
 thms     sorted(s∘s')   ⇐   sorted(s), sorted(s')
          makeBag(s∘s') ≡ makeBag(s) ∪ makeBag(s')
          makeBag(s) ≡ makeBag(s') ∪ makeBag(s")   ⇐   filter(x,s) ≡ (s',s")
          makeBag(s') ≤ x   ⇐   filter(x,s) ≡ (s',s")
          x ≤ makeBag(s")   ⇐   filter(x,s) ≡ (s',s")
 conjects sorted(quicksort(s))
          makeBag(quicksort(s)) ≡ makeBag(s)
```

Here is a *one-to-one* translation of the (constructor-based) axioms for quicksort and filter into SML programs (cf. Sect. 2.6):

```
fun     quicksort(nil) = nil |
        quicksort(x::s) =  let val (s',s") = filter(x,s)
                           in quicksort(s')@(x::quicksort(s")) end
and     filter(x,nil) = (nil,nil) |
        ilter(x,y::s) =  let val (s',s") = filter(x,s)
                         in if x ≤ y then (s',y::s") else (y::s',s") end
```

8.3.2 Heapsort

We proceed with the *heapsort* algorithm (cf., e.g., [Baa88]), which uses binary trees as intermediate representations of sequences to be sorted. Such a tree T is called a *heap* if T is *decreasing,* i.e., if the key at each node is not greater than the key at the corresponding parent node and if T has a certain structure that can be maintained effectively if T is implemented as an array. Using the specification refinement schema of Sect. 7.6, we start with a specification HEAPSORT for heapsort on trees and, subsequently, present heapsort on arrays as a correct implementation of HEAPSORT by ARRAY (cf. Ex. 7.20).[1]

HEAPSORT

base	NSB	
sorts	tree	
	symbol	*type*
functs	Ω	tree
	_•_•_	tree,nat,tree ⟶ tree
	domain	tree ⟶ seq
	domainL	tree,nat,seq ⟶ seq
	sift	tree ⟶ tree
	heapify	tree ⟶ tree
	heapsort	tree ⟶ seq
preds	Rep	tree
	all	seq,nat
	_ ∈ _	nat,seq
	decr	tree
	cutLeaf	tree,nat,tree

[1]The treatment of heapsort in [BD77], Sect. 8, follows the same idea. In addition, the authors derive an implementation of a function corresponding to *sift* in HEAPSORT from their abstract specification. We leave it to the reader to work out such a program synthesis here (cf. Ex. 5.12).

```
vars      x,y,z : nat;  T,T',U,U',V,V' : tree
axms      Rep(T)  ⇐  all(domain(T),n)                                   (REP)
          domain(T) ≡ domainL(T,1,ε)
          domainL(Ω,n,s) ≡ ε
          domainL(T•x•T',n,s) ≡ domainL(T,n*2,domainL(T',n*2+1,n&s))
          all(s,0)
          all(s,n+1)  ⇐  n+1 ∈ s,  all(s,n)
          n ∈ n&s
          m ∈ n&s  ⇐  m ∈ s
          decr(Ω)
          decr(Ω•x•Ω)
          decr((T•y•T')•x•Ω)  ⇐  x ≤ y
          decr((T•y•T')•x•(U•z•U'))  ⇐  x ≤ y,  x ≤ z
          sift(Ω) ≡ Ω                                                     (SI1)
          sift(Ω•x•Ω) ≡ Ω•x•Ω                                             (SI2)
          sift(T•x• Ω) ≡ T•x•Ω  ⇐  T ≡ Ω•y•Ω,  x ≤ y                      (SI3)
          sift(T•x• Ω) ≡ (Ω•x•Ω)•y•Ω  ⇐  T ≡ Ω•y•Ω,  x > y                (SI4)
          sift(T•x•T') ≡ T•x•T'
                  ⇐  T ≡ U•y•U',  T' ≡ V•z•V',  x ≤ y,  x ≤ z             (SI5)
          sift(T•x•T') ≡ sift(U•x•U')•y•T'
                  ⇐  T ≡ U•y•U',  T' ≡ V•z•V',  x > y,  y ≤ z             (SI6)
          sift(T•x•T') ≡ T•z•sift(V•x•V')
                  ⇐  T ≡ U•y•U',  T' ≡ V•z•V',  x > z,  y > z             (SI7)
          heapify(Ω) ≡ Ω
          heapify(T•x•T') ≡ sift(heapify(T)•x•heapify(T'))
          heapsort(Ω) ≡ ε                                                 (HS1)
          heapsort(Ω•x•Ω) ≡ x&ε                                           (HS2)
          heapsort(T•x•T') ≡ x&heapsort(sift(U•z•U'))
                      ⇐  T ≡ V•y•V',  cutLeaf(T•x•T',z,U•x•U')            (HS3)
          cutLeaf(Ω•x•Ω,x,Ω)
          cutLeaf(T•x•T',z,U•x•T')  ⇐  T ≡ V•y•V',  cutLeaf(T,z,U)
          cutLeaf(T•x•T',z,T•x•U)  ⇐  T ≡ V•y•V',  cutLeaf(T',z,U)
thms      decr(heapify(T))  ⇐  Rep(T)
conjects  sorted(heapsort(heapify(T)))  ⇐  Rep(T)
```

REP defines the structural heap condition on a tree T in terms of the domain of T. In other words, it reads as follows:

(1) T has 2^n nodes at all non-bottom levels n of T;

(2) all leaves at the first level above the bottom level are located to the right of all internal nodes of that level.

From (2) we conclude that, for instance, the term `Ω•x•(T•y•T')` does not represent a heap. The predicate `decr` checks whether a tree is decreasing (see above). `Sift` produces a rearranged tree with the root key moved down a branch, as far as possible over greater keys. `Heapify` performs the rearrangement on all subtrees of a tree T and thus makes T decreasing. In terms of divide-and-conquer algorithms, `sift` is the join operation of `heapify` (cf. Ex. 5.12).

`Heapsort` returns an increasing sequence of all keys of a heapified tree. On non-empty trees with at least two nodes (cf. HS3), a recursion step of `heapsort` consists of four operations:

- calling the non-deterministic function `cutleaf`, which deletes a leaf, `z`, from the tree `T•x•T'` and returns `z` together with the pruned tree `U•x•U'`;
- changing the root key of `U•x•U'` into `z`;
- sifting and sorting the modified tree `U•z•U'`;
- appending `x` to the left of the sorted sequence of the elements of `U•z•U'`.

```
IMPLA
  base    ARRAY(index←nat, entry←nat)    (cf. Ex. 7.20)
          .. signature of HEAPSORT ...
          symbol        type
  functs  abs           nat,array,nat ⟶ tree
          sift'         nat,array,nat ⟶ array
          heapify'      nat,array,nat,nat ⟶ array
          heapsort'     array,nat ⟶ seq
          makeSeq       array,nat ⟶ seq
  vars    a,a',a" : array;  m,n,q,r,x,y,z : nat;  U,U' : tree
  axms    Ω ≡ abs(m,a,n)  ⇐  m > n                                        (A1)
          abs(m*2,a,n)•x•abs(m*2+1,a,n) ≡ abs(m,a',n)
                                  ⇐  a' ≡ put(a,m,x),  0 < m ≤ n           (A2)
          sift(abs(m,a,n)) ≡ abs(m,sift'(m,a,n),n)                         (SA1)
          sift'(m,a,n) ≡ a  ⇐  m*2 > n                                     (SA2)
          sift'(m,a,n) ≡ a  ⇐  a[m] ≤ a[m*2],  m*2 ≤ n < m*2+1             (SA3)
          sift'(m,a,n) ≡ a' ⇐ a' ≡ put(put(a,m,a[m*2]),m*2,a[m]),
                              a[m] > a[m*2],  m*2 ≤ n < m*2+1              (SA4)
          sift'(m,a,n) ≡ a  ⇐  a[m] ≤ a[m*2], a[m]  ≤  a[m*2+1],  n ≥ m*2+1  (SA5)
          sift'(m,a,n) ≡ sift'(m*2,a',n)
                    ⇐  a' ≡ put(put(a,m,a[m*2]),m*2,a[m]),
                       a[m] > a[m*2],  a[m*2] ≤ a[m*2+1],  n ≥ m*2+1       (SA6)
          sift'(m,a,n) ≡ sift'(m*2+1,a',n)
                    ⇐  a' ≡ put(put(a,m,a[m*2+1]),m*2+1,a[m]),
                       a[m] > a[m*2+1],  a[m*2] > a[m*2+1],  n ≥ m*2+1     (SA7)
```

```
       heapify(abs(m,a,n)) ≡ abs(m,heapify'(m,a,n,q),n) ⇐  div(n,0+1+1) ≡ (q,r)¹
       heapify'(m,a,n,q) ≡ a  ⇐  m > q
       heapify'(m,a,n,q+1) ≡ heapify'(m,sift'(q+1,a,n),n,q)  ⇐  m ≤ q+1
       heapsort(abs(m,a,n)) ≡ makeSeq(m,heapsort'(m,a,n),n)
       heapsort'(m,a,n) ≡ a  ⇐  m ≥ n
       heapsort'(m,a,n+1)
          ≡ heapsort'(m,sift'(m,put(put(a,m,a[n+1]),n+1,a[m]),n),n)  ⇐  m < n+1
       makeSeq(m,a,n) ≡ ε  ⇐  m > n
       makeSeq(m,a,n+1) ≡ a[n+1]&makeSeq(m,a,n) ⇐ m ≤ n+1
thms   {U ≡ abs(m*2,a,n), U' ≡ abs(m*2+1,a,n)}  ⇐  abs(m,a,n) ≡ U•y•U'          (L1)
       {abs(m*2+1,a,n) ≡ abs(m*2+1,a",n),
        abs(m*2*2,a,n) ≡ abs(m*2*2,a",n),
        abs(m*2*2+1,a,n)  ≡  abs(m*2*2+1,a",n)}
                ⇐   a" ≡ put(put(a',m,y),m*2,z),  a' ≡ put(a,m,x)                (L2)
       {a[m] ≡ x,  a'[m*2] ≡ a[m*2],  a'[m*2+1] ≡ a[m*2+1]}
                       ⇐   a' ≡ put(a,m,x),  0 < m                               (L3)
       {a[m] ≡ y,  m ≤ n}  ⇐   abs(m,a,n) ≡ U•y•U'                               (L4)
       a ≡ put(a,m*2,x)  ⇐   a ≡ put(a',m*2,x)                                   (L5)
       abs(m*2+1,a,n) ≡ abs(m*2+1,sift'(m*2,a,n),n)  ⇐  0 < m                    (L6)
       sift'(m*2,a,n) ≡ put(sift'(m*2,a,n),m,y) ⇐ a ≡ put(a,m,y),  0 < m ≤ n     (L7)
       a ≡ put(a,m,y)  ⇐   a ≡ put(put(a',m,y),m*2,x),  0 < m                    (L8)
       0 < m ≤ n  ⇐   abs(m,a,n) ≡ U•y•U'                                        (L9)
       {0 < m ≤ n,  T ≡ abs(m*2,a,n),  T' ≡ abs(m*2+1,a,n)}
                  ⇐   T ≡ U•y•U',  T' ≡ V•z•V'                                   (L10)
```

Note the main idea of IMPLA: in contrast to the functions sift, heapify and heapsort, which are given as recursive programs on trees, their implementations sift', heapify' and heapsort' are specified as iterative programs on arrays.

Let IMPLR = HEAPSORT. As in Ex. 7.23, most of the conditions of Thm. 7.22 are easy to verify. The ground confluence proof again follows Cor. 6.16 provided that A1 and A2 were inverted. As a part of 7.22(a) let us show by inductive expansion that SI6 is inductively valid w.r.t. IMPL' (cf. Sect. 7.6).

goal	*rules applied*
sift(T•x•T') ≡ sift(U•x•U')•y•T' T ≡ U•y•U', T' ≡ V•z•V', x > y, y ≤ z	-- conclusion of SI6 -- generator of SI6
sift(abs(m,a',n)) ≡ sift(U•x•U')•y•abs(m*2+1,a,n) T ≡ abs(m*2,a,n), T' ≡ abs(m*2+1,a,n)	paramodulation upon A2

[1] *q* is the greatest index of *a* that denotes an internal node of *abs(m,a,n)*.

```
a' ≡ put(a,m,x),  0 < m ≤ n
T ≡ U•y•U',  T' ≡ V•z•V',  x > y,  y ≤ z
═══════════════════════════════════════════════════════════════
abs(m,sift'(m,a',n),n) ≡ sift(U•x•U')•y•abs(m*2+1,a,n)
T ≡ abs(m*2,a,n),  T' ≡ abs(m*2+1,a,n)              paramodulation upon SA1
a' ≡ put(a,m,x),  0 < m ≤ n
T ≡ U•y•U',  T' ≡ V•z•V',  x > y,  y ≤ z
═══════════════════════════════════════════════════════════════
abs(m,sift'(m,a',n),n)
≡ sift(abs(m*2*2,a,n)•x•abs(m*2*2+1,a,n))•y• abs(m*2+1,a,n)
abs(m*2,a,n) ≡ U•y•U'                                paramodulation upon L1
T ≡ abs(m*2,a,n),  T' ≡ abs(m*2+1,a,n)
a' ≡ put(a,m,x),  0 < m ≤ n
T ≡ U•y•U',  T' ≡ V•z•V',  x > y,  y ≤ z
═══════════════════════════════════════════════════════════════
abs(m,sift'(m*2,a",n),n)
≡ sift(abs(m*2*2,a,n)•x•abs(m*2*2+1,a,n))•y• abs(m*2+1,a,n)
a" ≡ put(put(a',m,a'[m*2]),m*2,a'[m])                paramodulation upon SA6
a'[m] > a'[m*2],  a'[m*2] ≤ a'[m*2+1],  n ≥ m*2+1
abs(m*2,a,n) ≡ U•y•U'
T ≡ abs(m*2,a,n),  T' ≡ abs(m*2+1,a,n)
a' ≡ put(a,m,x),  0 < m ≤ n
T ≡ U•y•U',  T' ≡ V•z•V',  x > y,  y ≤ z
═══════════════════════════════════════════════════════════════
abs(m,sift'(m*2,a",n),n)
≡ sift(abs(m*2*2,a",n)•x•abs(m*2*2+1,a",n))•y• abs(m*2+1,a",n)
a" ≡ put(put(a',m,a'[m*2]),m*2,a'[m])                paramodulation upon L2
a'[m] > a'[m*2],  a'[m*2] ≤ a'[m*2+1],  n ≥ m*2+1
abs(m*2,a,n) ≡ U•y•U'
T ≡ abs(m*2,a,n),  T' ≡ abs(m*2+1,a,n)
a' ≡ put(a,m,x),  0 < m ≤ n
T ≡ U•y•U',  T' ≡ V•z•V',  x > y,  y ≤ z
═══════════════════════════════════════════════════════════════
abs(m,sift'(m*2,a",n),n) ≡
sift(abs(m*2*2,a",n)•x•abs(m*2*2+1,a",n))•y• abs(m*2+1,a",n)
a" ≡ put(put(a',m,a[m*2]),m*2,x)                     paramodulation upon L3
x > a[m*2],  a[m*2] ≤ a[m*2+1],  n ≥ m*2+1
abs(m*2,a,n) ≡ U•y•U'
T ≡ abs(m*2,a,n),  T' ≡ abs(m*2+1,a,n)
a' ≡ put(a,m,x),  0 < m ≤ n
T ≡ U•y•U',  T' ≡ V•z•V',  x > y,  y ≤ z
═══════════════════════════════════════════════════════════════
abs(m,sift'(m*2,a",n),n)
≡ sift(abs(m*2*2,a",n)•x•abs(m*2*2+1,a",n))•y• abs(m*2+1,a",n)
a" ≡ put(put(a',m,y),m*2,x)                          paramodulation upon L4
```

```
abs(m*2,a,n) ≡ U•y•U'
abs(m*2+1,a,n) ≡ V•z•V'
T ≡ abs(m*2,a,n),  T' ≡ abs(m*2+1,a,n)
a' ≡ put(a,m,x),  0 < m ≤ n
T ≡ U•y•U',  T' ≡ V•z•V',  x > y,  y ≤ z
```

```
abs(m,sift'(m*2,a",n),n)
≡ sift(abs(m*2,a",n))•y• abs(m*2+1,a",n)          paramodulation upon A2
a" ≡ put(a",m*2,x),  0 < m*2 ≤ n
a" ≡ put(put(a',m,y),m*2,x)
abs(m*2,a,n) ≡ U•y•U'
abs(m*2+1,a,n) ≡ V•z•V'
T ≡ abs(m*2,a,n),  T' ≡ abs(m*2+1,a,n)
a' ≡ put(a,m,x),  0 < m ≤ n
T ≡ U•y•U',  T' ≡ V•z•V',  x > y,  y ≤ z
```

```
abs(m,sift'(m*2,a",n),n) ≡ sift(abs(m*2,a",n))•y•abs(m*2+1,a",n)
0 < m*2 ≤ n                                        resolution upon L5
a" ≡ put(put(a',m,y),m*2,x)
abs(m*2,a,n) ≡ U•y•U'
abs(m*2+1,a,n) ≡ V•z•V'
T ≡ abs(m*2,a,n),  T' ≡ abs(m*2+1,a,n)
a' ≡ put(a,m,x),  0 < m ≤ n
T ≡ U•y•U',  T' ≡ V•z•V',  x > y,  y ≤ z
```

```
abs(m,sift'(m*2,a",n),n) ≡ abs(m*2,sift'(m*2,a",n),n)•y•abs(m*2+1,a",n)
a" ≡ put(put(a',m,y),m*2,x)                        paramodulation upon SA1
abs(m*2,a,n) ≡ U•y•U'                              resolution upon L9
abs(m*2+1,a,n) ≡ V•z•V'
T ≡ abs(m*2,a,n),  T' ≡ abs(m*2+1,a,n)
a' ≡ put(a,m,x),  0 < m ≤ n
T ≡ U•y•U',  T' ≡ V•z•V',  x > y,  y ≤ z
```

```
abs(m,sift'(m*2,a",n),n)
≡ abs(m*2,sift'(m*2,a",n),n)•y•  abs(m*2+1,sift'(m*2,a",n),n)
a" ≡ put(put(a',m,y),m*2,x)                        paramodulation upon L6
abs(m*2,a,n) ≡ U•y•U'
abs(m*2+1,a,n) ≡ V•z•V'
T ≡ abs(m*2,a,n),  T' ≡ abs(m*2+1,a,n)
a' ≡ put(a,m,x),  0 < m ≤ n
T ≡ U•y•U',  T' ≡ V•z•V',  x > y,  y ≤ z
```

```
sift'(m*2,a",n) ≡ put(sift'(m*2,a",n),m,y)         resolution upon A2
a" ≡ put(put(a',m,y),m*2,x)
```

```
abs(m*2,a,n) ≡ U•y•U'
abs(m*2+1,a,n) ≡ V•z•V'
T ≡ abs(m*2,a,n), T' ≡ abs(m*2+1,a,n)
a' ≡ put(a,m,x), 0 < m ≤ n
T ≡ U•y•U', T' ≡ V•z•V', x > y, y ≤ z
=======================================================================
a" ≡ put(a",m,y)                                    resolution upon L7
a" ≡ put(put(a',m,y),m*2,x)
abs(m*2,a,n) ≡ U•y•U'
abs(m*2+1,a,n) ≡ V•z•V'
T ≡ abs(m*2,a,n), T' ≡ abs(m*2+1,a,n)
a' ≡ put(a,m,x), 0 < m ≤ n
T ≡ U•y•U', T' ≡ V•z•V', x > y, y ≤ z
=======================================================================
a" ≡ put(put(a',m,y),m*2,x)                         resolution upon L8
abs(m*2,a,n) ≡ U•y•U'
abs(m*2+1,a,n) ≡ V•z•V'
T ≡ abs(m*2,a,n), T' ≡ abs(m*2+1,a,n)
a' ≡ put(a,m,x), 0 < m ≤ n
T ≡ U•y•U', T' ≡ V•z•V', x > y, y ≤ z
=======================================================================
abs(m*2,a,n) ≡ U•y•U'                               unification
abs(m*2+1,a,n) ≡ V•z•V'
T ≡ abs(m*2,a,n), T' ≡ abs(m*2+1,a,n)
a' ≡ put(a,m,x), 0 < m ≤ n
T ≡ U•y•U', T' ≡ V•z•V', x > y, y ≤ z
=======================================================================
abs(m*2,a,n) ≡ U•y•U'                               unification
abs(m*2+1,a,n) ≡ V•z•V'
T ≡ abs(m*2,a,n), T' ≡ abs(m*2+1,a,n)
0 < m ≤ n
T ≡ U•y•U', T' ≡ V•z•V', x > y, y ≤ z
=======================================================================
T ≡ abs(m*2,a,n), T' ≡ abs(m*2+1,a,n)               resolution upon
0 < m ≤ n                                           U ≡ U' ⇐ T ≡ U, T ≡ U'
T ≡ U•y•U', T' ≡ V•z•V', x > y, y ≤ z
=======================================================================
T ≡ U•y•U', T' ≡ V•z•V', x > y, y ≤ z               resolution upon L10
=======================================================================
```

8.4 Balanced trees

We start with a specification of *AVL trees* as labelled binary trees with a key and a *balance value* at each node (cf., e.g., [Qui87], Sect. 5-2). The balance value is 0, +1 or -1. An AVL tree with left subtree L, key x, balance value i and right subtree R is represented by the term L•x|i•R.

```
AVL-TREE
   base       NSB
   sort vars  S
   sorts      tree, balVal
              symbol          type
   functs     Ω               tree
              _•_|_•_         tree,S,balVal,tree ⟶ tree
              0, -1, +1       balVal
              height          tree ⟶ nat
   preds      balanced        tree
              Def             tree
   vars       T,T',L,R : tree;  x : S;  n : nat;  i : balVal
   axms       balanced(T)  ⇐  Def(height(T))
              height(Ω) ≡ 0
              height(L•x|0•R) ≡ n+1   ⇐  height(L) ≡ n,  height(R) ≡ n
              height(L•x|-1•R) ≡ n+2  ⇐  height(L) ≡ n+1,  height(R) ≡ n
              height(L•x|+1•R) ≡ n+2  ⇐  height(L) ≡ n,  height(R) ≡ n+1
              Def(Ω)
              Def(L•x|i•R)  ⇐  Def(L),  Def(R)
   thms       height(L)+i ≡ height(R)  ⇐  balanced(L•x|i•R)
```

AVL-TREE is extended by a combined insertion and rebalancing operator insert. insert calls the function insertProg, which returns the modified tree together with a height increment 0 or 1. 0 indicates that the height of the tree has not changed, 1 indicates that the height has increased by 1.

```
AVL-TREE-INSERT
   base       AVL-TREE
              symbol          type
   functs     insert          tree,S ⟶ tree
              insertProg      tree,S ⟶ tree×nat
              rotate          tree ⟶ tree
   preds      _<_             S,S
```

vars T,T',L,R,L',R',LL,LR,RL,RR,LRL,LRR,RLL,RLR : tree; x,y,z : S;
i : balVal; k : nat

axms insert(T,z) ≡ T' ⇐ insertProg(T,z) ≡ (T',k)

insertProg(L•z|i•R,z) ≡ (L•z|i•R,0) (IC1)

insertProg(L•x|i•R,z) ≡ (L'•x|i•R,0)
⇐ z < x, insertProg(L,z) ≡ (L',0) (IC2)

insertProg(L•x|i•R,z) ≡ (L•x|i•R',0)
⇐ x < z, insertProg(R,z) ≡ (R',0) (IC3)

insertProg(Ω,z) ≡ (Ω•z|0•Ω,1) (IC4)

insertProg(L•x|0•R,z) ≡ (L'•x|-1•R,1)
⇐ z < x, insertProg(L,z) ≡ (L',1) (IC5)

insertProg(L•x|0•R,z) ≡ (L•x|+1•R',1)
⇐ x < z, insertProg(R,z) ≡ (R',1) (IC6)

insertProg(L•x|+1•R,z) ≡ (L'•x|0•R,0)
⇐ z < x, insertProg(L,z) ≡ (L',1) (IC7)

insertProg(L•x|-1•R,z) ≡ (L•x|0•R',0)
⇐ x < z, insertProg(R,z) ≡ (R',1) (IC8)

insertProg(L•x|-1•R,z) ≡ (rotate(L'•x|-1•R),0)
⇐ z < x, insertProg(L,z) ≡ (L',1) (IC9)

insertProg(L•x|+1•R,z) ≡ (rotate(L•x|+1•R'),0)
⇐ x < z, insertProg(R,z) ≡ (R',1) (IC10)

constrs ∀ x,y : x < y ∨ x ≡ y ∨ y < x (cf. Ex. 7.20)

conjects balanced(insert(T,x)) ⇐ balanced(T), Def(T) (BAL)

height(T') ≡ height(T)+i
⇐ balanced(T), Def(T), insertProg(T,x) ≡ (T',i) (HEI)

IC1-IC3 capture the cases where the tree does not change. IC4 generates a new leaf: an empty tree becomes a tree with height 1. In cases IC5 and IC6, the height of a tree with balance value 0 increases by 1. In cases IC7 and IC8, the height remains the same. Rebalancing is only necessary in cases IC9 and IC10 where the height first increases by 2, but tree rotations provide for a subsequent decrease by 1. Rotate works as follows:

rotate(L•x|-1•R) ≡ LL•y|0•(LR•x|0•R) ⇐ L ≡ LL•y|-1•LR (ROT1)

rotate(L•x|+1•R) ≡ (L•x|0•RL)•y|0•RR ⇐ R ≡ RL•y|+1•RR (ROT2)

rotate(L•x|-1•R) ≡ (LL•y|0•LRL)•z|0•(LRR•x|+1•R)
⇐ L ≡ LL•y|+1•(LRL•z|-1•LRR) (ROT3)

rotate(L•x|-1•R) ≡ (LL•y|-1•LRL)•z|0•(LRR•x|0•R)
⇐ L ≡ LL•y|+1•(LRL•z|+1•LRR) (ROT4)

rotate(L•x|+1•R) ≡ (L•x|0•RLL)•z|0•(RLR•y|+1•RR)
⇐ R ≡ (RLL•z|-1•RLR)•y|-1•RR (ROT5)

rotate(L•x|+1•R) ≡ (L•x|-1•RLL)•z|0•(RLR•y|0•RR)
⇐ R ≡ (RLL•z|-1•RLR)•y|+1•RR (ROT6)

These axioms consider all trees T with height n that `insertProg` can generate from a tree with height n-2. L (R) denotes the left (right) subtree of T, LL (LR) denotes the left (right) subtree of L, etc. ROTi, i = 1,...,6, handles the cases where the new leaf belongs to LL, RR, LRL, LRR, RLL, RLR, respectively. HEI comes up as the necessary generalization of BAL. Can it be obtained by applying known generalization techniques?

The specification of *2-3 trees* (cf., e.g., [HO82]) is quite similar. Each node of a 2-3 tree has one or two labels and, accordingly, two or three successors.

```
2-3-TREE
   base       NSB
   sort vars  S
   sorts      tree
              symbol         type
   functs     Ω              tree
              _•_•_          tree,S,tree ⟶ tree
              _•_•_•_•_      tree,S,tree,S,tree ⟶ tree
              height         tree ⟶ nat
   preds      balanced       tree
              Def            tree
   vars       T,T',L,M,R : tree;  x,y : S;  n : nat
   axms       balanced(T)  ⇐  Def(height(T))
              height(Ω) ≡ 0
              height(L•x•R) ≡ n+1  ⇐  height(L) ≡ n, height(R) ≡ n
              height(L•x•M•y•R) ≡ n+1 ⇐ height(L) ≡ n, height(M) ≡ n, height(R) ≡ n
              Def(Ω)
              Def(L•x•R)  ⇐  Def(L), Def(R)
              Def(L•x•M•y•R)  ⇐  Def(L), Def(M), Def(R)
   thms       height(L) ≡ height(R)  ⇐  balanced(L•x•R)
              {height(L) ≡ height(M), height(M) ≡ height(R)} ⇐ balanced(L•x•M•y•R)

2-3-TREE-INSERT
   base    2-3-TREE
           symbol            type
   functs  insert            tree,S ⟶ tree
           insertProg        tree,S ⟶ tree×nat
   preds   _<_    S,S

   vars    T,T',L,M,R,L',M',R',LL,LR,ML,MR,RL,RR : tree;  x,y,z : S;  i : balVal;  k : nat

   axms    insert(T,z) ≡ T'  ⇐  insertProg(T,z) ≡ (T',k)

           insertProg(L•z•R,z) ≡ (L•z•R,0)                                  (IC1)

           insertProg(L•z•M•y•R,z) ≡ (L•z•M•y•R,0)                          (IC2)

           insertProg(L•x•M•z•R,z) ≡ (L•x•M•z•R,0)                          (IC3)
```

$$\texttt{insertProg}(L\circ x\circ R,z) \equiv (L'\circ x\circ R,0) \Leftarrow z < x,\ \texttt{insertProg}(L,z) \equiv (L',0) \qquad \text{(IC4)}$$

$$\texttt{insertProg}(L\circ x\circ R,z) \equiv (L\circ x\circ R',0) \Leftarrow x < z,\ \texttt{insertProg}(R,z) \equiv (R',0) \qquad \text{(IC5)}$$

$$\texttt{insertProg}(L\circ x\circ M\circ y\circ R,z) \equiv (L'\circ x\circ M\circ y\circ R,0) \Leftarrow z < x,\ \texttt{insertProg}(L,z) \equiv (L',0) \qquad \text{(IC6)}$$

$$\texttt{insertProg}(L\circ x\circ M\circ y\circ R,z) \equiv (L\circ x\circ M'\circ y\circ R,0) \Leftarrow x < z,\ z < y,\ \texttt{insertProg}(M,z) \equiv (M',0) \qquad \text{(IC7)}$$

$$\texttt{insertProg}(L\circ x\circ M\circ y\circ R,z) \equiv (L\circ x\circ M\circ y\circ R',0) \Leftarrow y < z,\ \texttt{insertProg}(R,z) \equiv (R',0) \qquad \text{(IC8)}$$

$$\texttt{insertProg}(\Omega,z) \equiv (\Omega\circ z\circ\Omega,1) \qquad \text{(IC9)}$$

$$\texttt{insertProg}(L\circ x\circ R,z) \equiv (LL\circ x'\circ LR\circ x\circ R,0) \Leftarrow z < x,\ \texttt{insertProg}(L,z) \equiv (LL\circ x'\circ LR,1) \qquad \text{(IC10)}$$

$$\texttt{insertProg}(L\circ x\circ R,z) \equiv (L\circ x\circ RL\circ x'\circ RR,0) \Leftarrow x < z,\ \texttt{insertProg}(R,z) \equiv (RL\circ x'\circ RR,1) \qquad \text{(IC11)}$$

$$\texttt{insertProg}(L\circ x\circ M\circ y\circ R,z) \equiv ((LL\circ x'\circ LR)\circ x\circ(M\circ y\circ R),1) \Leftarrow z < x,\ \texttt{insertProg}(L,z) \equiv (LL\circ x'\circ LR,1) \qquad \text{(IC12)}$$

$$\texttt{insertProg}(L\circ x\circ M\circ y\circ R,z) \equiv ((L\circ x\circ ML)\circ x'\circ(MR\circ y\circ R),1) \Leftarrow x < z,\ z < y,\ \texttt{insertProg}(M,z) \equiv (ML\circ x'\circ MR,1) \qquad \text{(IC13)}$$

$$\texttt{insertProg}(L\circ x\circ M\circ y\circ R,z) \equiv ((L\circ x\circ M)\circ y\circ(RL\circ x'\circ RR),1) \Leftarrow y < z,\ \texttt{insertProg}(R,z) \equiv (RL\circ x'\circ RR,1) \qquad \text{(IC14)}$$

constrs $\forall\, x,y : x < y \ \vee\ x \equiv y \ \vee\ y < x$

conjects $\texttt{balanced}(\texttt{insert}(T,x)) \Leftarrow \texttt{balanced}(T),\ \texttt{Def}(T)$ (BAL)

$$\texttt{height}(T') \equiv \texttt{height}(T)+i \Leftarrow \texttt{balanced}(T),\ \texttt{Def}(T),\ \texttt{insertProg}(T,x) \equiv (T',i) \qquad \text{(HEI)}$$

IC1-IC9 capture the cases where the tree does not change. IC9 generates a new leaf: an empty tree becomes a tree with height 1. IC10 and IC11 rebalance a tree by merging its root with the root of one of its subtrees, thereby turning a 2-tree into a 3-tree. Conversely, IC12-IC14 transform a debalanced 3-tree into a 2-tree that will be balanced later by IC10 or IC11. By virtue of the axioms for `insertProg`, the proof of HEI by inductive expansion splits into 14 subexpansions (cf. Sect. 5.3):

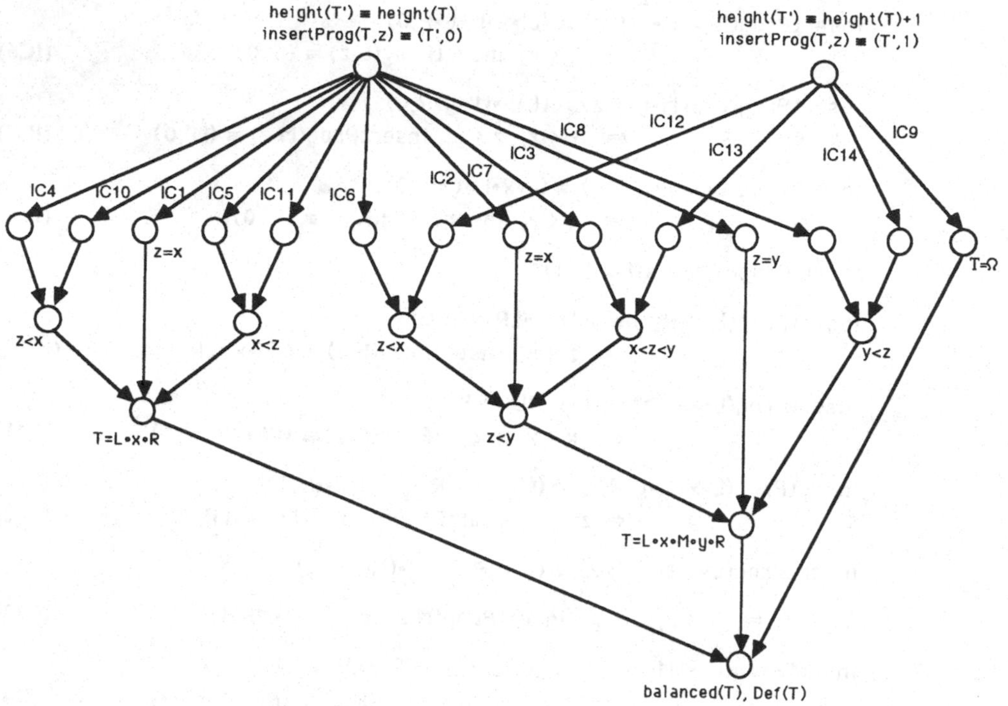

Figure 8.1 Schema of an expansion of HEI.

Let us translate the (constructor-based) axioms for insert and insertProg into SML programs. Note how the case analysis given by the axioms for insertProg is represented in SML.

```
datatype 'S tree = empty |
                   c2 of ('S tree) * 'S * ('S tree) |
                   c3 of ('S tree) * 'S * ('S tree) * 'S * ('S tree)
fun    insert(T,z) = let val (T',k) = insertProg(T,z) in T' end
and    insertProg(empty,z) = (c2(empty,z,empty),1) |
       insertProg(c2(L,x,R),z)
       =  if z = x then (c2(L,x,R),0) else
          if z < x then case insertProg(L,z) of
                  (L',0) => (c2(L',x,R),0) |
                  (c2(LL,x',LR),1) => (c3(LL,x',LR,x,R),0) |
                  _ => raise error else
          if x < z then case insertProg(R,z) of
                  (R',0) => (c2(L,x,R'),0) |
```

```
                (c2(RL,x',RR),1) => (c3(L,x',RL,x,RR),0) |
                _ => raise error
      else raise error |
   insertProg(c3(L,x,M,y,R),z)
   =  if z = x orelse z = y then (c3(L,x,M,y,R),0) else
      if z < x then case insertProg(L,z) of
                (L',0) => (c3(L',x,M,y,R),0) |
                (c2(LL,x',LR),1) => (c2(c2(LL,x',LR),x,c2(M,y,R)),0) |
                _ => raise error else
      if x < z andalso z < y then case insertProg(M,z) of
                      (M',0) => (c3(L,x,M',y,R),0) |
                      (c2(ML,x',MR),1) => (c2(c2(LL,x,LR),x',c2(M,y,R)),0) |
                      _ => raise error else
      if y < z then case insertProg(R,z) of
                    (R',0) => (c3(L,x,M,y,R'),0) |
                    (c2(RL,x',RR),1) => (c2(c2(LL,x,LR),y,c2(M,x',R)),0) |
                    _ => raise error
      else raise error
```

8.5 Game trees

Sets of possible moves in a two-person zero-sum game are structured with the help of a game tree (cf., e.g., [Qui87], Sect. 9-3). Game states are represented by nodes, while edges denote direct transitions between successive states. In states at even (odd) tree levels, the first (second) player goes ahead. Each leaf is labelled with the profit of the first player, provided that the game reaches the state corresponding to that leaf.

The leaf labels are regarded as weights of the game states they denote. Starting out from the leaves, one wants to compute the weights of all nodes. Of course, the computation depends on the perspective: the first player tries to maximize the weight, the second player attempts to minimize it. Therefore, the functions maximize and minimize (see below) are called alternatingly, when the computation proceeds from an even (odd) to an odd (even) tree level.

INT

sorts	int	
	symbol	*type*
functs	0	int
	_+1	int ⟶ int
	∞	int

```
              -_          int ⟶ int
              min         int ⟶ int
              max         int ⟶ int
   preds      _ ≤ _       int,int
              _ < _       int,int
              _ ≢ _       int,int
   vars       x,y : int
   axms       -0 ≡ 0
              --x ≡ x
              -(x+1)+1 ≡ -x
              ∞+1 ≡ ∞
              x ≤ ∞
              x ≤ x
              x ≤ y+1   ⇐   x ≤ y
              x ≤ -y   ⇐   y ≤ -x
              x < y   ⇐   x+1 ≤ y
              x ≢ y   ⇐   x < y
              x ≢ y   ⇐   y < x
              min(x,y) ≡ x   ⇐   x ≤ y
              min(x,y) ≡ y   ⇐   y < x
              max(x,y) ≡ -min(-x,-y)
GAME-TREE
  base        INT
  sort vars   S,S'
  sorts       int, tree, seq(S)
              symbol            type
  functs      ε                 seq(S)
              _&_               S,seq(S) ⟶ seq(S)
              _@_               int,seq(tree) ⟶ tree
              minseq            seq(int) ⟶ int
              maxseq            seq(int)⟶ int
              minimize          tree ⟶ int
              maximize          tree ⟶ int
              minimizeseq       seq(tree) ⟶ int
              maximizeseq       seq(tree) ⟶ int
              map(F)            seq(S) ⟶ seq(S')
  preds       _ > _             int×int×seq(tree)×int,int×int×seq(tree)×int
              _ > _             seq(tree),seq(tree)
```

```
vars    x,y,a,b,c,d : int;  xs : seq(int);  F : S⟶S';
        T : tree;  Ts,Us : seq(tree);  el : S;  s : seq(S)
axms    minseq(ε) ≡ ∞
        minseq(x&xs) ≡ min(x,minseq(xs))
        maxseq(ε) ≡ -∞
        maxseq(x&xs) ≡ max(x,maxseq(xs))
        minimize(x@ε) ≡ x                                      (M1)
        minimize(x@T&Ts) ≡ minimizeseq(T&Ts)                   (M2)
        maximize(x@ε) ≡ x                                      (M3)
        maximize(x@T&Ts) ≡ maximizeseq(T&Ts)                   (M4)
        minimizeseq(Ts) ≡ minseq(map(maximize)(Ts))
        maximizeseq(Ts) ≡ maxseq(map(minimize)(Ts))
        map(F)(ε) ≡ ε
        map(F)(el&s) ≡ F(el)&map(F)(s)
        (a,x,Ts,b) > (c,y,Us,d)  ⇐  Ts > Us                    (GR1)
        (x@Ts)&Us > Ts                                         (GR2)
        (x@Ts)&Us > Us                                         (GR3)
thms    minimizeseq(ε) ≡ ∞                                     (L1)
        minimizeseq(T&Ts) ≡ min(minimizeseq(Ts),maximize(T))   (L2)
        maximizeseq(ε) ≡ -∞                                    (L3)
        maximizeseq(T&Ts) ≡ max(minimize(T),maximizeseq(Ts))   (L4)
        min(min(x,y),z) ≡ min(x,min(y,z))                      (L5)
        max(x,max(y,z)) ≡ max(max(x,y),z)                      (L6)
        max(x,min(y,z)) ≡ min(max(x,y),max(x,z))               (L7)
        min(max(x,y),z) ≡ max(min(x,z),min(y,z))               (L8)
        min(max(x,y),z) ≡ max(x,min(y,z))  ⇐  x ≤ z            (L9)
        x ≤ max(x,min(y,z))  ⇐  x ≤ z                          (L10)
        max(x,min(y,z)) ≤ z  ⇐  x ≤ z                          (L11)
        min(∞,x) ≡ x                                           (L12)
        min(-∞,x) ≡ -∞                                         (L13)
        max(x,-∞) ≡ x                                          (L14)
        max(x,y) ≡ y  ⇐  x ≤ y                                 (L15)
        ∃ {x,Ts} T ≡ x@Ts                                      (L16)
        Ts ≡ ε  ∨  ∃ {x,Us,Ts'} Ts ≡ (x@Us)&Ts'                (L17)
```

`Minimize` and `maximize` traverse the entire tree without taking into account that their values range between given upper and lower bounds, namely the minimum (maximum) of the set of leaf labels. The branch-and-bound algorithm called *alpha-beta pruning* leads to optimized versions

ABminimize, ABmaximize : int,tree,int ⟶ int

of minimize and maximize by moving stepwise the lower and upper bounds closer together. If both bounds coincide, the tree need no longer be visited: ABminimize and ABmaximize only return the bound.[1] The correctness condition on these functions in terms of minimize and maximize reads as follows:

{ABminimize(a,x@Ts,b) ≡ minimize(x@Ts),

ABmaximize(a,x@Ts,b) ≡ maximize(x@Ts)} ⇐ a ≤ b. (ABM0)

In fact, one must establish the following generalization:

{ABminimize(a,x@Ts,b) ≡ max(a,min(minimize(x@Ts),b)),

ABmaximize(a,x@Ts,b) ≡ max(a,min(maximize(x@Ts),b))} ⇐ a ≤ b. (ABM)

ABM0 follows from ABM whenever the labels of x@Ts range between a and b. When executing ABminimize(a,x@Ts,b), we may come up with a recursive call ABminimize(a',x'@Ts',b') such that a' and b' do not enclose the labels of x'@Ts'. Therefore, ABM0 is indeed too weak for an inductive proof. Moreover, the structure of trees requires functions

ABminimizeseq, ABmaximizeseq : int,seq(tree),int ⟶ int

on tree *sequences* and a corresponding extension of ABM:

conjects {ABminimize(a,x@Ts,b) ≡ max(a,min(minimize(x@Ts),b)),

ABmaximize(a,x@Ts,b) ≡ max(a,min(maximize(x@Ts),b)),

ABminimizeseq(a,Ts,b) ≡ max(a,min(minimizeseq(Ts),b)),

ABmaximizeseq(a,Ts,b) ≡ max(a,min(maximizeseq(Ts),b))}⇐ a ≤ b. (ABMS)

We derive functional programs for all AB-functions from an inductive expansion of ABMS:

	goal	*rules applied*
G1	ABminimize(a,x@Ts,b) ≡ max(a,min(minimize(x@Ts),b))	-- conclusion of ABMS
	ABmaximize(a,x@Ts,b) ≡ max(a,min(maximize(x@Ts),b))	
	ABminimizeseq(a,Ts,b) ≡ max(a,min(minimizeseq(Ts),b))	
	ABmaximizeseq(a,Ts,b) ≡ max(a,min(maximizeseq(Ts),b))	

[1]For functional programs implementing alpha-beta pruning, cf. [BW88], Sect. 9.7, or [Hug89], Sect. 5. Our correctness condition ABMS is inspired by [BW88]: *bmx* and *cmx* correspond to *ABmaximize* and *ABmaximizeseq*, respectively.

Ts ≡ ε
ABminimize(a,x@ε,b) ≡ max(a,min(x,b))
ABmaximize(a,x@ε,b) ≡ max(a,min(x,b))
ABminimizeseq(a,ε,b) ≡ max(a,min(∞,b))
ABmaximizeseq(a,ε,b) ≡ max(a,min(-∞,b))

paramodulation upon M1, M3, L1, L3

G1

Ts ≡ ε
ABminimizeseq(a,ε,b) ≡ max(a,b)
ABmaximizeseq(a,ε,b) ≡ max(a,-∞)

resolution upon P1, P3 (see (see below), paramodulation upon L12, L13

G1

Ts ≡ ε
ABminimizeseq(a,ε,b) ≡ b
a ≤ b
ABmaximizeseq(a,ε,b) ≡ a

paramodulation upon L14, L15

G1

G2 Ts ≡ ε
a ≤ b

resolution upon P5, P7 see below)

G1

G2

Ts ≡ T'&Ts'
ABminimize(a,x@T'&Ts',b) ≡ max(a,min(minimizeseq(T'&Ts'),b))
ABmaximize(a,x@T'&Ts',b) ≡ max(a,min(maximizeseq(T'&Ts'),b))
ABminimizeseq(a,T'&Ts',b) ≡ max(a,min(minimizeseq(T'&Ts'),b))
ABmaximizeseq(a,T'&Ts',b) ≡ max(a,min(maximizeseq(T'&Ts'),b))

paramodulation upon M2, M4

G2

Ts ≡ T'&Ts'
ABminimize(a,x@T'&Ts',b) ≡ ABminimizeseq(a,T'&Ts',b)
ABmaximize(a,x@T'&Ts',b) ≡ ABmaximizeseq(a,T'&Ts',b)
ABminimizeseq(a,T'&Ts',b) ≡ max(a,min(minimizeseq(T'&Ts'),b))
ABmaximizeseq(a,T'&Ts',b) ≡ max(a,min(maximizeseq(T'&Ts'),b))

paramodulation upon a symmetry axiom

```
G2
--------------------------------------------------------------------------
Ts ≡ T'&Ts'
ABminimizeseq(a,T'&Ts',b) ≡ max(a,min(minimizeseq(T'&Ts'),b))
                                             resolution upon P2, P4
                                             (see below)
ABmaximizeseq(a,T'&Ts',b) ≡ max(a,min(maximizeseq(T'&Ts'),b))
==========================================================================
G2
--------------------------------------------------------------------------
Ts ≡ T'&Ts'                                  paramodulation upon
ABminimizeseq(a,T'&Ts',b) ≡                  L2, L4
     max(a,min(min(minimizeseq(Ts'), maximize(T')), b))
ABmaximizeseq(a,T'&Ts',b) ≡
     max(a,min(max(minimize(T'),maximizeseq(Ts')),b))
==========================================================================
G2
--------------------------------------------------------------------------
Ts ≡ T'&Ts'                                  paramodulation upon
ABminimizeseq(a,T'&Ts',b)≡                   L5, L8
     max(a,min(minimizeseq(Ts'),min(maximize(T'),b)))
ABmaximizeseq(a,T'&Ts',b) ≡
     max(a,max(min(minimize(T'),b),min(maximizeseq(Ts'),b)))
==========================================================================
G2
--------------------------------------------------------------------------
Ts ≡ T'&Ts'                                  paramodulation upon
ABminimizeseq(a,T'&Ts',b) ≡                  L7, L6
     min(max(a,minimizeseq(Ts')),max(a,min(maximize(T'),b)))
ABmaximizeseq(a,T'&Ts',b) ≡
     max(max(a,min(minimize(T'),b)),min(maximizeseq(Ts'),b))
==========================================================================
G2
--------------------------------------------------------------------------
Ts ≡ T'&Ts'                                  paramodulation upon L9
ABminimizeseq(a,T'&Ts',b) ≡
     max(a,min(minimizeseq(Ts'),max(a,min(maximize(T'),b))))
a ≤ max(a,min(maximize(T'),b))
ABmaximizeseq(a,T'&Ts',b) ≡
     max(max(a,min(minimize(T'),b)),min(maximizeseq(Ts'),b))
==========================================================================
G2
--------------------------------------------------------------------------
Ts ≡ T'&Ts'
ABminimizeseq(a,T'&Ts',b) ≡
     ABminimizeseq(a,Ts',max(a,min(maximize(T'),b)))
```

(a,x,T'&Ts',b) > (a,x,Ts',max(a,min(maximize(T'),b)))	inductive
a ≤ max(a,min(maximize(T'),b))	paramodulation
ABmaximizeseq(a,T'&Ts',b) ≡ ABmaximizeseq(max(a,min(minimize(T'),b)),Ts',b)	
(a,x,T'&Ts',b) > (max(a,min(minimize(T'),b)),x,Ts',b)	inductive
max(a,min(minimize(T'),b)) ≤ b	paramodulation

G2

Ts ≡ (y@Us)&Ts'	
ABminimizeseq(a,(y@Us)&Ts',b) ≡ ABminimizeseq(a,Ts',max(a,min(maximize(y@Us),b)))	
(a,x,(y@Us)&Ts',b) > (a,x,Ts',max(a,min(maximize(y@Us),b)))	
a ≤ max(a,min(maximize(y@Us),b))	
ABmaximizeseq(a,(y@Us)&Ts',b) ≡ ABmaximizeseq(max(a,min(minimize(y@Us),b)),Ts',b)	
(a,x,(y@Us)&Ts',b) > (max(a,min(minimize(y@Us),b)),x,Ts',b)	
max(a,min(minimize(y@Us),b)) ≤ b	paramodulation upon L16

G2

Ts ≡ (y@Us)&Ts'	
ABminimizeseq(a,(y@Us)&Ts',b) ≡ ABminimizeseq(a,Ts',ABmaximize(y@Us))	
(a,x,(y@Us)&Ts',b) > (a,y,Us,b)	inductive
a ≤ b	paramodulation
(a,x,(y@Us)&Ts',b) > (a,x,Ts',max(a,min(maximize(y@Us),b)))	
a ≤ max(a,min(maximize(y@Us),b))	
ABmaximizeseq(a,(y@Us)&Ts',b) ≡ ABmaximizeseq(ABminimize(y@Us),Ts',b)	
(a,x,(y@Us)&Ts',b) > (max(a,min(minimize(y@Us),b)),x,Ts',b)	inductive
max(a,min(minimize(y@Us),b)) ≤ b	paramodulation

G2

Ts ≡ (y@Us)&Ts'	resolution upon P6, P8
(y@Us)&Ts' > Us	(see below), GR1, L10,
a ≤ b	L11
(y@Us)&Ts' > Ts'	

G2

Ts ≡ (y@Us)&Ts'	resolution upon GR2,
a ≤ b	GR3

a ≤ b	resolution upon L17

The following program has been derived:

```
ABminimize(a,x@ε,b) ≡ max(a,min(x,b))                                    (P1)
ABminimize(a,x@T&Ts,b) ≡ ABminimizeseq(a,T&Ts,b)                         (P2)
ABmaximize(a,x@ε,b) ≡ max(a,min(x,b))                                    (P3)
ABmaximize(a,x@T&Ts,b) ≡ ABmaximizeseq(a,T&Ts,b)                         (P4)
ABminimizeseq(a,ε,b) ≡ b                                                 (P5)
ABminimizeseq(a,T&Ts,b) ≡ ABminimizeseq(a,Ts,ABmaximize(a,T,b))
                                                                         (P6)
ABmaximizeseq(a,ε,b) ≡ a                                                 (P7)
ABmaximizeseq(a,T&Ts,b) ≡ ABmaximizeseq(ABminimize(a,T,b),Ts,b)
                                                                         (P8)
```

Since for all AB-functions F, the equation F(a,X,a)≡a is INT∪{ABMS}-valid, P6 and P8 can be optimized:

```
ABminimizeseq(a,T&Ts,a) ≡ a
ABminimizeseq(a,T&Ts,b) ≡ ABminimizeseq(a,Ts,ABmaximize(a,T,b))
        ⇐  a ≢ b
ABmaximizeseq(a,T&Ts,a) ≡ a
ABmaximizeseq(a,T&Ts,b) ≡ ABmaximizeseq(ABminimize(a,T,b),Ts,b)
        ⇐  a ≢ b.
```

8.6 Binary graphs

Given a set N of nodes, binary graphs are functions from N to N×N. We start with a specification of finite (node) sets:

SET

sort vars	S	
sorts	set	
	symbol	*type*
functs	∅	set
	insert	S,set ⟶ set
preds	_ ≢ _	S,S
	_ ∈ _	S,set
	_ ∉ _	S,set
	_ ⊆ _	set,set
	_ ⊃ _	set,set
vars	k,k',m,m',n,n' : S; s,s' : set	
axms	insert(n,insert(n,s)) ≡ insert(n,s)	
	insert(m,insert(n,s)) ≡ insert(n,insert(m,s))	

```
            n ∈ insert(n,s)                                              (SET1)
            m ∈ insert(n,s)  ⇐  m ∈ s
            m ∉ Ø
            m ∉ insert(n,s)  ⇐  m ≢ n, m ∉ s
            Ø ⊆ s
            insert(n,s) ⊆ s'  ⇐  n ∈ s', s ⊆ s'
            s ⊃ s'  ⇐  k ∈ s, k ∉ s', s' ⊆ s                             (SET2)
thms        s ⊆ insert(k,s)                                              (SET3)
            insert(k,s) ⊃ s  ⇐  k ∉ s                                    (SET4)
            k ∈ s  ∨  k ∉ s                                              (SET5)
constrs     ∀ m,n : m ≡ n ∨ m ≢ n

BINGRAPH
  base      SET
  sorts     graph
            symbol              type
  functs    init                graph
            _[_⟶_×_]            graph,S,S,S ⟶ graph
            _[_]                graph ⟶ S×S
            remove              set,graph ⟶ graph
            nodes               graph ⟶ set
            nodesAcc            graph,set ⟶ set
  vars      k,k',m,m',n,n' : S;  s,s' : set;  g : graph;  w,w' : seq(S)
  axms      g[k⟶m×n][k⟶m'×n'] ≡ g[k⟶m×n]
            g[k⟶m×n][k'⟶m'×n'] ≡ g[k'⟶m'×n'][k⟶m×n]  ⇐  k ≢ k'
            g[k⟶m×n][k] ≡ (m,n)
            g[k⟶m×n][k'] ≡ g[k']  ⇐  k ≢ k'
            remove(s,init) ≡ init
            remove(s,g[k⟶m×n]) ≡ remove(s,g)  ⇐  k ∈ s
            remove(s,g[k⟶m×n]) ≡ remove(s,g)[k⟶m×n]  ⇐  k ∉ s
            nodes(g) ≡ nodesAcc(g,Ø)
            nodesAcc(init,s) ≡ s
            nodesAcc(g[k⟶m×n],s) ≡ nodesAcc(g,s)  ⇐  k ∈ s
            nodesAcc(g[k⟶m×n],s) ≡ nodesAcc(g,insert(k,s))  ⇐  k ∉ s
```

SML admits the direct translation of functional structures, such as binary graphs, into function types and associated higher order operations:

```
type 'S graph = 'S -> ('S * 'S)
```

For instance, the assignment operator _[_→_×_] of BINGRAPH is of second order:

```
fun assign(k,m,n)(g) = fn(x) => if x = k then (m,n) else g(x)
```

With the composition operator •, defined by

```
fun f • g = fn(x) => g(f(x)),
```

binary graphs can be entered as expressions of the form

$$\text{assign}(x_1,y_1,z_1) \circ \text{assign}(x_2,y_2,z_2) \circ \ldots \circ \text{assign}(x_n,y_n,z_n).$$

Node sets may be implemented by sequences, and the membership predicates ∈ and ∉ become a Boolean function:

```
fun  k ∈ nil  =  false |
     k ∈ n::s  =  k = n orelse k ∈ s
```

8.6.1 Depth-first marking

DEPTHFIRST

base	BINGRAPH	
sorts	seq(S)	
	symbol	*type*
functs	depthfirst	S,set,graph ⟶ set
	DFLoop	S,set,graph,seq(S) ⟶ set
	ε	seq(S)
	_&_	S,seq(S) ⟶ seq(S)
	makeSet	seq(S) ⟶ set
preds	_>_	S×set×graph×seq(S),S×set×graph×seq(S)
vars	k,k',m,n : S; s,s' : set; g : graph; w,w' : seq(S)	

axms

depthfirst(k,s,g) ≡ s ⇐ k ∈ s (DF1)

depthfirst(k,s,g) ≡ depthfirst(n,depthfirst(m,insert(k,s),g),g)
⇐ k ∉ s, g[k] ≡ (m,n) (DF2)

DFLoop(k,s,g,w) ≡ DFLoop(m,insert(k,s),g,k&w)
⇐ k ∉ s, g[k] ≡ (m,n) (DFL1)

DFLoop(k,s,g,k'&w) ≡ DFLoop(n,s,g,w)
⇐ k ∈ s, g[k'] ≡ (m,n) (DFL2)

DFLoop(k,s,g,ε) ≡ s ⇐ k ∈ s (DFL3)

makeSet(ε) ≡ ∅

makeSet(k&w) ≡ insert(k,makeSet(w))

(k,s,g,w) > (k',s',g,w')

	⇐ nodes(remove(s,g)) ⊃ nodes(remove(s',g))	(GR1)
	(k,s,g,n&w) > (k',s,g,w)	(GR2)
thms	k ∈ depthfirst(k,s,g)	(L1)
	depthfirst(m,insert(k,s),g) ⊃ s ⇐ k ∉ s	(L2)
	nodes(remove(s,g)) ⊃ nodes(remove(s',g)) ⇐ s' ⊃ s	(L3)
	m ∈ nodes(g) ⇐ g[k] ≡ (m,n)	(L4)
	n ∈ nodes(g) ⇐ g[k] ≡ (m,n)	(L5)
	∃ {m,n} g[k] ≡ (m,n) ⇐ k ∈ nodes(g)	(L6)
	w ≡ ε ∨ ∃ {k,w'} w ≡ k&w'	(L7)
	k ∈ nodes(g) ⇐ makeSet(k&w) ⊆ nodes(g)	(L8)
	makeSet(k&w) ⊆ nodes(g) ⇐ k ∈ nodes(g), makeSet(w) ⊆ nodes(g)	(L9)
conjects	DFLoop(k,∅,g,ε) ≡ depthfirst(k,∅,g) ⇐ k ∈ nodes(g)	(C1)
	DFLoop(k,s,g,w) ≡ DFLoop(k',s',g,w) ⇐ k ∈ nodes(g), k' ∈ nodes(g), depthfirst(k,s,g) ≡ s', makeSet(w) ⊆ nodes(g)	(C2)

The (constructor-based) axioms for depthfirst and its iterative version DFLoop yield the following SML programs:

```
fun depthfirst(k,s,g) =   if k ∈ s
                          then s
                          else  let val (m,n) = g(k)
                                in depthfirst(n,depthfirst(m,k::s,g),g) end

fun DFLoop(k,s,g,w) =     if k ∈ s
                          then case w of nil => s |
                                         k'::w' =>   let val (m,n) = g(k')
                                                     in DFLoop(k,s,g,w') end
                          else  let val (m,n) = g(k)
                                in DFLoop(m,k::s,g,k::w) end
```

Conjecture C2 generalizes C1: DFL3, L1 and C2 imply C1. GR1 and GR2 define the descent predicate used in the following inductive expansion of C2. Since {C2} is a constructor-based clause set with input variables k,s,g,w, guard {k ∈ nodes(g)} and generator {depthfirst(k,s,g) ≡ s'}, we can apply Cor. 5.6.

---

goal	*substitution of X_{out}*	*rules applied*

G1	DFLoop(k,s,g,w) ≡ DFLoop(k',s',g,w) depthfirst(k,s,g) ≡ s'		-- conclusion of C2 -- generator of C2
G2	DFLoop(k,s,g,w) ≡ DFLoop(k',s,g,w) k ∈ s	s/s'	resolution upon DF1
	G1		
	s ≡ s w ≡ ε, k ∈ s		paramodulation upon DFL3
	G2		
	G1		
	w ≡ ε, k ∈ s		unification
	G2		
	G1		
	w ≡ ε, k ∈ s		
	DFLoop(n,s,g,w') ≡ DFLoop(n,s,g,w') w ≡ k"&w', k ∈ s, g[k"] ≡ (m,n)		paramodulation upon DFL2
	G1		
	w ≡ ε, k ∈ s		
	w ≡ k"&w', k ∈ s, g[k"] ≡ (m,n)		unification
	G1		
	w ≡ ε, k ∈ s		
	w ≡ k"&w', k ∈ s, k" ∈ nodes(g)		resolution upon L6
	G1		
	w ≡ ε, k ∈		
	w ≡ k"&w', k ∈ s, makeSet(k"&w') ⊆ nodes(g)		resolution upon L8
	G1		

w ≡ ε, k ∈ s	
w ≡ k"&w', k ∈ s, makeSet(w) ⊆ nodes(g)	equational replacement
G1	
k ∈ s, makeSet(w) ⊆ nodes(g)	resolution upon L7
G1	
k ∈ s, makeSet(w) ⊆ nodes(g)	
DFLoop(m,insert(k,s),g,k&w) ≡ DFLoop(k',s',g,w) k ∉ s, g[k] ≡ (m,n) depthfirst(k,s,g) ≡ s'	paramodulation upon DFL1
k ∈ s, makeSet(w) ⊆ nodes(g)	
DFLoop(m,s",g,k&w) ≡ DFLoop(k',s',g,w) m ∈ nodes(g) depthfirst(m,insert(k,s),g) ≡ s" makeSet(k&w) ⊆ nodes(g) (k,s,g,w) > (m,insert(k,s),g,k&w) k ∉ s, g[k] ≡ (m,n) depthfirst(k,s,g) ≡ s'	inductive paramodulation
k ∈ s, makeSet(w) ⊆ nodes(g)	
DFLoop(m,s",g,k&w) ≡ DFLoop(k',s',g,w) k ∈ nodes(g), makeSet(w) ⊆ nodes(g) depthfirst(m,insert(k,s),g) ≡ s" (k,s,g,w) > (m,insert(k,s),g,k&w) k ∉ s, g[k] ≡ (m,n) depthfirst(k,s,g) ≡ s'	resolution upon L4 resolution upon L9
k ∈ s, makeSet(w) ⊆ nodes(g)	
DFLoop(n,s",g,w) ≡ DFLoop(k',s',g,w) k ∈ nodes(g), makeSet(w) ⊆ nodes(g) m ∈ s" depthfirst(m,insert(k,s),g) ≡ s" (k,s,g,w) > (m,insert(k,s),g,k&w) k ∉ s, g[k] ≡ (m,n) depthfirst(k,s,g) ≡ s'	paramodulation upon DFL2

```
k ∈ s,  makeSet(w) ⊆ nodes(g)
-----------------------------------------------------------------------------
n ∈ nodes(g),  k' ∈ nodes(g)                          inductive resolution
depthfirst(n,s",g) ≡ s'
(k,s,g,w) > (n,s",g,w)
k ∈ nodes(g),  makeSet(w) ⊆ nodes(g)
m ∈ s"
depthfirst(m,insert(k,s),g) ≡ s"
(k,s,g,w) > (m,insert(k,s),g,k&w)
k ∉ s,  g[k] ≡ (m,n)
depthfirst(k,s,g) ≡ s'
=============================================================================
k ∈ s,  makeSet(w) ⊆ nodes(g)
-----------------------------------------------------------------------------
k' ∈ nodes(g)                                         resolution upon L5
depthfirst(n,s",g) ≡ s'
(k,s,g,w) > (n,s",g,w)
k ∈ nodes(g),  makeSet(w) ⊆ nodes(g)
m ∈ s"
depthfirst(m,insert(k,s),g) ≡ s"
(k,s,g,w) > (m,insert(k,s),g,k&w)
k ∉ s,  g[k] ≡ (m,n)
depthfirst(k,s,g) ≡ s'
=============================================================================
k ∈ s,  makeSet(w) ⊆ nodes(g)
-----------------------------------------------------------------------------
k' ∈ nodes(g)
depthfirst(n,depthfirst(m,insert(k,s),g),g) ≡ s'      unification
(k,s,g,w) > (n,depthfirst(m,insert(k,s),g),g,w)
k ∈ nodes(g),  makeSet(w) ⊆ nodes(g)
m ∈ depthfirst(m,insert(k,s),g)
(k,s,g,w) > (m,insert(k,s),g,k&w)
k ∉ s,  g[k] ≡ (m,n)
depthfirst(k,s,g) ≡ s'
=============================================================================
k ∈ s,  makeSet(w) ⊆ nodes(g)
-----------------------------------------------------------------------------
(k,s,g,w) > (n,depthfirst(m,insert(k,s),g),g,w)
k ∈ nodes(g),  makeSet(w) ⊆ nodes(g)
(k,s,g,w) > (m,insert(k,s),g,k&w)                     resolution upon L1
k ∉ s,  g[k] ≡ (m,n)
depthfirst(k,s,g) ≡ s'                                paramodulation upon DF2
=============================================================================
k ∈ s,  makeSet(w) ⊆ nodes(g)
-----------------------------------------------------------------------------
nodes(remove(s,g)) ⊃ nodes(remove(depthfirst(m,insert(k,s),g),g))
```

```
k ∈ nodes(g), makeSet(w) ⊆ nodes(g)                      resolution upon GR1
nodes(remove(s,g)) ⊃ nodes(remove(insert(k,s),g))
k ∉ s, g[k] ≡ (m,n)                                      resolution upon s≡s
==============================================================================
k ∈ s, makeSet(w) ⊆ nodes(g)
------------------------------------------------------------------------------
depthfirst(m,insert(k,s),g) ⊃ s                          resolution upon L3
k ∈ nodes(g), makeSet(w) ⊆ nodes(g)
insert(k,s) ⊃ s
k ∉ s, g[k] ≡ (m,n)
==============================================================================
k ∈ s, makeSet(w) ⊆ nodes(g)
------------------------------------------------------------------------------
k ∈ nodes(g), makeSet(w) ⊆ nodes(g)
k ∉ s, g[k] ≡ (m,n)                                      resolution upon SET4, L2
==============================================================================
k ∈ s, makeSet(w) ⊆ nodes(g)
------------------------------------------------------------------------------
k ∈ nodes(g), makeSet(w) ⊆ nodes(g)
k ∉ s                                                    resolution upon L6
==============================================================================
k ∈ nodes(g), makeSet(w) ⊆ nodes(g)                      resolution upon SET5
==============================================================================
```

8.6.2 Recursive Schorr-Waite marking

Like `depthfirst`, the *Schorr-Waite graph marking algorithm* (cf. [SW67]) traverses a binary graph and returns the set of all visited nodes. [BP82] develops a functional program involving two recursive calls, which connect the three visits of each node. The transitions following these visits are illustrated below in the picture taken from [DF77].

curr yields the node currently processed. *prev* is the node visited in the directly preceding state. The algorithm avoids explicit backtracking by "rotating" the outgoing edges of *curr* each time *curr* is visited. Each transition consists of setting the left child of *curr* to the right child of *curr*, setting the left child of *curr* to *prev*, setting *prev* to *curr* and setting *curr* to the left child of *curr*. The rotation following the third visit of *curr* redirects the outgoing edges of *curr* to their original targets. Hence, upon termination of the algorithm, the original graph is retained. For the formal desciption, we follow [BP82] and add a sort `egraph` (extended graph) for triples consisting of a graph and the actual values of *curr* and *prev*.

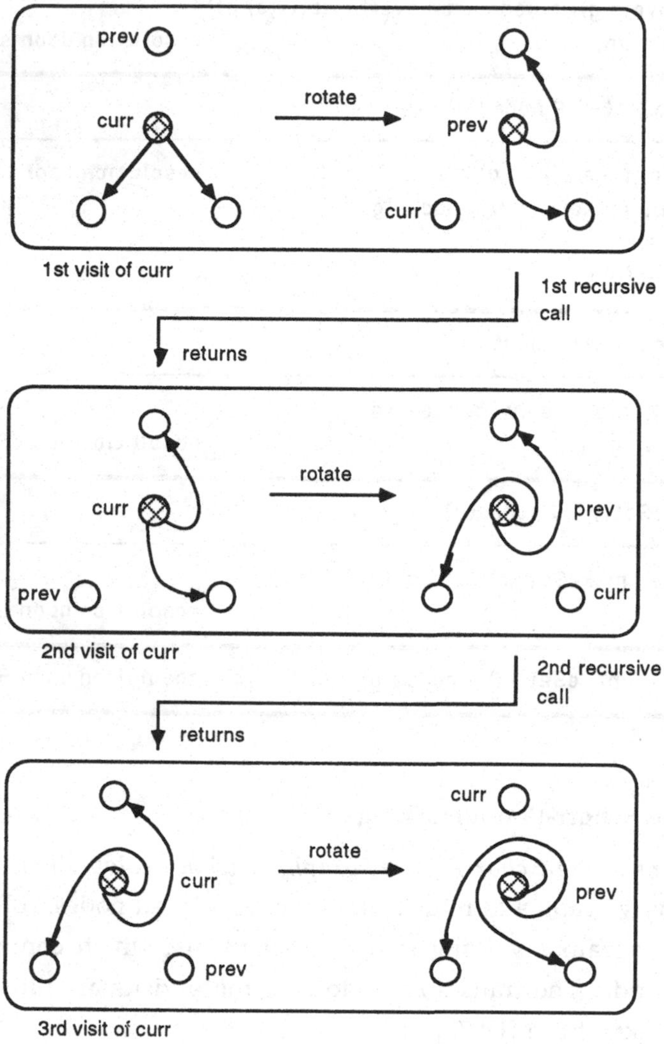

Figure 8.2 The Schorr-Waite algorithm.

SCHORR-WAITE

base	DEPTHFIRST	
sorts	`egraph = graph×S×S`	
	symbol	*type*
functs	`rotate`	`egraph ⟶ egraph`
	`exchange`	`egraph ⟶ egraph`
	`SchorrWaite`	`egraph,set ⟶ egraph×set`
preds	`_ > _`	`egraph×set,egraph×set`
vars	`g,g' : graph; k,k',m,m',n : S; e,e' : egraph; s,s',s" : set`	
axms	`rotate((g,k,k')) ≡ (g[k⟶n×k'],m,k) ⇐ g[k] ≡ (m,n)`	(ROT)

```
        SchorrWaite((g,k,k'),s) ≡ ((g,k',k),s)  ⇐  k ∈ s                    (SW1)
        SchorrWaite((g,k,k'),s) ≡ (rotate(e'),s")
                   ⇐ k ∉ s,
                          SchorrWaite(rotate((g,k,k')),insert(k,s)) ≡ (e,s'),
                          SchorrWaite(rotate(e),s') ≡ (e',s")                 (SW2)
        exchange((g,k,k')) ≡ (g,k',k)                                         (EX)
        ((g,k,k'),s) > ((g',m,m'),s')
                 ⇐  nodes(remove(s,g)) ⊃ nodes(remove(s',g'))                 (GR3)
thms    remove(Ø,g) ≡ g                                                       (REM)
        remove(s,g)[k] ≡ g[k]  ⇐  k ∉ s                                       (L10)
        rotate(exchange(rotate(exchange(rotate((g,k,k')))))) ≡ (g,k',k)       (L11)
        depthfirst(k,s,g) ≡ depthfirst(k,s,remove(s,g))                       (L12)
        remove(s,remove(s',g)) ≡ remove(s,g)  ⇐  s' ⊆ s                       (L13)
        remove(s,g) ≡ remove(s,g')
                 ⇐  k ∈ s,  k ∈ nodes(g),  rotate((g,k,k')) ≡ (g',m,n         (L14)
        remove(s,g) ≡ remove(s,g")
                 ⇐  k ∈ s,  k ∈ nodes(g), rotate((g,k,k')) ≡ (g',m,n),
                    rotate((g',m,n)) ≡ (g",m',n')                             (L15)
        n' ∈ nodes(g')  ⇐  n' ∈ nodes(g),  rotate((g,k,k')) ≡ (g',m,n)        (L16)
        g[k] ≡ (m,m')
                 ⇐ rotate((g,k,k')) ≡ (g',m,n),  rotate((g',m,n)) ≡ (g",m',n') (L17)
        {k ∈ s',  s ⊆ s'}  ⇐  SchorrWaite(e,insert(k,s)) ≡ (e',s')            (L18)
        ∃ {g,k,k'} rotate(e) ≡ (g,k,k')                                       (L19)
        ∃ {e',s'} SchorrWaite(e,s) ≡ (e',s')                                  (L20)
conjects {depthfirst(k,Ø,g) ≡ s',  e ≡ (g,k',k)}
                 ⇐  k ∈ nodes(g),  SchorrWaite((g,k,k'),Ø) ≡ (e,s')           (C3)
        , {depthfirst(k,s,remove(s,g)) ≡ s',  e ≡ (g,k',k)}
                 ⇐  k ∈ nodes(g),  SchorrWaite((g,k,k'),s) ≡ (e,s')           (C4)
```

Using the graph primitives of Sect. 8.6.1, the constructor-based axioms for `rotate` and `SchorrWaite` are translated into SML programs:

```
fun rotate(g,k,k') = let val (m,n) = g(k) in (assign(k,n,k')(g),m,k) end

fun SchorrWaite((g,k,k'),s) = if k ∈ s then ((g,k',k),s)

                              else  let  val (e,s) = SchorrWaite(rotate(g,k,k'),k::s)

                                         val (e,s) = SchorrWaite(rotate(e),s)

                                    in (rotate(e),s) end
```

Conjecture C3 states the correctness of SchorrWaite with respect to depthfirst. C4 generalizes C3: REM and C4 imply C3. Why do we have remove(s,g) instead of g? Because g does not provide a sufficiently strong induction hypothesis. C3 assumes that the graph processed by SchorrWaite does not change. But the recursive calls of SchorrWaite in SW2 work on a rotated graph, which may differ from the original graph g. The differences are confined to the subgraph generated by the set s of already visited nodes. Hence its complement remove(s,g) does not change.

GR3 defines the descent predicate used in the following inductive expansions of C4 and C6 (cf. Sect. 8.6.3). Since {C4} is a constructor-based clause set with input variables k,k',s,g,w, guard {k ∈ nodes(g)} and generator {SchorrWaite((g,k,k'),s) ≡ (e,s')}, we may apply Cor. 5.6.

	goal	*substitution of X_{out}*	*rules applied*
G1	depthfirst(k,s,remove(s,g)) ≡ s' e ≡ (g,k',k) SchorrWaite((g,k,k'),s) ≡ (e,s')		-- conclusion of C4 -- generator of C4
	k ∈ s (g,k',k) ≡ (g,k',k)	s/s' (g,k',k)/e	resolution upon DF1, SW1
	G1		
	k ∈ s		unification
	G1		
	k ∈ s		
	k ∉ s depthfirst(n,depthfirst(m,insert(k,s),remove(s,g)),remove(s,g)) ≡ s' remove(s,g)[k] ≡ (m,n) rotate(e') ≡ (g,k',k) SchorrWaite(rotate((g,k,k')),insert(k,s)) ≡ (e_1,s_1) SchorrWaite(rotate(e_1),s_1) ≡ (e',s')	 rotate(e')/e	 resolution upon DF2 resolution upon SW2
	k ∈ s		
	k ∉ s depthfirst(n,depthfirst(m,insert(k,s),remove(s,g)),remove(s,g)) ≡ s' g[k] ≡ (m,n) rotate(e') ≡ (g,k',k) SchorrWaite(rotate((g,k,k')),insert(k,s)) ≡ (e_1,s_1) SchorrWaite(rotate(e_1),s_1) ≡ (e',s')		 paramodulation upon L10
	k ∈ s		

k ∉ s
depthfirst(n,depthfirst(m,insert(k,s),g'),remove(s,g)) ≡ s'
g' ≡ remove(insert(k,s),remove(s,g)) paramodulation upon L12
rotate(e') ≡ (g,k',k)
g[k] ≡ (m,n)
SchorrWaite(rotate((g,k,k')),insert(k,s)) ≡ (e_1,s_1)
SchorrWaite(rotate(e_1),s_1) ≡ (e',s')

---

k ∈ s

---

k ∉ s
depthfirst(n,depthfirst(m,insert(k,s),g'),g") ≡ s' paramodulation upon L12
g' ≡ remove(insert(k,s),remove(s,g))
g" ≡ remove(depthfirst(m,insert(k,s),g'),remove(s,g))
rotate(e') ≡ (g,k',k)
g[k] ≡ (m,n)
SchorrWaite(rotate((g,k,k')),insert(k,s)) ≡ (e_1,s_1)
SchorrWaite(rotate(e_1),s_1) ≡ (e',s')

---

k ∈ s

---

k ∉ s
depthfirst(n,depthfirst(m,insert(k,s),g'),g") ≡ s'
g' ≡ remove(insert(k,s),g) paramodulation upon L13
s ⊆ insert(k,s)
g" ≡ remove(depthfirst(m,insert(k,s),g'),g) paramodulation upon L13
s ⊆ depthfirst(m,insert(k,s),g')
rotate(e') ≡ (g,k',k)
g[k] ≡ (m,n)
SchorrWaite(rotate((g,k,k')),insert(k,s)) ≡ (e_1,s_1)
SchorrWaite(rotate(e_1),s_1) ≡ (e',s')

---

k ∈ s

---

k ∉ s
depthfirst(n,depthfirst(m,insert(k,s),g'),g") ≡ s'
g' ≡ remove(insert(k,s),g_1) paramodulation upon L14
k ∈ insert(k,s)
k ∈ nodes(g)
rotate((g,k,k')) ≡ (g_1,m,n_1)
s ⊆ insert(k,s)
g" ≡ remove(depthfirst(m,insert(k,s),g'),g_2) paramodulation upon L15
k ∈ depthfirst(m,insert(k,s),g')
rotate((g_1,n_1,m)) ≡ (g_2,n,n_2)
s ⊆ depthfirst(m,insert(k,s),g')
rotate(e') ≡ (g,k',k)
g[k] ≡ (m,n)
SchorrWaite(rotate((g,k,k')),insert(k,s)) ≡ (e_1,s_1)
SchorrWaite(rotate(e_1),s_1) ≡ (e',s')

---

k ∈ s

---

k ∉ s
depthfirst(n,depthfirst(m,insert(k,s),g'),g") ≡ s'
g' ≡ remove(insert(k,s),g_1)
k ∈ nodes(g) resolution upon SET1, SET3
rotate((g,k,k')) ≡ (g_1,m,n_1)
g" ≡ remove(depthfirst(m,insert(k,s),g'),g_2)
k ∈ depthfirst(m,insert(k,s),g')
rotate((g_1,n_1,m)) ≡ (g_2,n,n_2)
s ⊆ depthfirst(m,insert(k,s),g')
rotate(e') ≡ (g,k',k)
g[k] ≡ (m,n)
SchorrWaite(rotate((g,k,k')),insert(k,s)) ≡ (e_1,s_1)
SchorrWaite(rotate(e_1),s_1) ≡ (e',s')

---

k ∈ s

---

k ∉ s
depthfirst(n,depthfirst(m,insert(k,s),g'),g") ≡ s'
g' ≡ remove(insert(k,s),g_1)
k ∈ nodes(g)
rotate((g,k,k')) ≡ (g_1,m,n_1)
g" ≡ remove(depthfirst(m,insert(k,s),g'),g_2)
k ∈ depthfirst(m,insert(k,s),g')
rotate((g_1,n_1,m)) ≡ (g_2,n,n_2)
s ⊆ depthfirst(m,insert(k,s),g')
rotate(e') ≡ (g,k',k)
g[k] ≡ (m,n) (g_1,n_1,m)/e_1
SchorrWaite((g_1,m,n_1),insert(k,s)) ≡ ((g_1,n_1,m),s_1) paramodulation
SchorrWaite((g_2,n,n_2),s_1) ≡ (e',s') upon a symmetry axiom

---

k ∈ s

---

k ∉ s
depthfirst(n,depthfirst(m,insert(k,s),g'),g") ≡ s'
g' ≡ remove(insert(k,s),g_1)
k ∈ nodes(g)
rotate((g,k,k')) ≡ (g_1,m,n_1)
g" ≡ remove(depthfirst(m,insert(k,s),g'),g_2)
k ∈ depthfirst(m,insert(k,s),g')
rotate((g_1,n_1,m)) ≡ (g_2,n,n_2)
s ⊆ depthfirst(m,insert(k,s),g') resolution upon L11
g[k] ≡ (m,n) exchange(rotate(exchange(rotate((g,k,k')))))/e
SchorrWaite((g_1,m,n_1),insert(k,s)) ≡ ((g_1,n_1,m),s_1)
SchorrWaite((g_2,n,n_2),s_1) ≡ (exchange(rotate(exchange(rotate((g,k,k'))))),s')

---

k ∈ s

---

k ∉ s
depthfirst(n,depthfirst(m,insert(k,s),g'),g") ≡ s'

g' ≡ remove(insert(k,s),g_1)

k ∈ nodes(g)

rotate((g,k,k')) ≡ (g_1,m,n_1)

g" ≡ remove(depthfirst(m,insert(k,s),g'),g_2)

k ∈ depthfirst(m,insert(k,s),g')

rotate((g_1,n_1,m)) ≡ (g_2,n,n_2)

s ⊆ depthfirst(m,insert(k,s),g')

g[k] ≡ (m,n)

SchorrWaite((g_1,m,n_1),insert(k,s)) ≡ ((g_1,n_1,m),s_1) paramodulation upon a

SchorrWaite((g_2,n,n_2),s_1) ≡ ((g_2,n_2,n),s') symmetry axiom and EX

---

k ∈ s

---

k ∉ s

depthfirst(n,depthfirst(m,insert(k,s),g'),g") ≡ s'

g' ≡ remove(insert(k,s),g_1)

k ∈ nodes(g)

rotate((g,k,k')) ≡ (g_1,m,n_1)

g" ≡ remove(depthfirst(m,insert(k,s),g'),g_2)

k ∈ depthfirst(m,insert(k,s),g')

rotate((g_1,n_1,m)) ≡ (g_2,n,n_2)

s ⊆ depthfirst(m,insert(k,s),g')

g[k] ≡ (m,n)

SchorrWaite((g_1,m,n_1),insert(k,s)) ≡ (e_1,s_1) paramodulation upon

e_1 ≡ (g_1,n_1,m) a symmetry axiom

SchorrWaite((g_2,n,n_2),s_1) ≡ (e',s')

e' ≡ (g_2,n_2,n)

---

k ∈ s

---

k ∉ s

depthfirst(n,s_1,g") ≡ s' inductive paramodulation

m ∈ nodes(g_1)

((g,k,k'),s) > ((g_1,m,n_1),insert(k,s))

g' ≡ remove(insert(k,s),g_1)

k ∈ nodes(g)

rotate((g,k,k')) ≡ (g_1,m,n_1)

g" ≡ remove(s_1,g_2)

k ∈ s_1

rotate((g_1,n_1,m)) ≡ (g_2,n,n_2)

s ⊆ s_1

g[k] ≡ (m,n)

SchorrWaite((g_1,m,n_1),insert(k,s)) ≡ (e_1,s_1)

SchorrWaite((g_2,n,n_2),s_1) ≡ (e',s')

---

k ∈ s

---

k ∉ s

n ∈ nodes(g_2) inductive resolution

((g,k,k'),s) > ((g_2,n,n_2),s_1)

$m \in nodes(g_1)$
$((g,k,k'),s) > ((g_1,m,n_1),insert(k,s))$
$g' \equiv remove(insert(k,s),g_1)$
$k \in nodes(g)$
$rotate((g,k,k')) \equiv (g_1,m,n_1)$
$g'' \equiv remove(s_1,g_2)$
$k \in s_1$
$rotate((g_1,n_1,m)) \equiv (g_2,n,n_2)$
$s \subseteq s_1$
$g[k] \equiv (m,n)$
$SchorrWaite((g_1,m,n_1),insert(k,s)) \equiv (e_1,s_1)$
$SchorrWaite((g_2,n,n_2),s_1) \equiv (e',s')$

* * *

$k \in s$

* * *

$k \notin s$
$n \in nodes(g_2)$
$nodes(remove(s,g)) \supset nodes(remove(s_1,g_2))$ resolution upon GR3
$m \in nodes(g_1)$
$nodes(remove(s,g)) \supset nodes(remove(insert(k,s),g_1))$
$k \in nodes(g)$ resolution upon GR3
$rotate((g,k,k')) \equiv (g_1,m,n_1)$ $remove(s_1,g_2)/g''$
$rotate((g_1,n_1,m)) \equiv (g_2,n,n_2)$ $remove(insert(k,s),g_1)/g'$
$k \in s_1$ unification
$s \subseteq s_1$
$g[k] \equiv (m,n)$
$SchorrWaite((g_1,m,n_1),insert(k,s)) \equiv (e_1,s_1)$
$SchorrWaite((g_2,n,n_2),s_1) \equiv (e',s')$

* * *

$k \in s$

* * *

$k \notin s$
$n \in nodes(g_2)$
$nodes(remove(s,g)) \supset nodes(remove(s_1,g))$ paramodulation upon L15
$m \in nodes(g_1)$
$nodes(remove(s,g)) \supset nodes(remove(insert(k,s),g))$
$k \in insert(k,s)$ paramodulation upon L14
$k \in nodes(g)$
$rotate((g,k,k')) \equiv (g_1,m,n_1)$
$rotate((g_1,n_1,m)) \equiv (g_2,n,n_2)$
$k \in s_1$
$s \subseteq s_1$
$g[k] \equiv (m,n)$
$SchorrWaite((g_1,m,n_1),insert(k,s)) \equiv (e_1,s_1)$
$SchorrWaite((g_2,n,n_2),s_1) \equiv (e',s')$

* * *

$k \in s$

* * *

$k \notin s$
$n \in nodes(g_2)$

$s_1 \supset s$ resolution upon L3
$m \in nodes(g_1)$
$insert(k,s) \supset s$ resolution upon L3
$k \in nodes(g)$ resolution upon SET1
$rotate((g,k,k')) \equiv (g_1,m,n_1)$
$rotate((g_1,n_1,m)) \equiv (g_2,n,n_2)$
$k \in s_1$
$s \subseteq s_1$
$g[k] \equiv (m,n)$
$SchorrWaite((g_1,m,n_1),insert(k,s)) \equiv (e_1,s_1)$
$SchorrWaite((g_2,n,n_2),s_1) \equiv (e',s')$

$k \in s$

$k \notin s$
$n \in nodes(g_2)$
$m \in nodes(g_1)$ resolution upon
$k \in nodes(g)$ SET2, SET4
$rotate((g,k,k')) \equiv (g_1,m,n_1)$
$rotate((g_1,n_1,m)) \equiv (g_2,n,n_2)$
$k \in s_1$
$s \subseteq s_1$
$g[k] \equiv (m,n)$
$SchorrWaite((g_1,m,n_1),insert(k,s)) \equiv (e_1,s_1)$
$SchorrWaite((g_2,n,n_2),s_1) \equiv (e',s')$

$k \in s$

$k \notin s$
$n \in nodes(g)$
$m \in nodes(g)$ resolution upon L16
$k \in nodes(g)$
$rotate((g,k,k')) \equiv (g_1,m,n_1)$
$rotate((g_1,n_1,m)) \equiv (g_2,n,n_2)$
$g[k] \equiv (m,n)$
$SchorrWaite((g_1,m,n_1),insert(k,s)) \equiv (e_1,s_1)$ resolution upon L18
$SchorrWaite((g_2,n,n_2),s_1) \equiv (e',s')$

$k \in s$

$k \notin s$
$k \in nodes(g)$
$rotate((g,k,k')) \equiv (g_1,m,n_1)$ resolution upon L4, L5
$rotate((g_1,n_1,m)) \equiv (g_2,n,n_2)$
$g[k] \equiv (m,n)$
$SchorrWaite((g_1,m,n_1),insert(k,s)) \equiv (e_1,s_1)$
$SchorrWaite((g_2,n,n_2),s_1) \equiv (e',s')$

$k \in s$

$k \notin s$

```
k ∈ nodes(g)
rotate((g,k,k')) ≡ (g1,m,n1)                              resolution upon L17
rotate((g1,n1,m)) ≡ (g2,n,n2)
SchorrWaite((g1,m,n1),insert(k,s)) ≡ (e1,s1)
SchorrWaite((g2,n,n2),s1) ≡ (e',s')
─────────────────────────────────────────────
k ∈ s
─────────────────────────────────────────────
k ∉ s                                                     resolution upon L19, L20
k ∈ nodes(g)
─────────────────────────────────────────────
k ∈ nodes(g)                                              resolution upon SET5
─────────────────────────────────────────────
```

8.6.3 Iterative Schorr-Waite marking

The iterative version of the Schorr-Waite algorithm needs only a bit sequence instead of the node sequence of `DFLoop` (cf. Sect. 8.6.1) and calls the auxiliary functions `up` and `down`, which are defined by mutual recursion. The names of these functions indicate the actual direction of graph traversal, while the bit sequence represents the path from the start node to the current node: "0" stands for a left turn, "1" denotes a right turn. If the current node *curr* has not yet been visited (`k ∉ s`), `down` proceeds to the left child (cf. SWL2). Otherwise the traversal changes its direction from `down` to `up` and starts working off the bit sequence (cf. SWL3). If it begins with a "0", control is passed on to `down`, which proceeds to the right child of *curr* (cf. SWL4). If it begins with a "1", control is returned to the parent node of *curr* (cf. SWL5). If it is empty, the initial node has been reached (cf. SWL6).

```
SCHORR-WAITE-LOOP
  base     SCHORR-WAITE
           symbol          type
  functs   SWLoop          egraph ⟶ egraph×set
           up              egraph,set,seq ⟶ egraph×set
           down            egraph,set,seq ⟶ egraph×set
  vars     g,g' : graph;  k,k' : S;  e: egraph;  s,s' : set;  w : seq(nat)
  axms     SWLoop(e) ≡ down(e,∅,ε)                                   (SWL1)
           down((g,k,k'),s,w) ≡ down(rotate((g,k,k')),insert(k,s),0&w)
                                  ⇐  k ∉ s                            (SWL2)
           down((g,k,k'),s,w) ≡ up((g,k',k),s,w)  ⇐  k ∈ s           (SWL3)
           up(e,s,0&w) ≡ down(rotate(e),s,1&w)                       (SWL4)
           up(e,s,1&w) ≡ up(rotate(e),s,w)                           (SWL5)
           up(e,s,ε) ≡ (e,s)                                         (SWL6)
```

conjects SWLoop((g,k,k')) ≡ SchorrWaite((g,k,k'),Ø)
⇐ k ∈ nodes(g) (C5)

down((g,k,k'),s,w) ≡ up(e,s',w)
⇐ k ∈ nodes(g), SchorrWaite((g,k,k'),s) ≡ (e,s') (C6)

Based on the graph primitives of Sect. 8.6.1, the constructor-based axioms for SWLoop are translated into SML programs:

```
fun  SWLoop(e) = down(e,nil,nil)

and  down((g,k,k'),s,w) = if k ∈ s   then up((g,k',k),s,w)
                                     else down(rotate(g,k,k'),k::s,0::w)

and  up(e,s,nil) = (e,s) |
     up(e,s,0::w) = down(rotate(e),s,1::w) |
     up(e,s,1::w) = up(rotate(e),s,w)
```

Conjecture C5 states the correctness of SWLoop with respect to SchorrWaite. SWL1, SWL6, L20 and C6 imply C5. Since {C6} is a constructor-based clause set with input variables e,s,w, guard {k ∈ nodes(g)} and generator {SchorrWaite((g,k,k'),s) ≡ (e,s')}, we may apply Cor. 5.6.

	goal	*substitution of X_{out}*	*rules applied*
G1	down((g,k,k'),s,w) ≡ up(e,s',w) SchorrWaite((g,k,k'),s) ≡ (e,s')		-- conclusion of C6 -- generator of C6
	k ∈ s SchorrWaite((g,k,k'),s) ≡ ((g,k',k),s)	(g,k',k)/e s/s'	resolution upon SWL3
	G1		
	k ∈ s		resolution upon SW1
	G1		
	k ∈ s		
	down(rotate((g,k,k')),insert(k,s),0&w) ≡ up(e,s',w) k ∉ s SchorrWaite((g,k,k'),s) ≡ (e,s')		paramodulation upon SWL2
	k ∈ s		
	down((g_1,m,n_1),insert(k,s),0&w) ≡ up(e,s',w) rotate((g,k,k')) ≡ (g_1,m,n_1) k ∉ s SchorrWaite((g,k,k'),s) ≡ (e,s')		paramodulation upon e≡(g,m,n) ⇐ e≡(g,m,n)

$k \in s$

$up(e',s'',0\&w) \equiv up(e,s',w)$
$SchorrWaite((g_1,m,n_1),insert(k,s)) \equiv (e',s'')$
$m \in nodes(g_1)$
$((g,k,k'),s) > ((g_1,m,n_1),insert(k,s))$
$rotate((g,k,k')) \equiv (g_1,m,n_1)$
$k \notin s$
$SchorrWaite((g,k,k'),s) \equiv (e,s')$

inductive paramodulation

$k \in s$

$down(rotate(e'),s'',1\&w) \equiv up(e,s',w)$
$SchorrWaite((g_1,m,n_1),insert(k,s)) \equiv (e',s'')$
$m \in nodes(g_1)$
$((g,k,k'),s) > ((g_1,m,n_1),insert(k,s))$
$rotate((g,k,k')) \equiv (g_1,m,n_1)$
$k \notin s$
$SchorrWaite((g,k,k'),s) \equiv (e,s')$

paramodulation upon SWL4

$k \in s$

$down((g_2,n,n_2),s'',1\&w) \equiv up(e,s',w)$
$rotate(e') \equiv (g_2,n,n_2)$
$SchorrWaite((g_1,m,n_1),insert(k,s)) \equiv (e',s'')$
$m \in nodes(g_1)$
$((g,k,k'),s) > ((g_1,m,n_1),insert(k,s))$
$rotate((g,k,k')) \equiv (g_1,m,n_1)$
$k \notin s$
$SchorrWaite((g,k,k'),s) \equiv (e,s')$

paramodulation upon $e \equiv (g,m,n) \Leftarrow e \equiv (g,m,n)$

$k \in s$

$up(e_1,s_1,1\&w) \equiv up(e,s',w)$
$SchorrWaite((g_2,n,n_2),s'') \equiv (e_1,s_1)$
$n \in nodes(g_2)$
$((g,k,k'),s) > ((g_2,n,n_2),s'')$
$rotate(e') \equiv (g_2,n,n_2)$
$SchorrWaite((g_1,m,n_1),insert(k,s)) \equiv (e',s'')$
$m \in nodes(g_1)$
$((g,k,k'),s) > ((g_1,m,n_1),insert(k,s))$
$rotate((g,k,k')) \equiv (g_1,m,n_1)$
$k \notin s$
$SchorrWaite((g,k,k'),s) \equiv (e,s')$

inductive paramodulation

$k \in s$

$SchorrWaite((g_2,n,n_2),s'') \equiv (e_1,s_1)$
$n \in nodes(g_2)$
$((g,k,k'),s) > ((g_2,n,n_2),s'')$
$rotate(e') \equiv (g_2,n,n_2)$
$SchorrWaite((g_1,m,n_1),insert(k,s)) \equiv (e',s'')$
$m \in nodes(g_1)$
$((g,k,k'),s) > ((g_1,m,n_1),insert(k,s))$
$rotate((g,k,k')) \equiv (g_1,m,n_1)$
$k \notin s$
$SchorrWaite((g,k,k'),s) \equiv (rotate(e_1),s_1)$

$rotate(e_1)/e$
s_1/s'

resolution upon SWL5

$k \in s$

$\mathrm{SchorrWaite}((g_2,n,n_2),s'') \equiv (e_1,s_1)$	resolution upon SW2
$n \in \mathrm{nodes}(g_2)$	
$((g,k,k'),s) > ((g_2,n,n_2),s'')$	
$\mathrm{rotate}(e') \equiv (g_2,n,n_2)$	
$\mathrm{SchorrWaite}((g_1,m,n_1),\mathrm{insert}(k,s)) \equiv (e',s'')$	
$m \in \mathrm{nodes}(g_1)$	
$((g,k,k'),s) > ((g_1,m,n_1),\mathrm{insert}(k,s))$	
$\mathrm{rotate}((g,k,k')) \equiv (g_1,m,n_1)$	
$k \notin s$	

$k \in s$

$\mathrm{SchorrWaite}((g_2,n,n_2),s'') \equiv (e_1,s_1)$	
$n \in \mathrm{nodes}(g_2)$	
$\mathrm{nodes}(\mathrm{remove}(s,g)) \supset \mathrm{nodes}(\mathrm{remove}(s'',g_2))$	resolution upon GR3
$\mathrm{rotate}(e') \equiv (g_2,n,n_2)$	
$\mathrm{SchorrWaite}((g_1,m,n_1),\mathrm{insert}(k,s)) \equiv (e',s'')$	
$m \in \mathrm{nodes}(g_1)$	
$\mathrm{nodes}(\mathrm{remove}(s,g)) \supset \mathrm{nodes}(\mathrm{remove}(\mathrm{insert}(k,s),g_1))$	resolution upon GR3
$\mathrm{rotate}((g,k,k')) \equiv (g_1,m,n_1)$	
$k \notin s$	

$k \in s$

$\mathrm{SchorrWaite}((g_2,n,n_2),s'') \equiv (e_1,s_1)$	
$n \in \mathrm{nodes}(g_2)$	
$\mathrm{nodes}(\mathrm{remove}(s,g)) \supset \mathrm{nodes}(\mathrm{remove}(s'',g))$	paramodulation upon L15
$k \in s''$	
$k \in \mathrm{nodes}(g)$	
$\mathrm{rotate}((g_1,n_1,m)) \equiv (g_2,n,n_2)$	
$\mathrm{rotate}(e') \equiv (g_2,n,n_2)$	
$\mathrm{SchorrWaite}((g_1,m,n_1),\mathrm{insert}(k,s)) \equiv (e',s'')$	
$m \in \mathrm{nodes}(g_1)$	
$\mathrm{nodes}(\mathrm{remove}(s,g)) \supset \mathrm{nodes}(\mathrm{remove}(\mathrm{insert}(k,s),g))$	paramodulation upon L14
$k \in \mathrm{insert}(k,s)$	
$\mathrm{rotate}((g,k,k')) \equiv (g_1,m,n_1)$	
$k \notin s$	

$k \in s$

$\mathrm{SchorrWaite}((g_2,n,n_2),s'') \equiv (e_1,s_1)$	
$n \in \mathrm{nodes}(g_2)$	
$s'' \supset s$	resolution upon L3
$k \in s''$	
$k \in \mathrm{nodes}(g)$	
$\mathrm{rotate}((g_1,n_1,m)) \equiv (g_2,n,n_2)$	
$\mathrm{rotate}(e') \equiv (g_2,n,n_2)$	
$\mathrm{SchorrWaite}((g_1,m,n_1),\mathrm{insert}(k,s)) \equiv (e',s'')$	
$m \in \mathrm{nodes}(g_1)$	
$\mathrm{insert}(k,s) \supset s$	resolution upon L3
$\mathrm{rotate}((g,k,k')) \equiv (g_1,m,n_1)$	resolution upon SET1
$k \notin s$	

$k \in s$

$\mathrm{SchorrWaite}((g_2,n,n_2),s'') \equiv (e_1,s_1)$	
$n \in \mathrm{nodes}(g_2)$	
$s \subseteq s''$	resolution upon
$k \in s''$	SET2, SET4
$k \in \mathrm{nodes}(g)$	
$\mathrm{rotate}((g_1,n_1,m)) \equiv (g_2,n,n_2)$	paramodulation upon
$e' \equiv (g_1,n_1,m)$	a symmetry axiom
$\mathrm{SchorrWaite}((g_1,m,n_1),\mathrm{insert}(k,s)) \equiv (e',s'')$	
$m \in \mathrm{nodes}(g_1)$	
$\mathrm{rotate}((g,k,k')) \equiv (g_1,m,n_1)$	
$k \notin s$	

===

$k \in s$

$\mathrm{SchorrWaite}((g_2,n,n_2),s'') \equiv (e_1,s_1)$	
$n \in \mathrm{nodes}(g_2)$	
$k \in \mathrm{nodes}(g)$	
$\mathrm{rotate}((g_1,n_1,m)) \equiv (g_2,n,n_2)$	
$\mathrm{SchorrWaite}((g_1,m,n_1),\mathrm{insert}(k,s)) \equiv (e',s'')$	resolution upon C4, L18
$m \in \mathrm{nodes}(g_1)$	
$\mathrm{rotate}((g,k,k')) \equiv (g_1,m,n_1)$	
$k \notin s$	

===

$k \in s$

$\mathrm{SchorrWaite}((g_2,n,n_2),s'') \equiv (e_1,s_1)$	
$n \in \mathrm{nodes}(g)$	
$k \in \mathrm{nodes}(g)$	
$\mathrm{rotate}((g_1,n_1,m)) \equiv (g_2,n,n_2)$	resolution upon L16
$\mathrm{SchorrWaite}((g_1,m,n_1),\mathrm{insert}(k,s)) \equiv (e',s'')$	
$m \in \mathrm{nodes}(g)$	
$\mathrm{rotate}((g,k,k')) \equiv (g_1,m,n_1)$	
$k \notin s$	

===

$k \in s$

$\mathrm{SchorrWaite}((g_2,n,n_2),s'') \equiv (e_1,s_1)$	
$g{\vee}k{\wedge} \equiv (m,n)$	resolution upon L4, L5
$k \in \mathrm{nodes}(g)$	
$\mathrm{rotate}((g_1,n_1,m)) \equiv (g_2,n,n_2)$	
$\mathrm{SchorrWaite}((g_1,m,n_1),\mathrm{insert}(k,s)) \equiv (e',s'')$	
$\mathrm{rotate}((g,k,k')) \equiv (g_1,m,n_1)$	
$k \notin s$	

===

$k \in s$

$\mathrm{SchorrWaite}((g_2,n,n_2),s'') \equiv (e_1,s_1)$	
$k \in \mathrm{nodes}(g)$	
$\mathrm{rotate}((g_1,n_1,m)) \equiv (g_2,n,n_2)$	resolution upon L17
$\mathrm{SchorrWaite}((g_1,m,n_1),\mathrm{insert}(k,s)) \equiv (e',s'')$	
$\mathrm{rotate}((g,k,k')) \equiv (g_1,m,n_1)$	
$k \notin s$	

===

$k \in s$

$k \in \mathrm{nodes}(g)$	resolution upon L19, L20

k ∉ s	
k ∈ nodes(g)	resolution upon SET5

8.7 Streams and networks

An *alternating bit protocol* (cf. [BSW69]) controls the transfer of messages in the following way. The sender releases a message several times until it gets an acknowledgement from the receiver that the message has arrived correctly. Both the channel transmitting messages to the receiver and the channel transmitting acknowledgements to the sender may damage transmitted items, i.e., turn them into error messages.[1] Acknowledgements alternate between the values 0 and 1. If the sender releases a message with 0 (1), the receiver expects a message with 0 (1). If the receiver obtains such a message, it sends 0 (1) to the sender, which equips the next message with 1 (0) and initiates a new transfer cycle.

For simulating the non-determinism involved in this problem, we follow [Str87] and specify channels as functions with a stream parameter to control the channel output:

```
STREAM
  base       NSB
  sort vars  S
  sorts      seq(S), stream
             symbol     type
  functs     _&_        nat,stream → stream
             error      S
             ε          seq(S)
             _&_        S,seq(S) → seq(S)
             channel    seq(S),stream → seq(S)
             _•_        seq,seq → seq
             _•_        seq,stream → stream
             _•_        seq(S),seq(S) → seq(S)
             lg         seq → nat
             _–         S,nat → seq(S)
  preds      fair       stream
             fairStep   nat,stream → stream
```

[1] Another alternating bit protocol also takes into account the loss of messages (see the end of this section).

	Def seq(S)	
vars	i : nat; s,s' : seq; st,st' : stream; m : S; ms,ms' : seq(S)	
axms	channel(ε,st) ≡ ε	(CH1)
	channel(m&ms,st) ≡ m&channel(ms,st') ⇐ st ≡ 0&st'	(CH2)
	channel(m&ms,st) ≡ error&channel(ms,st') ⇐ st ≡ (i+1)&st'	(CH3)
	ε∘s ≡ s	
	(i&s)∘s' ≡ i&(s∘s')	
	ε∘st ≡ st	
	(i&s)∘st ≡ i&(s∘st)	
	ε∘ms ≡ ms	
	(m&ms)∘ms' ≡ m&(ms∘ms')	
	lg(ε) ≡ 0	
	lg(i&s) ≡ lg(s)+1	
	m^0 ≡ ε	
	m^{i+1} ≡ m&m^i	
	fair(st) ⇐ ∀ i : fairStep(i,st)	(FAIR)
	fairStep(0,st)	(FS1)
	fairStep(i+1,st) ⇐ st ≡ s∘(0&st'), fairStep(i,st')	(FS2)
	Def(ε)	(DS1)
	Def(m&ms) ⇐ Def(ms)	(DS2)
thms	ms ≡ ε ∨ ∃ {m,ms'} ms ≡ m&ms' ⇐ Def(ms)	(DS^{-1})

We restrict ourselves to streams of natural numbers. Note that, in contrast to stream, the sorts seq (in NSB) and seq(S) stand for *finite* sequences over nat and S, resp. The leading element of a stream determines the actions of channel: a zero indicates the correct transfer, other numbers the damage of a message. A stream is *fair* if each released message is received eventually, formally: if it contains infinitely many zeros. Fair is specified along the step function or predicate schema explained in Sect. 1.2 and treated in more detail in [Pad90], Sect. 8.

STREAM does not admit the construction of ground terms of the sort stream. Analogously to the semantics of a polymorphic specification (cf. Ex. 7.20 and Sect. 8.5), STREAM stands for any inhabited extension of STREAM by individual streams. But what are individual streams? Ground terms on their own cannot be suitable representations because they always denote finite objects. Instead, streams are the (implicit) solutions of *regular equations* defining stream generating (sometimes constant) functions:

	symbol	*type*
functs	alt	stream

```
          nats         nat ⟶ stream
          repeat(F)    nat ⟶ stream
vars      i : nat; F : nat⟶nat
axms      1&0&alt ≡ alt
          i&nats(i+1) ≡ nats(i)
          i&repeat(F)(F(i)) ≡ repeat(F)(i)
```

From an operational viewpoint, these stream defining equations are written from right to left. We do so to preserve the strong termination of STREAM. Ground confluence can also be guaranteed, provided that the left-hand sides of other equational axioms do not overlap the left-hand sides of stream defining equations. This holds true automatically if the only terms of the sort `stream` occurring on the left-hand side of those equational axioms are variables (cf. CH1-CH3).

The above interpretation of STREAM as an inhabited extension allows us to stay within (finitary) initial semantics, however, at the expense of the possibility of inducing on streams. In fact, many verification problems dealing with streams, such as the correctness of our bit protocol, can be solved without induction on streams.

Besides their use in simulating non-determinism, streams come up when two functions f and g must be synchronized via a sequence s built up from values of f and determining the values of g (cf. [Hug89]). Then s is potentially infinite, i.e., s is a stream, and f is embedded into a stream generating function that computes only as many elements of s as are needed for the "next" value of g. For realizing the stepwise computation of streams, they are often regarded as functions. For instance, number streams can be implemented in SML as follows:

```
infix &
datatype stream = & of int * (unit -> stream)
fun first(st : unit->stream) = let val i&st' = st() in i end
fun rest(st : unit->stream) = let val i&st' = st() in st' end
```

The above axioms for `alt`, `nat`, `repeat` and `channel` can then be translated into SML programs:

```
fun alt() = let fun st() = 0&alt in 1&st end
fun nats(i)() = i&nats(i+1)
fun repeat(F)(i)() = i&repeat(F)(F(i))
fun channel(nil, st : unit->stream) = nil |
```

```
channel(m::ms, st : unit->stream) = case st() of 0&st' => m::channel(ms,st') |
                                              _&st' => channel(ms,st')
```

st denotes a closure, i.e., a non-evaluated stream, while st() yields the partially evaluated object consisting of the first element of the corresponding stream and the closure of the rest.

With the help of STREAM, we specify the alternating bit protocol:

PROTOCOL

base	STREAM	
sorts	bool, errorbool	
	symbol	*type*
functs	send	seq(S),seq(errorbool),bool ⟶ seq(S×bool)
	receive	seq(S×bool),bool ⟶ seq(S)×seq(errorbool)
	true	bool
	false	bool
	¬_	bool ⟶ bool
	_	bool ⟶ errorbool
	error	errorbool
	error	S×bool
preds	net	seq(S),bool,stream,stream
	_ > 0	seq
	_ > _	seq(S)×bool×stream×stream,seq(S)×bool×stream×stream
vars	b : bool; i : nat; s : seq; st,st',w,w' : stream; m : S; ms : seq(S); bs,bs' : seq(errorbool); mbs,mbs' : seq(S×bool)	

axms

send(ε,ε,b) ≡ ε (S1)

send(m&ms,b&bs,b) ≡ (m,b)&send(ms,bs,¬b) (S2)

send(m&ms,¬b&bs,b) ≡ (m,b)&send(m&ms,bs,b) (S3)

send(m&ms,error&bs,b) ≡ (m,b)&send(m&ms,bs,b) (S4)

receive(ε,b) ≡ (ε,ε) (R1)

receive((m,b)&mbs,b) ≡ (m&ms,b&bs)
 ⇐ receive(mbs,¬b) ≡ (ms,bs) (R2)

receive((m,¬b)&mbs,b) ≡ (ms,¬b&bs)
 ⇐ receive(mbs,b) ≡ (ms,bs) (R3)

receive(error&mbs,b) ≡ (ms,¬b&bs)
 ⇐ receive(mbs,b) ≡ (ms,bs) (R4)

net(ms,b,st,st')

$\Leftarrow$ send(ms,bs,b) ≡ mbs, channel(mbs,st) ≡ mbs',
receive(mbs',b) ≡ (ms,bs'), channel(bs',st') ≡ bs (NET)

¬true ≡ false

¬false ≡ true

ε > 0

(i+1)&s > 0 $\Leftarrow$ s > 0

(m&ms,b,st,st') > (ms,b',w,w') (GR)

The axioms for send and receive follow the informal protocol description given above. NET determines the correct cooperation of send, receive and channel as a functional network whose "internal wires" coincide with the fresh variables of NET:

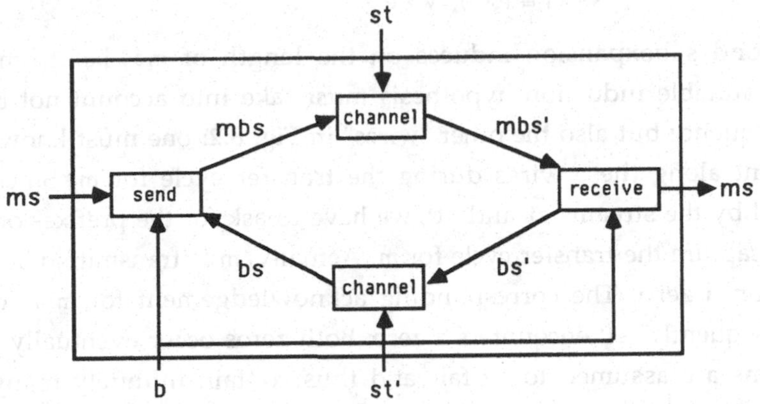

Figure 8.3 The ABP network.

Given a message m, PROTOCOL neglects the time passing between the release of m and the acknowledgement that m has been received. Hence the axioms for send consider only those cases where the message sequence ms and the acknowledgement sequence bs are both empty or both non-empty.

The protocol works correctly if all released messages are received in the order they have been sent, assumed that both channels are fair, i.e., do not damage the same message infinitely often:

conjects net(ms,b,st,st') $\Leftarrow$ fair(st), fair(st'), Def(ms) (ABP)

Using Cor. 5.7, we prove ABP by inductive expansion. After a resolution step upon NET the proof splits into two subexpansions. By applying S1, R1 and CH1, the first leads directly to the goal {ms≡ε}, while the following iterations of S2-S4, R2-R4, CH2 and CH3 are needed for achieving the goal {ms ≡ m&ms', fair(st), fair(st'), Def(ms)}:

thms $\mathsf{send(ms,channel((\neg b)^i \circ bs, v \circ w),b) \equiv (m,b)^i \circ mbs}$

$\Leftarrow \mathsf{send(ms,channel(bs,w),b) \equiv mbs,\ i \equiv lg(v)}$ (LS1)

$\mathsf{send(m\&ms,error^i \circ b\&bs,b) \equiv (m,b)^{i+1} \circ mbs}$

$\Leftarrow \mathsf{send(ms,bs,\neg b) \equiv mbs}$ (LS2)

$\mathsf{receive(error^i \circ (m,b)\&mbs,b) \equiv (m\&ms,(\neg b)^i \circ b\&bs)}$

$\Leftarrow \mathsf{receive(s,\neg b) \equiv (ms,bs)}$ (LR1)

$\mathsf{receive(channel((m,b)^i\&mbs,v \circ w),\neg b) \equiv (ms,b^i \circ bs)}$

$\Leftarrow \mathsf{receive(channel(mbs,w),\neg b) \equiv (ms,bs),\ i \equiv lg(v)}$ (LR2)

$\mathsf{channel(m^{i+1} \circ ms,v \circ 0\&w) \equiv error^i \circ m\&channel(ms,w)}$

$\Leftarrow \mathsf{i \equiv lg(v),\ v > 0}$ (LCH)

The second subexpansion induces on the length of ms, i.e., from ms' to m&ms'. A suitable induction hypothesis must take into account not only the message sequence but also the other "wires" in Fig. 8.2: one must know exactly what is sent along these wires during the transfer cycle for m. Since this is determined by the streams st and st', we have to ask for the prefixes of st and st', which capture the transfer cycle for m. Actually, m is transmitted as soon as st hits upon a zero. The corresponding acknowledgement for m is received when, subsequently, st' encounters a zero. Both zeros occur eventually because both streams are assumed to be fair and thus contain infinitely many zeros. Hence the crucial lemma for establishing the induction hypothesis follows from the axioms for fair (cf. STREAM):

$\exists \mathsf{\{v,v',v'',w,w',w''\}}$ $\mathsf{\{st \equiv v \circ 0\&w' \circ w'',\ v > 0,\ lg(v) \equiv lg(v'),}$

$\mathsf{st' \equiv v' \circ v'' \circ 0\&w,\ v'' > 0,\ lg(w') \equiv lg(v''),}$

$\mathsf{fair(w''),\ fair(w)\} \Leftarrow fair(st),\ fair(st')}$ (FAIR-L)

Here is the complete expansion of ABP:

	goal	*substitution*	*rules applied of* X_{out}
	net(ms,b,st,st')		-- conclusion of ABP
G1	send(ms,bs,b) ≡ mbs channel(mbs,st) ≡ mbs' receive(mbs',b) ≡ (ms,bs') channel(bs',st') ≡ bs		resolution upon NET

ms ≡ ε   ε/bs, ε/mbs   resolution upon
            ε/mbs', ε/bs'   S1, R1, CH1

G1

---

ms ≡ ε

---

ms ≡ m&ms'
st ≡ v•0&w   resolution upon LCH
k ≡ lg(v), v > 0 $(m,b)^{k+1}$•mbs1/mbs
send(m&ms',b,bs) ≡ $(m,b)^{k+1}$•mbs1
receive($error^{k}$•(m,b)&channel(mbs1,w),b) ≡ (m&ms',bs')
channel(bs',st') ≡ mbs' $error^{k}$•(m,b)&channel(mbs1,w)/mbs'

---

ms ≡ ε

---

ms ≡ m&ms'
st ≡ v•0&w
k ≡ lg(v), v > 0 $(\neg b)^{k}$•b&bs1'/bs'
send(m&ms',b,bs) ≡ $(m,b)^{k+1}$•mbs1
receive(channel(mbs1,w),¬b) ≡ (ms',bs1')   resolution upon LR1
channel($(\neg b)^{k}$•b&bs1',st') ≡ bs

---

ms ≡ ε

---

ms ≡ m&ms'
st ≡ v•0&w
k ≡ lg(v), v > 0   channel($(\neg b)^{k}$•b&bs1',st')/bs
send(m&ms',b,channel($(\neg b)^{k}$•b&bs1',st')) ≡ $(m,b)^{k+1}$•mbs1
receive(channel(mbs1,w),¬b) ≡ (ms',bs1')   unification

---

ms ≡ ε

---

ms ≡ m&ms'
st ≡ v•0&w
k ≡ lg(v), v > 0
send(m&ms',b,channel(b&bs1',w')) ≡ (m,b)&mbs1   resolution upon LS1
st' ≡ v'•w'
k ≡ lg(v')
receive(channel(mbs1,w),¬b) ≡ (ms',bs1')

---

ms ≡ ε

---

ms ≡ m&ms'
st ≡ v•0&w
k ≡ lg(v), v > 0 b^{i}•bs2'/bs1'

send(m&ms',b,error^{i}•b&channel(bs2',w")) ≡ (m,b)&mbs1
st' ≡ v'•v"•0&w" v"•0&w"/w'
i ≡ lg(v") paramodulation upon LCH
v" > 0
k ≡ lg(v')
receive(mbs1,w),¬b) ≡ (ms',b^{i}•bs2')

---

ms ≡ ε

---

ms ≡ m&ms'
st ≡ v•0&w resolution upon LS2
k ≡ lg(v), v > 0
send(ms',¬b,channel(bs2',w")) ≡ mbs2
st' ≡ v'•v"•0&w" (x,b)^{i}&mbs2/mbs1
i ≡ lg(v")
v" > 0
k ≡ lg(v')
receive(channel((m,b)^{i}&mbs2,w),¬b) ≡ (ms',b^{i}•bs2')

---

ms ≡ ε

---

ms ≡ m&ms'
st ≡ v•0&w$_{o}$•w$_{1}$ w$_{o}$•w$_{1}$/w
k ≡ lg(v), v > 0
send(ms',¬b,channel(bs2',w")) ≡ mbs2
st' ≡ v'•v"•0&w"
i ≡ lg(v")
v" > 0
k ≡ lg(v')
receive(channel(mbs2,w$_{1}$),¬b) ≡ (ms',bs2') resolution upon LR2
i ≡ lg(w$_{o}$)

---

ms ≡ ε

---

ms ≡ m&ms'
st ≡ v•0&w$_{o}$•w$_{1}$
v > 0 lg(v)/k unification
send(ms',¬b,channel(bs2',w")) ≡ mbs2
st' ≡ v'•v"•0&w"
lg(w$_{o}$) ≡ lg(v") lg(w$_{o}$)/i unification
v" > 0
lg(v) ≡ lg(v')
receive(channel(mbs2,w$_{1}$),¬b) ≡ (ms',bs2')

---

ms ≡ ε

$ms \equiv m\&ms'$
$st \equiv v \circ 0\&w_o \circ w_1$
$v > 0$
$net(ms', \neg b, w_1, w'')$ resolution upon NET^{-1}
$st' \equiv v' \circ v'' \circ 0\&w''$
$lg(w_o) \equiv lg(v'')$
$v'' > 0$
$lg(v) \equiv lg(v')$

* * *

$ms \equiv \varepsilon$

* * *

$ms \equiv m\&ms'$
$st \equiv v \circ 0\&w_o \circ w_1$
$v > 0$
$fair(w_1)$, $fair(w'')$, $Def(ms')$ inductive resolution
$(m\&ms', b, st, st') > (ms', \neg b, w_1, w'')$
$st' \equiv v' \circ v'' \circ 0\&w''$
$lg(w_o) \equiv lg(v'')$
$v'' > 0$
$lg(v) \equiv lg(v')$

* * *

$ms \equiv \varepsilon$

* * *

$ms \equiv m\&ms'$
$st \equiv v \circ 0\&w_o \circ w_1$
$v > 0$
$fair(w_1)$, $fair(w'')$, $Def(ms')$ resolution upon GR
$st' \equiv v' \circ v'' \circ 0\&w''$
$lg(w_o) \equiv lg(v'')$
$v'' > 0$
$lg(v) \equiv lg(v')$

* * *

$ms \equiv \varepsilon$

* * *

$ms \equiv m\&ms'$
$fair(st)$, $fair(st')$, $Def(ms')$ resolution upon FAIR-L

* * *

$ms \equiv \varepsilon$

* * *

$ms \equiv m\&ms'$ resolution upon $DS2^{-1}$
$fair(st)$, $fair(st')$, $Def(m\&ms')$

* * *

$ms \equiv \varepsilon$

* * *

$ms \equiv m\&ms'$ equational replacement
$fair(st)$, $fair(st')$, $Def(ms)$

---

fair(st), fair(st'), Def(ms) resolution upon DS^{-1}

How must PROTOCOL be changed if not only the damage but also the loss of a message is to be modelled? First, CH3 may be turned into the clauses

$$\text{channel(m\&ms,st)} \equiv \text{channel(ms,st')} \Leftarrow \text{st} \equiv \text{1\&st'}$$
$$\text{channel(m\&ms,st)} \equiv \text{error\&channel(ms,st')} \Leftarrow \text{st} \equiv \text{(i+2)\&st'}$$

where a "1" in the stream st indicates the loss of m. Furthermore, a function lg_{-1} : seq→nat is needed for counting all elements of a number sequence that are different from "1". As to the proof of ABP, one may use lemmas LS2 and LR1 unchanged, but LCH, LS1, LR2 and FAIR-L need to be adapted as follows:

$$\text{channel}(m^{i+1}\circ ms, v\circ 0\& w) \equiv \text{error}^{j}\circ m\&\text{channel}(ms,w)$$
$$\Leftarrow i \equiv lg(v),\ j \equiv lg_{-1}(v),\ v > 0 \qquad \text{(LCH')}$$

$$\text{send}(ms,\text{channel}((\neg b)^{i}\circ bs, v\circ w),b) \equiv (m,b)^{j}\circ mbs$$
$$\Leftarrow \text{send}(ms,\text{channel}(bs,w),b) \equiv mbs,\ i \equiv lg(v),\ j \equiv lg_{-1}(v) \qquad \text{(LS1')}$$

$$\text{receive}(\text{channel}((m,b)^{i}\& mbs, v\circ w),\neg b) \equiv (ms, b^{j}\circ bs)$$
$$\Leftarrow \text{receive}(\text{channel}(mbs,w),\neg b) \equiv (ms,bs),\ i \equiv lg(v),\ j \equiv lg_{-1}(v) \qquad \text{(LR2')}$$

$$\exists \{v,v',v'',w,w',w''\}\ \{st \equiv v\circ 0\& w'\circ w'',\ v > 0,\ lg_{-1}(v) \equiv lg(v'),$$
$$st' \equiv v'\circ v''\circ 0\& w,\ v'' > 0,\ lg_{-1}(w') \equiv lg(v''),$$
$$\text{fair}(w''),\ \text{fair}(w)\} \Leftarrow \text{fair}(st),\ \text{fair}(st'). \qquad \text{(FAIR-L')}$$

9: EXPANDER: Inductive Expansion in SML

EXPANDER is a proof support system for reasoning about data type specifications and declarative programs. EXPANDER applies the rules of inductive expansion (cf. Chapter 5) to correctness conditions that are given as single Gentzen clauses or sets of guarded Horn clauses (cf. Chapter 2). The system provides a kernel for special-purpose theorem provers, which are tailored to restricted application areas and implement specific proof plans, strategies or tactics. It is written in the functional language SML/NJ.

EXPANDER executes single inference steps. Each proof is a sequence of goal sets. The user has full control over the proof process. He may backtrack the sequence, interactively modify the underlying specification and add lemmas or induction orderings suggested by subgoals obtained so far. When a proof has been finished, the system can generate the theorems actually proved and, if necessary, the remaining subconjectures.

We first describe the kind of specifications that can be processed, then present the commands currently provided and, finally, document the implementation. The latter serves for illustrating the suitability of functional languages for encoding deductive methods.

9.1 The specifications

Specifications to be processed by EXPANDER are generated by the following context-free grammar in extended Backus-Naur form, i.e., `[_]`, `*`, `|` denote the usual operators for building regular expressions. Key words are enclosed in "...".

```
spec      ::= signat ["axioms" clause*] ["theorems" clause*]
                     ["conjects" clause*]
signat    ::= spec_name ["base" spec_name *] ["consts" const*]
                     ["functs" funct*] ["preds" pred*]
                     ["infixes" (funct | pred)*] ["vars" var*]
clause    ::= "(" number ")" (goals | goals "<==" goal)
goals     ::= goal | goal "\/" goals
```

```
goal        ::= "{" atoms "}"
atoms       ::= atoms | atom "," atoms
atom        ::= pred "(" termlist ")" | term restatom
restatom    ::= pred term
term        ::= (const | var) restterm |
                     (funct | var) "(" termlist ")" restterm |
                     "(" term "," termlist ")" restterm |
                     "(" term ")" restterm
restterm ::=  funct term | "(" termlist ")" restterm | ε
termlist ::=  term | term "," termlist
```

`spec_name`, `const`, `funct`, `pred` and `var` reduce into arbitrary strings. The parser processes specifications with infix functions, infix predicates, products of any finite arity and higher-order functions. For simplicity, sorts and function types are omitted and λ-expressions are not handled. Specifications can be built up hierarchically.

Here is an example (cf. Ex. 5.4):

EVEN_ODD

consts	0
functs	s double
preds	EvenOrOdd = Def >>
infixes	= >>
vars	x y
axioms	(1) { EvenOrOdd(x) } <== { x = double(y) }
	(2) { EvenOrOdd(x) } <== { x = s(double(y)) }
	(3) { double(0) = 0 }
	(4) { double(s(x)) = s(s(double(x))) }
	(6) { Def(0) }
	(7) { Def(s(x)) } <== { Def(x) }
	(8) { s(s(x)) >> x }
theorems	(1) { x = double(ex)}V{ x = s(double(ey)) } <== { EvenOrOdd(x) }
	(2) { x = 0 }V{ x = s(0) }V{ x = s(s(ex)) } <== { Def(x) }
	(3) { Def(x) } <== { Def(s(s(x))) }
conjects	(1) { EvenOrOdd(x) } <== { Def(x) }

The parser copies the specification, if necessary, with error messages, into the standard file PARSE. The following context conditions are presupposed.

- Undeclared identifiers occurring in axioms, theorems or conjectures are regarded as existential variables.
- Equality and descent predicates are declared as infix predicates and denoted by = and >> respectively.
- Axioms are Horn clauses. Theorems and conjectures may be arbitrary Gentzen clauses.
- A resolution redex is an arbitrary goal or a disjunction of goals such that each goal consists of a single atom: If $\exists X_1 g_1 \vee ... \vee \exists X_n g_n \Leftarrow g$ is the clause to be resolved with the current goal set GS, then
  $n = 1$ and there is a subset g_1' of g_1 such that GS is actually resolved with $\exists X_1 g_1' \Leftarrow g$ or
  $n > 1$ and for all $1 \le i \le n$ there is $p_i \in g_i$ such that GS is actually resolved with $\exists X_1 p_1 \vee ... \vee \exists X_n p_n \Leftarrow g$.
- A paramodulation redex is a disjunction of goals such that each goal consists of a single atom: If $\exists X_1 g_1 \vee ... \vee \exists X_n g_n \Leftarrow g$ is the clause to be paramodulated with the current goal set GS, then for all $1 \le i \le n$ there is $p_i \in g_i$ such that GS is actually paramodulated with $\exists X_1 p_1 \vee ... \vee \exists X_n p_n \Leftarrow g$.

9.2 The commands

Each EXPANDER command is an SML function that generates or modifies the quintuple

$$PR = (SP, XIN, INI, PROOF, FIN),$$

which consists of

- a specification SP,
- a set XIN of input variables,
- an expansion PROOF, given as a list of goal lists,
- an initial goal list INI,
- a final goal FIN that is to be derived.

EXPANDER records PROOF together with the corresponding command sequence in the standard file EXPANSION.

The start commands `st` and `std` turn conjectures of SP into the goal list INI and the goal FIN. To finish an expansion and, perhaps, to resume it later, we provide the commands `fi` and `fid`, which translate the last goal list GL of PROOF together with FIN into (the remaining) conjectures of SP. The command `et` extracts from INI and GL the new theorems that have been obtained so far. If an expansion succeeds as expected, i.e., if FIN has been accomplished, the new theorem is given by INI⇐FIN.

We use the SML notation for lists and list operations. Given a list L and a number i, L(i) denotes the i-th element of L. Given a list J of numbers between 1 and n,

$$L(J) = [L(i) \mid 1 \le i \le n, i \in J] \quad \text{and} \quad L(-J) = [L(i) \mid 1 \le i \le n, i \notin J].$$

In particular, L(-i) = L(-[i]).

```
re "s";
```

reads the file s, parses the contents of s as a specification and assigns the latter to SP. All subspecifications whose names are listed in s below the key word base are expanded. Hence SP is a *flat* specification, i.e., A(SP) and T(SP) include the axioms and theorems respectively of all base specifications. C(SP), however, is restricted to the conjectures listed in s.

Let A(SP), T(SP) and C(SP) be the respective lists of axioms, theorems and conjectures of SP.

9.2.1 Starting an expansion

Given a list c_nos and a number guard_no, the command

```
st c_nos guard_no;
```

starts an expansion by constructing XIN, INI and FIN from a sublist CL of C(SP) consisting of k *Horn* clauses. We assume that there is a goal g with no guard_no atoms that for all $1 \le i \le k$, $g_i \Leftarrow g @ g_i' = C(SP)(c\_nos(i))$ for some g_i'. We regard g as the guard of CL (cf. Sect. 2.2). GM = $[g_1',\ldots,g_k']$ is assumed to be a constructor-based matrix, i.e., GM consists of lists of equations with constructors on their right-hand sides (cf. Sect. 2.3). XIN becomes the set of all variables of CL that do not occur on a right-hand side of an equation of GM. Moreover,

$$INI := [g_1@g_1',\ldots,g_k@g_k'],\ FIN := g,\ PROOF := [INI].$$

Given a number c_no, the command

```
std c_no;
```

starts an expansion by constructing XIN, INI and FIN from the Gentzen clause $c = C(SP)(c\_no) = \exists X_1 g_1 \vee \ldots \vee \exists X_k g_k \Leftarrow g$. In contrast with **st**, the conclusion of c may be a proper **disjunction**. XIN becomes the set of all universal variables of c. Moreover,

$$\text{INI} := [g_1,\ldots,g_k],\ \text{FIN} := g,\ \text{PROOF} := [\text{INI}].$$

In the sequel, let GL = $[g_1,\ldots,g_k]$ be the last element of PROOF.

9.2.2 Resolving

Given a goal number g_no and a clause number c_no such that GL(g_no) has m elements and the **axiom** A(SP)(c_no) (**theorem** T(SP)(c_no), resp.) is a Horn clause $c = g \Leftarrow g'$ and given lists p_poss and q_poss of $n \le m$ numbers, the respective commands

```
ra g_no p_poss c_no q_poss;
rt g_no p_poss c_no q_poss;
```

unify GL(g_no)(p_poss) with g(q_poss) and construct the **resolvent** RS according to Sect. 5.1, provided that the conclusion of c consists of a single goal with at least n atoms and that the applicability conditions on the existential variables of c hold true (cf. Sect. 5.1). Moreover,

$$\text{PROOF} := \text{PROOF} \mathbin{@} [\text{RS} :: \text{GL}(\text{-g\_no})].$$

Given a clause number c_no such that the **axiom** A(SP)(c_no) (**theorem** T(SP)(c_no), resp.) reads as $c = \exists X_1 g'_1 \vee \ldots \vee \exists X_n g'_n \Leftarrow g$ with $n \le k$ and given lists g_nos, p_poss and q_poss of n numbers, the respective commands

```
rad g_nos p_poss c_no q_poss;
rtd g_nos p_poss c_no q_poss;
```

unify GL(g_nos(i))(p_poss(i)) with g'_i(q_poss(i)) for all $1 \le i \le n$ and construct the **resolvent** RS, provided that the applicability conditions on the existential variables of c hold true (cf. Sect. 5.1). In contrast with `ra` and `rt`, the conclusion of c may be a proper **disjunction**. Moreover,

$$\text{PROOF} := \text{PROOF} \mathbin{@} [\text{RS} :: \text{GL}(\text{-g\_nos})].$$

The commands

```
ras g_no p_poss c_no q_poss;
rts g_no p_poss c_no q_poss;
```

work the same as `ra` (and `rt` respectively) except that GL is **split**, i.e.,

$$\text{PROOF} := \text{PROOF} \mathbin{@} [\text{RS} :: \text{GL}].$$

The commands

```
rads g_nos p_poss c_no q_poss;
rtds g_nos p_poss c_no q_poss;
```

work the same as **rad** (and **rtd** respectively) except that GL is **split**, i.e.,

$$\text{PROOF} := \text{PROOF} @ [\text{RS} :: \text{GL}].$$

Given a goal number g_no and a clause number c_no such that GL(g_no) has m elements and the **conjecture** C(SP)(c_no) is a Horn clause $g \Leftarrow g'$ and given lists p_poss and q_poss of at most m numbers, the command

```
rc g_no p_poss c_no q_poss;
```

unifies GL(g_no)(p_poss) with g(q_poss) and constructs the **resolvent** RS together with a descent condition DC (cf. Sect. 5.2). Moreover,

$$\text{PROOF} := \text{PROOF} @ [\text{DC} :: \text{RS} :: \text{GL}(\text{-g\_no})].$$

9.2.3 Paramodulating

Given a clause number c_no such that the **axiom** A(SP)(c_no) (**theorem** T(SP)(c_no), resp.) reads as $c = \exists X_1 u_1 \equiv t \vee \ldots \vee \exists X_n u_n \equiv t \Leftarrow g$ with $n \leq k$ and given lists g_nos, p_poss and q_poss of n numbers and a list t_poss of n number lists such that, for all $1 \leq i \leq n$, t_i is the term at position t_poss(i) in GL(g_nos(i))(p_poss(i)), the respective commands

```
pa g_nos p_poss t_poss c_no q_poss;
pt g_nos p_poss t_poss c_no q_poss;
```

unify $[t_1,\ldots,t_n]$ with $[u_1,\ldots,u_n]$ and construct the **paramodulant** PM, provided that the applicability conditions on the existential variables of c hold true (cf. Sect. 5.1). Moreover,

$$\text{PROOF} := \text{PROOF} @ [\text{PM} :: \text{GL}(\text{-g\_nos})].$$

The commands

```
pai g_nos p_poss t_poss c_no q_poss;
pti g_nos p_poss t_poss c_no q_poss;
```

work the same as **pa** (and **pt** respectively) except that c has the form $\exists X_1 t \equiv u_1 \vee \ldots \vee \exists X_n t \equiv u_n \Leftarrow g$, i.e., the **inverse** of c is applied.

The commands

```
pas g_nos p_poss t_poss c_no q_poss;
pts g_nos p_poss t_poss c_no q_poss;
```

work the same as **pa** (and **pt** respectively) except that GL is **split**, i.e.,

PROOF := PROOF @ [PM :: GL].

The commands

pais g_nos p_poss t_poss c_no q_poss;

ptis g_nos p_poss t_poss c_no q_poss;

work the same as **pai** (and **pti** respectively) except that GL is **split**, i.e.,

PROOF := PROOF @ [PM :: GL].

Given a goal number g_no and a clause number c_no such that the **conjecture** C(SP)(c_no) is a conditional equation g⇐g' and given numbers p_pos and q_pos and a number list t_pos, the command

pc g_no p_pos t_pos c_no q_pos;

unifies the term at position t_pos in GL(g_no)(p_pos) with the left-hand side of g(q_pos) and constructs the **paramodulant** PM together with a descent condition DC (cf. Sect. 5.2). Moreover,

PROOF := PROOF @ [DC :: PM :: GL(-g_no)].

The command

pci g_no p_pos t_pos c_no q_pos;

works in the same way as **pc**, but unifies t with the right-hand side of g(q_pos), i.e., an **inverse** of c is applied.

9.2.4 Composed rules

The command

fa g_no p_pos q_pos;

factors the goal GL(g_no), i.e., computes a most general unifier f of GL(g_no)(p_pos) and GL(g_no)(q_pos). Let FA be the instance of GL(g_no)(-q_pos) by f. Moreover,

PROOF := PROOF @ [FA :: GL(-g_no)].

The command

un g_no eq_pos;

computes a most general **unifier** f of the left- and right-hand sides of the *equation* GL(g_no)(p_pos). Moreover,

PROOF := PROOF @ [REST :: GL(-g_no)]

where REST is the instance of GL(g_no)(-p_pos) by f.

Given a goal number g_no such that GL(g_no) has m elements and given a list p_poss of n≤m numbers and a list t_poss of n number lists such that, for all 1≤i≤n, t_i is the term at position t_poss(i) in GL(g_no)(p_poss(i)), the commands

```
eql g_no eq_pos p_poss t_poss;
eqr g_no eq_pos p_poss t_poss;
```

substitute the **left**-hand and **right**-hand sides respectively of the **equation** GL(g_no)(eq_pos) for t_i. Moreover,

PROOF := PROOF @ [NEW :: GL(-g_no)].

where NEW is the changed goal.

The command

```
de g_no;
```

deletes GL(g_no) from GL, i.e.,

PROOF := PROOF @ [GL(-g_no)].

9.2.5 Stopping an expansion

The command

```
et();
```

appends the clause list TH = [INI⇐GL(i) | 1≤i≤k] to the **theorem** list of SP. Note that the validity of TH is guaranteed only if the induction hypotheses used in PROOF are not stronger than TH.

Given a list ge_poss of k number lists, the command

```
fi ge_poss;
```

finishes an expansion by adding the clause

g_i(-ge_poss(i)) ⇐ FIN @ g_i(ge_poss(i)),

1≤i≤k, to the conjecture list of SP. The variables of GL are added to the variable list of SP.

The command

```
fid();
```

finishes an expansion by adding the clause $c = \exists X_1 g_1 \vee ... \vee \exists X_k g_k \Leftarrow FIN$ to the conjecture list of SP. In contrast with `fi`, the conclusion of c may be a proper **disjunction**. The sets $X_1,...,X_k$ of existential variables are identified automatically as those that have not been declared in SP.

9.2.6 Miscellaneous

```
ba n;
```

backtracks the expansion by deleting the last n goal lists from PROOF.

```
ct c_nos;
```

moves the sublist C(SP)(c_nos) of the **conjecture** list of SP to the **theorem** list of SP.

```
wrs "s";
wre "s";
```

write the current **specification** SP (and **expansion** PROOF respectively) on the file s.

```
shs();
she();
```

show the current **specification** SP (and **expansion** PROOF respectively) on the screen.

```
shp();
```

shows the contents of **PARSE** (cf. Sect. 9.1) on the screen.

```
sh "s";
```

shows the contents of file s on the screen.

9.2.7 Sample expansions

Example 9.1 (even or odd) For proving Conjecture 1 of EVEN_ODD (cf. Sect. 9.1) by inductive expansion we start the expansion by entering the command

```
st [1] [1];
```

and come up with the following final contents of the standard file EXPANSION (cf. Ex. 5.4):

initial goal set:
(1) { EvenOrOdd(x) }

atom 1 in goal 1 resolved with axiom 1
(1) { x = double(y) }
(2) { EvenOrOdd(x) }

atom 1 at position 2 in goal 1 paramodulated with axiom 3
(1) { x = 0 }
(2) { x = double(y) }
(3) { EvenOrOdd(x) }

atom 1 at position 2 in goal 2 paramodulated with axiom 4
(1) { x = s(s(double(x1))) }
(2) { x = 0 }
(3) { EvenOrOdd(x) }

atom 1 in goal 3 resolved with axiom 2
(1) { x = s(double(y)) }
(2) { x = s(s(double(x1))) }
(3) { x = 0 }

atom 1 at position 2 1 in goal 1 paramodulated with axiom 3
(1) { x = s(0) }
(2) { x = s(double(y)) }
(3) { x = s(s(double(x1))) }
(4) { x = 0 }

atom 1 at position 2 1 in goal 2 paramodulated with axiom 4
(1) { x = s(s(s(double(x1)))) }
(2) { x = s(0) }
(3) { x = s(s(double(x1))) }
(4) { x = 0 }

atoms 1 1 at positions 2 1 1, 2 1 1 in goals 3 1 paramodulated with theorem 1
(1) { x = s(s(x1)), EvenOrOdd(x1) }
(2) { x = s(0) }
(3) { x = 0 }

atom 2 in goal 1 resolved with conjecture 1
(1) { s(s(x1)) >> x1, Def(x1), x = s(s(x1)) }

(2) { x = s(0) }
(3) { x = 0 }

atom 1 in goal 1 resolved with axiom 7
(1) { Def(x1), x = s(s(x1)) }
(2) { x = s(0) }
(3) { x = 0 }

atom 1 in goal 1 resolved with theorem 3
(1) { Def(s(s(x1))), x = s(s(x1)) }
(2) { x = s(0) }
(3) { x = 0 }

atom 1 at position 1 replaced with equation 2 in goal 1
(1) { Def(x), x = s(s(x1)) }
(2) { x = s(0) }
(3) { x = 0 }

atoms 1 1 2 in goals 3 2 1 resolved with theorem 2
(1) { Def(x) }

Example 9.2 (recursive division) Axioms and lemmas used in a proof of the last conjecture of Exercise 5.11 constitute the following specification:

```
DIV
    consts      0
    functs      s + - * div divS
    preds       = Def < > >= >>
    infixes     + - * = < > >= >>
    vars        x y z x' y' q r
    axioms      (1)  { 0+x = x }
                (2)  { s(x)+y = s(x+y) }
                (3)  { 0*x = 0 }
                (4)  { s(x)*y = (x*y)+y }
                (5)  { div(x,y) = (0,x) } <== { x < y }
                (6)  { div(x,y) = (s(q),r) } <== { x >= y, y > 0, div(x-y,y) = (q,r) }
                (7)  { divS(x,y) = (q,r) } <== { x = (q*y)+r, r < y }
                (8)  { (x,y) >> (x',y') } <== { x > x' }
    theorems    (1)  { Def(x-y) } <== { Def(x), Def(y) }
                (2)  { (x+y)+z = (x+z)+y }
```

(3) { x = z+y } <== { x-y = z, x >= y }
(4) { x > x-y } <== { x >= y, y > 0 }
(5) { x < y }V{ x >= y } <== { Def(x), Def(y) }
(6) { x = (eq*y)+er, er < y } <== { y > 0, Def(x), Def(y) }
conjects (1) { div(x,y) = divS(x,y) } <== { y > 0, Def(x), Def(y) }

An expansion of Conjecture 1 is started by entering the command

```
st [1] [3];
```

It ends up with the following contents of EXPANSION:

initial goal set:
(1) { div(x, y) = divS(x, y) }

atom 1 at position 2 in goal 1 paramodulated with axiom 7
(1) { div(x, y) = (q, r), x = (q*y)+r, r < y }

atom 1 in goal 1 resolved with axiom 5
(1) { x = (0*y)+x, x < y }
(2) { div(x, y) = (q, r), x = (q*y)+r, r < y }

atom 1 at position 2 1 in goal 1 paramodulated with axiom 3
(1) { x = 0+x, x < y }
(2) { div(x, y) = (q, r), x = (q*y)+r, r < y }

atom 1 at position 2 in goal 1 paramodulated with axiom 1
(1) { x = x, x < y }
(2) { div(x, y) = (q, r), x = (q*y)+r, r < y }

equation 1 in goal 1 unified
(1) { x < y }
(2) { div(x, y) = (q, r), x = (q*y)+r, r < y }

atom 1 in goal 2 resolved with axiom 6
(1) { x = (s(q)*y)+r, r < y, x >= y, y > 0, div(x-y, y) = (q, r) }
(2) { x < y }

atom 5 at position 1 in goal 1 paramodulated with conjecture 1

(1) {(x, y) >> (x-y, y), divS(x-y, y) = (q, r), y > 0, Def(x-y), Def(y), r < y, x >= y, x = (s(q)*y)+r}
(2) { x < y }

atom 1 in goal 1 resolved with axiom 8
(1) { divS(x-y, y) = (q, r), y > 0, Def(x-y), Def(y), r < y, x >= y, x = (s(q)*y)+r, x > x-y }
(2) { x < y }

atom 1 in goal 1 resolved with axiom 7
(1) { y > 0, Def(x-y), Def(y), r < y, x >= y, x = (s(q)*y)+r, x > x-y }
(2) { x < y }

atom 7 in goal 1 resolved with theorem 4
(1) { y > 0, Def(x-y), Def(y), r < y, x >= y, x = (s(q)*y)+r }
(2) { x < y }

atom 6 at position 2 1 in goal 1 paramodulated with axiom 4
(1) { x = ((q*y)+y)+r, y > 0, Def(x-y), Def(y), r < y, x >= y }
(2) { x < y }

atom 1 at position 2 in goal 1 paramodulated with theorem 2
(1) { x = ((q*y)+r)+y, y > 0, Def(x-y), Def(y), r < y, x >= y }
(2) { x < y }

atom 1 in goal 1 resolved with theorem 3
(1) { x-y = (q*y)+r, x >= y, y > 0, Def(x-y), Def(y), r < y }
(2) { x < y }

atoms 1 6 in goal 1 resolved with theorem 6
(1) { y > 0, Def(x-y), Def(y), x >= y }
(2) { x < y }

atom 2 in goal 1 resolved with theorem 1
(1) { Def(x), Def(y), y > 0, x >= y }
(2) { x < y }

atoms 1 4 in goals 2 1 resolved with theorem 5

(1) { Def(x), Def(y), y > 0 }

Example 9.3 (iterative division) Here is a suitable extension of DIV for recapitulating Ex. 5.9:

```
ITER_DIV
   base       DIV
   functs     Loop
   vars       x y q r x' y' q' r'
   axioms     (9)  { Loop(x,y,q,r) = (q,r) } <== { r < y }
             (10)  { Loop(x,y,q,r) = Loop(x,y,s(q),r-y) } <== { r >= y, y > 0 }
             (11)  { (x,y,q,r) >> (x',y',q',r') } <== { r > r' }
   theorems   (7)  { x+0 = x }
              (8)  { x+s(y) = s(x+y) }
              (9)  { div(x,y) = (ex,ey) } <== { y > 0, Def(x), Def(y) }
             (10)  { x+s(y) = s(x)+y }
   conjects   (1)  { Loop(x,y,q,r) = (q+q',r') }
                     <== { y > 0, Def(r), Def(y), div(r,y) = (q',r') }
```

An expansion of Conjecture 1 is started by entering the command

```
st [1] [3];
```

Hence the first three atoms of the premise of Conjecture 1 constitute the guard (cf. Sect. 9.2.1). Note that the internal specification is constructed from DIV *and* ITER_DIV.

Here are the contents of EXPANSION after repeating the proof given in Ex. 5.9:

initial goal set:
(1) { Loop(x, y, q, r) = (q+q', r'), div(r, y) = (q', r') }

atom 2 in goal 1 resolved with axiom 5
(1) { r = r', r' < y, Loop(x, y, q, r') = (q+0, r') }
(2) { Loop(x, y, q, r) = (q+q', r'), div(r, y) = (q', r') }

equation 1 in goal 1 unified
(1) { r < y, Loop(x, y, q, r) = (q+0, r) }
(2) { Loop(x, y, q, r) = (q+q', r'), div(r, y) = (q', r') }

atom 2 at position 2 1 in goal 1 paramodulated with theorem 7

```
(1) { Loop(x, y, q, r) = (q, r), r < y }
(2) { Loop(x, y, q, r) = (q+q', r'), div(r, y) = (q', r') }

atom 1 in goal 1 resolved with axiom 9
(1) { r < y }
(2) { Loop(x, y, q, r) = (q+q', r'), div(r, y) = (q', r') }

atom 2 in goal 2 resolved with axiom 6
(1) { r >= y, y > 0, div(r-y, y) = (q1, r'), Loop(x, y, q, r) = (q+s(q1), r') }
(2) { r < y }

atom 4 at position 2 1 in goal 1 paramodulated with theorem 10
(1) { Loop(x, y, q, r) = (s(q)+q1, r'), r >= y, y > 0, div(r-y, y) = (q1, r') }
(2) { r < y }

atom 1 at position 2 in goal 1 paramodulated with conjecture 1
(1) { (x, y, q, r) >> (x1, y1, s(q), r1), Loop(x, y, q, r) = Loop(x1, y1, s(q), r1), y1 > 0,
    Def(r1), Def(y1), div(r1, y1) = (q1, r'), r >= y, y > 0, div(r-y, y) = (q1, r') }
(2) { r < y }

atom 1 in goal 1 resolved with axiom 11
(1) { r > r1, Loop(x, y, q, r) = Loop(x1, y1, s(q), r1), y1 > 0, Def(r1), Def(y1),
    div(r1, y1) = (q1, r'), r >= y, y > 0, div(r-y, y) = (q1, r') }
(2) { r < y }

atom 6 factored with atom 9 in goal 1
(1) { r > r-y, Loop(x, y, q, r) = Loop(x1, y, s(q), r-y), y > 0, Def(r-y), Def(y),
    div(r-y, y) = (q1, r'), r >= y }
(2) { r < y }

atom 6 in goal 1 resolved with theorem 9
(1) { y > 0, Def(r-y), Def(y), r > r-y, Loop(x, y, q, r) = Loop(x1, y, s(q), r-y), r >= y }
(2) { r < y }

atom 2 in goal 1 resolved with theorem 1
(1) { Def(r), Def(y), y > 0, r > r-y, Loop(x, y, q, r) = Loop(x1, y, s(q), r-y), r >= y }
(2) { r < y }
```

```
atom 4 in goal 1 resolved with theorem 4
 (1) { r >= y, y > 0, Def(r), Def(y), Loop(x, y, q, r) = Loop(x1, y, s(q), r-y) }
 (2) { r < y }

atom 5 in goal 1 resolved with axiom 10
 (1) { r >= y, y > 0, Def(r), Def(y) }
 (2) { r < y }

atoms 1 1 in goals 2 1 resolved with theorem 5
 (1) { Def(r), Def(y), y > 0 }
```

Example 9.4 (bubblesort) A suitable specification for proving conjecture C of BUBBLESORT (cf. Sect. 8.3.1) reads as follows:

```
BUBBLESORT
   consts     eps mt
   functs     & add bubblesort bubble makeBag lg
   preds      <= > = sorted >>
   infixes    & <= > = >>
   vars       x y s s' s"
   axioms     (1)  { eps&x = x&eps }
              (2)  { (x&s)&y = x&(s&y) }
              (3)  { makeBag(eps) = mt }
              (4)  { makeBag(x&s) = add(x, makeBag(s)) }
              (5)  { sorted(eps) }
              (6)  { sorted(x&eps) }
              (7)  { sorted(x&(y&s)) } <== { x <= y, sorted(y&s) }
              (8)  { bubblesort(eps) = eps }
              (9)  { bubblesort(x&s) = bubblesort(s')&y } <== { bubble(x&s) = s'&y }
             (10)  { bubble(x&eps) = x&eps }
             (11)  {bubble(x&(y&s)) = x&bubble(y&s) } <== { x <= y }
             (12)  {bubble(x&(y&s)) = y&bubble(x&s) } <== { x > y }
             (13)  { s >> s' } <== { lg(s) > lg(s') }
 theorems     (1)  {sorted(s&x) } <== { sorted(s), bubble(y&s) = s"&x }
              (2)  {makeBag(s) = makeBag(bubblesort(s)) }
              (3)  {lg(s&x) > lg(s) }
              (4)  {lg(s) = lg(s') } <== { bubble(s) = s' }
              (5)  {s = eps }V{ s = ex&es }
              (6)  {bubble(x&s) = es&ex }
 conjects     (1)  {sorted(s') } <== { bubblesort(s) = s' }
```

The crucial lemma used the following expansion of Conjecture 1 is given by Theorem 1. It translates the recursive definition of bubblesort into an inductive property of sorted: substitute bubblesort(s') for s in Theorem 1.[1] The expansion is started by entering the command

```
st [1] [0];
```

It ends up with the following contents of EXPANSION:

initial goal set:
(1) { sorted(s'), bubblesort(s) = s' }

atom 1 in goal 1 resolved with theorem 1
(1) { sorted(s1), bubble(y&s1) = s"&x, makeBag(s") = makeBag(s1),
bubblesort(s) = s1&x }
(2) { sorted(s'), bubblesort(s) = s' }

atom 1 in goal 1 resolved with conjecture 1
(1) { s >> s2, bubblesort(s2) = s1, bubble(y&s1) = s"&x,
makeBag(s") = makeBag(s1), bubblesort(s) = s1&x }
(2) { sorted(s'), bubblesort(s) = s' }

equation 2 in goal 1 unified
(1) { s >> s2, bubble(y&s1) = s"&x, makeBag(s") = makeBag(bubblesort(s2)),
bubblesort(s) = bubblesort(s2)&x }
(2) { sorted(s'), bubblesort(s) = s' }

atom 3 in goal 1 resolved with theorem 2
(1) { s >> s2, bubble(y&s1) = s2&x, bubblesort(s) = bubblesort(s2)&x }
(2) { sorted(s'), bubblesort(s) = s' }

atom 1 in goal 1 resolved with axiom 13
(1) { lg(s) > lg(s2), bubble(y&s1) = s2&x, bubblesort(s) = bubblesort(s2)&x }
(2) { sorted(s'), bubblesort(s) = s' }

atom 1 at position 1 in goal 1 paramodulated with theorem 4

---

[1]Cf. Ex. 5.12 for the corresponding lemma LEM1 used for proving the correctness of sort-by-insertion.

(1) { lg(s'1) > lg(s2), bubble(s) = s'1, bubble(y&s1) = s2&x,
bubblesort(s) = bubblesort(s2)&x }
(2) { sorted(s'), bubblesort(s) = s' }

atom 2 factored with atom 3 in goal 1
(1) { lg(s2&x) > lg(s2), s = y&s1, bubble(y&s1) = s2&x, bubblesort(y&s1) =
bubblesort(s2)&x }
(2) { sorted(s'), bubblesort(s) = s' }

atom 1 in goal 1 resolved with theorem 3
(1) { s = y&s1, bubble(y&s1) = s2&x, bubblesort(y&s1) = bubblesort(s2)&x }
(2) { sorted(s'), bubblesort(s) = s' }

atom 3 in goal 1 resolved with axiom 9
(1) { s = y&s1, bubble(y&s1) = s2&x }
(2) { sorted(s'), bubblesort(s) = s' }

atom 2 in goal 1 resolved with theorem 6
(1) { s = y&s1 }
(2) { sorted(s'), bubblesort(s) = s' }

atom 1 in goal 2 resolved with axiom 5
(1) { bubblesort(s) = eps }
(2) { s = y&s1 }

atom 1 in goal 1 resolved with axiom 8
(1) { s = eps }
(2) { s = y&s1 }

atoms 1 1 in goals 1 2 resolved with theorem 5
(1)

An inductive proof of Theorem 1 calls for a generalization. After several trials we came up with the conjunction of Theorem 7 and Conjecture 1 of the following extension of BUBBLESORT:

BUBBLE
base BUBBLESORT
vars x y z s s' s" b

axioms (14) { mt <= x }
(15) { add(x,b) <= y } <== { x <= y, b <= y }
(16) { (x,y&s) >> (y,s) }
theorems (7) { sorted(s&x) } <== { sorted(s), makeBag(s) <= x }
(8) { x <= x }
(9) { x <= z } <== { x <= y, y <= z }
(10) { x <= z } <== { y > x, y <= z }
(11) { x <= y }V{ x > y }
(12) { s = x&s' } <== { bubble(s) = s"&y }
conjects (1) { x <= y, makeBag(s) <= y } <== { bubble(x&s) = s'&y }

An expansion of Conjecture 1 is started by entering the command

```
st [1] [0];
```

It ends up with the following contents of EXPANSION.

initial goal set:
(1) { x <= x', makeBag(s) <= x', bubble(x&s) = s'&x' }

atom 3 at position 1 in goal 1 paramodulated with axiom 10
(1) { s = eps, x&eps = s'&x', x <= x', makeBag(eps) <= x' }
(2) { x <= x', makeBag(s) <= x', bubble(x&s) = s'&x' }

atom 2 at position 2 in goal 1 paramodulated with axiom 1
(1) { x&eps = x'&eps, s = eps, x <= x', makeBag(eps) <= x' }
(2) { x <= x', makeBag(s) <= x', bubble(x&s) = s'&x' }

equation 1 in goal 1 unified
(1) { s = eps, x <= x, makeBag(eps) <= x }
(2) { x <= x', makeBag(s) <= x', bubble(x&s) = s'&x' }

atom 2 in goal 1 resolved with theorem 8
(1) { s = eps, makeBag(eps) <= x }
(2) { x <= x', makeBag(s) <= x', bubble(x&s) = s'&x' }

atom 2 at position 1 in goal 1 paramodulated with axiom 3
(1) { mt <= x, s = eps }
(2) { x <= x', makeBag(s) <= x', bubble(x&s) = s'&x' }

```
atom 1 in goal 1 resolved with axiom 14
(1) { s = eps }
(2) { x <= x', makeBag(s) <= x', bubble(x&s) = s'&x' }

atom 3 at position 1 in goal 2 paramodulated with axiom 11
(1) { s = y&s1, x&bubble(y&s1) = s'&x', x <= y, x <= x', makeBag(y&s1) <= x' }
(2) { x <= x', makeBag(s) <= x', bubble(x&s) = s'&x' }
(3) { s = eps }

atom 2 at position 2 in goal 1 paramodulated with axiom 2
(1) { x&bubble(y&s1) = x1&(s1&x'), s = y&s1, x <= y, x <= x',
      makeBag(y&s1) <= x' }
(2) { x <= x', makeBag(s) <= x', bubble(x&s) = s'&x' }
(3) { s = eps }

atom 5 at position 1 in goal 1 paramodulated with axiom 4
(1) { add(y, makeBag(s1)) <= x', x&bubble(y&s1) = x1&(s2&x'), s = y&s1,
      x <= y, x <= x' }
(2) { x <= x', makeBag(s) <= x', bubble(x&s) = s'&x' }
(3) { s = eps }

atom 1 in goal 1 resolved with axiom 15
(1) { y <= x', makeBag(s1) <= x', x&bubble(y&s1) = x1&(s2&x'), s = y&s1,
      x <= y, x <= x' }
(2) { x <= x', makeBag(s) <= x', bubble(x&s) = s'&x' }
(3) { s = eps }

atom 1 in goal 1 resolved with theorem 9
(1) { y <= x', makeBag(s1) <= x', x&bubble(y&s1) = x&(s2&x'), s = y&s1, x <= y }
(2) { x <= x', makeBag(s) <= x', bubble(x&s) = s'&x' }
(3) { s = eps }

atoms 1 2 in goal 1 resolved with conjecture 1
(1) { (x, y&s1) >> (y, s1), bubble(y&s1) = s3&x', x&bubble(y&s1) = x&(s2&x'),
      s = y&s1, x <= y }
(2) { x <= x', makeBag(s) <= x', bubble(x&s) = s'&x' }
(3) { s = eps }
```

atom 1 in goal 1 resolved with axiom 16
(1) { bubble(y&s1) = s3&x', x&bubble(y&s1) = x&(s2&x'), s = y&s1, x <= y }
(2) { x <= x', makeBag(s) <= x', bubble(x&s) = s'&x' }
(3) { s = eps }

atom 3 at position 1 2 replaced with equation 1 in goal 1
(1) { bubble(y&s1) = s3&x', x&(s3&x') = x&(s2&x'), s = y&s1, x <= y }
(2) { x <= x', makeBag(s) <= x', bubble(x&s) = s'&x' }
(3) { s = eps }

equation 3 in goal 1 unified
(1) { bubble(y&s1) = s2&x', s = y&s1, x <= y }
(2) { x <= x', makeBag(s) <= x', bubble(x&s) = s'&x' }
(3) { s = eps }

atom 1 in goal 1 resolved with theorem 6
(1) { s = y&s1, x <= y }
(2) { x <= x', makeBag(s) <= x', bubble(x&s) = s'&x' }
(3) { s = eps }

atom 3 at position 1 in goal 2 paramodulated with axiom 12
(1) { s = y&s1, y&bubble(x&s1) = s'&x', x > y, x <= x', makeBag(y&s1) <= x' }
(2) { s = y&s1, x <= y }
(3) { s = eps }

atom 2 at position 2 in goal 1 paramodulated with axiom 2
(1) { y&bubble(x&s1) = x1&(s2&x'), s = y&s1, x > y, x <= x',
makeBag(y&s1) <= x' }
(2) { s = y&s1, x <= y }
(3) { s = eps }

atom 5 at position 1 in goal 1 paramodulated with axiom 4
(1) { add(y, makeBag(s1)) <= x', y&bubble(x&s1) = x1&(s2&x'), s = y&s1,
x > y, x <= x' }
(2) { s = y&s1, x <= y }
(3) { s = eps }

atom 1 in goal 1 resolved with axiom 15

(1) { y <= x', makeBag(s1) <= x', y&bubble(x&s1) = x1&(s2&x'), s = y&s1,
x > y, x <= x' }
(2) { s = y&s1, x <= y }
(3) { s = eps }

atom 1 in goal 1 resolved with theorem 10
(1) { makeBag(s1) <= x', y&bubble(x&s1) = x1&(s2&x'), s = y&s1, x > y, x <= x' }
(2) { s = y&s1, x <= y }
(3) { s = eps }

atoms 5 1 in goal 1 resolved with conjecture 1
(1) { (x, x&s1) >> (x, s1), bubble(x&s1) = s3&x', y&bubble(x&s1) = x1&(s2&x'),
s = y&s1, x > y }
(2) { s = y&s1, x <= y }
(3) { s = eps }

atom 1 in goal 1 resolved with axiom 16
(1) { bubble(x&s1) = s3&x', y&bubble(x&s1) = x1&(s2&x'), s = y&s1, x > y }
(2) { s = y&s1, x <= y }
(3) { s = eps }

atom 2 at position 1 2 replaced with equation 1 in goal 1
(1) { bubble(x&s1) = s3&x', y&(s3&x') = x1&(s2&x'), s = y&s1, x > y }
(2) { s = y&s1, x <= y }
(3) { s = eps }

equation 2 in goal 1 unified
(1) { bubble(x&s1) = s3&x', s = y&s1, x > y }
(2) { s = y&s1, x <= y }
(3) { s = eps }

atom 1 in goal 1 resolved with theorem 6
(1) { s = y&s1, x > y }
(2) { s = y&s1, x <= y }
(3) { s = eps }

atoms 2 2 in goals 2 1 resolved with theorem 11
(1) { s = y&s1 }
(2) { s = eps }

atoms 1 1 in goals 2 1 resolved with theorem 5

(1)

The expansions of Exs. 9.1-9.4 are optimal in the sense that each subgoal is removed as soon as it is not used as a redex in a subsequent expansion step. As long as it is not clear which goals are needed later as resolution and paramodulation redices, one may preserve them by entering the commands `ras`, `rads`, `pas`, `pais` instead of `ra`, `rad`, `pa`, `pai`, resp. Conversely, a goal can always be eliminated from a (non-singleton) goal list by calling the command `de`.

The specifications upon which our sample expansions are based include all lemmas employed in the proofs, although most of these lemmas are actually unknown at the beginning of a proof. Instead, they became more or less obvious only after several proof steps. Alternatively, one may start out from a partial specification, add axioms and lemmas as needed and proceed with the modified specification by entering the read command `re` (cf. Sect. 9.2.6). Remember that the intermediate addition of axioms is the essence of program synthesis (cf. Sects. 2.1 and 5.5).

The backtrack command `ba` permits returning to a preceding goal list. If, for instance, one hits upon an unsolvable element in the current goal list (cf. Sects. 5.4 and 7.2), one may go back to a goal list consisting of solvable goals. Backtracking is also convenient for "massaging" a proof, i.e., for reducing a sequence of axiom applications to the application of a single, well-chosen, lemma.

9.3 The implementation

We start with auxiliary functions:

```
structure Aux = struct

  fun   front(s,0) = nil |
        front(x::s,n) = x::front(s,n-1)
  fun   mapconc(f)(s) = fold(fn(s,s')=>s@s')(map(f)(s))(nil)
  val   implod = mapconc(fn(x)=>x)
  fun   Max(s) = fold(fn(x,y)=>max(x,y))(s)(~1)
  fun   map2(f)(nil,nil) = (nil,nil) |
        map2(f)(x::s,y::s') = let val (fst,snd) = f(x,y)
                                  val (rest1,rest2) = map2(f)(s,s')
                              in (fst::rest1,snd::rest2) end
```

```
fun  forall(p)(nil) = true |
     forall(p)(x::s) = p(x) andalso forall(p)(s)
fun  forall2(p)(nil,nil) = true |
     forall2(p)(x::s,y::s') = p(x,y) andalso forall2(p)(s,s')
fun  filter(f,p)(nil,nil) = nil |
     filter(f,p)(x::s,y::s') = if p(x,y) then filter(f,p)(s,s') else f(x,y)::filter(f,p)(s,s')
fun  Member(eq)(x,nil) = false |
     Member(eq)(x,y::s) = eq(x,y) orelse Member(eq)(x,s)
val  member = Member(fn(x,y)=>x=y)
fun  diff(nil,s) = nil |
     diff(x::s,s') = if member(x,s') then diff(s,s') else x::diff(s,s')
fun  disjoint(nil,s) = true |
     disjoint(x::s,s') = not(member(x,s')) andalso disjoint(s,s')
fun  is_set(s) = is_setLoop(s,nil)
and  is_setLoop(nil,s) = true |
     is_setLoop(x::s,s') = not(member(x,s')) andalso is_setLoop(s,x::s')
fun  Makeset(is_in)(nil,s) = nil |
     Makeset(is_in)(x::s,s') = if is_in(x,s') then Makeset(is_in)(s,s')
                                               else x::Makeset(is_in)(s,x::s')
fun  makeset(s) = Makeset(member)(s,nil)
fun  mapstring(nil) = "" |
     mapstring(x::s) = makestring(x:int)^" "^mapstring(s)
fun  mapstrings(nil) = "" |
     mapstrings([x]) = mapstring(x) |
     mapstrings(x::s) = mapstring(x)^", "^mapstrings(s)
fun  instring(s,acc) = if end_of_stream(s) then acc else instring(s,acc^input_line(s))
fun  distr3(nil) = (nil,nil,nil) |
     distr3((a,b,c)::s) = let val (a',b',c') = distr3(s) in (a::a',b@b',c@c') end
fun  distr5(nil) = (nil,nil,nil,nil,nil) |
     distr5((a,b,c,d,e)::s) = let val (a',b',c',d',e') = distr5(s)
                              in (a@a',b@b',c@c',d@d',makeset(e@e')) end

end (*Aux*)
```

9.3.1 Scanning

The scanner reads characters and groups them into words. A string forms a word if it is preceded and followed by a delimiter, the disjunction symbol ∨ or the implication sign ⇐.

```
structure Scanner = struct

  fun  delimiter(x) = Aux.member(x,[",","(",")","{","}","+","-","*","&","@","#"])
                         orelse empty_space(x)
  and  empty_space(x) = Aux.member(x,[" ","\n","\t"])
  fun  words(s) = wordsLoop(s,"",nil)
  and  wordsLoop("\\"::"/"::s,w,acc) = if w = "" then wordsLoop(s,"",acc@["\\/"])
                                       else wordsLoop(s,"",acc@[w]@["\\/"]) |
       wordsLoop("<"::"="::"="::s,w,acc) = if w = "" then wordsLoop(s,"",acc@["<=="])
                                       else wordsLoop(s,"",acc@[w]@["<=="]) |
       wordsLoop(x::s,w,acc) = if delimiter(x)
                               then if empty_space(x)
                                    then if w = "" then wordsLoop(s,"",acc)
                                         else wordsLoop(s,"",acc@[w])
                                    else if w = "" then wordsLoop(s,"",acc@[x])
                                         else wordsLoop(s,"",acc@[w]@[x])
                               else wordsLoop(s,w^x,acc) |
       wordsLoop(nil,w,acc) = if w = "" then acc else acc@[w]

end (*Scanner*)
```

9.3.2 Abstract syntax

The internal representation of terms, goals and clauses is given by lists of objects built up of constructors for the datatype Term:

```
structure AbstractSyntax = struct
  datatype symbol_mode = vart | evart | varg | evarg of int | con | opn | opi | pre | pri
  datatype Term =  Var of string * symbol_mode |
                   Op of string * Term list * symbol_mode |
                   Pr of string * Term list * symbol_mode | err_term
  fun    Vars(Pr(_,tlist,_)) = Aux.mapconc(Vars)(tlist) |
         Vars(Op(_,tlist,_)) = Aux.mapconc(Vars)(tlist) |
         Vars(Var(x)) = [x]
```

```
fun   InVars(Pr(_,tlist,_)) = Aux.mapconc(InVars)(tlist) |
      InVars(Op(_,tlist,_)) = Aux.mapconc(InVars)(tlist) |
      InVars(Var(x,vart)) = [x] |
      InVars _ = nil
fun   occurs(x)(Var(y)) = x = y |
      occurs(x)(Op(_,tlist,_)) = exists(occurs(x))(tlist) |
      occurs(x)(Pr(_,tlist,_)) = exists(occurs(x))(tlist)
fun   eq_term(Var(x),Var(y)) = x = y |
      eq_term(Op(F,tlist,_),Op(G,tlist',_))
      = F = G andalso Aux.forall2(eq_term)(tlist,tlist') |
      eq_term(Pr(P,tlist,_),Pr(Q,tlist',_))
      = P = Q andalso Aux.forall2(eq_term)(tlist,tlist') |
      eq_term _ = false
fun   equal(x,t) = (Var(x,varg) = t)
fun   build_eq(x,t) = Pr("=",[Var(x,varg),t],pri)
fun   build_descent([t],[t']) = Pr(">>",[t,t'],pri) |
      build_descent(s,s') = Pr(">>",[Op("",s,opn),Op("",s',opn)],pri)
fun   lhs(Pr("=",[lhs,_],_)) = lhs
fun   rhs(Pr("=",[_,rhs],_)) = rhs

end (*AbstractSyntax*)
```

vart (evart) denotes the mode of a universal (existential) variable of SP, while varg (evarg(n)) denotes the mode of an input (output) variable of a goal occurring in the current expansion. Theorem variables must be distinguished from goal variables because a term of a theorem and a term of a goal are unifiable only if their variable sets are disjoint. Realizing the distinction by different variable modes relieves us of inventing different names for theorem variables on the one hand and goal variables on the other hand.

Moreover, the modes varg and vart allow us to distinguish the input variable set Xin of a conjecture c from their instances z1,...,zk in induction hypotheses used in a proof of c (cf. Sect. 5.2): the assignments

```
val t1_tk = apply_sub(Search.EQ(Xin,gl,id)&g,varg)(Xin)
val z1_zk = apply_sub(g,vart)(Xin)
```

in the body of ind_resolve and ind_paramodulate (cf. Sects. 9.3.10-9.3.11) attach the mode varg to Xin and the mode vart to z1,...,zk.

con stands for constants, opn (opi) for (infix) functions and pre (pri) for (infix) predicates.

9.3.3 Parsing

inspec reads a specification from a file and writes it, possibly equipped with error messages, on the file PARSE:

```
structure Parser = struct

  open AbstractSyntax

  fun    inspec(s) = let  val file = open_in(s)
                          val str = Aux.instring(file,"")
                          val charlist = explode(str)
                          val name::wordlist = Scanner.words(charlist)
                          val (sp,parse) = spec(wordlist)
                          val _ = close_in(file)
                          val check = open_out("PARSE")
                          val _ = output(check,parse)
                          val _ = close_out(check)
                      in sp end
```

The parser works by recursive descent, i.e., it breaks up into several functions, most of them associated with a nonterminal of the grammar given in Sect. 9.1.

```
  and    spec(s) = let val (sign,rest) = signat(s)
                       val (sign,axms,thms) = flatten(sign)
                       val (axms',rest,parse) = axioms(rest,sign)
                       val (thms',rest,parse) = theorems(rest,sign,parse)
                       val (conjs,rest,parse) = conjects(rest,sign,parse)
                   in ((sign,axms@axms',thms@thms',conjs),parse) end

  and    flatten(bs,cs,fs,ps,is,vs)
           = let fun f(b) = let val (sign,axms,thms,_) = inspec(b) in (sign,axms,thms) end
                 val specs = map(f)(bs)
                 val (signs,axms,thms) = Aux.distr3(specs)
                 val sign = Aux.distr5((cs,fs,ps,is,vs)::signs)
             in (sign,axms,thms) end

  and    axioms("axioms"::s,sign) = clauses(s,sign,nil,"\naxioms") |
         axioms(s,_) = (nil,s,"")

  and    theorems("theorems"::s,sign,parse) = clauses(s,sign,nil,parse^"\ntheorems") |
```

```
              theorems(s,_,parse) = (nil,s,parse)
and     conjects("conjects"::s,sign,parse) = clauses(s,sign,nil,parse^"\nconjects") |
              conjects(s,_,parse) = (nil,s,parse)
```

The signature returned by signat is a sextuple (bs,cs,fs,ps,is,vs) of base specification names and constant, function, predicate, infix and variable symbols, resp. The function flatten expands the base specifications such that the internal signature becomes a quintuple (cs,fs,ps,is,vs) (cf. Sect. 9.2.1).

```
and     signat(s) =  let  val (bs,rest) = base(s)
                          val (cs,rest) = consts(rest)
                          val (fs,rest) = functs(rest)
                          val (ps,rest) = preds(rest)
                          val (is,rest) = infixes(rest)
                          val (vs,rest) = vars(rest)
                     in ((bs,cs,fs,ps,is,vs),rest) end

and     base("base"::s) = symbols(s,nil) | base(s) = (nil,s)
and     consts("consts"::s) = symbols(s,nil) | consts(s) = (nil,s)
and     functs("functs"::s) = symbols(s,nil) | functs(s) = (nil,s)
and     preds("preds"::s) = symbols(s,nil) | preds(s) = (nil,s)
and     infixes("infixes"::s) = symbols(s,nil) | infixes(s) = (nil,s)
and     vars("vars"::s) = symbols(s,nil) | vars(s) = (nil,s)
and     symbols(x::s,acc)
        = ifAux.member(x,["consts", "functs","preds","infixes","vars", "axioms",
                                "theorems", "conjects"])
          then (acc,x::s) else symbols(s,acc@[x]) |
        symbols(nil,acc) = (acc,nil)
```

Clauses and goals are parsed into (pairs of) lists:

```
and     clauses("("::x::")"::s,sign,acc,parse)
        = let val tab = if String.length(x) = 1 then " " else ""
              val (cl,rest,parse) = clause(s,sign,parse^"\n"^tab^"("^x^")")
          in clauses(rest,sign,acc@[cl],parse) end |
        clauses(x::s,sign,acc,parse)
        = if Aux.member(x,["theorems","conjects"])
          then (acc,x::s,parse) else clauses(s,sign,acc,parse^x) |
        clauses(nil,_,acc,parse) = (acc,nil,parse)
and     clause(s,sign,parse)
```

```
        = case goals(s,sign,parse) of
          (concl,"<==="::rest,parse) => let val (prem,rest,parse)
                                              = goal(rest,sign, parse^"<==")
                                        in ((concl,prem),rest,parse) end |
          (concl,x::rest,parse) => if Aux.member(x,["(","theorems","conjects"])
                                   then ((concl,nil),x::rest,parse)
                                   else ((nil,nil),rest,parse^x^" NO CLAUSE ") |
          (concl,nil,parse) => ((concl,nil),nil,parse)
and     goals(s,sign,parse) = goalsLoop(s,sign,nil,parse)
and     goalsLoop(s,sign,acc,parse)
        = case goal(s,sign,parse) of
          (g,"\V"::rest,parse) => goalsLoop(rest,sign,acc@[g],parse^"\V") |
          (g,x::rest,parse) =>
                  if Aux.member(x,["<==","(","theorems","conjects"])
                  then (acc@[g],x::rest,parse) else (nil,rest,parse^x^" NO GOALS ") |
          (g,nil,parse) => (acc@[g],nil,parse)

and     goal("{"::s,sign,parse) = goalLoop(s,sign,nil,parse^" { ") |
        goal(s,_,parse) = (nil,s,parse^" NO GOAL ")
and     goalLoop(s,sign,acc,parse)
        = case atom(s,sign,parse) of
          (at,","::rest,parse) => goalLoop(rest,sign,acc@[at],parse^", ") |
          (at,"}"::rest,parse) => (acc@[at],rest,parse^" } ") |
          (at,rest,parse) => (nil,rest,parse^" NO GOAL ")
```

According to the signature (cs,fs,ps,is,vs), the function first_mode attaches a symbol mode to the first element of a word sequence (cf. Sect. 9.3.2). Undeclared words are regarded as existential theorem variables.

```
and     first_mode(sym::s,(cs,fs,ps,is,vs))
        = if Aux.member(sym,cs) then (sym,s,con)
          else if Aux.member(sym,fs) then if Aux.member(sym,is) then (sym,s,opi)
          else (sym,s,opn)
          else if Aux.member(sym,ps) then if Aux.member(sym,is) then (sym,s,pri)
          else (sym,s,pre)
          else if Aux.member(sym,vs) then (sym,s,vart) else (sym,s,evart)
```

first_mode controls the parsing of atoms and terms:

```
and     atom(s,sign,parse)
```

```
    = case first_mode(s,sign) of
        (P,"("::rest,pre) => let val (tlist,rest,parse) = termlist(rest,sign,parse^P^"(")
                              in (Pr(P,tlist,pre),rest,parse) end |
        _ => let val (t,rest,parse) = term(s,sign,parse)
                              in rest_atom(t,rest,sign,parse) end

and rest_atom(t,nil,_,parse) = (err_term,nil,parse^" NO ATOM ") |
    rest_atom(t,s,sign,parse)
    = case first_mode(s,sign) of
        (P,rest,pri) => let val(t',rest,parse) = term(rest,sign,parse^" "^P^" ")
                        in (Pr(P,[t,t'],pri),rest,parse) end |
        (x,rest,_) => (err_term,rest,parse^x^" NO ATOM ")

and term(s,sign,parse)
    = case first_mode(s,sign) of
        ("(",rest,_) => (case termlist(rest,sign,parse^"(") of
                        ([t],rest,parse) => rest_term(t,rest,sign,parse) |
                        (tlist,rest,parse) => rest_term(Op("",tlist,opn),rest,sign,parse))|
        (F,"("::rest,opn) =>  let val (tlist,rest,parse) = termlist(rest,sign,parse^F^"(")
                              in rest_term(Op(F,tlist,opn),rest,sign,parse) end |
        (x,"("::rest,vart) =>  let val (tlist,rest,parse) = termlist(rest,sign,parse^x^"(")
                              in rest_term(Op("APPLY",Var(x,vart)::tlist,opn),
                              rest,sign, parse) end |
        (x,"("::rest,evart) => let val (tlist,rest,parse) = termlist(rest,sign,parse^x^"(")
                              in rest_term(Op("APPLY",Var(x,evart)::tlist,opn),
                              rest,sign, parse) end |
        (C,rest,con) => rest_term(Op(C,nil,con),rest,sign,parse^C) |
        (C,rest,opn) => rest_term(Op(C,nil,opn),rest,sign,parse^C) |
        (C,rest,opi) => rest_term(Op(C,nil,opi),rest,sign,parse^C) |
        (x,rest,mode) => if Scanner.delimiter(x)
                              then (err_term,rest,parse^x^" NO TERM ")
                         else rest_term(Var(x,mode),rest,sign,parse^x)

and rest_term(t,nil,_,parse) = (t,nil,parse) |
    rest_term(t,s,sign,parse)
    = case first_mode(s,sign) of
        ("(",rest,_) => let val (tlist,rest,parse) = termlist(rest,sign,parse^"(")
                        in rest_term(Op("APPLY",t::tlist,opn),rest,sign,parse) end |
```

```
        (F,rest,opi) => let val (t',rest,parse) = term(rest,sign,parse^F)
                        in (Op(F,[t,t'],opi),rest,parse) end |
        _ => (t,s,parse)

and     termlist(s,sign,parse) = termlistLoop(s,sign,nil,parse)

and     termlistLoop(s,sign,acc,parse)
        = case term(s,sign,parse) of
          (t,","::rest,parse) => termlistLoop(rest,sign,acc@[t],parse^", ") |
          (t,")"::rest,parse) => (acc@[t],rest,parse^")") |
          (t,rest,parse) => (nil,rest,parse^" NO TERMLIST ")

end (*Parser*)
```

9.3.4 Unparsing

The following SML structure provides functions for transforming the internal representation of a specification into a string.

```
structure Unparser = struct

  open AbstractSyntax

  fun   symbols(s) = implode(map(fn(x)=>x^" ")(s))

  fun   outspec(sp,s) = let val file = open_out(s)
                            val _ = output(file,spec(sp))
                        in close_out(file) end

  and   spec((cs,fs,ps,is,vs),axms,thms,conjs)
        = "\nconsts "^symbols(cs)^"\nfuncts "^symbols(fs)^"\npreds  "^symbols(ps)^
          "\ninfixes "^symbols(is)^"\nvars   "^symbols(vs)^"\naxioms"^clauses(axms)^
          "\ntheorems"^clauses(thms)^"\nconjects"^clauses(conjs)

  and   clauses(cls) = clausesLoop(cls,1)
  and   clausesLoop(nil,_) = "" |
        clausesLoop((concl,prem)::axms,n)
        = let val premise = if prem = nil then "" else " <== "^goal(prem)
              val tab = if n < 10 then " " else ""
```

```
            in "\n"^tab^"("^makestring(n:int)^") "^conclusion(concl)^premise^
               clausesLoop(axms,n+1) end

and     goal(nil) = "" |
        goal(g) = "{ "^termlist(g)^" }"

and     conclusion(nil) = "" |
        conclusion([g]) = goal(g) |
        conclusion(g::gs) = goal(g)^"\/"^conclusion(gs)

and     term(Var(x,evarg(n))) = if n = 0 then x else x^makestring(n:int) |
        term(Var(x,_)) = x |
        term(Op(C,nil,_)) = C |
        term(Op("APPLY",t::tlist,opn)) = term(t)^"("^termlist(tlist)^")" |
        term(Op(F,tlist,opn)) = F^"("^termlist(tlist)^")" |
        term(Op(F,[t,t'],opi))
        = (case (t,t') of (Op(_,_,opi),Op(_,_,opi)) => "("^term(t)^")"^F^"("^term(t')^")"|
                          (Op(_,_,opi),_)  => "("^term(t)^")"^F^term(t') |
                          (_,Op(_,_,opi)) => term(t)^F^"("^term(t')^")" |
                          _ => term(t)^F^term(t')) |
        term(Pr(P,tlist,pre)) = P^"("^termlist(tlist)^")" |
        term(Pr(P,[t,t'],pri)) = term(t)^" "^P^" "^term(t')

and     termlist(nil) = "" |
        termlist([t]) = term(t) |
        termlist(t::tlist) = term(t)^", "^termlist(tlist)

fun     goals(gs) = goalsLoop(gs,1)
and     goalsLoop(nil,_) = "" |
        goalsLoop(g::gs,n) = let val tab = if n < 10 then " " else ""
                             in "\n"^tab^"("^makestring(n:int)^") "^goal(g)^
                                goalsLoop (gs,n+1) end

end (*Unparser*)
```

9.3.5 Unifying

Substitutions are implemented as functions of the type (string * symbol_mode) -> Term (cf. Sect. 9.3.2). They are created and modified by the following operations:

```
structure Unifier = struct

    open  AbstractSyntax

    val     id = fn(x) => Var(x)
    fun     t/x = fn(y) => if y = x then t else Var(y)
    fun     apply_sub(f,mode) = map(fn(x)=>f(x,mode))

    fun     substitute(f)(Var(x)) = f(x) |
            substitute(f)(Op("APPLY",Var(x)::tlist,opn))
             = (case f(x) of
                Op(F,nil,mode) => Op(F,map(substitute(f))(tlist),mode) |
                _ => Op("APPLY",f(x)::map(substitute(f))(tlist),opn)) |
            substitute(f)(Op(F,tlist,mode)) = Op(F,map(substitute(f))(tlist),mode) |
            substitute(f)(Pr(P,tlist,mode)) = Pr(P,map(substitute(f))(tlist),mode)

    infix   &
    fun     f&g = fn(x) => substitute(g)(f(x))

    exception
            mismatch and occur_check_fails

    fun     unify(Var(x,evart),Var(y),Evars) = (Var(y)/(x,evart),y::Evars) |
            unify(Var(x,evart),_,_) = raise mismatch |
            unify(Var(x,vart),Var(y),Evars) = (Var(y)/(x,vart),Evars) |
            unify(Var(x,varg),Var(y),Evars) = (Var(x,varg)/y,Evars) |
            unify(Var(x,evarg(m)),Var(y,evarg(n)),Evars)
                = (Var(x,evarg(m))/(y,evarg(n)), Evars) |
            unify(Var(x,evarg(n)),Var(y),Evars) = unify(Var(y),Var(x,evarg(n)),Evars) |
            unify(t,Var(x),Evars)
                = if occurs(x)(t) then raise occur_check_fails else(t/x,Evars) |
            unify(Var(x),t,Evars) = unify(t,Var(x),Evars) |
            unify(Op("APPLY",tlist,_),Op("APPLY",tlist',_),Evars)
            = let val (f,Evarslist) = unifyall(tlist,tlist')
```

```
        in (f,Aux.implod(Evars::Evarslist)) end |
      unify(Op("APPLY",Var(x)::tlist,_),Op(F,tlist',mode),Evars)
      = if exists(occurs(x))(tlist') then raise occur_check_fails
        else let val f = Op(F,nil,mode)/x
                 val (g,Evarslist) = unifyall(tlist,tlist')
             in (f&g,Aux.implod(Evars::Evarslist)) end |
      unify(Op(F,tlist,mode),Op("APPLY",tlist',opn),Evars)
      = unify(Op("APPLY",tlist',opn),Op(F,tlist,mode),Evars) |
      unify(Op(F,tlist,_),Op(G,tlist',_),Evars)
      = if F = G then let val (f,Evarslist) = unifyall(tlist,tlist')
                      in (f,Aux.implod(Evars::Evarslist)) end
                 else raise mismatch |
      unify(Pr(P,tlist,_),Pr(Q,tlist',_),Evars)
      = if P = Q then let val (f,Evarslist) = unifyall(tlist,tlist')
                      in (f,Aux.implod(Evars::Evarslist)) end
                 else raise mismatch |
      unify _ = raise mismatch
and   unifyall(nil,nil) = (id,nil) |
      unifyall(t::tlist,t'::tlist')
      = let val (f,Evars) = unify(t,t',nil)
            val newtlist = map(substitute(f))(tlist)
            val newtlist' = map(substitute(f))(tlist')
            val (g,Evarslist) = unifyall(newtlist,newtlist')
        in (f&g,Evars::Evarslist) end |
      unifyall _ = raise mismatch

end (*Unifier*)
```

unify and unifyall return respectively a most general unifier of two terms, term lists, atoms or atom lists together with the list Evars of all variables that were substituted for existential theorem variables (cf. Sect. 9.3.2). Evars is needed for checking the applicability conditions of lemma resolution and paramodulation upon a given lemma (cf. Sects. 5.1 and 9.3.10-9.3.11).

Two terms or atoms t and t' are not unifiable if unify creates from t and t' two terms that must be unified, but which have common variables. This leads to the exception occur_check_fails. The exception mismatch is raised if

- an existential theorem variable would be substituted by a term that is not a variable,[1] or
- the terms to be unified start with different function or predicate symbols.

Note that unify prefers substituting goal variables for theorem variables to substituting theorem variables for goal variables.

9.3.6 Renaming

The commands `st` and `std` extract from conjectures a goal list to be expanded. This includes the initialization of theorem variables as goal variables. In fact, only symbol modes must be changed:

```
structure Renamer = struct

  open AbstractSyntax Unifier

  fun   initialize(gs) = map(initialize_goal)(gs)
  and   initialize_goal(g) = map(initialize_atom)(g)
  and   initialize_atom(at) = let fun f(x,vart) = Var(x,varg) |
                                      f(x,evart) = Var(x,evarg(0)) |
                                      f(x) = Var(x)
                              in substitute(f)(at) end
```

Conversely, the commands `et`, `fi` and `fid`, which construct theorems or conjectures from an expansion, turn goal variables into theorem variables:

```
  fun   finalize(gs) = map(finalize_goal)(gs)
  and   finalize_goal(g) = map(finalize_atom)(g)
  and   finalize_atom(at) = let fun f(x,varg) = Var(x,vart) |
                                    f(x,evarg(n)) = Var(if n = 0 then x
                                                        else x^makestring(n:int),evart) |
                                    f(x) = Var(x)
                            in substitute(f)(at) end
```

An expansion step often introduces new theorem variables into the current goal list. These are turned into output variables as soon as the step has been finished: the assignment

---

[1]This violates the applicability condition "g(X⁻)⊆X" of lemma resolution and paramodulation (cf. Sect. 5.1).

```
val reduct = Renamer.rename(make_goal(reduct))
```

in the body of resolve and paramodulate (cf. Sects. 9.3.10/11) eliminates multiple atom occurrences from the reduct and renames theorem variables by goal variables in such a way that name conflicts are avoided by increasing the parameter of evarg(n):

```
fun    rename(g) = map(rename_atom(g))(g)
and    rename_atom(g)(p) = let fun f(x,vart) = Var(x,evarg(next(x,g))) |
                                   f(x,evart) = Var(x,evarg(next(x,g))) |
                                   f(x) = Var(x)
                           in substitute(f)(p) end

and    next(x,g) = Aux.Max(Aux.mapconc(evarg_nos(x))(g))+1

and    evarg_nos(x)(Pr(_,tlist,_)) = Aux.mapconc(evarg_nos(x))(tlist) |
       evarg_nos(x)(Op(_,tlist,_)) = Aux.mapconc(evarg_nos(x))(tlist) |
       evarg_nos(x)(Var(y,evarg(n))) = if x = y then [n] else nil |
       evarg_nos(x)(Var(y,varg)) = if x = y then [0] else nil |
       evarg_nos _ _ = nil

end (*Renamer*)
```

9.3.7 Searching and recording

Without comment we present the SML structures Search and Record, which provide a number of functions for respectively searching clauses, goals, etc., at given positions and recording expansion steps.

```
structure Search = struct

  open AbstractSyntax Unifier

  exception
          clause_not_found and goal_not_found and atom_not_found

  fun     clauses(cls,ns) = clausesLoop(cls,ns,1,nil,nil)
  and     clausesLoop(cl::cls,n::ns,k,acc,rest)
            = if n = k then clausesLoop(cls,ns,k+1,acc@[cl],rest)
```

```
                else clausesLoop(cls,n::ns,k+1,acc,rest@[cl]) |
        clausesLoop(nil,n::ns,_,acc,rest) = clausesLoop(rest,n::ns,1,acc,nil) |
        clausesLoop(cls,nil,_,acc,rest) = (acc,rest@cls)

and     clause(cls,n) = let val (_,cl,_) = clause_in_context(cls,n) in cl end

and     clause_in_context(cls,n) = clause_in_contextLoop(cls,n,1,nil)
and     clause_in_contextLoop(cl::cls,n,k,cls')
          = if n = k then (cls',cl,cls) else clause_in_contextLoop(cls,n,k+1,cls'@[cl]) |
        clause_in_contextLoop _ = raise clause_not_found

and     disjunct(gs,ns) = disjunctLoop(gs,ns,nil,nil)
and     disjunctLoop(g::gs,n::ns,acc,rest)
        = let val (g1,at,g2)
        = atom(g,n) in disjunctLoop(gs,ns,acc@[at],rest@g1@g2) end |
        disjunctLoop(nil,_,acc,rest) = (acc,rest)

and     goals(gs,ns) = goalsLoop(gs,ns,1,nil,nil)
and     goalsLoop(g::gs,n::ns,k,acc,rest)
          = if n = k then goalsLoop(gs,ns,k+1,acc@[g],rest)
            else goalsLoop(gs,n::ns,k+1,acc,rest@[g]) |
        goalsLoop(nil,n::ns,_,acc,rest) = goalsLoop(rest,n::ns,1,acc,nil) |
        goalsLoop(gs,nil,_,acc,rest) = (acc,rest@gs)

and     goal(gs,n) = goalLoop(gs,n,1,nil)
and     goalLoop(g::gs,n,k,gs') = if n = k then (gs',g,gs)
                                  else goalLoop(gs,n,k+1,gs'@[g]) |
        goalLoop _ = raise goal_not_found

and     atoms(g,ns) = atomsLoop(g,ns,1,nil,nil)
and     atomsLoop(at::g,n::ns,k,acc,rest)
          = if n = k then atomsLoop(g,ns,k+1,acc@[at],rest)
            else atomsLoop(g,n::ns,k+1,acc,rest@[at]) |
        atomsLoop(nil,n::ns,_,acc,rest) = atomsLoop(rest,n::ns,1,acc,nil) |
        atomsLoop(g,nil,_,acc,rest) = (acc,rest@g)

and     atom(g,n) = atomLoop(g,n,1,nil)
and     atomLoop(at::g,n,k,g') = if n = k then (g',at,g)
                                 else atomLoop(g,n,k+1,g'@[at]) |
        atomLoop _ = raise atom_not_found
```

```
and     term(t,nil,context) = (context,t) |
        term(t,k::w,context) = case t of Var(x) => (context,t) |
                                         Op(C,nil,_) => (context,t) |
                                         Op(F,tlist,mode) =>
                                                termlist(tlist,k,1,nil,w,context,F,mode) |
                                         Pr(P,tlist,mode) =>
                                                termlist(tlist,k,1,nil,w,context,P,mode)

and     termlist(t::tlist,k,k',tlist',w,context,F,mode)
        = if k = k' then let val x = ("YY",varg)
                          val c = case mode of opn => Op(F,tlist'@(Var(x)::tlist),opn) |
                                               opi => Op(F,tlist'@(Var(x)::tlist),opi) |
                                               pre => Pr(F,tlist'@(Var(x)::tlist),pre) |
                                               pri => Pr(F,tlist'@(Var(x)::tlist),pri)
                         in term(t,w,substitute(c/x)(context)) end
          else termlist(tlist,k,k'+1,tlist'@[t],w,context,F,mode)

and     EQ(vs,nil,f) = f |
        EQ(vs,at::g,f) = case at of Pr("=",[Var(x,varg),t],_) =>
                                            if Aux.member(x,vs)
                                            then EQ(vs,g,(t/(x,varg))&f)
                                            else EQ(vs,g,f) |
                                    _ => EQ(vs,g,f)

end (*Search*)

structure Record = struct

  datatype clause_mode = axm | axmd | thm | thmd | conj

  fun   start(gs)
        = let val file = open_out("EXPANSION")
              val str = "\ninitial goal set:"^Unparser.goals(gs)^"\n"
              val _ = output(std_out,str^"\n")
              val _ = output(file,str)
          in close_out(file) end

  fun   resolve(gs,g_nos,p_poss,c_no,c_mode)
        = let val file = open_append("EXPANSION")
```

```
        val str1 = case c_mode of axm => "axiom " | axmd => "axiom " |
                                  thm => "theorem " |
                                  thmd => "theorem " | conj => "conjecture "
        val str2 = case g_nos of [_] => " " | _ => "s "
        val str3 = case p_poss of [_] => " " | _ => "s "
        val str4 = "\natom"^str3^Aux.mapstring(p_poss)^"in goal"^str2^
                   Aux. mapstring(g_nos)^
                  "resolved with "^str1^makestring(c_no:int)^
                   Unparser.goals(gs)^"\n"
        val _ = output(std_out,str4^"\n")
        val _ = output(file,str4)
      in close_out(file) end

fun     paramodulate(gs,g_nos,p_poss,t_poss,c_no,c_mode)
      = let val file = open_append("EXPANSION")
        val str1 = case c_mode of axm => "axiom " | thm => "theorem " |
                                         conj => "conjecture "
        val str2 = case g_nos of [_] => " " | _ => "s "
        val str3 = "\natom"^str2^Aux.mapstring(p_poss)^"at position"^str2^
             Aux.mapstrings(t_poss)^"in goal"^str2^Aux.mapstring(g_nos)^
             "paramodulated with "^str1^makestring(c_no:int)^
              Unparser. goals(gs)^"\n"
        val _ = output(std_out,str3^"\n")
        val _ = output(file,str3)
      in close_out(file) end

fun     factor(gs,g_no,p_pos,q_pos)
      = let val file = open_append("EXPANSION")
        val str = "\natom "^makestring(p_pos:int)^" factored with atom "^
                   makestring(q_pos:int)^
                  " in goal "^makestring(g_no:int)^Unparser.goals(gs)^"\n"
        val _ = output(std_out,str^"\n")
        val _ = output(file,str)
            in close_out(file) end
fun     unify(gs,g_no,eq_pos)
      = let val file = open_append("EXPANSION")
        val str = "\nequation "^makestring(eq_pos:int)^" in goal"^
                  makestring(g_no:int)^" unified"^
                  Unparser.goals(gs)^"\n"
```

```
            val _ = output(std_out,str^"\n")
            val _ = output(file,str)
              in close_out(file) end

  fun     replace(gs,g_no,eq_pos,p_poss,t_poss)
           = let val file = open_append("EXPANSION")
                 val str1 = case p_poss of [_] => " " | _ => "s "
                 val str2 = "\natom"^str1^Aux.mapstring(p_poss)^"at position"^str1^
                          Aux.mapstrings(t_poss)^replaced with equation "^
                          makestring(eq_pos:int)^" in goal "^makestring(g_no:int)^
                          Unparser.goals(gs)^"\n"
                 val _ = output(std_out,str2^"\n")
                 val _ = output(file,str2)
             in close_out(file) end

  fun     delete(gs,g_no)
           = let val file = open_append("EXPANSION")
                 val str = "\ngoal "^makestring(g_no:int)^
                         "deleted"^Unparser.goals(gs)^"\n"
                 val _ = output(std_out,str^"\n")
                 val _ = output(file,str)
             in close_out(file) end

  fun     backtrack(gs)
           = let val file = open_append("EXPANSION")
                 val str = "\ncurrent goal set:"^Unparser.goals(gs)^"\n"
                 val _ = output(std_out,str^"\n")
                 val _ = output(file,str)
             in close_out(file) end

  fun     change_spec(cls,n,str)
           = let val str1 = case cls of [_] => " " | _ => "s "
                 val str2 = case cls of [_] => "is" | _ => "are"
                 val str3 = "\nthe "^str^str1^Unparser.clausesLoop(cls,n)^"\n"^str2^
                         " added to the specification\n"
             in output(std_out,str3^"\n") end

end (*Record*)
```

9.3.8 The commands

The following SML structure Commands initializes the quintuple PR (cf. Sect. 9.2) and defines each command in terms of functions defined by the structure Expander (cf. Sects. 9.3.9-9.3.13).

```
structure Commands = struct

  open AbstractSyntax

  val    pr = ref((((nil,nil,nil,nil,nil),nil,nil,nil),nil,nil,nil,nil)
                 :((string list * string list * string list * string list *string list) *
                 (Term list list * Term list) list *
                 (Term list list * Term list) list *
                 (Term list list * Term list) list) *
                 string list * Term list list * Term list list list * Term list)

  fun    st c_nos guard_no = pr := Expander.start_proof(!pr,c_nos,guard_no)
  fun    std c_no = pr := Expander.start_proof_dis(!pr,c_no)
  fun    ra g_no p_poss c_no q_poss
         = pr := Expander.resolve(!pr,[g_no],p_poss,c_no,q_poss,Record.axm,0)
  fun    rad g_nos p_poss c_no q_poss
         = pr := Expander.resolve(!pr,g_nos,p_poss,c_no,q_poss,Record.axmd,0)
  fun    ras g_no p_poss c_no q_poss
         = pr := Expander.resolve(!pr,[g_no],p_poss,c_no,q_poss,Record.axm,1)
  fun    rads g_nos p_poss c_no q_poss
         = pr := Expander.resolve(!pr,g_nos,p_poss,c_no,q_poss,Record.axmd,1)
  fun    rt g_no p_poss c_no q_poss
         = pr := Expander.resolve(!pr,[g_no],p_poss,c_no,q_poss,Record.thm,0)
  fun    rtd g_nos p_poss c_no q_poss
         = pr := Expander.resolve(!pr,g_nos,p_poss,c_no,q_poss,Record.thmd,0)
  fun    rts g_no p_poss c_no q_poss
         = pr := Expander.resolve(!pr,[g_no],p_poss,c_no,q_poss,Record.thm,1)
  fun    rtds g_nos p_poss c_no q_poss
         = pr := Expander.resolve(!pr,g_nos,p_poss,c_no,q_poss,Record.thmd,1)
  fun    rc g_no p_poss c_no q_poss
         = pr := Expander.resolve(!pr,[g_no],p_poss,c_no,q_poss,Record.conj,0)
  fun    pa g_nos p_poss t_poss c_no q_poss
```

```
       = pr := Expander.paramodulate(!pr,g_nos,p_poss,t_poss,c_no,q_poss,0,
                                                          Record.axm,0)
fun    pai g_nos p_poss t_poss c_no q_poss
       = pr := Expander.paramodulate(!pr,g_nos,p_poss,t_poss,c_no,q_poss,1,
                                                          Record.axm,0)
fun    pas g_nos p_poss t_poss c_no q_poss
       = pr := Expander.paramodulate(!pr,g_nos,p_poss,t_poss,c_no,q_poss,0,
                                                          Record.axm,1)
fun    pais g_nos p_poss t_poss c_no q_poss
       = pr := Expander.paramodulate(!pr,g_nos,p_poss,t_poss,c_no,q_poss,1,
                                                          Record.axm,1)
fun    pt g_nos p_poss t_poss c_no q_poss
       = pr := Expander.paramodulate(!pr,g_nos,p_poss,t_poss,c_no,q_poss,0,
                                                          Record.thm,0)
fun    pti g_nos p_poss t_poss c_no q_poss
       = pr := Expander.paramodulate(!pr,g_nos,p_poss,t_poss,c_no,q_poss,1,
                                                          Record.thm,0)
fun    pts g_nos p_poss t_poss c_no q_poss
       = pr := Expander.paramodulate(!pr,g_nos,p_poss,t_poss,c_no,q_poss,0,
                                                          Record.thm,1)
fun    ptis g_nos p_poss t_poss c_no q_poss
       = pr := Expander.paramodulate(!pr,g_nos,p_poss,t_poss,c_no,q_poss,1,
                                                          Record.thm,1)
fun    pc g_no p_pos t_pos c_no q_pos
       = pr := Expander.paramodulate(!pr,[g_no],[p_pos],[t_pos],c_no,[q_pos],0,
                                                          Record.conj,0)
fun    pci g_no p_pos t_pos c_no q_pos
       = pr := Expander.paramodulate(!pr,[g_no],[p_pos],[t_pos],c_no,[q_pos],1,
                                                          Record.conj,0)
fun    fa g_no p_pos q_pos = pr := Expander.factor(!pr,g_no,p_pos,q_pos)
fun    un g_no eq_pos = pr := Expander.unify_eq(!pr,g_no,eq_pos)
fun    eql g_no eq_pos p_poss t_poss
       = pr := Expander.replace(!pr,g_no,eq_pos,0,p_poss,t_poss)
fun    eqr g_no eq_pos p_poss t_poss
       = pr := Expander.replace(!pr,g_no,eq_pos,1,p_poss,t_poss)

fun    de g_no = pr := Expander.delete(!pr,g_no)
fun    et() = pr := Expander.expansion_to_thms(!pr)
```

```
fun   fi ge_poss = pr := Expander.finish_proof(!pr,ge_poss)
fun   fid() = pr := Expander.finish_proof_dis(!pr)

fun   re s = let val (sp,Xin,ini,proof,fin) = !pr
       in pr := (Parser.inspec(s),Xin,ini,proof,fin) end

fun   ba n = let val (sp,Xin,ini,proof,fin) = !pr
                val proof = nthtail(proof,n)
                val _ = Record.backtrack(hd(proof))
             in pr := (sp,Xin,ini,proof,fin) end

fun   ct c_nos = let val ((sign,axms,thms,conjs),Xin,ini,proof,fin) = !pr
                     val (cls,rest) = Search.clauses(conjs,c_nos)
                     val sp = (sign,axms,thms@cls,rest)
                     val _ = Record.change_spec(cls,length(thms)+1,"theorem")
                 in pr := (sp,Xin,ini,proof,fin) end

fun   wrs s = let val (sp,Xin,ini,proof,fin) = !pr
              in Unparser.outspec(sp,s) end

fun   wre s = let val file = open_in("EXPANSION")
                  val str = Aux.instring(file,"")
                  val _ = close_in(file)
                  val file = open_out(s)
                  val _ = output(file,str)
              in close_out(file) end

fun   shs() = let val (sp,Xin,ini,proof,fin) = !pr
              in output(std_out,Unparser.spec(sp)^"\n") end

fun   she() = let val file = open_in("EXPANSION")
                  val str = Aux.instring(file,"")
                  val _ = close_in(file)
              in output(std_out,str^"\n") end

fun   shp() = let val file = open_in("PARSE")
                  val str = Aux.instring(file,"")
                  val _ = close_in(file)
```

```
                in output(std_out,str^"\n\n") end

    fun     sh s = let val file = open_in(s)
                       val str = Aux.instring(file,"")
                       val _ = close_in(file)
                   in output(std_out,str^"\n") end

  end (*Commands*)
```

9.3.9 Starting an expansion (cf. Sect. 9.2.1)

```
  structure Expander = struct

    open    AbstractSyntax Unifier

    fun     start_proof(((sign,axms,thms,conjs),Xin,ini,proof,fin),c_nos,guard_no)
              = let val (gs_Xin,fin) = make_goals(conjs,c_nos,guard_no)
                    val ini = Renamer.initialize(map(#1)(gs_Xin))
                    val Xin = Aux.makeset(Aux.mapconc(#2)(gs_Xin))
                    val proof = [ini]
                    val _ = Record.start(ini)
                      in ((sign,axms,thms,conjs),Xin,ini,proof,fin) end

    and     make_goals(cls,ms,n) = make_goalsLoop(cls,ms,n,1,nil)
    and     make_goalsLoop(cl::cls,m::ms,n,k,acc)
            = if m = k then make_goalsLoop(cls,ms,n,k+1,acc@[(cl,n)])
                      else make_goalsLoop(cls,m::ms,n,k+1,acc) |
            make_goalsLoop(_,nil,n,_,acc)
            = let val (_,prem) = hd(acc)
                in (extract_goals(acc,n),Aux.front(prem,n)) end

    and     extract_goals(([concl],prem)::rest,n)
             = let val gens = nthtail(prem,n)
                   val g = concl@gens
                   val allvars = Aux.makeset(Aux.mapconc(InVars)(g))
                   val outvars = Aux.makeset(Aux.mapconc(InVars)(map(rhs)(gens)))
                   val Xin = Aux.diff(allvars,outvars)
               in (g,Xin)::extract_goals(rest) end |
```

```
          extract_goals(nil,n) = nil

fun   start_proof_dis(((sign,axms,thms,conjs),Xin,ini,proof,fin),c_no)
        = let val (gs,fin) = Search.clause(conjs,c_no)
              val Xin = Aux.makeset(Aux.mapconc(Aux.mapconc(InVars))(gs))
              val ini = Renamer.initialize(gs)
              val proof = [ini]
              val _ = Record.start(ini)
          in ((sign,axms,thms,conjs),Xin,ini,proof,fin) end
```

9.3.10 Resolving (cf. Sect. 9.2.2)

```
exception ex_var_incorrectly_substituted

fun   resolve(((sign,axms,thms,conjs),Xin,ini,proof,fin),g_nos,p_poss, c_no,
            q_poss, c_mode,split)
        = let val (redex,rest) = Search.goals(hd(proof),g_nos)
              val reduct = case c_mode of
                              Record.axm => lem_resolve(Xin,redex,p_poss,axms,
                                                        c_no,q_poss,1) |
                              Record.axmd => lem_resolve(Xin,redex,p_poss,axms,
                                                        c_no,q_poss,2) |
                              Record.thm => lem_resolve(Xin,redex,p_poss,thms,
                                                        c_no,q_poss,1) |
                              Record.thmd => lem_resolve(Xin,redex,p_poss,thms,
                                                        c_no,q_poss,2) |
                              Record.conj => ind_resolve(Xin,hd(redex), p_poss,
                                                        conjs, c_no,q_poss)
              val reduct = Renamer.rename(make_goal(reduct))
              val gs = if split = 0 then reduct::rest else reduct::redex@rest
              val proof = gs::proof
              val _ = Record.resolve(gs,g_nos,p_poss,c_no,c_mode)
          in ((sign,axms,thms,conjs),Xin,ini,proof,fin) end

and   make_goal(g) = Aux.Makeset(Aux.Member(eq_term))(g,nil)

and   lem_resolve(Xin,gs,p_poss,thms,c_no,q_poss,sum_no)
        = let val (p1_pn,rest) = if sum_no = 1 then Search.atoms(hd(gs),p_poss)
```

```
                                          else Search.disjunct(gs,p_poss)
          val (concl,prem) = Search.clause(thms,c_no)
          val (q1_qn,_) = if sum_no = 1 then Search.atoms(hd(concl),q_poss)
                                          else Search.disjunct(concl,q_poss)
          val (g,Evarslist) = unifyall(p1_pn,q1_qn)
          val Evarslist = if sum_no = 1 then [Aux.implod(Evarslist)]
                                          else Evarslist
          val gXin = apply_sub(g,varg)(Xin)
          val EQgin = Aux.filter(build_eq,equal)(Xin,gXin)
          val rest = map(substitute(g))(rest)
          val varsOfRestAndgXin = Aux.mapconc(Vars)(rest@gXin)
       in if Aux.disjoint(Aux.implod(Evarslist),varsOfRestAndgXin)
             andalso Aux.forall(Aux.is_set)(Evarslist)
          then EQgin @ map(substitute(g))(prem) @ rest
          else raise ex_var_incorrectly_substituted end
```

..disjoint(..Evarslist..,varsOfRestAndgXin) and ..is_set(Evarslist) check the applicability condition of lemma resolution with unifier g: given that $\exists X_1\gamma_1\vee\ldots\vee\exists X_n\gamma_n \Leftarrow\gamma$ is the clause resolved upon, the variables of Evarslist = map(g)[$X_1,\ldots,X_n$] must neither occur in the g-instance of an atom, which does not belong to the redex, nor in the g-instance of an input variable (cf. Sect. 5.1). Moreover, g must be injective on all X_i, i.e., each variable may occur at most once in g(X_i).

```
and   ind_resolve(Xin,gl,p_poss,conjs,c_no,q_poss)
        = let val (p1_pn,rest) = Search.atoms(gl,p_poss)
              val ([concl],prem) = Search.clause(conjs,c_no)
              val (q1_qn,_) = Search.atoms(concl,q_poss)
              val (g,_) = unifyall(p1_pn,q1_qn)
              val gXin = apply_sub(g,varg)(Xin)
              val EQgin = Aux.filter(build_eq,equal)(Xin,gXin)
              val t1_tk = apply_sub(Search.EQ(Xin,gl,id)&g,varg)(Xin)
              val z1_zk = apply_sub(g,vart)(Xin)
              val descent = build_descent(t1_tk,z1_zk)
          in descent :: EQgin @ map(substitute(g))(prem@rest) end
```

9.3.11 Paramodulating (cf. Sect. 9.2.3)

```
fun   paramodulate(((sign,axms,thms,conjs),Xin,ini,proof,fin),
                     g_nos,p_poss,t_poss,c_no,q_poss,c_dir,c_mode,split)
```

```
          = let val (redex,rest) = Search.goals(hd(proof),g_nos)
                val (p_pos,t_pos,q_pos) = map(hd)[p_poss,t_poss,q_poss]
                val reduct = case c_mode of
                      Record.axm => lem_paramodulate(Xin,redex,p_poss,t_poss,axms,
                                                          c_no,q_poss,c_dir) |
                      Record.thm => lem_paramodulate(Xin,redex,p_poss,t_poss,thms,
                                                          c_no,q_poss,c_dir) |
                      Record.conj => ind_paramodulate(Xin,hd(redex),p_pos,t_pos,conjs,
                                                          c_no,q_pos,c_dir)
                val reduct = Renamer.rename(make_goal(reduct))
                val gs = if split = 0 then reduct::rest else reduct::redex@rest
                val proof = gs::proof
                val _ = Record.paramodulate(gs,g_nos,p_poss,t_poss,c_no,c_mode)
             in ((sign,axms,thms,conjs),Xin,ini,proof,fin) end

and       lem_paramodulate(Xin,gs,p_poss,t_poss,thms,c_no,q_poss,c_dir)
          = let val (p1_pn,rest) = Search.disjunct(gs,p_poss)
                val (concl,prem) = Search.clause(thms,c_no)
                val (q1_qn,_) = Search.disjunct(concl,q_poss)
                val x = ("YY",varg)
                val search_terms = fn(y,z)=>Search.term(y,z,Var(x))
                val (contexts,t1_tn) = Aux.map2(search_terms)(p1_pn,t_poss)
                val u1_un = if c_dir = 0 then map(lhs)(q1_qn) else map(rhs)(q1_qn)
                val t = if c_dir = 0 then rhs(hd(q1_qn)) else lhs(hd(q1_qn))
                val (g,Evarslist) = unifyall(t1_tn,u1_un)
                val gXin = apply_sub(g,varg)(Xin)
                val EQgin = Aux.filter(build_eq,equal)(Xin,gXin)
                val reduct = map(substitute(t/x))(contexts)
                val reduct = map(substitute(g))(reduct)
                val rest = map(substitute(g))(rest)
                val varsOfReductAndgXin = Aux.mapconc(Vars)(reduct@rest@gXin)
             in if Aux.disjoint(Aux.implod(Evarslist),varsOfReductAndgXin)
                  andalso Aux.forall(Aux.is_set)(Evarslist)
                then EQgin @ reduct @ map(substitute(g))(prem) @ rest
                else raise ex_var_incorrectly_substituted end
```

..disjoint(gevart,varsOfRestAndgXin) and ..is_set(Evarslist) check the applicability condition of lemma paramodulation with unifier g: given that $\exists X_1 u_1 \equiv t \vee \ldots \vee \exists X_n u_n \equiv t \Leftarrow \gamma$ is the clause paramodulated upon, the variables of Evarslist

= map(g)[X_1,...,X_n] must neither occur in the g-instance of a subterm, which does not belong to the redex, nor in the g-instance of an input variable (cf. Sect. 5.1). Moreover, g must be injective on all X_i, i.e., each variable may occur at most once in g(X_i).

```
and    ind_paramodulate(Xin,gl,p_pos,t_pos,conjs,c_no,q_pos,c_dir)
        = let val (rest1,p,rest2) = Search.atom(gl,p_pos)
              val ([concl],prem) = Search.clause(conjs,c_no)
              val (_,q,_) = Search.atom(concl,q_pos)
              val x = ("YY",varg)
              val (context,t) = Search.term(p,t_pos,Var(x))
              val u = if c_dir = 0 then lhs(q) else rhs(q)
              val u' = if c_dir = 0 then rhs(q) else lhs(q)
              val (g,_) = unify(t,u,nil)
              val gXin = apply_sub(g,varg)(Xin)
              val EQgin = Aux.filter(build_eq,equal)(Xin,gXin)
              val t1_tk = apply_sub(Search.EQ(Xin,gl,id)&g,varg)(Xin)
              val z1_zk = apply_sub(g,vart)(Xin)
              val descent = build_descent(t1_tk,z1_zk)
              val reduct = substitute(u'/x)(context)
          in descent :: EQgin @ map(substitute(g))(reduct::prem@rest1@rest2) end
```

9.3.12 Composed rules (cf. Sect. 9.2.4)

```
fun    factor((sp,Xin,ini,proof,fin),g_no,p_pos,q_pos)
        = let val (rest1,redex,rest2) = Search.goal(hd(proof),g_no)
              val (_,p,_) = Search.atom(redex,p_pos)
              val (rest3,q,rest4) = Search.atom(redex,q_pos)
              val (g,_) = unify(p,q,nil)
              val gXin = apply_sub(g,varg)(Xin)
              val EQgin = Aux.filter(build_eq,equal)(Xin,gXin)
              val reduct = EQgin @ map(substitute(g))(rest3@rest4)
              val reduct = make_goal(reduct)
              val gs = rest1@reduct::rest2
              val proof = gs::proof
              val _ = Record.factor(gs,g_no,p_pos,q_pos)
          in (sp,Xin,ini,proof,fin) end
```

```
fun     unify_eq((sp,Xin,ini,proof,fin),g_no,eq_pos)
          = let val (rest1,redex,rest2) = Search.goal(hd(proof),g_no)
                val (rest3,eq,rest4) = Search.atom(redex,eq_pos)
                val (g,_) = unify(lhs(eq),rhs(eq),nil)
                val gXin = apply_sub(g,varg)(Xin)
                val EQgin = Aux.filter(build_eq,equal)(Xin,gXin)
                val reduct = EQgin @ map(substitute(g))(rest3@rest4)
                val reduct = make_goal(reduct)
                val gs = rest1@reduct::rest2
                val proof = gs::proof
                val _ = Record.unify(gs,g_no,eq_pos)
            in (sp,Xin,ini,proof,fin) end

fun     replace((sp,Xin,ini,proof,fin),g_no,eq_pos,dir,p_poss,t_poss)
          = let val (rest1,redex,rest2) = Search.goal(hd(proof),g_no)
                val (_,eq,_) = Search.atom(redex,eq_pos)
                val reduct = replace_list(p_poss,t_poss,redex,eq,dir)
                val gs = rest1@reduct::rest2
                val proof = gs::proof
                val _ = Record.replace(gs,g_no,eq_pos,p_poss,t_poss)
            in (sp,Xin,ini,proof,fin) end

and     replace_list(p_pos::p_poss,t_pos::t_poss,redex,eq,dir)
          = let val reduct = replace_single(p_pos,t_pos,redex,eq,dir)
            in replace_list(p_poss,t_poss,reduct,eq,dir) end |
        replace_list(nil,nil,redex,_,_) = redex

and     replace_single(p_pos,t_pos,redex,eq,dir)
          = let val x = ("YY",varg)
                val (rest1,p,rest2) = Search.atom(redex,p_pos)
                val (context,t) = Search.term(p,t_pos,Var(x))
                val reduct = if dir = 0 then substitute(lhs(eq)/x)(context)
                                        else substitute(rhs(eq)/x)(context)
            in rest1@reduct::rest2 end

fun     delete((sp,Xin,ini,proof,fin),g_no)
          = let val (rest1,redex,rest2) = Search.goal(hd(proof),g_no)
                val gs = rest1@rest2
```

```
                val proof = gs::proof
                val _ = Record.delete(gs,g_no)
            in (sp,Xin,ini,proof,fin) end
```

9.3.13 Stopping an expansion (cf. Sect. 9.2.5)

```
fun     expansion_to_thms((sign,axms,thms,conjs),Xin,ini,proof,fin)
          = let val concl = Renamer.finalize(ini)
                val gs = Renamer.finalize(hd(proof))
                val cls = map(fn(g)=>(concl,g))(gs)
                val sp = (sign,axms,thms@cls,conjs)
                val _ = Record.change_spec(cls,length(thms)+1,"theorem")
            in (sp,Xin,ini,proof,fin) end

fun     finish_proof(((sign,axms,thms,conjs),Xin,ini,proof,fin),ge_poss)
          = let val gs = Renamer.finalize(hd(proof))
                val cls = make_conjects(gs,ge_poss,fin)
                val (cs,fs,ps,is,vs) = sign
                val vs' = map(#1)(Aux.mapconc(Aux.mapconc(Vars))(gs))
                val sign = (cs,fs,ps,is,Aux.makeset(vs@vs'))
                val sp = (sign,axms,thms,conjs@cls)
                val _ = Record.change_spec(cls,length(conjs)+1,"conjecture")
            in (sp,Xin,ini,proof,fin) end

and     make_conjects(g::gs,ns::nss,prem)
          = let val (gens,concl) = Search.atoms(g,ns)
              in ([concl],prem@gens)::make_conjects(gs,nss,prem) end |
        make_conjects(nil,nss,prem) = nil

fun     finish_proof_dis((sign,axms,thms,conjs),Xin,ini,proof,fin)
          = let val gs = Renamer.finalize(hd(proof))
                val cls = [(gs,fin)]
                val sp = (sign,axms,thms,conjs@cls)
                val _ = Record.change_spec(cls,length(conjs)+1,"conjecture")
                    in (sp,Xin,ini,proof,fin) end

end (*Expander*)
```

References

[Baa88] S. Baase, *Computer Algorithms,* Addison-Wesley (1988)

[BDH86] L. Bachmair, N. Dershowitz, J. Hsiang, *Orderings for Equational Proofs*, Proc. LICS '86 (1986) 346-357

[BSW69] K.A. Bartlet, R.A. Scantlebury, P.T. Wilkinson, *A Note on Reliable Full-Duplex Transmission over Half-Duplex Links,* Comm. ACM 12 (1969) 260-261

[BW82] F.L. Bauer, H. Wössner, *Algorithmic Language and Program Development*, Springer (1982)

[BV87] C. Beierle, A. Voß, *Theory and Practice of Canonical Term Functors in Abstract Data Type Specifications,* Proc. TAPSOFT '87, Springer LNCS 250 (1987) 320-334

[Bir84] R. Bird, *Using Circular Programs to Eliminate Multiple Traversals of Data*, Acta Informatica 21 (1984) 239-250

[BW88] R. Bird, P. Wadler, *Introduction to Functional Programming*, Prentice-Hall (1988)

[BP82] M. Broy, P. Pepper, *Combining Algebraic and Algorithmic Reasoning: An Approach to the Schorr-Waite Algorithm,* ACM TOPLAS 4 (1982) 362-381

[BPW84] M. Broy, C. Pair, M. Wirsing, *A Systematic Study of Models of Abstract Data Types,* Theoretical Comp. Sci. 33 (1984) 139-174

[BD77] R.M. Burstall, J. Darlington, *A Transformation System for Recursive Programs*, J. ACM 24 (1977) 44-67

[DF77] E. Denert, R. Franck, *Datenstrukturen*, B.I.-Wissenschaftsverlag (1977)

[Der83] N. Dershowitz, *Computing with Rewrite Systems*, Report ATR-83(8478)-1, Inform. Sci. Research Office, The Aerospace Corp., El Segundo CA (1983)

[Der87] N. Dershowitz, *Termination of Rewriting*, J. Symbolic Comp. 3 (1987) 69-115

[DJ90] N. Dershowitz, J.-P. Jouannaud, *Rewrite Systems*, in: J. van Leeuwen, ed., Handbook of Theoretical Computer Science, Vol. B: *Formal Models and Semantics*, Elsevier (1990) 243-320

[DM79] N. Dershowitz, Z. Manna, *Proving Termination with Multiset Orderings,* Comm. ACM (1979) 465-476

[DOS87] N. Dershowitz, M. Okada, G. Sivakumar, *Confluence of Conditional Rewrite Systems*, Proc. CTRS '87, Springer LNCS 308 (1988) 31-44

[DOS88] N. Dershowitz, M. Okada, G. Sivakumar, *Canonical Conditional Rewrite Systems*, Proc. CADE '88, Springer LNCS 310 (1988) 538-549

[DH87] M. Dincbas, P. van Hentenryck, *Extended Unification Algorithms for the Integration of Functional Programming into Logic Programming,* J. Logic Programming 4 (1987) 199-227

[Ech88] R. Echahed, *On Completeness of Narrowing Strategies,* Proc. CAAP '88, Springer LNCS 299 (1988) 89-101

[EKMP82] H. Ehrig, H.-J. Kreowski, B. Mahr, P. Padawitz, *Algebraic Implementation of Abstract Data Types,* Theoretical Comp. Sci. 20 (1982) 209-263

[EM85] H. Ehrig, B. Mahr, *Fundamentals of Algebraic Specification 1: Equations and Initial Semantics,* Springer (1985)

[Fay79] M. Fay, *First Order Unification in an Equational Theory,* Proc. 4th Workshop on Automated Deduction, Academic Press (1979) 161-167

[Fri89] L. Fribourg, *A Strong Restriction of the Inductive Completion Procedure*, J. Symbolic Comp. 8 (1989) 253-276

[FHS89] U. Furbach, S. Hölldobler, J. Schreiber, *Horn Equality Theories and Paramodulation*, J. Automated Reasoning 5 (1989) 309-338

[GS87] J.H. Gallier, W. Snyder, *A General Complete E-unification Procedure,* Proc. RTA '87, Springer LNCS 256 (1987) 216-227

[GHM87] A. Geser, H. Hußmann, A. Mück, *A Compiler for a Class of Conditional Term Rewriting Systems*, Proc. CTRS '87, Springer LNCS 308 (1987) 84-90

[GM85] J.A. Goguen, J. Meseguer, *EQLOG: Equality, Types, and Generic Modules for Logic Programming,* in: D. DeGroot, G. Lindstrom, eds., Logic Programming: Functions, Relations, and Equations, Prentice-Hall (1985) 295-363

[GM87] J.A. Goguen, J. Meseguer, *Unifying Functional, Object-Oriented and Relational Programming with Logical Semantics,* in: B. Shriver, P. Wegner, eds., Research Directions in Object-Oriented Programming, MIT Press (1987) 417-477

[GTW78] J.A. Goguen, J.W. Thatcher, E.G. Wagner, *An Initial Algebra Approach to the Specification, Correctness and Implementation of Abstract Data Types,* in: R. Yeh, ed., Current Trends in Programming Methodology, Vol. 4, Prentice-Hall (1978) 80-149

[Gol86] A.T. Goldberg, *Knowledge-Based Programming: A Survey of Program Design and Construction Techniques*, IEEE Transact. Softw. Engineer. 12 (1986) 752-768

[GB78] C. Green, D. Barstow, *On Program Synthesis Knowledge*, Artificial Intelligence 10 (1978) 241-279

[Gri79] D. Gries, *The Schorr-Waite Graph Marking Algorithm*, Acta Inform. 11 (1979) 223-232

[GL90] Y. Guo, H.C.R. Lock, *A Classification Scheme for Declarative Programming Languages,* GMD-Studien Nr. 182, GMD (1990)

[GM88] Y. Gurevich, J.M. Morris, *Algebraic Operational Semantics and Modula-2,* Proc. CSL '87, Springer LNCS 329 (1988) 81-101

[Gut77] J. Guttag, *Abstract Data Types and the Development of Data Structures,* Comm. ACM 20 (1977) 396-404

[HMM86] R. Harper, D. MacQueen, R. Milner, *Standard ML,* Report ECS-LFCS-86-2, Comp. Sci. Dept., Edinburgh University (1986)

[Hoa69] C.A.R. Hoare, *An Axiomatic Basis for Computer Programming,* Comm. ACM 12 (1969) 576-580

[Hoa72] C.A.R. Hoare, *Proof of Correctness of Data Representations,* Acta Informatica 1 (1972) 271-281

[Höl89] S. Hölldobler, *Foundations of Equational Logic Programming,* Springer (1989)

[HO82] C.M. Hoffmann, M.J. O'Donnell, *Programming with Equations*, ACM TOPLAS 4 (1982) 83-112

[HR87] J. Hsiang, M. Rusinowitch, *On Word Problems in Equational Theories*, Proc. ICALP '87, Springer LNCS 267 (1987) 54-71

[Hue86] G. Huet, *Formal Structures for Computation and Deduction,* Course Notes, Comp. Sci. Dept., Carnegie-Mellon University (1986)

[HH82] G. Huet, J.M. Hullot, *Proofs by Induction in Equational Theories with Constructors*, J. Comp. Syst. Sci. 25 (1982) 239-266

[HO80] G. Huet, D.C. Oppen, *Equations and Rewrite Rules: A Survey*, in: R.V. Book, ed., Formal Language Theory: Perspectives and Open Problems, Academic Press (1980)

[Hug89] J. Hughes, *Why Functional Programming Matters,* Comp. J. 32 (1989) 98-107

[Hul80] J.M. Hullot, *Canonical Forms and Unification,* Proc. 5th CADE, Springer LNCS 87 (1980) 318-334

[Huß85] H. Hußmann, *Unification in Conditional-Equational Theories,* Proc. EUROCAL '85, Springer LNCS 204 (1985) 543-553

[Huß88] H. Hußmann, *Nondeterministic Algebraic Specifications and Nonconfluent Term Rewriting,* Proc. ALP '88, Springer LNCS 343 (1988) 31-40

[Jor87] Ph. Jorrand, *Term Rewriting as a Basis for the Design of a Functional and Parallel Programming Language,* in: W. Bibel, Ph. Jorrand, eds., Fundamentals of Artificial Intelligence, Springer (1987) 221-276

[JKi86] J.-P. Jouannaud, H. Kirchner, *Completion of a Set of Rules Modulo a Set of Equations*, SIAM J. Comp. 15 (1986) 1155-1194

[JKo86] J.-P. Jouannaud, E. Kounalis, *Automatic Proofs by Induction in Equational Theories without Constructors*, Proc. LICS '86 (1986) 358-366

[KL80] S. Kamin, J.-J. Levy, *Attempts for Generalizing the Recursive Path Orderings*, unpublished manuscript, INRIA (1980)

[Kap84] S. Kaplan, *Conditional Rewrite Rules*, Theoretical Comp. Sci. 33 (1984) 175-194

[KM87] D. Kapur, D.R. Musser, *Proof by Consistency*, Artificial Intelligence 31 (1987) 125-157

[Klä84] H.A. Klaeren, *A Constructive Method for Abstract Algebraic Software Specification,* Theoretical Comp. Sci. 30 (1984) 139-204

[KS85] F. Kluzniak, S. Szpakowicz, *Prolog for Programmers,* Academic Press (1985)

[Knu68] D.E. Knuth, *Semantics of Context-Free Languages*, Math. Syst. Theory 2 (1968) 127-145

[KB70] D.E. Knuth, P.B. Bendix, *Simple Word Problems in Universal Algebras,* in: J. Leech, ed., Computational Problems in Abstract Algebra, Pergamon Press (1970) 263-297

[Küc89] W. Küchlin, *Inductive Completion by Ground Proof Transformation,* in: H. Ait-Kaci, M. Nivat, eds., *Resolution of Equations in Algebraic Structures,* Academic Press (1989)

[Lan75] D.S. Lankford, *Canonical Inference*, Report ATP-32, University of Texas at Austin (1975)

[Lin88] P.A. Lindsay, *A Survey of Mechanical Support for Formal Reasoning,* Software Engineering Journal (Jan. 1988) 3-27

[Llo87] J.W. Lloyd, *Foundations of Logic Programming*, 2nd edition, Springer (1987)

[Man74] Z. Manna, *Mathematical Theory of Computation*, McGraw-Hill (1974)

[MW80] Z. Manna, R. Waldinger, *A Deductive Approach to Program Synthesis*, ACM TOPLAS 2 (1980) 90-121

[MW87] Z. Manna, R. Waldinger, *How to Clear a Block: A Theory of Plans*, J. Automated Reasoning 3 (1987) 343-377

[MMR86] A. Martelli, C. Moiso, G.F. Rossi, *An Algorithm for Unification in Equational Theories,* Proc. Symp. on Logic Programming (1986) 180-186

[Mes90] J. Meseguer, *Rewriting as a Unified Model For Concurrency,* Report SRI-CSL-90-02R, SRI International (1990)

[MTW88] B. Möller, A. Tarlecki, M. Wirsing, *Algebraic Specifications of Reachable Higher-Order Algebras*, in: D. Sannella, A. Tarlecki, eds., Recent Trends in Data Type Specification, Springer LNCS 332 (1988) 154-169

[Nou81] F. Nourani, *On Induction for Programming Logic,* EATCS Bulletin 13 (1981) 51-64

[O'D85] M.J. O'Donnell, *Equational Logic as a Programming Language*, MIT Press (1985)

[Pad81] P. Padawitz, *Some Examples of Algebraic Specifications and Implementations: Part 3,* Report FB 20 81-5, TU Berlin (1981)

[Pad83] P. Padawitz, *Correctness, Completeness and Consistency of Equational Data Type Specifications,* Dissertation, Report FB 20 83-15, TU Berlin (1983)

[Pad87] P. Padawitz, *Strategy-Controlled Reduction and Narrowing,* Proc. RTA '87, Springer LNCS 256 (1987) 242-255

[Pad88a] P. Padawitz, *Computing in Horn Clause Theories,* Springer (1988)

[Pad88b] P. Padawitz, *Inductive Proofs of Constructor-based Horn Clauses,* Report MIP-8810, Universität Passau (1988)

[Pad89] P. Padawitz, *Proving the Correctness of Schorr-Waite Graph Marking by Inductive Expansion,* Proc. Information Processing '89, Elsevier (1989) 1121-1126

[Pad91] P. Padawitz, *Inductive Expansion: A Calculus for Verifying and Synthesizing Functional and Logic Programs,* J. Automated Reasoning 7 (1991) 27-103

[Par90] H.A. Partsch, *Specification and Transformation of Programs,* Springer (1990)

[PS87] A. Pettorrossi, A. Skowron, *Higher Order Generalization in Program Derivation,* Proc. TAPSOFT '87, Springer LNCS 250 (1987) 182-196

[Qui87] M.J. Quinn, *Designing Efficient Algorithms for Parallel Computers,* McGraw-Hill (1987)

[Rea89] C. Reade, *Elements of Functional Programming,* Addison-Wesley (1989)

[Red85] U. Reddy, *Narrowing as the Operational Semantics of Functional Languages,* Proc. IEEE Symp. on Logic Programming (1985) 138-151

[Rei78] R. Reiter, *On Closed World Data Bases,* Proc. Symp. Logic and Data Bases, Plenum Press (1978)

[RW69] G. Robinson, L. Wos, *Paramodulation and Theorem-Proving in First-Order Logic,* in: Machine Intelligence, Vol. 4, Edinburgh University Press (1969) 135-150

[Rob65] J.A. Robinson, *A Machine-Oriented Logic Based on the Resolution Principle,* J. ACM 12 (1965) 23-41

[SL89] G. Saake, U.W. Lipeck, *Using Finite-Linear Temporal Logic for Specifying Database Dynamics,* Proc. CSL '88, Springer LNCS 385 (1989) 288-300

[ST88] D.T. Sannella, A. Tarlecki, *Towards Formal Development of Programs from Algebraic Specifications: Implementations Revisited,* Acta Informatica 25 (1988) 233-281

[SW67] H. Schorr, W.M. Waite, *An Efficient Machine-Independent Procedure for Garbage Collection in Various List Structures,* Comm. ACM 10 (1967) 501-506

[Sel72] A. Selman, *Completeness of Calculi for Axiomatically Defined Classes of Algebras,* Algebra Universalis 2 (1972) 20-32

[Sha87] E. Shapiro, *Concurrent Prolog: A Progress Report,* in: W. Bibel, Ph. Jorrand, eds., Fundamentals of Artificial Intelligence, Springer (1987) 277-313

[Sha89] E. Shapiro, *The Family of Concurrent Logic Programming Languages,* ACM Comp. Surveys 21 (1989) 413-510

[Sla74] J.R. Slagle, *Automated Theorem Proving for Theories with Simplifiers, Commutativity and Associativity,* J. ACM 21 (1974) 622-642

[Smi85] D.R. Smith, *Top-Down Synthesis of Divide-and-Conquer Algorithms,* Artificial Intelligence 27 (1985) 43-96

[Str87] Th. Streicher, *A Verification Method for Finite Dataflow Networks with Constraints Applied to the Verification of the Alternating Bit Protocol,* Report MIP-8706, Universität Passau (1987)

[Ued86] K. Ueda, *Guarded Horn Clauses,* Proc. Symp. Logic Programming, Springer LNCS 221 (1986) 168-179

[WB83] F. Winkler, B. Buchberger, *A Criterion for Eliminating Unnecessary Reductions in the Knuth-Bendix Algorithm,* Proc. Coll. Algebra, Combinatorics and Logic in Comp. Sci., North-Holland (1983)

[WF86] T. Winograd, F. Flores, *Understanding Computers and Cognition,* Ablex Publishing Corp. (1986)

[You88] J.-H. You, *Outer Narrowing for Equational Theories based on Constructors,* Proc. ICALP '88, Springer LNCS 317 (1988) 727-741

Index